# SUMMARY of CHANGE

AR 670-1
Wear and Appearance of Army Uniforms and Insignia

This rapid action revision, dated 11 May 2012--

o  Integrates the Program Executive Office Soldier products list guidance into
   the Uniform Quality Control Program (para 2-8).

o  Makes administrative changes (app A: marked obsolete forms and publications;
   corrected forms and publication titles; and corrected Web site addresses;
   glossary: deleted unused acronyms and corrected titles/abbreviations as
   prescribed by Army Records Management and Declassification Agency).

(This page intentionally left blank)

**Headquarters**
**Department of the Army**
**Washington, DC**
**3 February 2005**

**\*Army Regulation 670–1**

**Effective 3 March 2005**

Uniforms and Insignia

# Wear and Appearance of Army Uniforms and Insignia

By Order of the Secretary of the Army:

RAYMOND T. ODIERNO
*General, United States Army*
*Chief of Staff*

Official:

JOYCE E. MORROW
*Administrative Assistant to the*
*Secretary of the Army*

**History.** This publication is a rapid action revision (RAR). This RAR is effective 11 June 2012. The portions affected by this RAR are listed in the summary of change.

**Summary.** This regulation prescribes Department of the Army policy for proper wear and appearance of Army uniforms and insignia, as worn by officers and enlisted personnel of the active Army and the U.S. Army Reserve, as well as by former Soldiers.

**Applicability.** This regulation applies to the active Army, the Army National Guard/Army National Guard of the United States, and the U.S. Army Reserve, unless otherwise stated. Also, it applies to the Reserve Officers' Training Corps and the

Corps of Cadets, United States Military Academy, only when their respective uniform regulations do not include sufficient guidance or instruction. It does not apply to generals of the Army, the Chief of Staff of the Army, or former Chiefs of Staff of the Army, each of whom may prescribe his or her own uniform. During mobilization, the proponent may modify chapters and policies contained in this regulation.

**Proponent and exception authority.** The proponent of this regulation is the Deputy Chief of Staff, G–1. The proponent has the authority to approve exceptions or waivers to this regulation that are consistent with controlling law and regulations. The proponent may delegate this approval authority, in writing, to a division chief within the proponent agency or its direct reporting unit or field operating agency, in the grade of colonel or the civilian equivalent. Activities may request a waiver to this regulation by providing justification that includes a full analysis of the expected benefits and must include formal review by the activity's senior legal officer. All waiver requests will be endorsed by the commander or senior leader of the requesting activity and forwarded through their higher headquarters to the policy proponent. Refer to AR 25–30 for specific guidance.

**Army management control process.** This regulation does not contain management control provisions.

**Supplementation.** Supplementation of this regulation and establishment of command and local forms are prohibited without prior approval from the Deputy Chief of Staff, G–1 (DAPE–HR–IRP), 300 Army Pentagon, Washington, DC 20310–0300.

**Suggested improvements.** Users are invited to send comments and suggested improvements on DA Form 2028 (Recommended Changes to Publications and Blank Forms) directly to the Deputy Chief of Staff, G–1 (DAPE–HR–IRP), 300 Army Pentagon, Washington, DC 20310–0300.

**Distribution.** This publication is available in electronic media only and is intended for command levels A, B, C, D, and E for the active Army, the Army National Guard/Army National Guard of the United States, and the U.S. Army Reserve.

# Contents (Listed by paragraph and page number)

*This regulation supersedes AR 670–1, dated 5 September 2003. This edition publishes a rapid action revision of AR 670–1.

AR 670–1 • 3 February 2005/RAR 11 May 2012

**UNCLASSIFIED**

i

# Contents—Continued

# Contents—Continued

# Contents—Continued

# Contents—Continued

Contents—Continued

## Contents—Continued

# Contents—Continued

## Chapter 28
## Wear of Insignia and Accouterments, *page 176*

# Contents—Continued

## Contents—Continued

# Contents—Continued

# Contents—Continued

## Contents—Continued

**Contents—Continued**

**Contents—Continued**

## Contents—Continued

## Contents—Continued

## Glossary

## Index

# Part One
## General Information and Responsibilities

## Chapter 1
## Introduction

### 1–1. Purpose
This regulation prescribes the authorization for wear, composition, and classification of uniforms, and the occasions for wearing all personal (clothing bag issue), optional, and commonly worn organizational Army uniforms. It also prescribes the awards, insignia, and accouterments authorized for wear on the uniform, and how these items are worn. General information is also provided on the authorized material, design, and uniform quality control system.

### 1–2. References
Required and related publications are listed in appendix A.

### 1–3. Explanation of abbreviations and terms
Abbreviations and special terms used in this regulation are explained in the glossary.

### 1–4. General
a. Only uniforms, accessories, and insignia prescribed in this regulation or in the common tables of allowance (CTA), or as approved by Headquarters, Department of the Army (HQDA), will be worn by personnel in the U.S. Army. Unless specified in this regulation, the commander issuing the clothing and equipment will establish wear policies for organizational clothing and equipment. No item governed by this regulation will be altered in any way that changes the basic design or the intended concept of fit as described in TM 10–227 and AR 700–84, including plating, smoothing, or removing detail features of metal items, or otherwise altering the color or appearance. All illustrations in this regulation should coincide with the text. The written description will control any inconsistencies between the text and the illustration.

b. AR 70–1 prescribes Department of the Army (DA) policies, responsibilities, and administrative procedures by which all clothing and individual equipment used by Army personnel are initiated, designed, developed, tested, approved, fielded, and modified.

c. AR 385–10 prescribes DA policies, responsibilities, and administrative procedures and funding for protective clothing and equipment.

d. In accordance with chapter 45, section 771, title 10, United States Code (10 USC 771), no person except a member of the U.S. Army may wear the uniform, or a distinctive part of the uniform of the U.S. Army unless otherwise authorized by law. Additionally, no person except a member of the U.S. Army may wear a uniform, any part of which is similar to a distinctive part of the U.S. Army uniform. This includes the distinctive uniforms and uniform items listed in paragraph 1–12 of this regulation. Further, soldiers are not authorized to wear distinctive uniforms or uniform items of the U.S. Army or of other U.S. Services with, or on civilian clothes, except as provided in chapters 27 through 30 of this regulation.

### 1–5. How to recommend changes to Army uniforms
a. *Army Ideas For Excellence Program (AIEP).* If a major Army command (MACOM) recommends approval of an AIEP suggestion, the recommendation will be forwarded to the Project Manager-Soldier Systems (SEQ), Bldg. 328, 5901 Putnam Road, Fort Belvoir, VA 22060–5852, for consideration. Each suggestion forwarded to the project manager will reflect the MACOM position; contain all appropriate supporting documentation; and be signed by the commander, deputy commander, chief of staff, or comparable level official. Suggestions not recommended for adoption at any level will not be forwarded to PM-Soldier. Suggestions forwarded without a MACOM position will be returned to the MACOM for action.

b. *General comments and suggestions.* Comments and suggestions regarding the policy, criteria, and administrative instructions concerning individual military decorations, the Good Conduct Medal, service medals and service ribbons, combat and special skill badges and tabs, and unit decorations will be processed in accordance with AR 600–8–22.

### 1–6. Classification of service and utility or field uniforms
a. The male class A service uniform consists of the Army green (AG) coat and trousers, a short- or long-sleeved AG shade 415 shirt with a black four-in-hand tie, and other authorized accessories.

b. The male class B service uniform is the same as class A, except the service coat is not worn. The black four-in-hand tie is required with the long-sleeved AG shade 415 shirt when the long-sleeved shirt is worn without the class A coat, as an outer garment; the tie is optional with the short-sleeved shirt.

c. The female class A service uniform consists of the Army green coat and skirt or slacks, a short- or long-sleeved AG shade 415 shirt with a black neck tab, and other authorized accessories. The Army green maternity uniform (slacks or skirt) is also classified as a class A service uniform when the tunic is worn. When the tunic is worn, females will wear the neck tab with both the short- and long-sleeved maternity shirts.

*d.* The female class B service uniform is the same as the class A, except that neither the service coat nor the maternity tunic are worn. The black neck tab is required only when wearing the long-sleeved AG shade 415 shirt or the long-sleeved maternity shirt without the class A coat or tunic; the neck tab is optional with the short-sleeved version of both shirts.

*e.* Class C uniforms are the utility, field, hospital duty, food service, and other organizational uniforms.

*f.* See the table of prescribed dress in appendix B.

### 1–7. Personal appearance policies

*a. General.* The Army is a uniformed service where discipline is judged, in part, by the manner in which a soldier wears a prescribed uniform, as well as by the individual's personal appearance. Therefore, a neat and well-groomed appearance by all soldiers is fundamental to the Army and contributes to building the pride and esprit essential to an effective military force. A vital ingredient of the Army's strength and military effectiveness is the pride and self-discipline that American soldiers bring to their Service through a conservative military image. It is the responsibility of commanders to ensure that military personnel under their command present a neat and soldierly appearance. Therefore, in the absence of specific procedures or guidelines, commanders must determine a soldier's compliance with standards in this regulation. Soldiers must take pride in their appearance at all times, in or out of uniform, on and off duty. Pride in appearance includes soldiers' physical fitness and adherence to acceptable weight standards, in accordance with AR 600–9.

*b.* Exceptions to appearance standards based on religious practices.

(1) As provided by AR 600–20, paragraph 5–6, and subject to temporary revocation because of health, safety, or mission requirements, the following applies to the wear of religious apparel, articles, or jewelry. The term "religious apparel" is defined as articles of clothing worn as part of the observance of the religious faith practiced by the soldier. Religious articles include, but are not limited to, medallions, small booklets, pictures, or copies of religious symbols or writing carried by the individual in wallets or pockets. Except as noted below, personnel may not wear religious items if they do not meet the standards of this regulation, and requests for accommodation will not be entertained (see AR 600–20, para 5–6g(2)(d)).

*(a)* Soldiers may wear religious apparel, articles, or jewelry with the uniform, to include the physical fitness uniform, if they are neat, conservative, and discreet. "Neat conservative, and discreet" is defined as meeting the uniform criteria of this regulation. In other words, when religious jewelry is worn, the uniform must meet the same standards of wear as if the religious jewelry were not worn. For example, a religious item worn on a chain may not be visible when worn with the utility, service, dress, or mess uniforms. When worn with the physical fitness uniform, the item should be no more visible than identification (ID) tags would be in the same uniform. The width of chains worn with religious items should be approximately the same size as the width of the ID tag chain.

*(b)* Soldiers may not wear these items when doing so would interfere with the performance of their duties or present a safety concern. Soldiers may not be prohibited, however, from wearing religious apparel, articles, or jewelry meeting the criteria of this regulation simply because they are religious in nature, if wear is permitted of similar items of a nonreligious nature. A specific example would be wearing a ring with a religious symbol. If the ring meets the uniform standards for jewelry and is not worn in a work area where rings are prohibited because of safety concerns, then wear is allowed and may not be prohibited simply because the ring bears a religious symbol.

*(c)* During a worship service, rite, or ritual, soldiers may wear visible or apparent religious articles, symbols, jewelry, and apparel that do not meet normal uniform standards. Commanders, however, may place reasonable limits on the wear of non-subdued items of religious apparel during worship services, rites, or rituals conducted in the field for operational or safety reasons. When soldiers in uniform wear visible religious articles on such occasions, they must ensure that these articles are not permanently affixed or appended to any prescribed article of the uniform.

*(d)* Chaplains may wear religious attire as described in this regulation, CTA 50–909, and AR 165–1 in the performance of religious services and other official duties, as required. Commanders may not prohibit chaplains from wearing religious symbols that are part of the chaplain's duty uniform. (See AR 600–20, para 5–6g(7).)

(2) Soldiers may wear religious headgear while in uniform if the headgear meets the following criteria.

*(a)* It must be subdued in color (black, brown, green, dark or navy blue, or a combination of these colors).

*(b)* It must be of a style and size that can be completely covered by standard military headgear, and it cannot interfere with the proper wear or functioning of protective clothing or equipment.

*(c)* The headgear cannot bear any writing, symbols, or pictures.

*(d)* Personnel will not wear religious headgear in place of military headgear when military headgear is required (outdoors, or indoors when required for duties or ceremonies).

(3) Personal grooming. Hair and grooming practices are governed by paragraph 1–8 of this regulation, and exceptions or accommodations based on religious practices will not be granted. As an exception, policy exceptions based on

religious practice given to soldiers in accordance with AR 600–20 on or prior to 1 January 1986 remain in effect as long as the soldier remains otherwise qualified for retention.

## 1–8. Hair and fingernail standards and grooming policies

*a.* Hair.

(1) General. The requirement for hair grooming standards is necessary to maintain uniformity within a military population. Many hairstyles are acceptable, as long as they are neat and conservative. It is not possible to address every acceptable hairstyle, or what constitutes eccentric or conservative grooming. Therefore, it is the responsibility of leaders at all levels to exercise good judgment in the enforcement of Army policy. All soldiers will comply with the hair, fingernail, and grooming policies while in any military uniform or while in civilian clothes on duty.

*(a)* Leaders will judge the appropriateness of a particular hairstyle by the appearance of headgear when worn. Soldiers will wear headgear as described in the applicable chapters of this regulation. Headgear will fit snugly and comfortably, without distortion or excessive gaps. Hairstyles that do not allow soldiers to wear the headgear properly, or that interfere with the proper wear of the protective mask or other protective equipment, are prohibited.

*(b)* Extreme, eccentric, or trendy haircuts or hairstyles are not authorized. If soldiers use dyes, tints, or bleaches, they must choose those that result in natural hair colors. Colors that detract from a professional military appearance are prohibited. Therefore, soldiers should avoid using colors that result in an extreme appearance. Applied hair colors that are prohibited include, but are not limited to, purple, blue, pink, green, orange, bright (fire-engine) red, and fluorescent or neon colors. It is the responsibility of leaders to use good judgment in determining if applied colors are acceptable, based upon the overall effect on soldiers' appearance.

*(c)* Soldiers who have a texture of hair that does not part naturally may cut a part into the hair. The part will be one straight line, not slanted or curved, and will fall in the area where the soldier would normally part the hair. Soldiers will not cut designs into their hair or scalp.

(2) Male haircuts will conform to the following standards.

*(a)* The hair on top of the head must be neatly groomed. The length and bulk of the hair may not be excessive or present a ragged, unkempt, or extreme appearance. The hair must present a tapered appearance. A tapered appearance is one where the outline of the soldier's hair conforms to the shape of the head, curving inward to the natural termination point at the base of the neck. When the hair is combed, it will not fall over the ears or eyebrows, or touch the collar, except for the closely cut hair at the back of the neck. The block-cut fullness in the back is permitted to a moderate degree, as long as the tapered look is maintained. In all cases, the bulk or length of hair may not interfere with the normal wear of headgear (see para 1–8*a*(1)(a), above) or protective masks or equipment. Males are not authorized to wear braids, cornrows, or dreadlocks (unkempt, twisted, matted, individual parts of hair) while in uniform or in civilian clothes on duty. Hair that is clipped closely or shaved to the scalp is authorized.

*(b)* Males will keep sideburns neatly trimmed. Sideburns may not be flared; the base of the sideburn will be a clean-shaven, horizontal line. Sideburns will not extend below the lowest part of the exterior ear opening.

*(c)* Males will keep their face clean-shaven when in uniform or in civilian clothes on duty. Mustaches are permitted; if worn, males will keep mustaches neatly trimmed, tapered, and tidy. Mustaches will not present a chopped off or bushy appearance, and no portion of the mustache will cover the upper lip line or extend sideways beyond a vertical line drawn upward from the corners of the mouth (see figure 1–1). Handlebar mustaches, goatees, and beards are not authorized. If appropriate medical authority prescribes beard growth, the length required for medical treatment must be specified. For example, "The length of the beard will not exceed ¼ inch" (see TB MED 287). Soldiers will keep the growth trimmed to the level specified by appropriate medical authority, but they are not authorized to shape the growth into goatees, or "Fu Manchu" or handlebar mustaches.

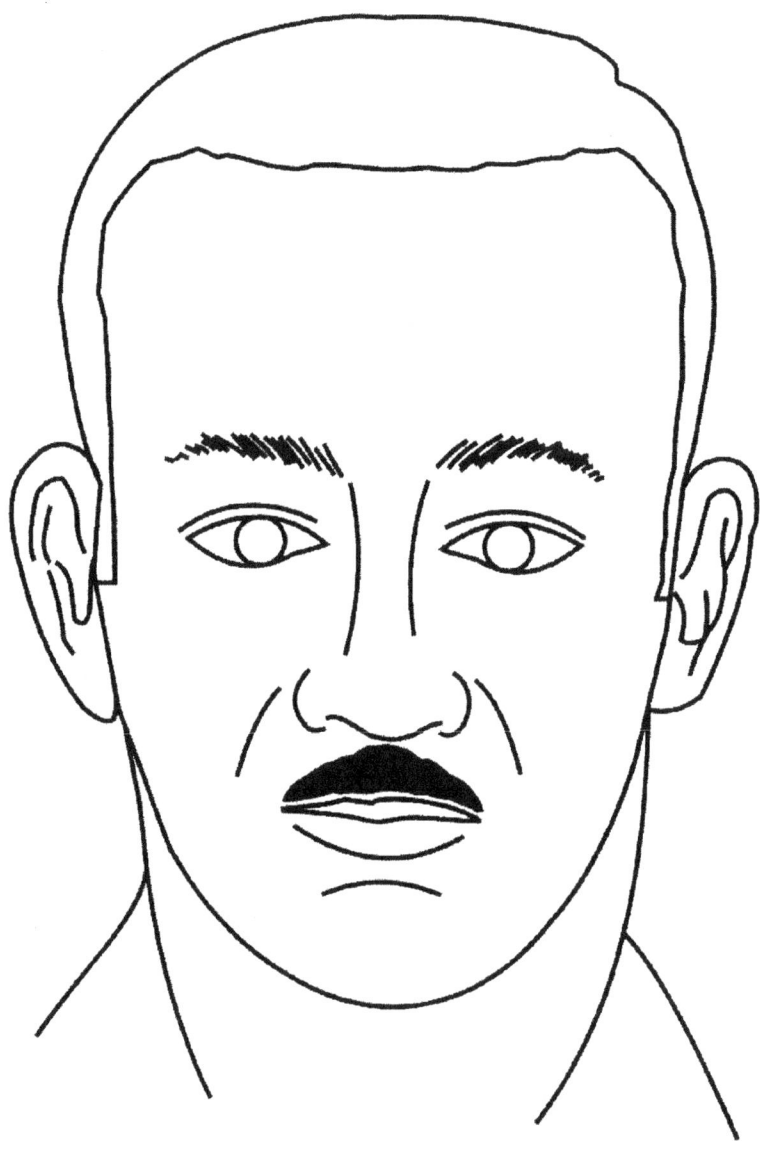

Figure 1–1. Wear of mustache

*(d)* Males are prohibited from wearing wigs or hairpieces while in uniform or in civilian clothes on duty, except to cover natural baldness or physical disfiguration caused by accident or medical procedure. When worn, wigs or hairpieces will conform to the standard haircut criteria as stated in 1–8a(2)(a), above.

(3) Female haircuts will conform to the following standards.

*(a)* Females will ensure their hair is neatly groomed, that the length and bulk of the hair are not excessive, and that the hair does not present a ragged, unkempt, or extreme appearance. Likewise, trendy styles that result in shaved portions of the scalp (other than the neckline) or designs cut into the hair are prohibited. Females may wear braids and cornrows as long as the braided style is conservative, the braids and cornrows lie snugly on the head, and any hair-holding devices comply with the standards in 1–8a(3)(d) below. Dreadlocks (unkempt, twisted, matted individual parts of hair) are prohibited in uniform or in civilian clothes on duty. Hair will not fall over the eyebrows or extend below the bottom edge of the collar at any time during normal activity or when standing in formation. Long hair that falls naturally below the bottom edge of the collar, to include braids, will be neatly and inconspicuously fastened or pinned,

so no free-hanging hair is visible. This includes styles worn with the physical fitness uniform/improved physical fitness uniform (PFU/IPFU).

*(b)* Styles that are lopsided or distinctly unbalanced are prohibited. Ponytails, pigtails, or braids that are not secured to the head (allowing hair to hang freely), widely spaced individual hanging locks, and other extreme styles that protrude from the head are prohibited. Extensions, weaves, wigs, and hairpieces are authorized; however, these additions must have the same general appearance as the individual's natural hair. Additionally, any wigs, extensions, hairpieces, or weaves must comply with the grooming policies set forth in this paragraph.

*(c)* Females will ensure that hairstyles do not interfere with proper wear of military headgear and protective masks or equipment at any time (see 1–8a(1)(a), above). When headgear is worn, the hair will not extend below the bottom edge of the front of the headgear, nor will it extend below the bottom edge of the collar.

*(d)* Hair-holding devices are authorized only for the purpose of securing the hair. Soldiers will not place hair-holding devices in the hair for decorative purposes. All hair-holding devices must be plain and of a color as close to the soldier's hair as is possible or clear. Authorized devices include, but are not limited to, small, plain scrunchies (elastic hair bands covered with material), barrettes, combs, pins, clips, rubber bands, and hair bands. Devices that are conspicuous, excessive, or decorative are prohibited. Some examples of prohibited devices include, but are not limited to, large, lacy scrunchies; beads, bows, or claw clips; clips, pins, or barrettes with butterflies, flowers, sparkles, gems, or scalloped edges; and bows made from hairpieces.

*(e)* Soldiers may not wear hairnets unless they are required for health or safety reasons, or in the performance of duties (such as those of a cook). No other type of hair covering is authorized in lieu of the hairnet. The commander will provide the hairnet to the soldier at no cost.

*b.* Cosmetics.

(1) General. As with hairstyles, the requirement for standards regarding cosmetics is necessary to maintain uniformity and to avoid an extreme or unmilitary appearance. Males are prohibited from wearing cosmetics, to include nail polish. Females are authorized to wear cosmetics with all uniforms, provided they are applied conservatively and in good taste and complement the uniform. Leaders at all levels must exercise good judgment in the enforcement of this policy.

*(a)* Females may wear cosmetics if they are conservative and complement the uniform and their complexion. Eccentric, exaggerated, or trendy cosmetic styles and colors, to include makeup designed to cover tattoos, are inappropriate with the uniform and are prohibited. Permanent makeup, such as eyebrow or eyeliner, is authorized as long as the makeup conforms to the standards outlined above.

*(b)* Females will not wear shades of lipstick and nail polish that distinctly contrast with their complexion, that detract from the uniform, or that are extreme. Some examples of extreme colors include, but are not limited to, purple, gold, blue, black, white, bright (fire-engine) red, khaki, camouflage colors, and fluorescent colors. Soldiers will not apply designs to nails or apply two-tone or multi-tone colors to nails.

(2) Females will comply with the cosmetics policy while in any military uniform or while in civilian clothes on duty.

*c.* Fingernails. All personnel will keep fingernails clean and neatly trimmed. Males will keep nails trimmed so as not to extend beyond the fingertip. Females will not exceed a nail length of ¼ inch, as measured from the tip of the finger. Females will trim nails shorter if the commander determines that the longer length detracts from the military image, presents a safety concern, or interferes with the performance of duties.

*d.* Hygiene and body grooming. Soldiers will maintain good personal hygiene and grooming on a daily basis and wear the uniform so as not to detract from their overall military appearance.

*e.* Tattoo policy

(1) Tattoos or brands anywhere on the head, face, and neck above the class A uniform collar are prohibited.

(2) Tattoos or brands that are extremist, indecent, sexist, or racist are prohibited, regardless of location on the body, as they are prejudicial to good order and discipline within units.

*(a)* Extremist tattoos or brands are those affiliated with, depicting, or symbolizing extremist philosophies, organizations, or activities. Extremist philosophies, organizations, and activities are those which advocate racial, gender or ethnic hatred or intolerance; advocate, create, or engage in illegal discrimination based on race, color, gender, ethnicity, religion, or national origin; or advocate violence or other unlawful means of depriving individual rights under the U.S. Constitution, Federal, or State law (see para 4–12, AR 600–20).

*(b)* Indecent tattoos or brands are those that are grossly offensive to modesty, decency, or propriety; shock the moral sense because of their vulgar, filthy, or disgusting nature or tendency to incite lustful thought; or tend reasonably to corrupt morals or incite libidinous thoughts.

*(c)* Sexist tattoos or brands are those that advocate a philosophy that degrades or demeans a person based on gender, but that may not meet the same definition of "indecent."

*(d)* Racist tattoos or brands are those that advocate a philosophy that degrades or demeans a person based on race, ethnicity, or national origin.

(3) Counseling requirements.

*(a)* Commanders will ensure soldiers understand the tattoo policy.

*(b)* For soldiers who are not in compliance, commanders may not order the removal of a tattoo or brand. However, the commander must counsel soldiers, and afford them the opportunity to seek medical advice about removal or alteration of the tattoo or brand.

(4) If soldiers are not in compliance with the policy, and refuse to remove or alter the tattoos or brands, commanders will:

*(a)* Ensure the soldier understands the policy.

*(b)* Ensure the soldier has been afforded the opportunity to seek medical advice about removal or alteration.

*(c)* Counsel the soldier in writing. The counseling form will state that the soldier's refusal to remove extremist, indecent, sexist, or racist tattoos or brands anywhere on the body, or refusal to remove any type of tattoo or brand visible in the class A uniform (worn with slacks/trousers), will result in discharge.

(5) Existing tattoos or brands on the hands that are not extremist, indecent, sexist, or racist, but are visible in the class A uniform (worn with slacks/trousers), are authorized.

(6) Finality of determination.

*(a)* Recruiting battalion commanders or recruiting battalion executive officers (0–5 or above) will make initial entry determinations that tattoos or brands comply with this policy for Active Army and Army Reserve soldiers. This authority will not be delegated further.

*(b)* Unit commanders or unit executive officers will make determinations for soldiers currently on active duty. This authority will not be delegated further.

*(c)* Recruiting and retention managers (O–5 or above) will make initial entry determinations that tattoos or brands comply with this policy for National Guard soldiers. This authority will not be delegated further.

*(d)* Professors of military science (O-5 or above) will make initial entry determinations that tattoos or brands comply with this policy for ROTC cadets. This authority will not be delegated further.

*(e)* The Director of Admissions will make initial entry determinations that tattoos or brands comply with this policy for the U.S. Military Academy cadets. This authority will not be delegated further.

*(f)* Determinations will be fully documented in writing and will include a description of existing tattoos or brands and their location on the body. A copy of the determination will be provided to the soldier. Unless otherwise directed by the Army Deputy Chief of Staff, G-1, these determinations are final. If a tattoo or brand is discovered to violate this policy after an initial determination has been documented, commanders must submit requests for an exception to policy or for discharge through the soldier's chain of command to the MACOM for approval. Appeals to the MACOM decision will be forwarded to the Army Deputy Chief of Staff, G-1 for decision.

(7) Soldiers may not cover tattoos or brands in order to comply with the tattoo policy.

## 1–9. Uniform appearance and fit

*a.* Appearance.

(1) All personnel will maintain a high standard of dress and appearance. Uniforms will fit properly; trousers, pants, or skirts should not fit tightly; and personnel must keep uniforms clean and serviceable and press them as necessary. Soldiers must project a military image that leaves no doubt that they live by a common military standard and are responsible to military order and discipline. Soldiers will ensure that articles carried in pockets do not protrude from the pocket or present a bulky appearance.

(2) Wear of items on uniforms.

*(a)* When required and prescribed by the commander, soldiers may attach keys or key chains to the uniform when performing duties such as charge of quarters, armorer, duty officer/NCO, or other duties as prescribed by the commander. Keys or key chains will be attached to the uniform on the belt, belt loops, or waistband.

*(b)* At the discretion of the commander, and when required in the performance of duties listed above, soldiers may wear an electronic device on the belt, belt loops, or waistband of the uniform. Only one electronic device may be worn; it may be either a pager or a cell phone. The body of the device may not exceed 4x2x1 inches, and the device and carrying case must be black; no other colors are authorized. If security cords or chains are attached to the device, soldiers will conceal the cord or chain from view. Other types of electronic devices are not authorized for wear on the uniform. If the commander issues and requires the use of other electronic devices in the performance of duties, the soldier will carry them in the hand, pocket, briefcase, purse, bag, or in some other carrying container.

*(c)* Soldiers will not wear keys, key chains, or electronic devices on the uniform when the commander determines such wear is inappropriate, such as in formation, or during parades or ceremonies. Soldiers will not wear items or devices on the uniform when not performing required duties.

(3) While in uniform, personnel will not place their hands in their pockets, except momentarily to place or retrieve objects. Soldiers will keep uniforms buttoned, zipped, and snapped. They will ensure metallic devices such as metal insignia, belt buckles, and belt tips are free of scratches and corrosion and are in proper luster or remain properly subdued, as applicable; and that all medals and ribbons are clean and not frayed. Personnel will keep shoes and boots

cleaned and shined. Soldiers will replace the insignia listed in AR 700–84, paragraph 5–5, when it becomes unserviceable or no longer conforms to standards.

(4) Lapels and sleeves of service, dress, and mess coats and jackets will be roll-pressed, without creasing. Skirts will not be creased. Trousers, slacks, and the sleeves of shirts and blouses will be creased. Soldiers may add military creases to the AG shade 415 shirt and the BDU coat (not the field jacket). Personnel will center the front creases on each side of the shirt, centered on the pockets, for those garments that have front pockets. Soldiers may press a horizontal crease across the upper back of the shirt or coat (not necessary on the male shirt due to the yoke seam), and they may press three equally spaced vertical creases down the back, beginning at the yoke seam or the horizontal crease. Additionally, personnel may crease the sleeves of the battle dress uniform (BDU) coat. Personnel are not authorized to sew military creases into the uniform.

(5) Although some uniform items are made of wash-and-wear materials or are treated with a permanent-press finish, soldiers may need to press these items to maintain a neat, military appearance. However, before pressing uniform items, soldiers should read and comply with care instruction labels attached to the items. Soldiers may starch BDUs and the maternity work uniform, at their option. Commanders will not require soldiers to starch these uniforms, and soldiers will not receive an increase in their clothing replacement allowance to compensate for potential premature wear that may be caused by starching uniforms.

*b.* Fit. Fitting instructions and alterations of uniforms will be made in accordance with AR 700–84 and TM 10–227. The following is a summary of general fitting guidelines.

(1) Black all-weather coat.

*(a)* Males. The length of the sleeves of the all-weather coat will be ½ inch longer than the service coat. The bottom of the black all weather coat will reach to a point 1½ inches below the center of the knee.

*(b)* Females. The length of the sleeves of the all-weather coat will be ½ inch longer than the service coat. The bottom of the coat will reach a point at least 1 inch below the skirt hem, but not less than 1½ inches below the center of the knee.

(2) Uniform coats and jackets (male and female). The sleeve length will be 1 inch below the bottom of the wrist bone.

(3) Trousers and slacks.

*(a)* Trousers will be fitted and worn with the lower edge of the waistband at the top of the hipbone, plus or minus ½ inch. The front crease of the trousers will reach the top of the instep, touching the top of the shoe at the shoelaces. Trousers will be cut on a diagonal line to reach a point approximately midway between the top of the heel and the top of the standard shoe in the back. The trousers may have a slight break in the front.

*(b)* Slacks will be fitted and worn so that the center of the waistband is at the natural waistline. The front crease of the slacks will reach the top of the instep, touching the top of the foot or the shoe at the shoelaces. Slacks will be cut on a diagonal line to reach a point approximately midway between the top of the heel and the top of the standard shoe in the back. The slacks may have a slight break in the front.

(4) Knee-length skirts. Skirt lengths will be no more than 1 inch above or 2 inches below the center of the knee.

(5) Long-sleeved shirts. The sleeve length will extend to the center of the wrist bone.

(6) Other. Personnel will wear appropriate undergarments with all uniforms, in accordance with paragraph 27–28.

## 1–10. When the wear of the Army uniform is required or prohibited

*a.* All personnel will wear the Army uniform when on duty, unless granted an exception by the commander to wear civilian clothes. The wear of civilian clothing on duty is subject to the provisions of AR 700–84. The following personnel may grant exceptions:

(1) Commanders of major commands.

(2) Assistant Secretaries, the Secretary of Defense or his designee, or the Secretary of the Army.

(3) Heads of Department of Defense agencies.

(4) Heads of Department of the Army Staff agencies.

*b.* Personnel traveling on Air Mobility Command and non-Air Mobility Comand flights on permanent change of station (PCS) orders, temporary duty (TDY), emergency leave, or space-available flights, are authorized to wear civilian clothes. Personnel must ensure clothing worn is appropriate for the occasion and reflects positively on the Army. (See DOD 4500.54–G) for information concerning mandatory wear of civilian clothing in foreign countries. The individual's travel orders will reflect information authorizing the wear of civilian clothing.)

*c.* Soldiers may wear the BDU when deploying as part of a unit move and the mode of transportation is for the exclusive use of the military. Embarkation and debarkation points will be in military-controlled areas.

*d.* Soldiers may wear optional uniform items with the class A and B service uniforms, as prescribed in this regulation. All uniform combinations are authorized for year-round wear. However, soldiers should use appropriate discretion based upon weather conditions and duties. Wearing combinations of uniform items not prescribed in this regulation or in other authorization documents approved by HQDA, is prohibited. Commanders will not prescribe seasonal wear dates for uniform items.

*e.* Wear of military and civilian items.

(1) The wear of a combination of civilian and military clothing is prohibited, unless prescribed in this regulation or other authorization documents approved by HQDA.

(2) Soldiers may carry civilian gym bags, civilian rucksacks, or other similar civilian bags while in uniform. Soldiers may carry these bags by hand, on one shoulder using a shoulder strap, or over both shoulders using both shoulder straps. If the soldier opts to carry a bag over one shoulder, the bag must be carried on the same side of the body as the shoulder strap; therefore, soldiers may not carry the bag slung across the body with the strap over the opposite shoulder. If soldiers choose to carry a shoulder bag while in uniform, the bag must be black with no other colors and may not have any logos. The contents of the bag may not be visible; therefore, see-through plastic or mesh bags are not authorized. There is no restriction on the color of civilian bags carried in the hand. These rules do not apply to purses, which are covered in chapter 27 of this regulation. Commanders govern the wear of organizational issue rucksacks in garrison and field environments.

*f.* Soldiers may continue to wear uniform items changed in design or material as long as the item remains in serviceable condition, unless specifically prohibited. (See appendix D for a list of possession and wear-out dates for uniform items.)

*g.* Civilian clothing is considered appropriate attire for individuals who are participating in civilian outdoor activities such as volksmarches, orienteering, or similar activities. Soldiers who are spectators at these activities may wear the service uniform. Soldiers who are participating in, or observing these events are not authorized to wear utility or field uniforms. However, commanders of participating units or of those units that provide support personnel, such as medical and traffic control personnel, may prescribe appropriate uniforms, to include utility or organizational uniforms, if warranted by the occasion, weather conditions, or activity.

*h.* Soldiers may wear experimental uniform items while actively engaged in an experimental uniform test program approved by HQ, U.S. Army Training and Doctrine Command, HQ, Army Materiel Command (AMC), or the Army Uniform Board, HQDA. Soldiers will not wear experimental items after completion of the test unless such wear is approved by HQDA.

*i.* Army National Guard technicians who are also members of the Army National Guard will wear the appropriate Army duty uniform while engaged in their civil service status.

*j.* Wearing Army uniforms is prohibited in the following situations:

(1) In connection with the furtherance of any political or commercial interests, or when engaged in off-duty civilian employment.

(2) When participating in public speeches, interviews, picket lines, marches, rallies, or public demonstrations, except as authorized by competent authority.

(3) When attending any meeting or event that is a function of, or is sponsored by, an extremist organization.

(4) When wearing the uniform would bring discredit upon the Army.

(5) When specifically prohibited by Army regulations.

*k.* Soldiers will wear headgear with the Army uniform, except under the following circumstances:

(1) Headgear is not required if it would interfere with the safe operation of military vehicles. The wear of military headgear is not required while in or on a privately owned vehicle (to include a motorcycle, bicycle, or convertible automobile), a commercial vehicle, or on public conveyance (such as a subway, train, plane, or bus).

(2) Soldiers will not wear headgear indoors unless under arms in an official capacity, or when directed by the commander, such as for indoor ceremonial activities.

(3) Male and female soldiers are not required to wear headgear to evening social events (after Retreat) when wearing the Army blue and white uniforms, the enlisted green dress uniform, the Army green maternity dress uniform (females only), or the mess and evening mess uniforms.

(4) Soldiers will carry their headgear, when it is not worn, in their hands while wearing service, dress, and mess uniforms. Soldiers are authorized storage of the headgear, when it is not worn, in the BDU cargo pockets. Soldiers must fold the headgear neatly so as not to present a bulky appearance. Soldiers will not attach headgear to the uniform or hang it from the belt.

## 1–11. Uniformity of material

*a.* When soldiers exercise their option to choose among various fabrics authorized for uniforms, they must ensure that all garments (coats, trousers, skirts, and slacks) are made of the same material. However, junior and senior ROTC cadets may wear garrison caps made of polyester-wool blend (AG shade 489) or all polyester (AG shade 491) interchangeably with service uniforms of either shade.

*b.* When gold lace (sleeve or trouser ornamentation) or gold bullion is prescribed for wear with uniforms, personnel may substitute gold-colored nylon, rayon, or synthetic metallic gold. If trouser and sleeve ornamentation is gold bullion, the cap ornamentation and shoulder strap insignia must also be gold bullion.

*c.* Ornamentation on the visors of all service caps will be gold bullion or synthetic metallic gold yarn, or anodized aluminum in 24–karat yellow-gold color.

*d.* Anodized aluminum white-gold colored buttons are not authorized for wear.

## 1–12. Distinctive uniforms and uniform items

*a.* The following uniform items are distinctive and will not be sold to or worn by unauthorized personnel:

(1) All Army headgear, when worn with insignia.

(2) Badges and tabs (identification, marksmanship, combat, and special skill).

(3) Uniform buttons (U.S. Army or Corps of Engineers).

(4) Decorations, service medals, service and training ribbons, and other awards and their appurtenances.

(5) Insignia of any design or color that the Army has adopted.

*b.* Individuals will remove all distinctive items before disposing of unserviceable uniform items.

## 1–13. Wear of civilian clothing

*a.* Civilian clothing is authorized for wear when off duty, unless the wear is prohibited by the installation commander in CONUS or by the MACOM commander overseas. Commanders down to unit level may restrict the wear of civilian clothes by those soldiers who have had their pass privileges revoked, under the provisions of AR 600–8–10.

*b.* When on duty in civilian clothes, Army personnel will conform to the appearance standards in this regulation, unless specifically exempted by the commander for specific mission requirements.

## 1–14. Wear of jewelry

*a.* Soldiers may wear a wristwatch, a wrist identification bracelet, and a total of two rings (a wedding set is considered one ring) with Army uniforms, unless prohibited by the commander for safety or health reasons. Any jewelry soldiers wear must be conservative and in good taste. Identification bracelets are limited to medical alert bracelets and MIA/POW identification bracelets. Soldiers may wear only one item on each wrist.

*b.* No jewelry, other than that described in paragraph 1–14*a*, above, will appear exposed while wearing the uniform; this includes watch chains, or similar items, and pens and pencils. The only authorized exceptions are religious items described in para 1–7*b*, above; a conservative tie tack or tie clasp that male soldiers may wear with the black four-in-hand necktie; and a pen or pencil that may appear exposed on the hospital duty, food service, CVC, or flight uniforms.

*c.* Body piercing. When on any Army installation or other places under Army control, soldiers may not attach, affix, or display objects, articles, jewelry, or ornamentation to or through the skin while they are in uniform, in civilian clothes on duty, or in civilian clothes off duty (this includes earrings for male soldiers). The only exception is for female soldiers, as indicated in paragraph 1–14*d*, below. (The term "skin" is not confined to external skin, but includes the tongue, lips, inside the mouth, and other surfaces of the body not readily visible).

*d.* Females are authorized to wear prescribed earrings with the service, dress, and mess uniforms.

(1) Earrings may be screw-on, clip-on, or post-type earrings, in gold, silver, white pearl, or diamond. The earrings will not exceed 6 mm or ¼ inch in diameter, and they must be unadorned and spherical. When worn, the earrings will fit snugly against the ear. Females may wear earrings only as a matched pair, with only one earring per ear lobe.

(2) Females are not authorized to wear earrings with any class C (utility) uniform (BDU, hospital duty, food service, physical fitness, field, or organizational).

(3) When on duty in civilian attire, female soldiers must comply with the specifications listed in (1) above when wearing earrings, unless otherwise authorized by the commander. When females are off duty, there are no restrictions on the wear of earrings.

*e.* Ankle bracelets, necklaces (other than those described in para 1–7*b*), faddish (trendy) devices, medallions, amulets, and personal talismans or icons are not authorized for wear in any military uniform, or in civilian clothes on duty.

## 1–15. Wear of eyeglasses, sunglasses, and contact lenses

*a.* Wear of eyeglasses and sunglasses.

(1) Conservative civilian prescription eyeglasses are authorized for wear with all uniforms.

(2) Conservative prescription and nonprescription sunglasses are authorized for wear when in a garrison environment, except when in formation and while indoors. Individuals who are required by medical authority to wear sunglasses for medical reasons other than refractive error may wear them, except when health or safety considerations apply. Soldiers may not wear sunglasses in the field, unless required by the commander for safety reasons in high-glare, field environments.

(3) Restrictions on eyeglasses and sunglasses. Eyeglasses or sunglasses that are trendy, or have lenses or frames with initials, designs, or other adornments are not authorized for wear. Soldiers may not wear lenses with extreme or trendy colors, which include but are not limited to, red, yellow, blue, purple, bright green, or orange. Lens colors must be traditional gray, brown, or dark green shades. Personnel will not wear lenses or frames that are so large or so small that they detract from the appearance of the uniform. Personnel will not attach chains, bands, or ribbons to eyeglasses.

Eyeglass restraints are authorized only when required for safety purposes. Personnel will not hang eyeglasses or eyeglass cases on the uniform, and may not let glasses hang from eyeglass restraints down the front of the uniform.

*b.* Restrictions on contact lenses. Tinted or colored contact lenses are not authorized for wear with the uniform. The only exception is for opaque lenses that are prescribed medically for eye injuries. Additionally, clear lenses that have designs on them that change the contour of the iris are not authorized for wear with the uniform.

## 1–16. Wear of identification tags and security badges

*a.* Identification (ID) tags. The wear of ID tags is governed by AR 600–8–14.

(1) Soldiers will wear ID tags at all times when in a field environment, while traveling in aircraft, and when outside the continental United States.

(2) Personnel will wear ID tags around the neck, except when safety considerations apply (such as during physical training).

*b.* Security identification badges. In restricted areas, commanders may prescribe the wear of security identification badges, in accordance with AR 600–8–14 and other applicable regulations. Personnel will not wear security identification badges outside the area for which they are required. Personnel will not hang other items from the security badge(s). The manner of wear will be determined by the organization that requires wear of the badges.

## 1–17. Wear of personal protective or reflective clothing

*a.* Protective headgear. Soldiers are authorized to wear commercially designed, protective headgear with the uniform when operating motorcycles, bicycles, or other like vehicles, and are required to do so when installation regulations mandate such wear. Personnel will remove protective headgear and don authorized Army headgear upon dismounting from the vehicle.

*b.* Protective/reflective clothing. Soldiers may wear protective/reflective outer garments with uniforms when safety considerations make it appropriate and when authorized by the commander.

## 1–18. Wear of organizational protective or reflective clothing

When safety considerations apply, commanders may require the wear of organizational protective or reflective items, or other occupational health or safety equipment, with the uniform (such as during physical fitness training). If required, commanders will furnish protective or reflective clothing to soldiers at no cost.

## 1–19. Restrictions on the purchase, possession, and reproduction of heraldic items

*a.* The heraldic items listed below are authorized for purchase and possession. Variations from the prescribed specifications for these heraldic items are not permitted without the prior approval of The Institute of Heraldry (TIOH), U.S. Army.

(1) All insignia approved by HQDA.

(2) Appurtenances and devices for attachment to decorations, service medals, and ribbons.

(3) Miniature replicas of decorations, service medals, and ribbons.

(4) Oversize replicas of decorations and service medals for grave markers only. These replicas must be at least twice the size prescribed for the decoration or service medal.

(5) Ribbons pertaining to decorations and service medals.

(6) Unit award emblems, fourrageres, and the orange lanyard.

(7) Combat, special skill, and marksmanship badges, including miniatures and dress miniatures.

(8) Identification badges.

(9) Rosettes and lapel buttons.

*b.* The heraldic items listed below are not authorized for purchase.

(1) Medal of Honor.

(2) Items incorporating designs or the likeness of decorations, service medals, and service ribbons.

*c.* Possession, wear, and other uses of heraldic items.

(1) The possession of any of the items listed in paragraph 1–19*a*, above, or elsewhere in this regulation is authorized. The wear of any HQDA-prescribed decoration, service medal, badge, service ribbon, lapel button, or insignia by persons not authorized to do so, or their use of such items to defraud or to misrepresent their identification or status, is prohibited. Persons violating this provision are subject to punishment under the statutes listed in sections 701 and 704, title 18, U.S. Code (18 USC 701, 704).

(2) No organization, society, or other group of persons may use any of the articles or imitations specified in paragraph 1–19*a*, above, or elsewhere in this regulation without written approval of the Secretary of the Army.

*d.* Reproductions of heraldic items.

(1) The heraldic items listed in paragraph 1–19*a*, above, may not be reproduced, except as prescribed in AR 672–8.

(2) Certain designs, the likeness of insignia, and specified badges, such as combat, special skill, and marksmanship,

may be incorporated in articles manufactured for sale, provided The Institute of Heraldry has granted permission in writing.

## Chapter 2
## Responsibilities

### 2–1. Deputy Chief of Staff, G-1

*a.* Consistent with controlling law and regulation, the Deputy Chief of Staff, G-1 (DCS, G-1) has the authority to approve exceptions to this regulation. The DCS, G-1 may delegate this authority in writing to a division chief within the proponent agency who holds the grade of colonel or the civilian equivalent. The approval authority will coordinate all questions regarding the scope of authority to approve exceptions with HQDA, OTJAG, ATTN: DAJA–AL, Washington, DC 20310–2200.

*b.* The DCS, G-1 will develop and monitor the following Army policies:

(1) Standards of personal appearance.

(2) The standards for the wear of utility, service, dress, and mess uniforms and for the accessories, awards and decorations, accouterments, insignia, and other heraldic items worn with all authorized uniforms.

*c.* The DCS, G-1 will do the following:

(1) Function as a member of the Army Uniform Board

(2) Coordinate with the Army and Air Force Exchange Service (AAFES) and the Deputy Chief of Staff, G-4, as required in order to incorporate uniform changes or additions to this regulation.

### 2–2. Deputy Chief of Staff, G-4

*a.* The Deputy Chief of Staff, G-4 (DCS, G-4) is responsible for the life-cycle management of clothing and individual equipment, in accordance with AR 70–1.

*b.* The DCS, G-4 coordinates the Army Uniform Board meetings.

### 2–3. The Institute of Heraldry

The Institute of Heraldry (TIOH) will do the following:

*a.* Monitor the Heraldic Quality Control System in accordance with AR 672–8, to ensure heraldic items are manufactured according to government specifications or purchase descriptions.

*b.* Provide manufacturers with government-loaned tools and specifications for heraldic items.

*c.* Authorize the manufacture of heraldic items and issue certificates of authority to manufacture items under the provisions of AR 672–8.

*d.* Approve designs for distinctive unit insignia (DUI), regimental distinctive insignia (RDI), and shoulder sleeve insignia (SSI), as authorized by this regulation.

### 2–4. The U.S. Army Materiel Command

The Commanding General, AMC will do the following:

*a.* Operate the Project Manager-Soldier Systems Office.

*b.* Ensure the performance of Army materiel management functions for clothing and individual equipment and centrally procured heraldic items, to include quality control.

*c.* Operate the Uniform Quality Control Program (UQCP) for all optional uniforms and uniform items approved for wear by HQDA, except non-distinctive commercial component items of some optional uniforms, such as men's white shirts, cuff links, and brand name footwear.

### 2–5. The U.S. Army and Air Force Exchange Service

*a.* The U.S. Army and AAFES will operate, manage, and supervise the Army military clothing sales stores (AMCSS) program worldwide, in accordance with the terms of the memorandum of understanding between the Department of the Army and AAFES, Dallas, Texas.

*b.* Responsibilities include, but are not limited to, the control, storage, and distribution of "issue" AMCSS inventories and optional-wear military clothing items from certified manufacturers, according to DA specifications, and as developed by the PM Soldier (SEQ), Bldg. 328, 5901 Putnam Road, Fort Belvoir, VA 22060–5852, in conjunction with the textile technology team at the Natick Soldier Center, Natick, MA 01760. (Optional-wear items are those not considered "issue" items.) Responsibility does not include war reserve stock management.

### 2–6. Commanders

*a.* Commanders of MACOMs will thoroughly evaluate all proposals to change or add uniforms, accessories, or wear policies for uniforms, insignia, and awards that are submitted through the AIEP.

*b.* The installation commander may prescribe the uniform for wear in formations. When not prescribed by the installation or subordinate commander, the unit commander will prescribe the uniform for wear in formation. Commanders will not establish seasonal wear dates for uniforms.

*c.* Installation commanders in CONUS, MACOM commanders overseas, the Chief, Army Reserve for USAR, and State Adjutants General for the ARNG may publish, in writing, exceptions to the policy that authorizes the wear of utility and organizational uniforms off military installations (see para 3–3).

*d.* The commander in charge of units on maneuver may prescribe the uniform for wear within the maneuver area.

*e.* Ceremonial details and units.

(1) Members of honor guards, color guards, and similar details will wear the prescribed Army service, dress, or utility uniforms with authorized accouterments. These members may wear accessories authorized in CTA 50–900, such as individual equipment, belts, white gloves, and slings, when authorized by the commander. Commanders will prescribe uniform wear policies for these items.

(2) Only those units authorized to wear a distinctive uniform in accordance with CTA 50–900 for ceremonial duties, such as the Old Guard and the Army Band, are exempt from the policy to wear the Army service, dress, or utility uniforms in the performance of ceremonial duties. Commanders of special units will prescribe the wear policy for all distinctive uniform items and accouterments.

*f.* Commanders will not require individuals to purchase optional uniform items. Likewise, they will not restrict or discourage them from wearing optional uniform items authorized by this regulation, except in those instances where uniformity is required, such as parades or formations.

*g.* Commanders will conduct periodic inspections to ensure that all personnel under their command comply with the following:

(1) That soldiers possess the minimum quantities of uniforms prescribed in this regulation, AR 700–84, and CTA 50–900, tables 1, 2, and 3; and that the uniforms are properly fitted and in serviceable condition.

(2) That soldiers wear only authorized insignia and awards, as prescribed in this regulation.

(3) That soldiers wear only uniform and heraldic items produced by certified manufacturers, and that they meet the specifications for quality and design.

*h.* Commanders will promptly submit quality deficiency reports on uniforms and individual equipment, in accordance with AR 702–7–1 and DA Pam 738–750, regarding those items that do not meet the requirements in paras 2–6g(1–3), above.

*i.* Commanders may purchase heraldic items through local procurement procedures only from manufacturers certified by TIOH.

*j.* Overseas MACOM commanders will establish a service point of contact to provide information to local textile and uniform producers on optional uniforms and uniform items. Additionally, the point of contact will provide UQCP certification procedures to manufacturers desiring to sell these items to soldiers within the overseas theater.

## 2–7. Responsibilities of soldiers purchasing uniforms, uniform items, and heraldic items

*a.* Soldiers purchasing uniforms, uniform items, or heraldic items from establishments other than the AMCSS must ensure that the items are authorized for wear and that they conform to appropriate military specifications or are manufactured in accordance with the UQCP or the heraldic quality control system. When items appear deficient, soldiers should submit a SF 368 (Product Quality Deficiency Report) through their servicing MCSS, where forms are available. Commercially purchased items that are authorized for wear in lieu of military-issue items must conform to the basic specification of the military-issue item, unless otherwise specified in this regulation.

(1) All Army uniforms, uniform items, and heraldic items procured by the Defense Logistics Agency and sold in the AMCSS are procured in accordance with appropriate military specifications and are authorized for wear. However, in those MCSS with multi-service support agreements, some items are sold that are authorized for wear by members of other services, but not by Army personnel. Soldiers are responsible for verifying with their chain of command which items are authorized for wear by Army personnel. Uniform items with defects in workmanship or material should be returned to the AMCSS for replacement or repair.

(2) Optional uniforms and other uniform clothing items sold in the MCSS, in post exchanges, or by commercial sources will contain a label, stamp, or certificate issued by the textile technology team at the Natick Soldier Center. Components of some optional uniforms, such as men's commercial white shirts, studs, and cuff links, are not included in the UQCP.

(3) All heraldic items purchased from a post exchange, AMCSS, or commercial source will contain a hallmark or label certifying that the item was produced in accordance with the appropriate military specification by a manufacturer certified by TIOH, U.S. Army.

(4) All individuals purchasing uniform or insignia items from commercial sources must take care to ensure that the items conform to the requirements in 2–7a(1–3), above.

*b.* All enlisted personnel will do the following:

(1) Maintain their clothing bag items and any supplemental clothing items they are issued, as prescribed in AR 700–84 or CTA 50–900.

(2) Ensure that their uniforms and insignia conform with this regulation.

c. All officers will procure and maintain the uniforms and accessories appropriate to their assigned duties. Appendix C lists the minimum quantities of uniforms and other items normally prescribed by commanders for officers. (Note exceptions for officers on extended active duty for less than 6 months.) Officers are responsible for ensuring that their uniforms and insignia conform to specifications in this regulation.

## 2–8. Operation of the Uniform Quality Control Program

a. The program executive officer (Program Executive Office (PEO) Soldier) and project manager (Soldier Protection and Individual Equipment), in conjunction with the U.S. Army Natick Soldier Research, Development and Engineering Center (NSRDEC), will oversee UQCP operations and will execute the following tasks:

(1) Prepare and maintain military specifications, purchase descriptions, and master patterns for optional uniform items, as prescribed by the Army Uniform Board and approved by the Chief of Staff, Army.

(2) Publish and disseminate periodic bulletins to industry that provide guidance and information regarding changes in military specifications, testing and certification requirements, uniform regulations, or adoption of new optional uniform items.

(3) Furnish specifications, purchase descriptions, master patterns, shade standards, and other information about optional uniforms to industry when required.

(4) Receive and examine laboratory test reports, manufacturer certifications, and samples from commercial manufacturers, custom tailors, military tailors, and other suppliers of optional uniform items, as required. Require manufacturers to provide requested laboratory test reports, manufacturer certifications, and samples of optional uniform items at no cost to the Army.

(5) Issue certificates of authority to manufacturers whose samples meet or exceed standards established by specifications of purchase descriptions. Certificates will be supplemented by documents showing the specific optional uniform items that the manufacturer is authorized to produce. Provide a list of certified manufacturers and products that will be furnished to the AAFES and included on appropriate Army Web sites. Revoke or suspend certificates when the certificate holder has violated any of the expressed conditions under which the certification was granted, as determined by PEO Soldier.

(6) Conduct inspections and otherwise monitor manufacturers for compliance with certificate terms and conditions. Review optional uniform items to verify compliance with, or appropriate exemption/waiver from, applicable domestic source requirements as set forth in 10 USC 2533a.

b. The UQCP will be monitored overseas as follows: OCONUS Army service component command (ASCC) will establish a service POC who will inturn direct local textile and uniform producers desiring to sell optional uniform items to Soldiers within the theater to PEO Soldier, project manager (Soldier Protection and Individual Equipment), or to NSRDEC for follow-on coordination.

c. Manufacturers and suppliers of optional uniform items will—

(1) Obtain certification required under the UQCP from NSRDEC or project manager (Soldier Protection and Individual Equipment) before manufacturing any optional uniform items for sale.

(2) Affix a label with the following information certifying the optional uniform items were manufactured in accordance with the UQCP prior to offering the items for sale: This garment is warranted to meet or exceed the standards of specification number . . . and was produced under certificate number . . . from basic material warranted by the manufacturer as having been produced in accordance with the sample under current certification. This item is not authorized for turn-in to central issue facilities.

(3) Familiarize themselves with Army specifications, purchase descriptions, testing/certification requirements, shade standards, and other pertinent information for optional uniform items, and submit required samples and information to NSRDEC or project manager (Soldier Protection and Individual Equipment) for approval.

(4) Comply with all terms of the certification. Certificates may be revoked or suspended if the certificate holder has violated any of the expressed conditions of the certification.

# Part Two
# Utility and Selected Organization Uniforms

# Chapter 3
# Temperate, Hot-Weather, and Enhanced Hot-Weather Battle Dress Uniforms

## 3–1. Authorization for wear
The temperate, hot-weather, and enhanced hot-weather battle dress uniforms (BDUs) are authorized for year-round wear by all personnel when prescribed by the commander. (See figs 3–1 and 3–2.)

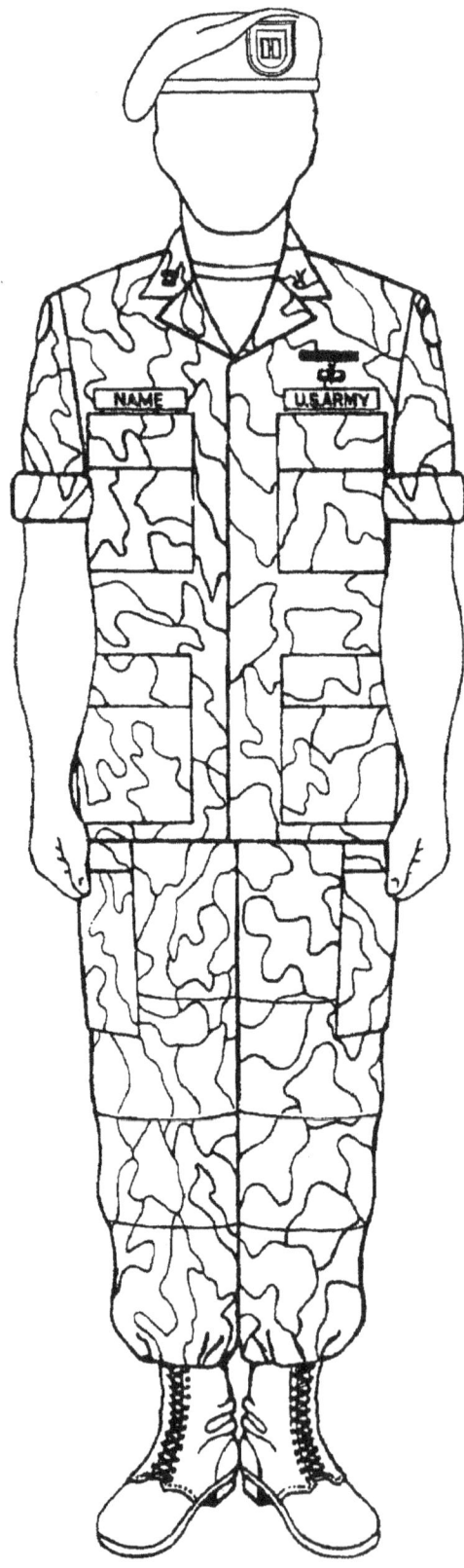

Figure 3–1. Temperate and hot-weather battle dress uniform, with beret, sleeves rolled

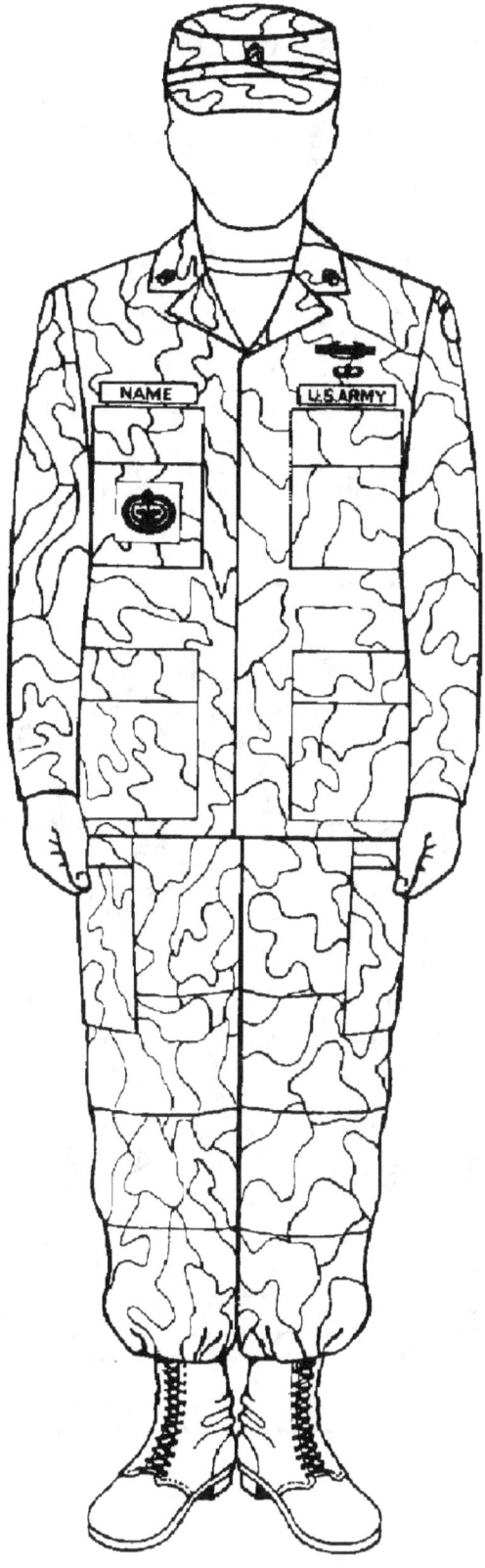

Figure 3–2. Temperate and hot-weather battle dress uniform, with patrol cap, sleeves down

### 3-2. Composition and classification

*a.* Material composition.

(1) Coat, cold weather, woodland camouflage pattern (field jacket). Fabric is nylon and cotton sateen, wind resistant.

(2) Enhanced hot-weather coat and trousers. Fabric is 50/50 ripstop nylon and cotton poplin, in a four-color woodland camouflage pattern.

(3) Hot-weather coat and trousers. Fabric is 100 percent ripstop cotton, in a four-color woodland camouflage pattern.

(4) Temperate coat and trousers. Fabric is 50/50 nylon and cotton twill, in a four-color woodland camouflage pattern.

*b.* Uniform composition.

(1) Beret. The black beret became the standard headgear for utility uniforms on 14 June 2001. The beret consists of a woolen knitted outer shell (lined or unlined) with a leather sweatband and an adjusting ribbon threaded through the binding. The beret is equipped with a stiffener on the left front for the attachment of organizational flashes and insignia.

(2) Cap, woodland camouflage pattern (patrol cap). The cap has a visor, a circular top crown, a side crown with an outside crown band, and retractable earflaps (temperate cap only; the hot-weather caps do not have retractable earflaps).

(3) Coat, cold weather, woodland camouflage pattern (field jacket). The coat is lined, hip length with a bi-swing back, with a convertible stand-up collar with concealed hood and a slide-fastener front closure, with two breast and two lower pockets. (See fig 3-3.)

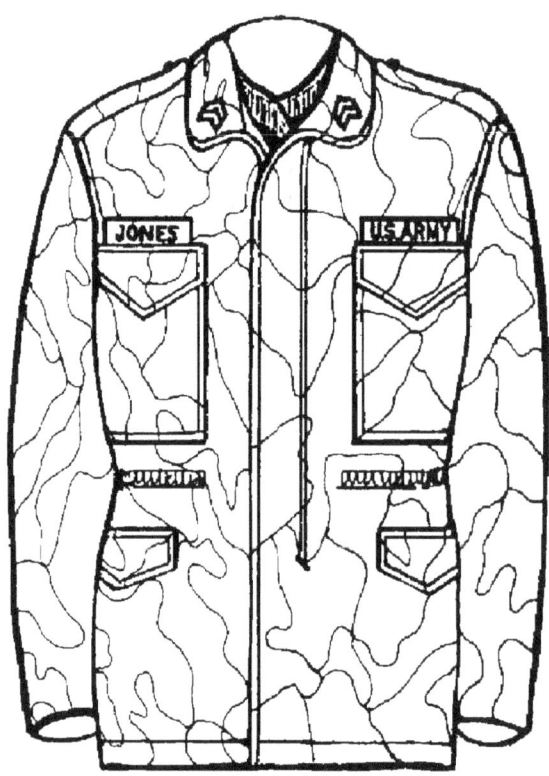

**Figure 3-3. Cold-weather coat, camouflage (field jacket)**

(4) Coat, woodland camouflage pattern. The coat is a single-breasted "bush type" design with a collar and four patch bellows-type pockets with flaps (two chest and two lower). The coat has a straight-cut bottom, waist take-up tabs on both sides (old version only), and cuffed sleeves with reinforcement patches at the elbows. The enhanced hot-weather coat has a fused collar and pocket flaps, a suppressed waist (3 inches), and no waist adjustment tabs.

(5) Trousers, woodland camouflage pattern. The trousers have four standard type pockets and two leg bellows-type pockets, and reinforcement patches at the knees and buttocks. The trousers have a buttonhole fly with protective flap (hot-weather battle dress uniform), adjustable waist tabs (old version only), and leg-hem draw cords. The hot-weather battle dress uniform trousers with knee pleats are authorized for wear until current stocks are exhausted. The knee pleats were removed from the enhanced hot-weather battle dress uniform (EHWBDU) trousers.

c. Accessories. The following accessories are normally worn with these uniforms:

(1) Belt, web with open-faced black buckle (para 27–2a and b).

(2) Boots, combat, leather black (para 27–3).

(3) Chaplain's apparel (para 27–7).

(4) Coat, black all weather (para 27–8).

(5) Gloves, black leather shell with inserts (para 27–12a).

(6) Handbags.

(a) Black, clutch type, optional purchase (para 27–13a).

(b) Black, shoulder (para 27–13d).

(7) Hat, drill sergeant (para 27–14).

(8) Military police accessories (para 27–16).

(9) Neckgaiter, optional purchase (para 27–17).

(10) Scarves.

(a) Black (with black overcoat only) (para 27–21a).

(b) Olive-green 208 (para 27–21b).

(11) Socks, black, cushion sole (para 27–24a).

(12) Undergarments (paras 27–28).

(13) Undershirt, brown (para 27–28e).

(14) Organizational clothing and equipment, as determined by the commander in accordance with CTA 50–900 or CTA 8–100 (medical personnel).

(15) Personal hydration systems, as determined by the commander.

d. Classification. The temperate, enhanced hot-weather, and hot-weather BDUs are clothing bag issue utility uniforms. The beret is an organizational issue item. DA Pam 710–2–1 governs turn-in and reissue of the beret.

## 3–3. Occasions for wear

a. Soldiers may wear BDUs on duty when prescribed by the commander. Soldiers may wear BDUs off post unless prohibited by the commander. They may not wear BDUs for commercial travel, unless authorized by para 1–10c of this regulation. Personnel may not wear BDUs in establishments that primarily sell alcohol. If the establishment sells alcohol and food, soldiers may not wear utility uniforms if their activities in the establishment center on drinking alcohol only.

b. Utility uniforms are not normally considered appropriate for social or official functions off the installation, such as memorial services and funerals. These uniforms are issued as utility, field, training, or combat uniforms and are not intended for wear as all-purpose uniforms when other uniforms are more appropriate.

## 3–4. Insignia and accouterments

The following insignia and accouterments are authorized for wear on these uniforms:

a. Badges (subdued).

(1) Combat and special skill badges (pin on or embroidered sew on) (para 29–17d).

(2) Special skill tabs (para 29–17d).

(3) Subdued identification badges (para 29–18d).

b. Brassards (para 28–29).

c. Branch insignia (paras 28–10b and 28–12b).

d. Combat leaders identification (para 28–21).

e. Grade insignia (paras 28–5 through 28–7).

f. Headgear insignia (para 28–3).

g. Subdued shoulder sleeve insignia, current organization (para 28–16e(2)).

*h.* Subdued shoulder sleeve insignia, former wartime service (para 28–17*c*(2)).

*i.* Name and U.S. Army distinguishing tapes (paras 28–24*a* and 28–24*b*).

*j.* Organizational flash (para 28–31*a*).

*k.* Foreign badges are not authorized for wear on these uniforms.

## 3–5. Headgear

*a.* Beret.

(1) General. The beret is the basic headgear for utility uniforms in garrison environments. The beret is not worn in the field, in training environments, or in environments where the wear of the beret is impractical, as determined by the commander. Additionally, the beret is not worn on deployments unless authorized by the commander. Personnel being transferred from one organization to another may continue to wear the beret and flash of the former unit until they report for duty at the new organization.

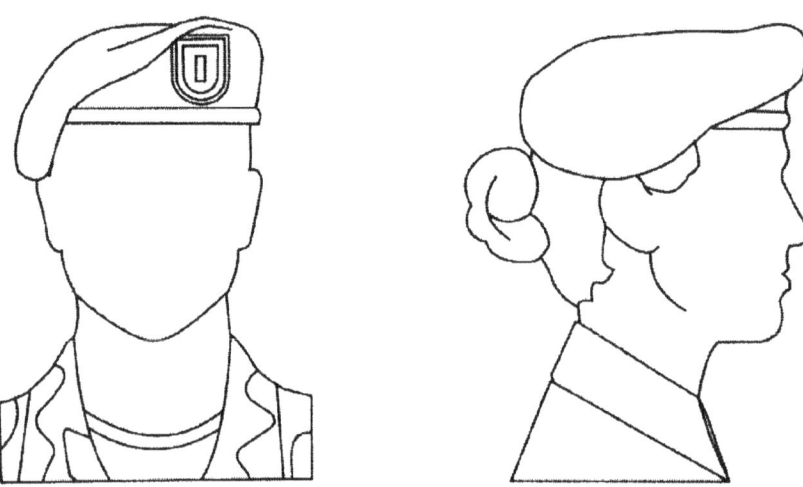

Figure 3–4. Wear of the beret, male and female

(2) Wear. The beret is worn so that the headband (edge binding) is straight across the forehead, 1 inch above the eyebrows. The flash is positioned over the left eye, and the excess material is draped over to the right ear, extending to at least the top of the ear, and no lower than the middle of the ear. Personnel will cut off the ends of the adjusting ribbon and secure the ribbon knot inside the edge binding at the back of the beret. When worn properly, the beret is formed to the shape of the head; therefore, soldiers may not wear hairstyles that cause distortion of the beret. Paragraph 3–5*c*, below, addresses wear of headgear insignia. Figures 3–1 and 3–4 show wear of the beret. Soldiers wear berets as indicated below:

(3) Black beret.

*(a)* Soldiers who are not assigned to units or positions authorized wear of the tan, green, or maroon berets will wear the black beret. This includes senior and junior ROTC instructors, unless otherwise indicated below.

*(b)* Soldiers are issued the black beret upon assignment to their first permanent duty assignment after the completion of initial entry training or officer/warrant officer basic courses. Cadets and officer/warrant officer candidates will not wear the black beret. Split-option soldiers or soldiers in the simultaneous membership program will wear the black beret only when performing duties with their units, and they will wear the patrol cap with the BDU, as described in paragraph 3–5*b* below, when in a cadet or trainee status. Soldiers who have not been issued or who do not wear the black beret will wear the patrol cap with the BDU, as indicated in paragraph 3–5*b* below. In those cases where beret sustainment levels are not sufficient for turn-in and reissue of unserviceable berets, the commander can authorize the temporary wear of the patrol cap until the beret can be replaced.

*(c)* The Army flash is the only flash authorized for wear on the black beret, unless authorization for another flash was granted before the implementation of the black beret as the standard Army headgear (for example, Opposing Forces (OPFOR) elements).

(4) Ranger tan beret. Soldiers currently assigned to the following units are authorized wear of the Ranger tan beret. Personnel will wear the approved flash of the unit to which they are assigned.

(a) 75th Ranger Regiment.

(b) Ranger Training Brigade.

(c) Ranger-qualified soldiers in the following units or positions, if they previously served in the 75th Ranger Regiment: U.S. Special Operations Command; U.S. Army Special Operations Command; U.S. Special Operations Command Joint Task Force; and Theater Special Operations Command. The 75th Ranger Regiment is the sole authority for validation of service in the Ranger Regiment.

(5) Green beret.

(a) If approved by local commanders, all Special Forces-qualified personnel (those carrying the Special Forces MOSs of 18A or 180A, CMF 18, and CSMs reclassified from 18Z to OOZ) are authorized to wear the green beret. This includes senior and junior ROTC instructors and those attending training at an Army service school in a student status (for example, Command and General Staff College, Defense Language Institute, or United States Army Sergeants Major Academy).

(b) Special Forces personnel will wear the approved flash of the unit to which they are assigned. Special Forces personnel who are assigned to an organization without an approved flash will wear the generic SF flash (the flash approved for personnel assigned to SF positions, but not assigned to SF units).

(6) Maroon beret. All personnel assigned to airborne units whose primary missions are airborne operations wear the maroon beret. The airborne designation for a unit is found in the unit modification table of organization and equipment (MTOE). Other soldiers authorized to wear the maroon beret are indicated below. Personnel will wear the approved flash of the unit to which they are assigned.

(a) Active Army advisors to reserve airborne units on jump status.

(b) All personnel assigned to the airborne departments of the U.S. Army Infantry School and the U.S. Army Quartermaster School.

(c) All personnel assigned to long-range surveillance detachments designated as airborne.

(d) All personnel assigned to the airborne/airlift action office.

(e) Recruiters of the Special Operations Recruiting Company (SORC), U.S. Army Recruiting Command. Personnel will wear the USASOC flash.

(f) All personnel assigned to the airborne procurement team.

(g) All personnel assigned to 55th Signal Company Airborne Combat Camera Documentation Team.

(h) All personnel assigned to 982d Combat Signal Company airborne platoons.

(i) All personnel assigned to rigger detachments.

b. Patrol cap.

(1) The patrol cap (formerly called the BDU cap) is worn with the BDU in field environments when the Kevlar helmet is not worn; on work details; or in other environments where the wear of the beret is impractical, as determined by the commander. Additionally, personnel in initial training categories who do not wear the black beret (see para 3–5a(3)(b), above) wear the patrol cap with the BDU. The patrol cap is available in the hot-weather and temperate fabrics.

(2) Personnel wear the patrol cap straight on the head so that the cap band creates a straight line around the head, parallel to the ground. The patrol cap will fit snugly and comfortably around the largest part of the head without distortion or excessive gaps. The cap is worn so that no hair is visible on the forehead beneath the cap. At their discretion, individuals may wear the earflaps down during cold weather, except in formation when the commander may prescribe wear policy (see fig 3–2).

c. Headgear insignia. (See para 28–3 for placement of headgear insignia and beret flashes.)

(1) Beret. Officers and warrant officers wear non-subdued grade insignia centered on the beret flash, and chaplains wear their branch insignia. Enlisted personnel wear their distinctive unit insignia (DUI) centered on the beret flash. Enlisted personnel assigned to units not authorized the DUI wear their regimental distinctive insignia (RDI). General officers may wear full-, medium-, or miniature-sized stars on the beret. Stars are centered horizontally on the flash point-to-point, and they may be mounted on a bar as an option. Overlap of the stars beyond the flash is authorized.

(2) Patrol cap. Commissioned and warrant officers wear non-subdued grade insignia on the patrol cap in garrison environments; chaplains wear non-subdued branch insignia. In field environments, commissioned and warrant officers wear subdued grade insignia; chaplains wear subdued branch insignia. Enlisted personnel wear subdued grade insignia on the patrol cap in garrison and field environments.

## 3–6. General guidelines

a. These uniforms are designed to fit loosely; alterations to make them fit tightly are not authorized. A tight fit reduces the airflow needed for ventilation and cooling. The only alterations authorized are those listed in AR 700–84. Personnel are authorized to mix and match hot-weather and enhanced hot-weather coats, trousers, and patrol caps. However, personnel may not mix hot-weather and temperate uniform items, to include the patrol cap.

*b.* The coat is worn outside the trousers, and the trousers are worn with a belt. The coat will not extend below the top of the cargo pocket on the pants and will not be higher than the bottom of the side pocket on the pants. Commanders may authorize exceptions to this policy under conditions deemed appropriate in the interest of health, comfort, and efficiency because of climatic conditions, or to accommodate a soldier's religious practices in accordance with AR 600–20, para 5–6.

*c.* Soldiers will wear the trousers bloused, using the draw cords or blousing rubbers, if the trousers are not tucked into the boots. Personnel will not wrap the trouser leg around the leg tightly enough to present a pegged appearance. Soldiers will not blouse the boots so that the trouser leg extends down to the ankle area. When bloused, the trousers should not extend below the third eyelet from the top of the boot. When soldiers wear the sleeves of the coat rolled up, the camouflage pattern will remain exposed. Personnel will roll the sleeves neatly above the elbow, no more than 3 inches above the elbow.

*d.* The commander may require that soldiers press these uniforms for special occasions when an especially sharp appearance is required, such as parades, reviews, inspections, or other ceremonial occasions. Although soldiers are authorized to starch the BDU, commanders may not require them to do so. Soldiers are authorized to press military creases in the BDU coat (see para 1–9*a*(4)).

*e.* When uniformity in appearance is required, commanders may prescribe a specific uniform for formations or ceremonial occasions, such as parades. When a specific uniform is not prescribed, soldiers may wear the enhanced hot-weather, hot-weather, or temperate BDU, or other authorized utility uniforms.

*f.* Soldiers may wear the black leather shell gloves with utility uniforms without cold-weather outer garments, provided that sleeves are rolled down. Personnel may wear the woodland camouflage cold-weather coat with all utility uniforms. Soldiers may wear the black all-weather coat as a raincoat with these uniforms only in a garrison environment when they have not been issued organizational raingear. When the cold-weather coat or other authorized cold-weather outer garments are worn, personnel may wear the olive-green scarf and the black leather shell gloves, but are not required to do so. Coats are worn buttoned and zipped, and the shirt collar is worn inside the cold-weather coat and other outer garments. Soldiers may wear the hood of the cold-weather coat at their option. However, when the hood is not worn, soldiers will tuck it into the jacket and will zip the zipper. Female personnel may carry handbags with these uniforms only while in a garrison environment.

*g.* Commanders may authorize the use of a camouflage personal hydration system only in the following situations: in a field environment, in high-heat areas, or on work details. Soldiers will not carry hydration systems in a garrison environment unless the commander has authorized it for one of the situations described above. Soldiers will not let the drinking tube hang from their mouths when the device is not in use.

## Chapter 4
## Maternity Work Uniform

### 4–1. Authorization for wear
The Army maternity work uniform is authorized for year-round duty wear by pregnant soldiers, when prescribed by the commander. (See fig 4–1.)

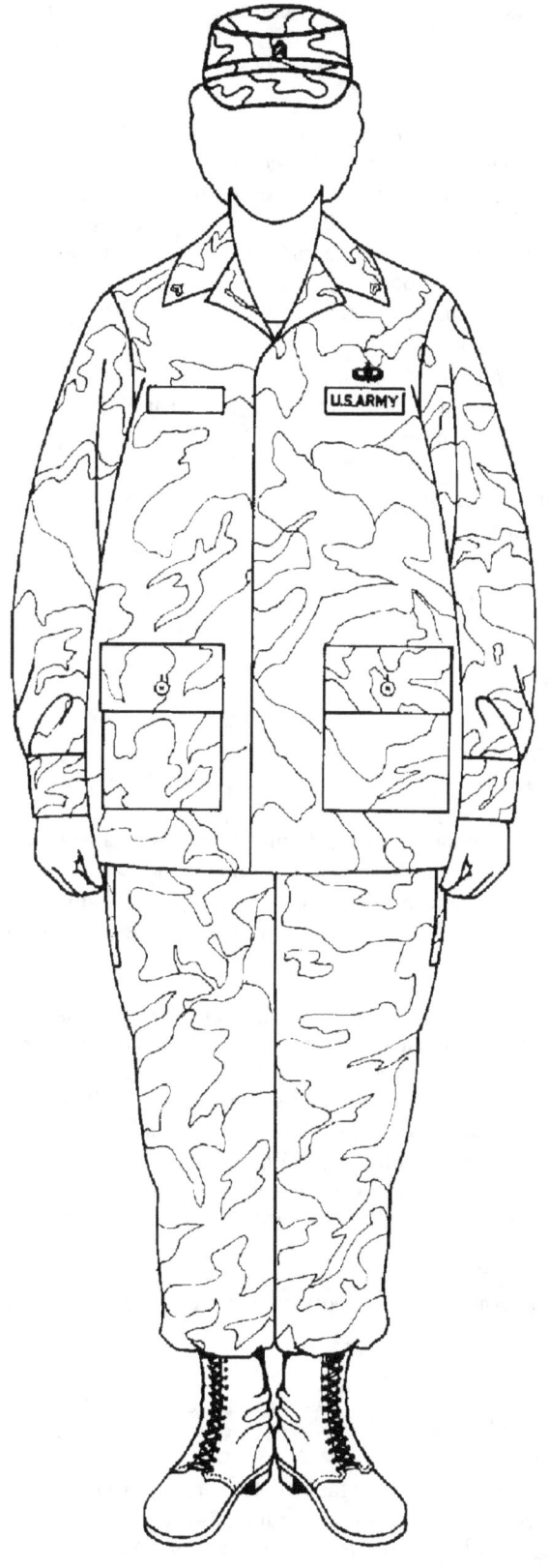

Figure 4–1. Maternity work uniform

## 4–2. Composition and classification

*a.* Material composition. Fabric is 100 percent ripstop cotton (old fabric blend), or a 50/50 nylon and cotton ripstop poplin (new fabric blend).

*b.* Uniform composition.

(1) Beret (para 3–2*b*(1)).

(2) Cap, patrol (formerly BDU) (para 3–2*b*(2)).

(3) Coat, cold weather, camouflage pattern (para 3–2*a*(1)).

(4) Coat, maternity, woodland camouflage pattern. A single-breasted coat style design with a collar, two patch pockets with flaps, a straight-cut bottom, sleeve tabs, and pleated side-body panels with take-up tabs.

(5) Trousers, maternity, woodland camouflage pattern. The trousers have a front stretch panel with an elasticized waistband and side pockets, with flaps on both legs.

*c.* Accessories. The following accessories are normally worn with this uniform.

(1) Boots, combat, leather, black (para 27–3).

(2) Chaplain's apparel (para 27–7)

(3) Coat, black all weather (para 27–8). (See para 4–5*d* for wear policy.)

(4) Gloves, black, leather shell, with inserts (para 27–12*a*).

(5) Handbags.

*(a)* Black, clutch type, optional purchase (para 27–13*a*).

*(b)* Black, shoulder (para 27–13*d*).

(6) Hat, drill sergeant (para 27–14*a*).

(7) Military Police accessories (para 27–16).

(8) Neckgaiter (para 27–17).

(9) Scarves.

*(a)* Black (with black overcoat only) (para 27–21*a*).

*(b)* Olive-green 208 (para 27–21*b*).

(10) Socks, black, cushion sole (para 27–24*a*).

(11) Undergarments (para 27–28).

(12) Undershirt, brown (para 27–28*e*).

(13) Organizational clothing and equipment, as determined by the commander, according to CTA 50–900.

(14) Personal hydration systems, as determined by the commander.

*d.* Classification. The maternity work uniform is an organizationally issued utility and field uniform. The beret is an organizational issue item. DA Pam 710–2–1 governs turn-in and reissue of the beret.

## 4–3. Occasions for wear

*a.* The maternity work uniform is worn on duty when prescribed by the commander. Females may wear the maternity work BDUs off post unless prohibited by the commander. They may not wear the maternity work uniform for commercial travel, unless authorized by para 1–10*c* of this regulation. Soldiers may not wear the maternity work uniform in establishments that primarily sell alcohol. If the establishment sells alcohol and food, soldiers may not wear utility uniforms if their activities in the establishment center on drinking alcohol only.

*b.* Utility uniforms are not normally considered appropriate for social or official functions off the installation, such as memorial services and funerals. The maternity work uniform is issued as an organizational utility or field maternity uniform and is not intended for wear when other maternity uniforms are more appropriate.

## 4–4. Insignia and accouterments

The following insignia and accouterments are authorized for wear on the maternity work uniform.

*a.* Badges, special skill (para 29–17).

*b.* Brassards (para 28–29).

*c.* Branch insignia (paras 28–10*b* and 28–12*b*).

*d.* Grade insignia (paras 28–5, 28–6, and 28–7).

*e.* Headgear insignia (para 28–3).

*f.* Subdued shoulder sleeve insignia, current organization (para 28–16*e*(2)).

*g.* Shoulder sleeve insignia-former wartime service (para 28–17*c*(2)).

*h.* Name and U.S. Army distinguishing tapes (paras 28–24*a* and 28–24*b*).

*i.* Organizational flash (para 28–31*a*).

*j.* Personnel will not wear foreign badges on this uniform.

## 4–5. General guidelines

*a.* This uniform is designed to fit loosely; alterations to make the uniform fit tightly are not authorized. A tight fit reduces the airflow needed for ventilation and cooling. The coat is worn outside the trousers. Soldiers will not wear a belt with this uniform. Soldiers will wear the trousers bloused, using the draw cords or blousing rubbers, if the trousers are not tucked into the boots. Personnel will not wrap the trouser legs around the leg tightly enough to present a pegged appearance. Soldiers will not blouse the boots so that the trouser leg extends down to the ankle area. When bloused, the trousers should not extend below the third eyelet from the top of the boot. When soldiers wear the sleeves of the coat rolled up, the camouflage pattern will remain exposed. Personnel will roll the sleeves neatly above the elbow, no more than 3 inches above the elbow.

*b.* The commander may require that soldiers press the maternity work uniform when an especially sharp appearance is required for special occasions, such as parades, reviews, inspections, or other ceremonial occasions. Soldiers are authorized to starch the maternity work uniform; however, commanders may not require soldiers to do so. Soldiers are authorized to press military creases in the BDU coat (see para 1–9*a*(4)).

*c.* The black beret became the basic headgear for this uniform on 14 June 2001. (See para 3–5 of this regulation for wear policy of the beret and other headgear.)

*d.* Soldiers may wear the black all-weather coat with the uniform in garrison. When coats are worn, soldiers may wear them unbuttoned and unzipped, if necessary. Soldiers may wear the black leather shell gloves with this uniform without cold weather outer garments, provided that the sleeves are rolled down. When the cold weather coat or other authorized cold-weather outer garments are worn, personnel may wear the olive-green scarf and the black leather shell gloves, but they are not required to do so. Soldiers will wear the shirt collar inside the cold-weather coat and other outer garments. Personnel may carry handbags with this uniform, but only while in a garrison environment.

*e.* Commanders may authorize the use of a camouflage personal hydration system only in the following situations: in a field environment, in high-heat areas, or on work details. Soldiers will not carry hydration systems in a garrison environment unless the commander has authorized it for one of the situations described above. Soldiers will not let the drinking tube hang from their mouths when the device is not in use.

## Chapter 5
## Desert Battle Dress Uniform

### 5–1. Authorization for wear

The desert battle dress uniform (DBDU) is authorized for year-round wear by all personnel when issued as organizational clothing and prescribed by the commander. (See figs 5–1 through 5–4.)

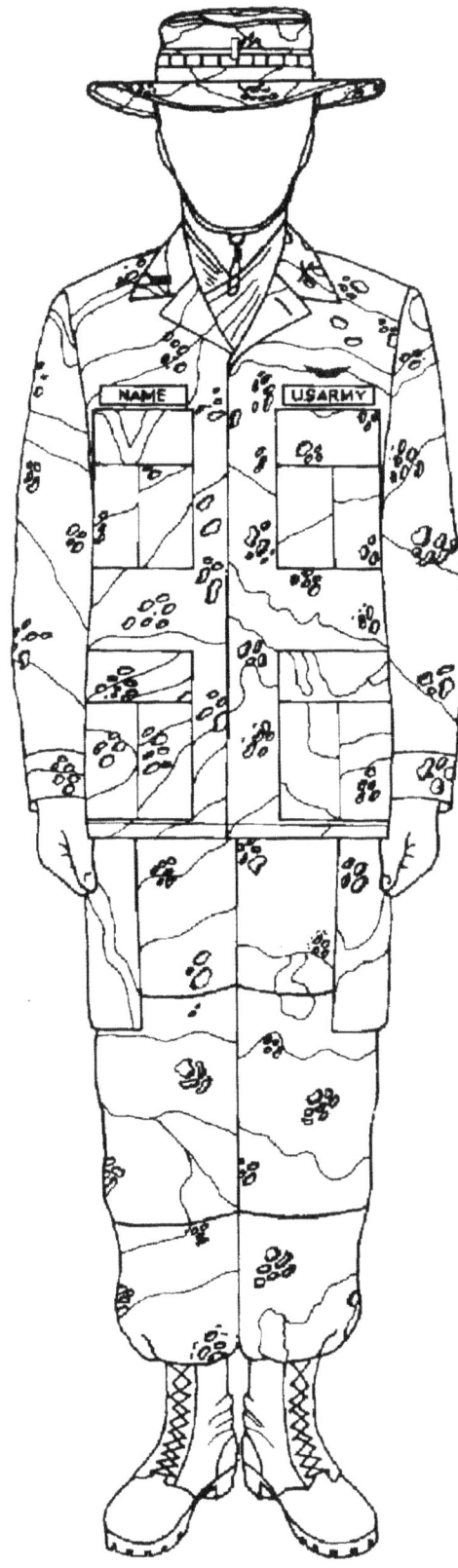

Figure 5–1. Desert battle dress uniform, daytime pattern, officer, with desert BDU hat

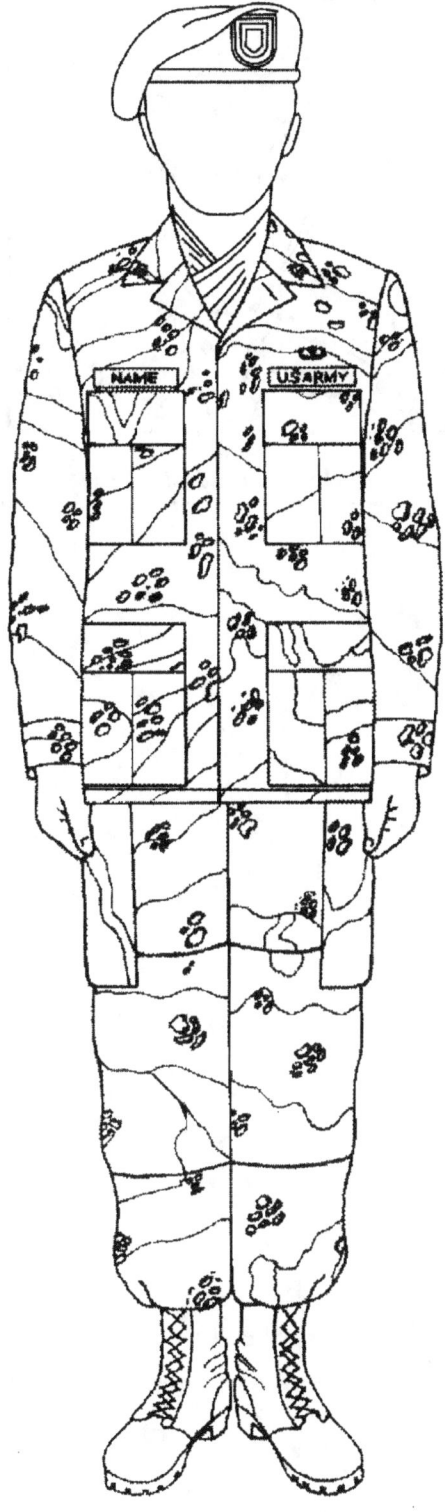

Figure 5–2. Desert battle dress uniform, daytime pattern, enlisted, with beret

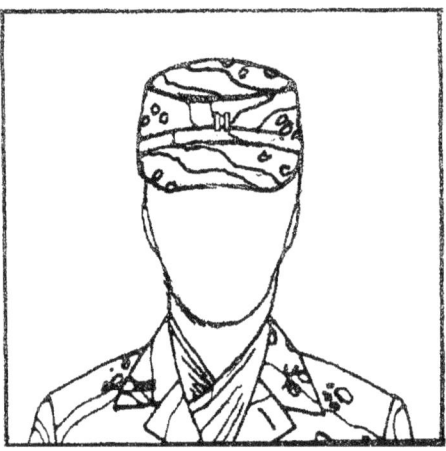

Figure 5–3. Desert BDU cap

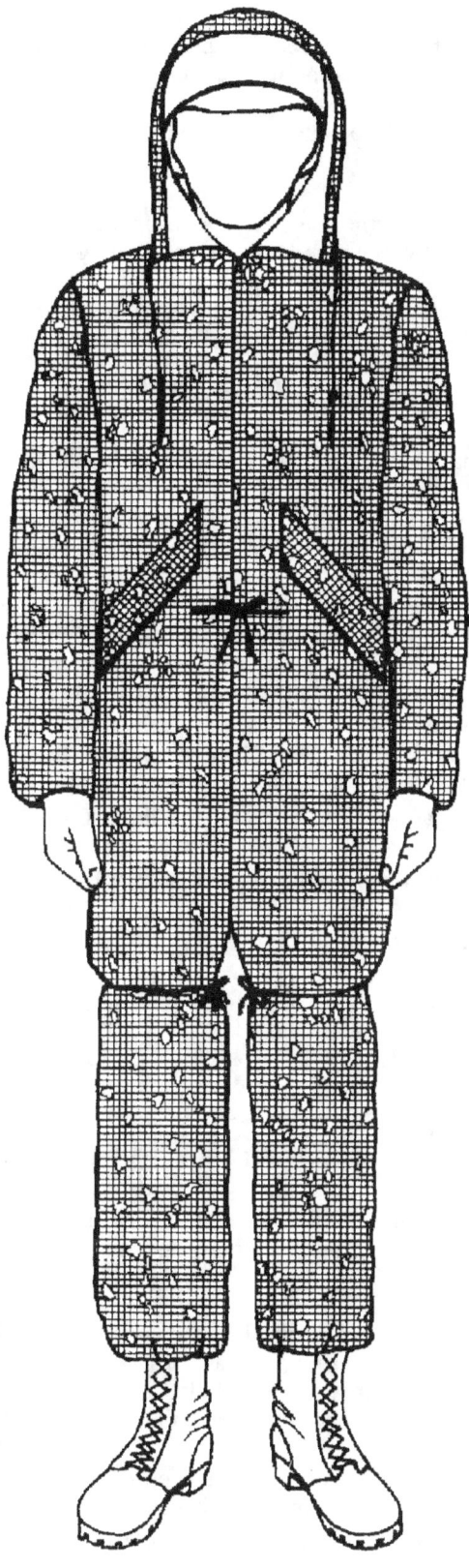

**Figure 5–4. Desert battle dress uniform, nighttime pattern**

## 5–2. Composition and classification

*a.* Material composition.

(1) Desert coat, trousers and hat. Fabric is 50/50 cotton and nylon twill (old weight material) or 50/50 cotton and nylon ripstop (new weight material), with infrared protection characteristics, and it is printed with a three-color desert camouflage pattern.

(2) Desert coat, cold weather. Fabric is 50/50 cotton and nylon sateen, wind resistant, and it is printed with a three-color desert camouflage pattern.

*b.* Uniform composition.

(1) Coat, desert camouflage, daytime pattern. The coat is a bush-type design with a collar and four patch bellows-type pockets with flaps (two chest and two lower). The coat has a straight-cut bottom, suppressed waist, and cuffed sleeves with reinforcement patches at the elbows.

(2) Coat, cold weather, desert. The coat is lined, hip length with a bi-swing back, a convertible stand-up collar with concealed hood, and a slide-fastener front closure with two breast, and two lower pockets.

(3) Beret (para 3–2*b*(1)).

(4) Hat, desert camouflage. The hat has a stiff crown with a standard width, quilted stitched brim, a chinstrap, and a camouflage band.

(5) Cap, patrol, desert. The cap has a visor, a circular top crown, a side crown with an outside crown band, and retractable earflaps.

(6) Parka, desert camouflage, night pattern. The parka has a hood, a button front closure, two slit-type hand openings with flaps, draw cords at neck, hood, waist, and hemline, and buttons on the inside for the attachment of a liner.

(7) Trousers, desert camouflage, daytime pattern. The trousers have four standard-type pockets, two leg bellows-type pockets, and reinforcement patches at the knees and buttocks, a buttonhole fly, adjustable waist tabs, and leg hem draw cords.

(8) Trousers, desert camouflage, night pattern. The trousers have a front opening, two side slit-type openings with flaps, and two hip patch pockets with flaps.

*c.* Accessories. The following accessories are normally worn with the DBDU.

(1) Belt, web with open-faced black buckle (paras 27–2*a* and *b*).

(2) Boots, combat, leather, black (para 27–3) or desert tan when issued in accordance with CTA 50–900.

(3) Chaplain's apparel (para 27–7).

(4) Gloves, black leather shell with inserts (para 27–12*a*).

(5) Handbags.

*(a)* Black, clutch type, optional purchase (para 27–13*a*).

*(b)* Black, shoulder (para 27–13*d*).

(6) Military Police accessories (para 27–17).

(7) Neckerchief, brown, LIN M95975, CTA 50–900.

(8) Socks, black, cushion sole (para 27–24*a*).

(9) Undergarments (paras 27–28).

(10) Undershirt, brown (para 27–28*e*).

(11) Organizational clothing and equipment, as prescribed by the commander in accordance with CTA 50–900.

(12) Desert personal hydration system, as determined by the commander.

*d.* Classification. The DBDU is an organizationally issued utility, field, training, or combat uniform. The beret is an organizational issue item. DA Pam 710–2–1 governs turn-in and reissue of the beret.

## 5–3. Occasions for wear

*a.* Personnel wear the DBDU on duty when prescribed by the commander. Soldiers may wear the DBDU off post, unless prohibited by the commander. They may not wear DBDUs for commercial travel, unless authorized by paragraph 1–10*c* of this regulation. Personnel may not wear DBDUs in establishments that primarily sell alcohol. If the establishment sells alcohol and food, soldiers may not wear utility uniforms if their activities in the establishment center on drinking alcohol only.

*b.* Utility uniforms are not normally considered appropriate for social or official functions off of the installation, such as memorial services and funerals. These uniforms are issued as organizational utility, field, training, or combat uniforms, and they are not intended for wear as all-purpose uniforms when other uniforms are more appropriate.

## 5–4. Insignia and accouterments

The following insignia and accouterments are authorized for wear on the DBDU.

   *a.* Badges (subdued).

   (1) Combat and special skill badges (pin-on or embroidered sew-on) (para 29–17*a*).

   (2) Special skill tabs (para 29–17*e*(1)(b)).

   (3) Subdued identification badges (para 29–18*d*).

   *b.* Brassards (para 28–29).

   *c.* Branch insignia (paras 28–10*b* and 28–12).

   *d.* Grade insignia (paras 28–5 through 28–7).

   *e.* Headgear insignia (para 28–3).

   *f.* Subdued shoulder sleeve insignia, current organization (para 28–16*e*(2)).

   *g.* Subdued shoulder sleeve insignia, former wartime service (SSI–FWTS) (para 28–17*c*(2)).

   *h.* Name and U.S. Army distinguishing tapes (paras 28–24*a* and 28–24*b*).

   *i.* Organizational flash (para 28–31*a*).

   *j.* Foreign badges are not authorized for wear on this uniform.

## 5–5. General guidelines

   *a.* The DBDU is designed to fit loosely and alterations are not authorized. The coat is worn outside the trousers, and the trousers are worn belted. Commanders may authorize exceptions to this policy under conditions deemed appropriate in the interest of health, comfort, and efficiency because of climatic conditions, or to accommodate a soldier's religious practices, in accordance with AR 600–20, para 5–6.

   *b.* Soldiers are required to wear the nametape, U.S. Army tape, and the SSI, current organization. However, they have the option of wearing the SSI–FWTS, and they may wear either pin-on or sew-on rank, branch insignia, and subdued badges. If soldiers choose to wear optional sew-on insignia, they will bear all costs associated with the application and removal of the insignia. This includes any damage to the organizational DBDU. All optional insignia must be removed from the DBDU prior to returning the garment to organizational stock.

   *c.* Soldiers will wear the trousers bloused, using the draw cords or blousing rubbers, if the trousers are not tucked into the boots. Personnel will not wrap the trouser legs around the leg tightly enough to present a pegged appearance. Soldiers will not blouse the boots so that the trouser leg extends down to the ankle area. When bloused, the trousers should not extend below the third eyelet from the top of the boot. When sleeves are rolled up, the camouflage pattern will remain exposed. Personnel will roll the sleeves neatly above the elbow, no more than 3 inches above the elbow.

   *d.* The commander may require that soldiers press this uniform for special occasions when an especially sharp appearance is required, such as for parades, reviews, inspections, or other ceremonial occasions. Soldiers may press the DBDU, but they are not authorized to starch the uniform.

   *e.* Headgear. The desert patrol cap, desert camouflage hat, and the beret are the authorized headgear for this uniform. The commander will determine which headgear soldiers wear on the basis of mission requirements. Soldiers wear the desert camouflage hat so that no hair is visible on the forehead, and with the chinstrap pulled up under the chin (see figure 5–1). The desert patrol cap is worn in the same fashion as the woodland patrol cap (formerly the BDU cap) (refer to para 3–5 for wear of the patrol cap and the beret). Figures 5–1, 5–2, and 5–3 show the wear of the desert camouflage hat, desert patrol cap, and the beret.

   *f.* Soldiers may wear the black leather shell gloves with utility uniforms without cold-weather outer garments, provided sleeves are rolled down. When the parka is worn, soldiers will wear it buttoned and will wear the shirt collar inside the parka. Soldiers may wear the black leather shell gloves with this uniform when they wear the parka, but they are not required to do so.

   *g.* Commanders may authorize the use of a desert camouflage personal hydration system only in desert environments. Soldiers will not let the drinking tube hang from their mouths when the device is not in use.

# Chapter 6
# Aircrew Battle Dress Uniform

## 6–1. Authorization for wear

The aircrew battle dress uniform (ABDU) is authorized for year-round wear by aircrew members, as specified in CTA 50–900, when prescribed by the commander. (See fig 6–1.)

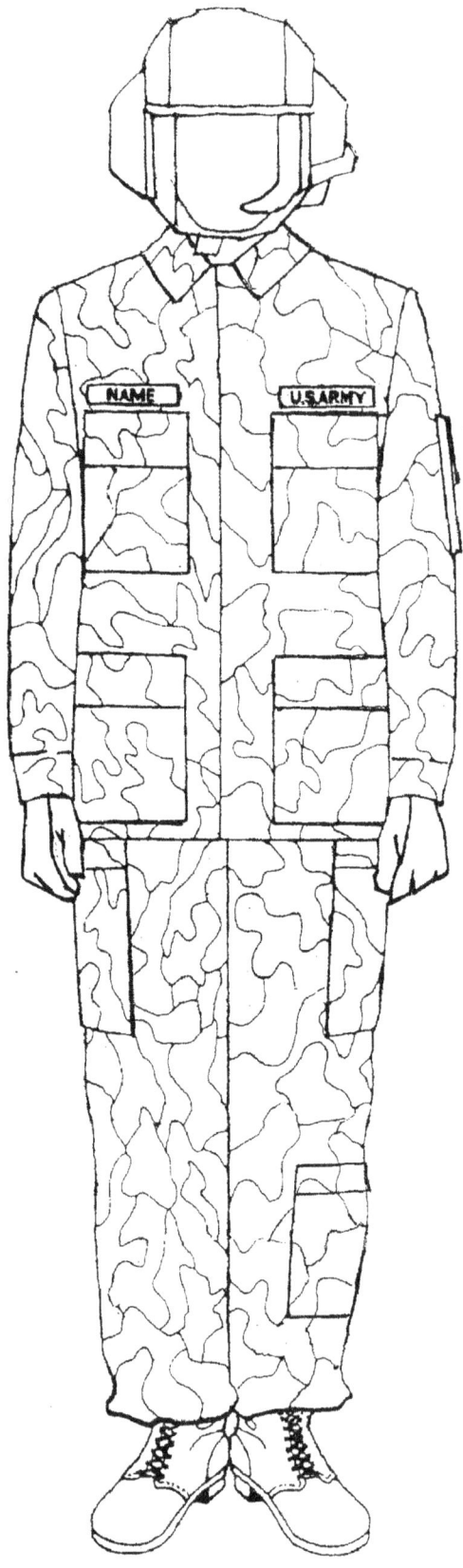

Figure 6–1. Aircrew battle dress uniform

AR 670–1 • 3 February 2005

## 6–2. Composition and classification

*a.* Material composition.

(1) Aircrew coat and trousers. The fabric is a blend of 92 percent NOMEX, 5 percent Kevlar, and 3 percent static dissipative fiber in a plain weave, printed with a four-color woodland camouflage pattern and tan 380.

(2) Aircrew cold-weather clothing system jacket, liner and hood. The jacket shell fabric is a blend of 92 percent NOMEX, 5 percent Kevlar, and 3 percent static dissipative fiber, oxford weave, in a four-color woodland camouflage. The lining is a blend of 92 percent NOMEX, 5 percent Kevlar, and 3 percent static dissipative fiber, plain weave, camouflage green in color. The jacket liner fabric is a quilted NOMEX batting, camouflage green in color. The hood main body is an oxford aramid cloth, in a woodland camouflage pattern, with a batting lining and synthetic fur ruff.

*b.* Uniform composition.

(1) Beret (para 3–2*b*(1)).

(2) Cap, patrol (formerly BDU) (para 3–2*b*(2)).

(3) Jacket, aircrew, cold-weather clothing system, woodland camouflage pattern. The jacket is a single-breasted design with a slide-fastener front closure, fully lined, and it has draw cords at the waist and hem. The jacket has a collar, two bellows-type chest pockets, two lower hanging pockets, a left-sleeve utility pocket, shoulder loops, reinforced elbows, and wrist tabs with hook-and-loop tape adjustments. The jacket has buttons located in the neck and inside facings for the cold-weather liner attachment. All pockets have flaps with hook-and-loop closures to meet aviator-specific needs. The jacket liner is a collarless cardigan style, with underarm vent openings and knitted cuffs. The liner can be buttoned into the jacket or self-buttoned for wear alone in cold-weather conditions. The hood attaches to the jacket with snap fasteners and closes with a draw cord and hook-and-pile fastener tape. The hood can be worn over the flyer's helmet.

(4) Coat, aircrew, woodland camouflage pattern. The coat is a single-breasted bush-type design with a slide-fastener front closure, collar, four patch-type pockets with flaps (two upper and two lower), and a left-sleeve utility pocket with flap. The coat has a straight-cut bottom, adjustment tabs with hook-and-loop tape at the waist, collar, and wrists, and reinforcement patches at the elbows. All pockets use hook-and-loop closures to meet aviator-specific needs.

(5) Trousers, aircrew, woodland camouflage pattern. The trousers contain four standard-type pockets, two side-opening, leg cargo-type pockets, and two top-opening calf patch pockets. All pockets have flaps, except for the front hanging pockets. Hook-and-loop closures are used on the pockets and pocket flaps to meet aviator-specific needs. The trousers have a slide-fastener fly closure, adjustable straps at the waist, and leg hem drawcords.

*c.* Accessories. The following accessories are normally worn with these uniforms.

(1) Balaclava, hood, LIN H46881, CTA 50–900.

(2) Belt, web, with open-faced black buckle (paras 27–2*a* and *b*).

(3) Bib, overall, LIN P37820.

(4) Boots, combat, black leather (para 27–3).

(5) Gloves, flyer's, LIN J67052.

(6) Handbags.

*(a)* Black, clutch type, optional purchase (para 27–13*a*).

*(b)* Black, shoulder (para 27–13*d*).

(7) Neckgaiter (para 27–17)

(8) Scarf, olive-green 208 (para 27–21*b*).

(9) Socks, black, cushion sole (para 27–24*a*).

(10) Undergarments (paras 27–28).

(11) Undershirt, brown (para 27–28*e*).

(12) Organizational clothing and equipment, as determined by the commander, in accordance with CTA 50–900.

(13) Sweater, wool, black or green.

(14) Sweater, wool, brown, with partial front buttons and short collar.

(15) Personal hydration system, as determined by the commander.

*d.* Classification. The aircrew battle dress uniform is an organizational issue flight utility uniform. The beret is an organizational issue item. DA Pam 710–2–1 governs turn-in and reissue of the beret.

## 6–3. Occasions for wear

*a.* Soldiers may wear ABDUs on duty when prescribed by the commander for flight operations. Soldiers may wear ABDUs off post, unless prohibited by the commander. They may not wear ABDUs for commercial travel, unless authorized by para 1–10*c* of this regulation. Personnel may not wear ABDUs in establishments that primarily sell alcohol. If the establishment sells alcohol and food, soldiers may not wear utility uniforms if their activities in the establishment center on drinking alcohol only.

*b.* Utility uniforms are not normally considered appropriate for social or official functions off the installation, such as memorial services and funerals. These uniforms are issued as utility uniforms and are not intended for wear as all-purpose uniforms when other uniforms are more appropriate.

## 6–4. Insignia and accouterments
The following insignia and accouterments are authorized for wear on these uniforms. Only embroidered insignia and accouterments are authorized for wear on the ABDU.

*a.* Badges (subdued).

(1) Combat and special skill badges (para 29–17*d*).

(2) Special skill tabs (para 29–17*e*).

(3) Identification badges (para 29–18).

*b.* Branch insignia (paras 28–10*b* and 28–12*b*).

*c.* Combat leaders identification (para 28–21).

*d.* Grade insignia (paras 28–5, 28–6, and 28–7).

*e.* Headgear insignia (para 28–3).

*f.* Subdued shoulder sleeve insignia, current organization (para 28–16*e*(2)).

*g.* Subdued shoulder sleeve insignia, former wartime service (SSI–FWTS) (para 28–17*c*(2)).

*h.* Name and U.S. Army distinguishing tapes (paras 28–24*a* and 28–24*b*).

*i.* Organizational flash (para 28–31*a*).

*j.* Foreign badges are not authorized for wear on this uniform.

## 6–5. General guidelines
*a.* Basic uniform. The ABDU is for use by flight crews and personnel in other selected MOSs (military occupational specialties), as prescribed in CTA 50–900. It will not be worn as a substitute for the BDU when the BDU is more appropriate. Insignia is worn on the ABDU the same way as on the BDU; personnel will not wear the leather nameplates that are worn on the flight uniform. These uniforms are designed to be slightly loose fitting; alterations to make them form fitting are not authorized. The coat is worn outside the trousers for all duties, to include flight. The trousers are worn with the standard black cotton web belt. The coat will not extend below the top of the cargo pocket on the pants, and it will not extend higher than the bottom of the side pocket on the pants. Soldiers will keep sleeves down on the ABDU during flight operations (see fig 6–1).

*b.* Soldiers are required to wear rank, nametape, U.S. Army tape, and the SSI, current organization. However, they have the option of wearing the SSI–FWTS, branch insignia, and badges. If soldiers choose to wear the optional insignia, they will bear all costs associated with the application and removal of the insignia. This includes any damage to the organizational ABDU. All optional insignia must be removed from the ABDU prior to returning the garment to organizational stock.

*c.* Soldiers are not authorized to blouse the trousers inside the boots during the execution of flight crew duties. When not performing flight duties and the trousers are bloused, soldiers will use the draw cords or blousing rubbers if the trousers are not tucked into the boots. Personnel will not wrap the trouser legs around the leg tightly enough to present a pegged appearance. Soldiers will not blouse the boots so that the trouser leg extends down to the ankle area. When bloused, the trousers should not extend below the third eyelet from the top of the boot. When soldiers wear the sleeves of the coat rolled up, the camouflage pattern will remain exposed. Personnel will roll the sleeves neatly above the elbow, no more than 3 inches above the elbow. Soldiers will not press or starch the ABDU.

*d.* The black beret became the basic headgear for this uniform on 14 June 2001. The beret will be worn when soldiers are not performing flight duties, unless the commander has prescribed wear of the patrol cap, as described in chapter 3 of this regulation. When soldiers wear the patrol cap, they may wear either the temperate or the hot-weather headgear with the ABDU. (See para 3–5 for wear policy concerning the beret and the patrol cap.)

*e.* The black leather combat boot and the black leather flyer's insulated boot (when authorized according to CTA 50–900) are the authorized footwear for the ABDU. Soldiers will not wear the jungle boot with the ABDU.

*f.* Soldiers may wear the black leather shell gloves with these uniforms when not performing crew duties. They may wear the gloves without cold-weather outer garments, provided sleeves are rolled down. The flight jacket is the only authorized cold-weather coat for wear with the ABDU. The aircrew cold weather clothing system jacket will serve as the ABDU flight jacket. Soldiers may wear the black all-weather coat as a raincoat with these uniforms when they have not been issued organizational raingear, but only in a garrison environment and only when they are not performing flight operations. Personnel will wear coats buttoned and zipped. The shirt collar will be worn inside the cold-weather coat and other outer garments. Soldiers may wear the hood of the cold-weather coat at their discretion. Female personnel may carry handbags with these uniforms only while in a garrison environment.

*g.* Commanders may authorize other uniforms for wear during administrative flights after performing the proper risk assessment. Local commanders may authorize the wear of solid baseball caps (when authorized per CTA 50–900) by aircraft and ground crewmembers while on the flight line or in the base operations area, as a safety and identification measure. Soldiers will wear standard headgear outside these areas. Personnel will wear insignia of grade on organizational baseball caps in accordance with paragraph 28–3f. Commanders will provide the caps to individuals at no cost.

*h.* Protective clothing and equipment for flight crews are specified in AR 95–1, paragraph 8–9.

*i.* Commanders may authorize the use of a camouflage personal hydration system only in the following situations: in a field environment, in high-heat areas, or on work details. Soldiers will not carry hydration systems in a garrison environment, unless the commander has authorized it for one of the situations described above. Soldiers will not let the drinking tube hang from their mouths when the device is not in use.

## Chapter 7
## Cold-Weather Uniform

### 7–1. Authorization for wear
The OG 108 cold-weather uniform is authorized for year-round wear by all personnel, when issued as organizational clothing and prescribed by the commander. (See fig 7–1.)

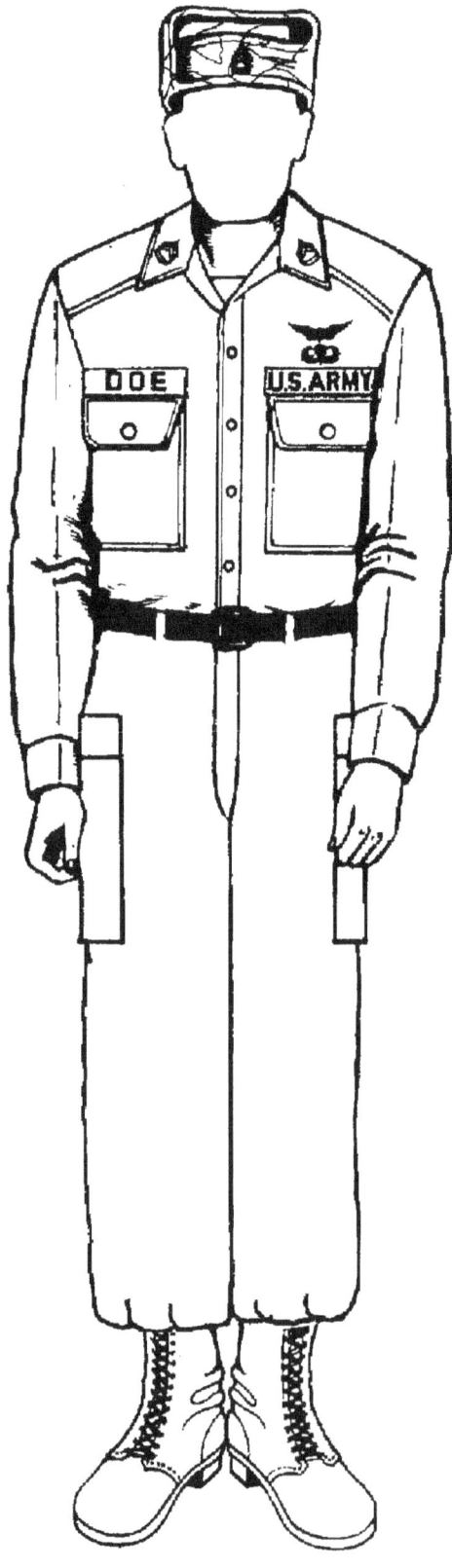

Figure 7–1. Cold-weather uniform

## 7–2. Composition and classification

*a.* Material composition. Fabric is wool serge, olive-green shade 108.

*b.* Uniform composition.

(1) Beret (para 3–2*b*(1)).

(2) Cap, patrol (formerly BDU) (para 3–2*b*(2)).

(3) Cap, cold-weather, woodland camouflage pattern or OG 107 (pile cap). The cap is a fully lined cold-weather head covering, with a turndown forehead flap, a three-piece crown, a stretch gusset with an elastic strip at the center back, and earflaps with a nylon fastener hook-and-pile type overlap closure. (See fig 7–2.)

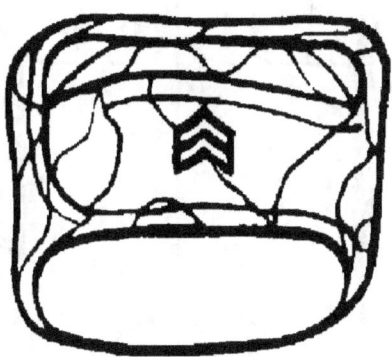

**Figure 7–2. Cold-weather cap, camouflage**

(4) Shirt, wool serge, OG 108 (male). The shirt has two buttoned chest pockets, cuffed, buttoned sleeves, and a front button closure.

(5) Shirt, wool serge, OG 108 (female). The shirt has three pockets, two chest pockets with buttoned flaps, an upper sleeve pocket, cuffed, buttoned sleeves, and a front button closure. (See fig 7–3.)

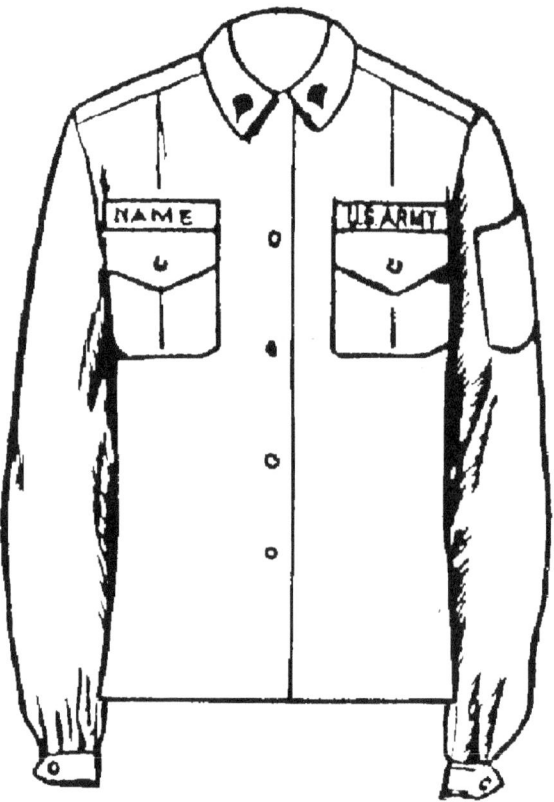

Figure 7–3. Wool serge shirt, female

(6) Trousers, cold-weather, OG 107. Fabric is cotton and nylon, wind resistant. The trousers have hip pockets, side front cargo pockets, waist adjustment straps, a slide-fastener fly, and leg draw cords.

(7) Trousers, wool serge, OG 108. The trousers have four patch pockets (two in front, two in back) with flaps and a covered front zipper opening.

*c.* Accessories. The following accessories are normally worn with the cold-weather uniform.

(1) Belt, web with open-faced black buckle (para 27–2*a* and *b*).

(2) Coat, cold-weather, woodland camouflage pattern (BDU field jacket) (para 3–2*b*(3)).

(3) Boots, combat, leather, black (para 27–3).

(4) Chaplain's apparel (para 27–7).

(5) Gloves, black leather shell with inserts (para 27–12*a*).

(6) Military Police accessories (para 27–16).

(7) Neckgaiter (para 27–17).

(8) Scarf, olive-green 208 (para 27–21*b*).

(9) Socks, black, cushion sole (para 27–24*a*).

(10) Undergarments (paras 27–28).

(11) Undershirt, brown (para 27–28*e*).

(12) Organizational clothing and equipment, as determined by the commander in accordance with CTA 50–900.

*d.* Classification. The OG 108 uniform is an organizationally issued field uniform. The beret is an organizational issue item. DA Pam 710–2–1 governs turn-in and reissue of the beret.

## 7–3. Occasions for wear

Soldiers may wear the OG 108 uniform only on duty, when prescribed by the commander. The OG 108 uniform is not authorized for travel or for wear off military installations, except in transit between the individual's quarters and duty station. (See para 1–10*c* for exceptions to this policy.) The OG 108 uniform is an organizationally issued field uniform and is not intended for wear as an all-purpose uniform when other uniforms are more appropriate. Personnel may wear components of this uniform with utility and other organizational uniforms as part of a cold-weather ensemble, when issued and prescribed by the commander.

## 7–4. Insignia and accouterments
The insignia and accouterments authorized for wear on the cold-weather uniform follow.

*a.* Badges, combat and special skill, subdued pin-on only (para 29–17).

*b.* Brassards (para 28–29).

*c.* Branch insignia, subdued pin-on only (paras 28–10*b* and 28–12*b*).

*d.* Combat leaders identification (on cold-weather coats (field jackets) and extended cold-weather clothing system (Gortex) parka only) (para 28–21).

*e.* Grade insignia, subdued pin-on (para 28–5, 28–6, and 28–7).

*f.* Headgear insignia (para 28–3).

*g.* Name and Army distinguishing tapes (paras 28–24*a* and 28–24*b*).

*h.* Shoulder sleeve insignia (current organization and former wartime service) is not authorized for wear on the OG 108 shirts. When the OG 108 shirt is prescribed for wear only as an undergarment, soldiers will not wear collar insignia and name and U.S. Army distinguishing tapes on the shirt.

*i.* Organizational flash (para 28–31*a*).

*j.* Foreign badges, sew-on badges, and sew-on grade insignia are not authorized for wear on this uniform.

## 7–5. General guidelines
*a.* The OG 108 uniform is designed to fit loosely, with tabs available for adjustment. Alterations are not authorized. Soldiers should not wear the OG 108 shirt and trousers as outer garments if they could become unduly soiled, snagged, or otherwise damaged in the performance of duties. When the shirt is worn as an outer garment, it is worn inside the trousers and a belt is worn with the trousers. When the trousers are worn as an outer garment, soldiers will blouse the trousers, using the draw cords or blousing rubbers, if the trousers are not tucked into the boots. Personnel will not wrap the trouser legs around the leg tightly enough to present a pegged appearance. Soldiers will not blouse the boots so that the trouser leg extends down to the ankle area. When bloused, the trousers should not extend below the third eyelet from the top of the boot. (See fig 7–1.) Soldiers will not roll up the sleeves of the OG 108 shirt. Female soldiers may wear either the male or female OG 108 shirt. Female Army Medical Department (AMEDD) officers may wear the cold-weather clothing as prescribed in CTA 50–900.

*b.* The beret, patrol cap, or the cold-weather caps are authorized for wear with this uniform. (See para 3–5 for wear policy of the beret and patrol cap.) When the cold-weather cap is worn properly, no hair is visible on the forehead. When the earflaps are worn down, they are fastened under the chin; when they are worn up, they are fastened to the cap.

*c.* Soldiers may wear the black leather shell gloves with utility uniforms without cold-weather outer garments, provided that sleeves are rolled down. When the cold-weather coat or other authorized cold-weather outer garments are worn, personnel may wear the olive-green scarf and the black leather shell gloves, but they are not required to do so. Coats are worn buttoned and zipped, and the shirt collar is worn inside the cold-weather coat and other outer garments. The cold-weather parka is authorized for wear with the cold-weather trousers (OG 107), or as prescribed by the commander. Figures 7–1 and 7–3 show the cold-weather uniform.

*d.* Commanders may authorize the use of a camouflage personal hydration system only in the following situations: in a field environment, in high-heat areas, or on work details. Soldiers will not carry hydration systems in a garrison environment, unless the commander has authorized it for one of the situations described above. Soldiers will not let the drinking tube hang from their mouths when the device is not in use.

## 7–6. Extended cold-weather clothing system
The extended cold-weather clothing system (ECWCS) is authorized for wear in accordance with CTA 50–900.

## 7–7. Composition and classification
*a.* The following are the components of the ECWCS.

(1) Parka, cold-weather, camouflage.

(a) The parka fabric is a triple-layer, laminated, waterproof, windproof, and moisture-vapor permeable nylon material. The garment repels water, but it is sufficiently porous to prevent moisture buildup from perspiration. The parka has a hood with an attachment piece that allows fastening of the fur ruff; inside map pockets that can be opened without unzipping the parka; two large lower cargo pockets, and a two-way, full-front slide fastener to provide full-face protection, leaving only the eyes uncovered. The parka is woodland camouflage and fully lined with a windskirt. There are elastic drawcords with barrel locks at the waist, and a woven nylon tape drawcord with barrel locks at the hood. Nylon hook-and-pile fastener tapes are located at the wrist tabs to allow for adjustment along the full-front closure on the overlay of the slide fastener, on the windskirt, and on the lower front pockets. The parka is authorized for wear as an organizational issue item.

*(b)* Soldiers will wear insignia of rank and the nametape on the parka. The insignia of rank is centered on the tab located in the center of the chest. Soldiers may wear either pin-on or embroidered slip-on cloth loop insignia of rank. The nametape is worn on the pocket flap of the left sleeve of the parka (see para 28–24*b*(2)(b)).

(2) Trousers, cold-weather, camouflage. The trousers are made from a triple-layer, laminated, waterproof, windproof, and moisture-vapor permeable nylon material that repels water, but the material is sufficiently porous to prevent moisture buildup from perspiration. The trousers have seat and knee patches, pass-through pockets, and zippered leg openings to allow easy donning and doffing without removing the footwear. Nylon hook-and-pile fastener tapes are located at the ankle tabs to allow for adjustment. The fly has a slide-fastener closure. Nylon tape suspender loops are located at the waist.

(3) Trousers, cold-weather, field, nylon and cotton. The trousers are made from a wind-resistant nylon and cotton fabric. Characteristics of the trousers are side-hanging pockets, hip pockets, cargo pockets, drawcords at the trousers bottoms, and adjustable waist straps. The trousers are worn over the liners as a durable, insulating layer when the cold-weather trouser is not needed.

(4) Liner, cold-weather parka. The coat liner is an olive-green undergarment of polyester-covered batting, covered with three plies of ripstop nylon cloth. The liner serves as an insulating layer for the upper body, and it may be worn independently of the parka.

(5) Liner, cold-weather trousers, field. The trouser liner is an olive-green undergarment of polyester-covered batting, covered with two plies of ripstop nylon cloth. The liner serves as the insulating layer for the lower body, and it may be worn independently of the cold-weather trousers.

(6) Shirt, cold weather, fleece. The shirt is made from a knitted polyester fiber pile. It has reinforced shoulder and elbow patches, a convertible turtleneck collar, front zipper, elastic drawcord waist, hook-and-pile cuff tabs, two chest cargo-style pockets, and two lower hand-warmer pockets. The shirt is the primary insulating layer for the upper body.

(7) Overalls, cold weather, fleece. The overalls are made from a knitted polyester fiber pile. They have elastic suspenders with quick release buckles, and full-length, side-seam slide fasteners. The overalls are worn as an additional layer when temperatures are -25 degrees to -60 degrees Fahrenheit.

(8) Undershirt, cold weather, polypropylene. The material used for the undershirt is a knitted, brushed, multi-filament polypropylene. It has a center-front zipper that extends to the middle of the chest area, allowing for ventilation of the neck and chest areas. The undershirt layer next to the skin acts as a moisture-wicking layer, serving to draw moisture away from the skin and transferring it to the outer layers of the system.

(9) Drawers, cold weather, polypropylene. The material used for the drawers is a knitted, brushed, multi-filament polypropylene. The drawers serve as the base layer for the lower extremities.

(10) Parka, snow camouflage, white. The parka is made from a lightweight, white nylon filament, water-repellant treated cloth. The parka has a snap-fastener front closure, storage pouch, elastic wrists, and drawcords at the waist, hood, and bottom. The parka is used as a camouflage outer layer in snow terrain, but it is not a substitute for the camouflage cold-weather parka.

(11) Trousers, snow camouflage, white. The trousers are made from a lightweight, white nylon filament, water-repellant, treated cloth. The trousers have front pass-through pockets, cargo pockets with flaps, suspender loops, inside button tabs for attaching a button-in liner, slide fastener openings on legs, a waist drawcord, storage pouch, and elastic cord leg bottoms. The trousers are used as a camouflage outer layer in snow terrain, but they are not a substitute for the camouflage cold-weather trouser, or for the field cold-weather trouser made from nylon and cotton.

(12) Hood, balaclava, cold weather. The hood is constructed of two plies of a black, knitted wool blend with a nylon wind-barrier interlining. The design is a pull-over-the-head style with an adjustable face opening.

(13) Ruff, parka, extended cold weather. The ruff is made from the same triple layer, laminated, waterproof, windproof, and moisture-vapor permeable nylon as the parka and trousers. One side of the ruff incorporates the synthetic fur, with hook-and-pile fasteners and snap fasteners on the opposite side. The fasteners allow attachment of the ruff to the camouflage cold-weather parka.

*b.* Accessories. The following accessories are normally worn with the ECWCS:

(1) Boots, combat, leather, black (para 27–3).

(2) Chaplain's apparel (para 27–7).

(3) Gloves, black leather shell with inserts (para 27–12*a*).

(4) Military Police accessories (para 27–16).

(5) Neckgaiter (para 27–17).

(6) Socks, black, cushion sole (para 27–24*a*).

(7) Undergarments (para 27–28).

(8) Organizational clothing and equipment, as determined by the commander in accordance with CTA 50–900.

*c.* Accouterments. The following insignia will be worn on the ECWCS (Gortex) parka.

(1) Grade insignia (paras 28–5, 28–6, and 28–7).

(2) Name-distinguishing tape (para 28–24*b*).

*d.* Commanders may authorize the use of a camouflage personal hydration system only in the following situations:

in a field environment, in high-heat areas, or on work details. Soldiers will not carry hydration systems in a garrison environment, unless the commander has authorized it for one of the situations described above. Soldiers will not let the drinking tube hang from their mouths when the device is not in use.

## Chapter 8
## Hospital Duty Uniform—Male

### 8–1. Authorization for wear
The male hospital duty uniform is authorized for year-round wear by all male officers in the Army Nurse Corps (ANC), the Army Medical Specialist Corps (AMSC), and by enlisted males with medical, dental, or veterinary military occupational specialties (MOSs). (See fig 8–1).

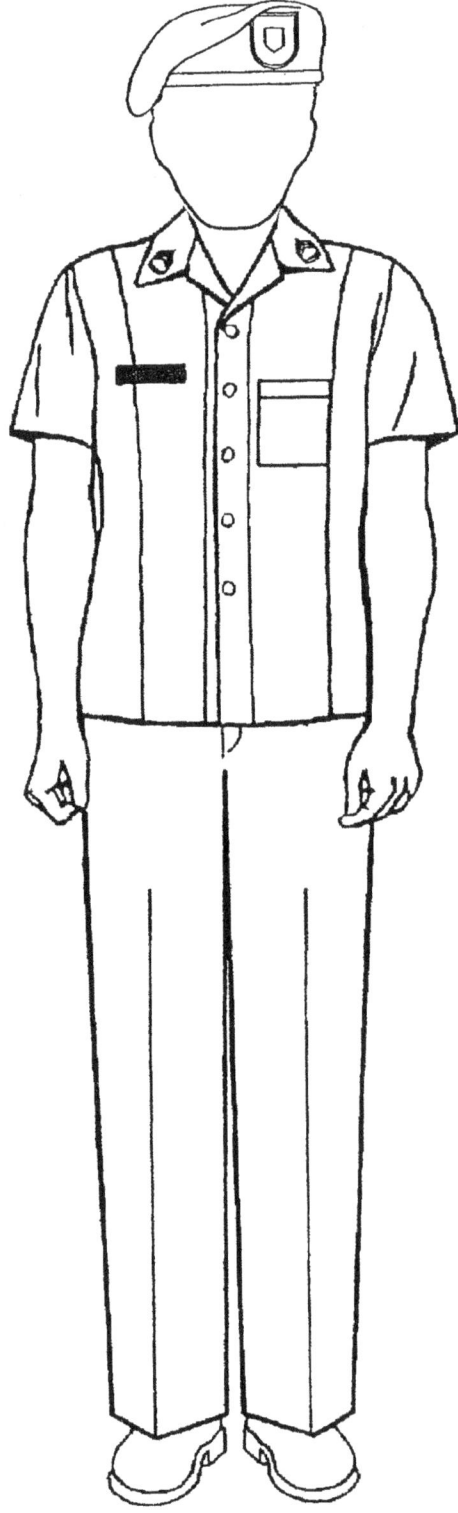

Figure 8–1. Hospital duty uniform, male

AR 670–1 • 3 February 2005

## 8–2. Composition and classification

*a.* Material composition. The fabric is white, durable-press cotton and polyester.

*b.* Uniform composition. The male hospital duty uniform normally comprises the items listed below. However, the medical facility commander may authorize variations to this uniform, using clothing items listed in CTA 50–900 and CTA 8–100.

(1) Smock, men's, medical assistant's. The smock is short-sleeved with a left breast pocket, a front button closure, and a straight-cut bottom.

(2) Smock, physician's white. The smock is knee-length with a front button closure, and upper and lower pockets.

(3) Trousers, men's, medical assistant's. The trousers have four pockets (two slash pockets in front, and two patch pockets in back), with a button closure on the left side, a front zipper closure, and belt loops.

*c.* Accessories. The following accessories are normally worn with the male hospital duty uniform.

(1) Belt, web, with open-faced black buckle (paras 27–2*a* and *b*).

(2) Coats.

*(a)* Black, all weather (para 27–8).

*(b)* Coat, cold weather, woodland camouflage pattern (BDU field jacket) (para 3–2*b*(3)).

(3) Gloves, black leather shell with inserts (para 27–12*a*).

(4) Headgear.

*(a)* Beret (para 3–2*b*(1)).

*(b)* Cap, service, cold weather, AG 489 (only with the black all-weather coat) (para 27–5).

(5) Scarves.

*(a)* Black (with black overcoat only)(para 27–21*a*).

*(b)* Olive-green 208 (with field jacket only) (para 27–21*b*).

(6) Shoes.

*(a)* Oxford, black (para 27–23*c*).

*(b)* Oxford, white (para 27–23*e*).

(7) Socks.

*(a)* Black, dress (para 27–24*b*).

*(b)* White (para 27–24*c*).

(8) Sweater, white unisex cardigan (para 27–26*b*).

(9) Undergarments (para 27–28).

(10) Undershirt, white (para 27–28*f*).

(11) Windbreaker, black (para 27–30).

(12) Organizational clothing and equipment, as determined by the medical facility commander for wear within the medical treatment facility, according to CTA 50–900 or CTA 8–100.

*d.* Classification. The hospital duty uniform is an organizational issue utility uniform. The beret is an organizational issue item. DA Pam 710–2–1 governs turn-in and reissue of the beret.

## 8–3. Occasions for wear

The male hospital duty uniform is worn on duty in Army health care facilities, as prescribed by the medical commander. The hospital duty uniform is not authorized for travel or for wear off military installations, except when in transit between an individual's quarters and duty station. The commander may authorize medical personnel to wear this uniform off post when providing support for activities in the civilian community, such as parades or ceremonies. (See para 2–6*c* for other exceptions to this policy.)

## 8–4. Insignia and accouterments

The following insignia and accouterments are authorized for wear on the male hospital duty uniforms.

*a.* Branch insignia, non-subdued (para 28–12*a*).

*b.* Grade insignia, non-subdued (paras 28–5, 28–6, and 28–7).

*c.* Headgear insignia (para 28–3).

*d.* Nameplate (para 28–24*c*).

*e.* Organizational flash (para 28–31*a*).

## 8–5. General guidelines

*a.* Enlisted and Army Nurse Corps personnel. When prescribed for wear, the hospital duty uniform is worn with the medical assistant's smock worn over the white trousers. Officer personnel wear white oxford shoes and white socks with these uniforms. Wear of the white oxfords and white socks by enlisted personnel is optional. Enlisted personnel will otherwise wear black oxford shoes and black socks with this uniform. Personnel may wear the optional purchase, black windbreaker with the uniform, except in formation (para 27–30). The optional purchase, white unisex cardigan is authorized for wear as an outer garment while on duty. Soldiers may wear the white unisex cardigan buttoned or unbuttoned while indoors; when outdoors, they will wear the cardigan buttoned. Soldiers will wear the collar of the smock outside the sweater so rank is visible.

*b.* The black beret became the basic headgear for this uniform on 14 June 2001 (see para 3–5 for wear policy). When the cold-weather coat or other authorized cold-weather outer garments are worn, personnel may wear the olive-green scarf and the black leather shell gloves, but they are not required to do so. Soldiers may wear the black scarf and AG 489 cold-weather cap with the black all-weather coat. Depending upon the uniform fabric, starching and pressing may damage the uniform material, so soldiers must exercise caution in this matter.

*c.* Warrant officers and commissioned officers. Warrant or commissioned officers of the medical, dental, veterinary, medical service, or medical specialty corps may wear the physician's white smock over either the service or utility uniforms, in a medical care facility, or on duty as directed by the commander of the medical facility.

*d.* Precautionary wear restrictions. Personnel should exercise caution because some of the materials used in these uniforms are inappropriate for use in areas where flammable gases are employed. Commanders will prohibit the wear of polyester hospital duty uniforms in flammable, anesthetizing locations and mixed facilities (as defined in National Fire Protection Association (NFPA) standards), or in any area where easily ignitable substances are present, such as anesthetizing agents. This restriction does not apply to inhalation therapy areas where oxygen is administered, providing that easily ignitable substances such as ether, cyclopropane, alcohol, acetone, oils, greases, or lotions are not present. The presence of such flammable substances in oxygen-enriched atmospheres is prohibited by NFPA standards.

*e.* Figure 8–1 shows the hospital duty uniform for males.


## Chapter 9
## Hospital Duty and Maternity Uniforms—Female

### 9–1. Authorization for wear
The female hospital duty uniforms are authorized for year-round wear by all female officers in the ANC and the AMSC, and by enlisted females with a medical, dental, or veterinary MOS. The term "hospital duty uniform" used throughout this chapter refers to both the hospital duty and hospital duty maternity uniforms. (See figs 9–1 and 9–2.)

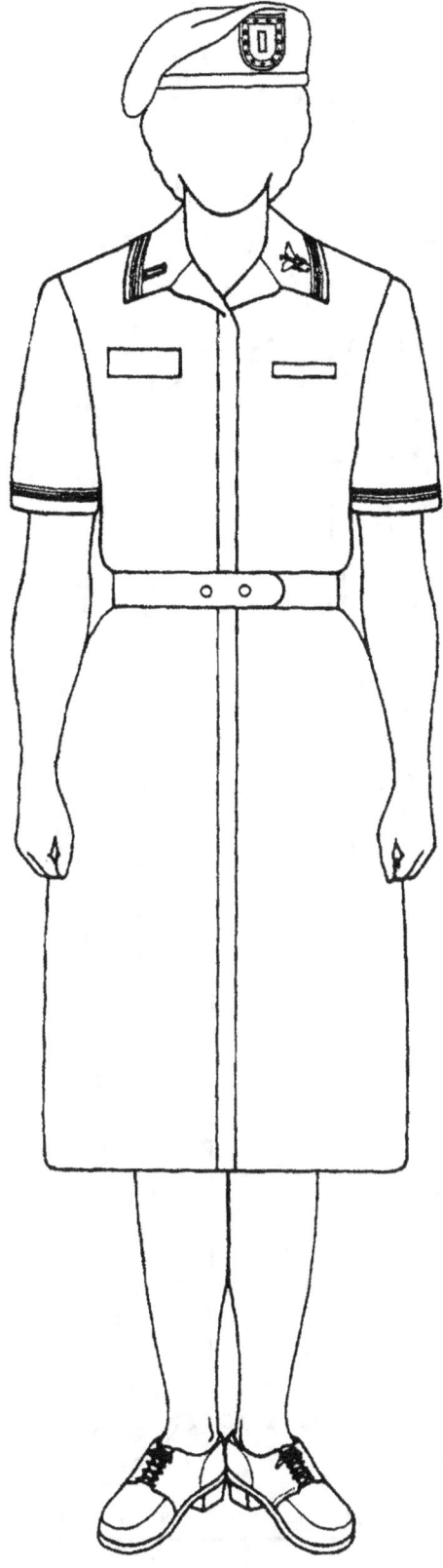

Figure 9–1. Hospital duty dress, with beret

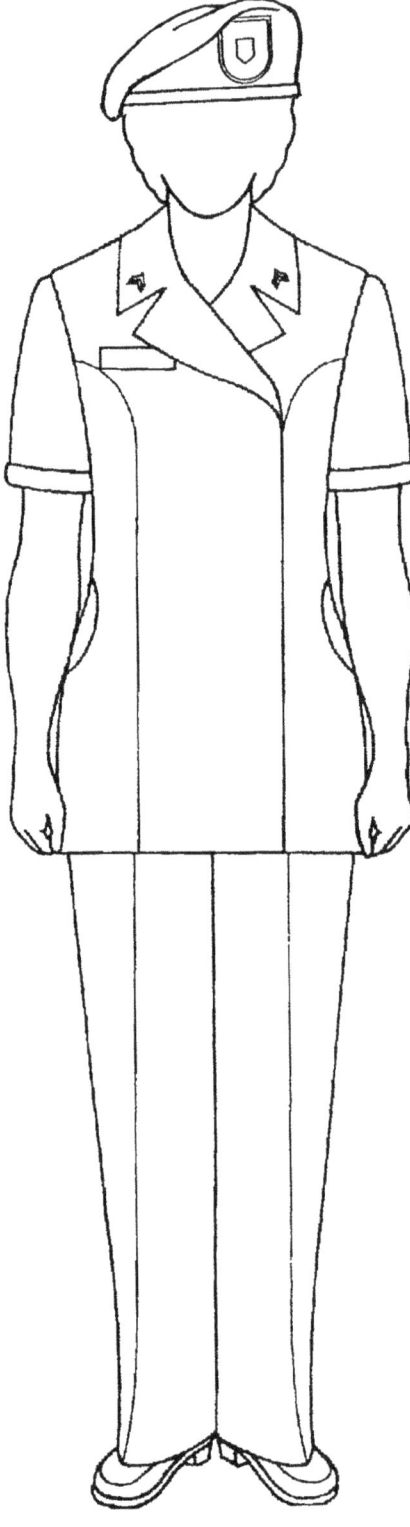

Figure 9–2. Hospital duty pantsuit

## 9–2. Composition and classification

a. *Material composition.* The fabric is white cotton or polyester.

b. *Uniform composition.* The female hospital duty uniform normally comprises the following items; however, the commander may authorize variations to this uniform using clothing items authorized in CTA 50–900 and CTA 8–100.

(1) Dress, maternity, white. The dress is any plain, white, unadorned commercial design, in an easy-care, durable-press and soil-release material, with wing collars suitable for placement of rank and branch insignia, as prescribed. Fabric content must comply with NFPA standards. Any closure method is acceptable, but it may not cause safety hazards or degradation of appearance.

(2) Dress, women's. The dress will be of an approved specification or pattern. It is knee-length with short sleeves and has a front button closure system, wing-tip collars, and a belt (see fig 9–1).

(3) Slacks and tunic, maternity, white. The slacks and tunic may be any plain, white, unadorned commercial design. The fabric is an easy-care, durable-press, and soil-release material, with wing collars suitable for placement of rank and branch insignia, as prescribed. Fabric content must comply with NFPA standards. Any closure method is acceptable, but it may not cause safety hazards or degradation of appearance.

(4) Smock, physician's, white. The smock is knee-length, with a front button closure and upper and lower pockets.

(5) Uniform, women's, tunic and pants, hospital duty. The uniform will be of an approved specification or pattern. The tunic is an over-the-hip style with winged collars, short sleeves, and side pockets; the pants are straight-legged (see fig 9–2).

(6) Headgear. The beret is authorized for wear with the hospital duty uniforms when outside the medical treatment facility (see para 3–5).

c. *Accessories.* The following accessories are normally worn with the female hospital duty uniform.

(1) Coats.

(a) Black, all weather (para 27–8).

(b) Coat, cold weather, woodland camouflage pattern (BDU field jacket) (para 3–2b(3)).

(2) Gloves, black leather shell, with inserts (para 27–12a).

(3) Handbags.

(a) Black, clutch type, optional purchase (para 27–13a).

(b) Black, shoulder (para 27–13d).

(4) Headgear.

(a) Beret (para 3–2b(1)).

(b) Cap, service, cold weather, AG 489 (only with the black all-weather coat) (para 27–5).

(5) Scarves.

(a) Black (with black overcoat only) (para 27–21a).

(b) Olive-green 208 (with field jacket only) (para 27–21b).

(6) Shoes.

(a) Oxford, black (para 27–23a).

(b) Oxford, white (para 27–23d).

(7) Socks.

(a) Black (para 27–24b).

(b) White (para 27–24c).

(8) Stockings.

(a) Sheer (para 27–24d).

(b) White (para 27–24e).

(9) Sweater, white unisex cardigan (para 27–26b).

(10) Undergarments (para 27–28).

(11) Windbreaker (para 27–30).

(12) Organizational clothing and equipment, as determined by the medical facility commander for wear within the medical treatment facility, according to CTA 50–900 or CTA 8–100.

d. *Classification.* The hospital duty uniform is an organizational issue utility uniform. The beret is an organizational issue item. DA Pam 710–2–1 governs turn-in and reissue of the beret.

## 9–3. Occasions for wear

The female hospital duty uniform is worn on duty in Army health care facilities, as prescribed by the medical commander. It is not authorized for travel or for wear off military installations, except when in transit between an individual's quarters and duty station. The commander may authorize medical personnel to wear this uniform off post when providing support for activities in the civilian community, such as parades or ceremonies. (See para 2–6c for other exceptions to this policy.)

## 9–4. Insignia and accouterments
The following insignia and accouterments are authorized for wear on the female hospital duty uniforms.

a. Branch insignia, non-subdued (para 28–12a).

b. Grade insignia, non-subdued (paras 28–5, 28–6, and 28–7).

c. Headgear insignia (para 28–3).

d. Nameplate (para 28–24c).

e. Organizational flash (para 28–31a).

## 9–5. General guidelines
a. Basic uniform.

(1) Enlisted and officer ANC and AMSC personnel.

(a) The dress is worn when prescribed for wear. The length of the dress will be no longer than 2 inches below, or more than 1 inch above the bend in the back of the knee. The dress is worn with the belt at all times. Only the dome-shaped, white polyester shank-type buttons issued with the dress are authorized for wear on the belt (secured with safety pins on the back of the belt). The white maternity dress does not have a belt.

(b) The tunic-and-pants uniform is worn when prescribed for wear. The tunic is worn outside the pants.

(c) The following pertains to both the dress and the tunic-and-pants uniforms. Officers will wear the white oxford shoes and white stockings with these uniforms. Wear of the white oxford shoes and stockings by enlisted personnel is optional. Enlisted personnel will otherwise wear black oxford shoes and sheer stockings with the hospital duty dress, and the black oxford shoes with black socks when wearing the tunic-and-pants uniforms.

(2) Soldiers may wear the white unisex cardigan sweater as an outer garment with this uniform while on duty. Personnel may wear the white unisex cardigan buttoned or unbuttoned while indoors; when outdoors, all except pregnant soldiers will wear the cardigan buttoned. Personnel will wear the collar of the dress or tunic outside the sweater so the rank is visible. The black windbreaker is authorized for wear with the tunic-and-pants uniform and the hospital duty dress (para 27–30). The other outer garments listed in paragraph 9–2c(1) also are authorized for wear with these uniforms.

(3) The black beret became the basic headgear for this uniform on 14 June 2001 (see para 3–5 for wear policy). When the cold-weather coat or other authorized cold-weather outer garments are worn, personnel may wear the olive-green scarf and the black leather shell gloves, but they are not required to do so. Soldiers may wear the black scarf and AG 489 cold-weather cap with the black all-weather coat. Depending upon the uniform fabric, starching and pressing may damage the uniform material, so soldiers must exercise caution in this matter.

(4) Warrant officers and commissioned officers. The commander may authorize the wear of the physician's white smock over the service or utility uniforms (except the hospital duty dress and tunic and pants) in a medical treatment facility.

b. Issue. The issue of the hospital maternity uniform to hospital duty female personnel has no bearing on the issue of the Army green maternity service uniform (chap 17) or the maternity work uniform (chap 4).

c. Precautionary wear restrictions. Personnel should exercise caution because some of the materials used in these uniforms are inappropriate for use in areas where flammable gases are employed. Commanders will prohibit the wear of hospital duty dresses and polyester pantsuits in flammable, anesthetizing locations and mixed facilities (as defined in NFPA standards), or in any area where easily ignitable substances are present, such as anesthetizing agents. This restriction does not apply to inhalation therapy areas where oxygen is administered, providing that easily ignitable substances such as ether, cyclopropane, alcohol, acetone, oils, greases, or lotions are not present. The presence of such flammable substances in oxygen-enriched atmospheres is prohibited by NFPA standards.

## Chapter 10
## Food Service Uniform—Male

## 10–1. Authorization for wear
The male food service utility uniforms are authorized for year-round wear by all enlisted soldiers in career management field (CMF) 92 who hold food service MOSs, when prescribed by CTA 50–900 and the commander. (See fig 10–1.)

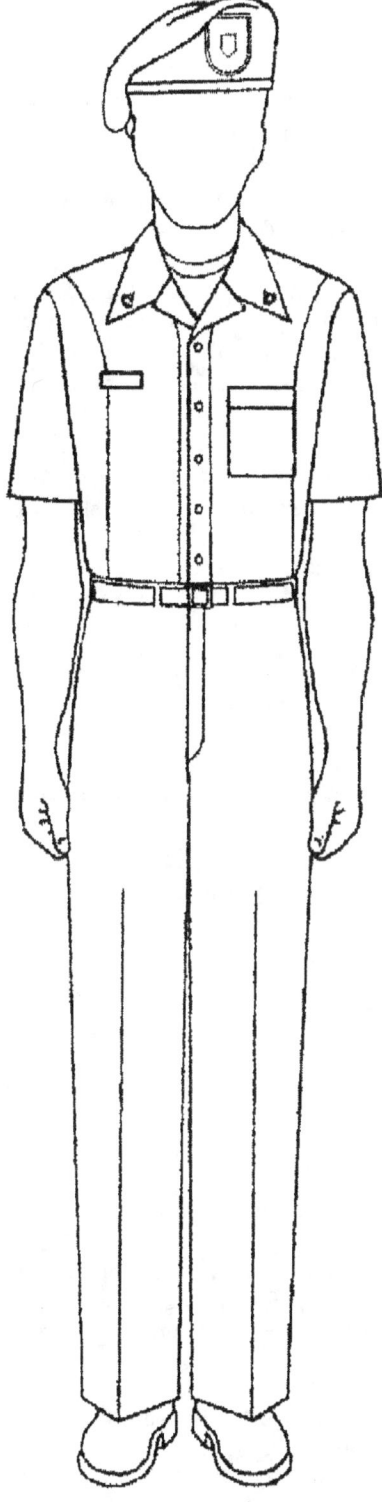

Figure 10–1. Food service uniform, male

## 10–2. Composition and classification

*a.* Material composition.

(1) White, cotton and polyester, durable press.

(2) Black, polyester, durable press.

*b.* Uniform composition.

(1) The male food service utility uniform comprises the following items:

*(a)* Smock, men's, medical assistant's (see para 8–2*b*(1)).

*(b)* Trousers, men's, medical assistant's (see para 8–2*b*(3)).

(2) The garrison food service supervisor uniform comprises the following items.

*(a)* Shirt, white dress. Commercial, short-sleeved shirt with a left chest pocket and a front button closure (local procurement according to CTA 50–900).

*(b)* Trousers, men's, food service, black. Commercial straight-legged trousers with two front slash pockets, two back patch pockets, and a front zipper closure with belt loops (local procurement according to CTA 50–900).

*c.* Accessories. The following accessories are normally worn with the food service utility uniforms.

(1) Belt, web, with open-faced black buckle (food service uniform), and belt, web, with brass buckle (food service supervisor) (para 27–2).

(2) Coats.

*(a)* Black, all weather (para 27–8).

*(b)* Coat, cold weather, woodland camouflage pattern (BDU field jacket) (para 3–2*b*(3)).

(3) Footwear.

*(a)* Boots, combat, leather, black (para 27–3).

*(b)* Shoes, oxford, black (para 27–23*c*).

(4) Gloves.

*(a)* Black leather shell with inserts (para 27–12*a*).

*(b)* Black, leather, dress, unisex (para 27–12*b*).

(5) Headgear.

*(a)* Beret, (para 3–2*b*(1)).

*(b)* Cap, service, cold weather, AG 489 (only with the black all-weather coat) (para 27–5).

(6) Scarves.

*(a)* Black (only with the black overcoat) (para 27–21*a*).

*(b)* Olive-green 208 (only with the BDU jacket) (para 27–21*b*).

(7) Socks.

*(a)* Black, cushion sole (worn with boots only) (para 27–24*a*).

*(b)* Black, dress (para 27–24*b*).

(8) Sweater, black unisex cardigan (para 27–26*a*) and black pullover (para 27–26*c*) (only with food service supervisor uniform).

(9) Sweater, white unisex cardigan (para 27–26*b*) (only with food service utility uniform).

(10) Undergarments (para 27–28).

(11) Undershirts, white (para 27–28*f*).

(12) Windbreaker (para 27–30).

(13) Smock, food inspector's, and other organizational clothing and equipment as determined by the commander, according to CTA 50–900 and CTA 50–970.

*d.* Classification. The food service utility and food service supervisor uniforms are organizationally issued utility uniforms. However, soldiers retain these uniforms for as long as they are assigned to food service duties. The beret is an organizational issue item. DA Pam 710–2–1 governs turn-in and reissue of the beret.

## 10–3. Occasions for wear

Enlisted soldiers in CMF 92 who hold food service MOSs wear the food service utility and food service supervisor uniforms on duty, when prescribed by the commander. The food service utility uniforms are not authorized for travel or for wear off military installations, except in transit between an individual's quarters and duty station. The commander may authorize food service personnel to wear these uniforms off post when providing support for activities in the civilian community, such as parades or ceremonies. (See para 2–6*c* for exceptions to this policy.) These uniforms are worn only in garrison and are not authorized for wear in the field.

## 10–4. Insignia and accouterments

The following insignia are authorized for wear on the male food service uniforms.

a. Grade insignia, non-subdued (paras 28–5, 28–6, and 28–7).

b. Headgear insignia (para 28–3).

c. Nameplate (para 28–24c).

d. Organizational flash (para 28–31a).

## 10–5. General guidelines

a. The food service uniform is worn with the smock tucked into the trousers. The commander may authorize exceptions to the prescribed wear of the smock for health and safety reasons. The black belt with black open-faced buckle is worn with this uniform. The food handler's apron and food handler's caps are worn only within the immediate vicinity of the dining facility. No insignia is worn on the food handler's cap.

b. The optional purchase, white unisex cardigan is authorized for wear as an outer garment with the food service uniform while on duty. However, soldiers may not wear the white cardigan when serving or preparing food. Soldiers may wear the white unisex cardigan buttoned or unbuttoned while indoors; when outdoors, they will wear the cardigan buttoned. Soldiers will wear the collar of the smock outside the sweater so rank is visible. Soldiers may wear the black all-weather coat and the cold-weather camouflage coat (field jacket) as outer garments with these uniforms. When the cold-weather coat or other authorized cold-weather outer garments are worn, personnel may wear the olive-green scarf and the black leather shell gloves, but they are not required to do so. Personnel may wear the optional purchase, black windbreaker (para 27–30), except in formation. Black oxford shoes or combat boots are worn with the food service uniforms, unless CTA 50–900 authorizes other footwear. Soldiers will not blouse the trousers when wearing boots. The black beret became the basic headgear for this uniform on 14 June 2001 (see para 3–5 for wear policy). Soldiers will wear the food handler's cap only while in the dining facility.

c. The food service supervisor may wear the white shirt, black trousers, black oxford shoes, and the beret, when authorized by the commander. The black windbreaker, black pullover and unisex cardigan sweaters, and the black all-weather coat are authorized for wear with this uniform. Food service supervisors may wear the black unisex cardigan buttoned or unbuttoned while indoors; when outdoors, they will button the sweater. The black belt with brass buckle is worn with this uniform. The food inspector's smock is authorized for wear with the food service supervisor uniform only while in the dining facility.

d. The black scarf, black dress gloves, and the AG 489 cold-weather service cap are authorized for wear with the black all-weather coat, with the food service uniforms.

e. Figure 10–1 shows the food service uniform for males.

## Chapter 11
## Food Service and Maternity Uniforms—Female

### 11–1. Authorization for wear

The female food service utility uniforms are authorized for year-round wear by enlisted soldiers in CMF 92 who hold food service MOSs, when prescribed by CTA 50–900 and the commander. (See fig 11–1.)

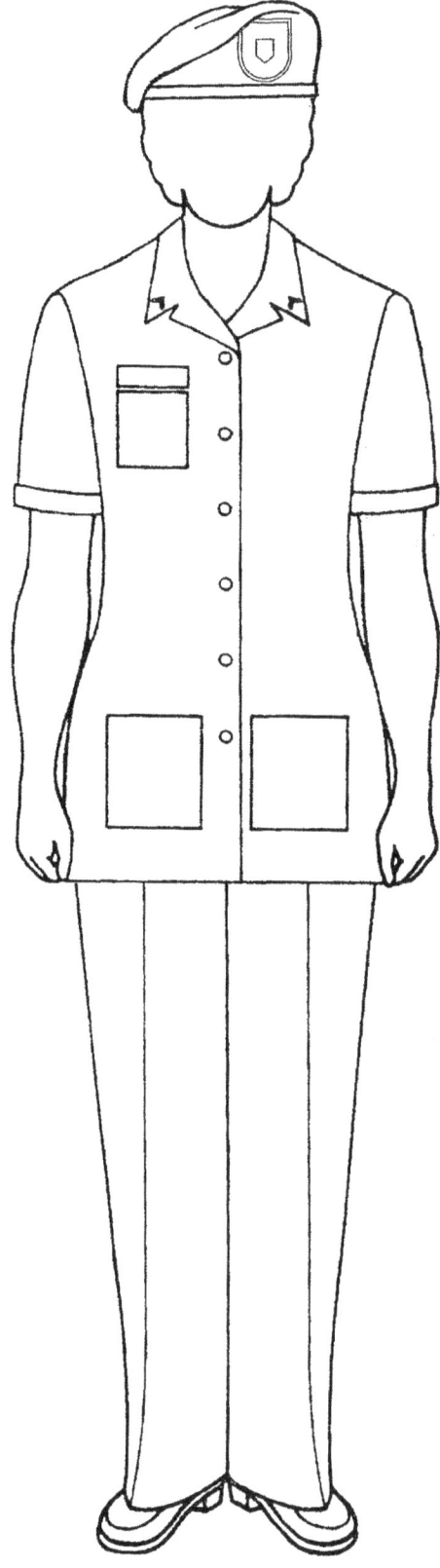

Figure 11–1. Food service uniform, female

AR 670–1 • 3 February 2005

## 11–2. Composition and classification

*a.* Material composition.

(1) White, cotton and polyester, durable press.

(2) Black, polyester, durable press.

*b.* Uniform composition.

(1) The female food service uniform comprises the following items (see chap 9).

*(a)* Dress, women's, hospital duty, white.

*(b)* Uniform, tunic and pants, women's, hospital duty, white.

*(c)* Dress, maternity, white.

*(d)* Slacks and tunic, maternity, white.

*(e)* Pantsuit, women's, cotton/polyester, white.

(2) The garrison food service supervisor uniform comprises the following items.

*(a)* Blouse, women's, food service, white. Commercial, short-sleeved blouse with a front button closure (local procurement according to CTA 50–900).

*(b)* Skirt, women's food service, black (local procurement according to CTA 50–900).

*(c)* Slacks, women's, food service, black (local procurement according to CTA 50–900).

*c.* Accessories. The following accessories are normally worn with the food service utility uniforms.

(1) Coats.

*(a)* Black, all weather (para 27–8).

*(b)* Coat, cold weather, woodland camouflage pattern (BDU field jacket) (para 3–2*b*(3)).

(2) Footwear.

*(a)* Boots, combat, leather, black (para 27–3).

*(b)* Shoes, oxford, black (para 27–23*a*).

(3) Gloves.

*(a)* Black leather shell, with inserts (para 27–12*a*).

*(b)* Black, leather, dress, unisex (para 27–12*b*).

(4) Handbags.

*(a)* Black, clutch type, optional purchase (para 27–13*a*).

*(b)* Black, shoulder (27–13*d*).

(5) Headgear.

*(a)* Beret (para 3–2*b*(1)).

*(b)* Cap, service, cold weather, AG 489 (only with the black all-weather coat) (para 27–5).

(6) Scarves.

*(a)* Black (only with the black overcoat) (para 27–21*a*).

*(b)* Olive-green 208 (only with the field jacket) (para 27–21*b*).

(7) Socks.

*(a)* Black, cushion sole (para 27–24*a*).

*(b)* Black, dress (para 27–24*b*).

(8) Stockings, sheer (para 27–24*d*).

(9) Sweater, black unisex cardigan and black pullover (paras 27–26*a* and *c*) (only with the food service supervisor uniform).

(10) Sweater, white unisex cardigan (para 27–26*b*) (only with the food service utility uniform).

(11) Undergarments (para 27–28).

(12) Windbreaker (para 27–30).

(13) Smock, food inspector's, and other organizational clothing and equipment, as determined by the commander, according to CTA 50–900 and CTA 50–970.

*d.* Classification. The food service utility and food service supervisor uniforms are organizationally issued utility uniforms. However, soldiers retain these uniforms for as long as they are assigned to food service duties. The beret is an organizational issue item. DA Pam 710–2–1 governs turn-in and reissue of the beret.

## 11–3. Occasions for wear

Enlisted soldiers in CMF 92 who hold food service MOSs wear the food service utility uniform on duty, when prescribed by the commander. The food service utility uniforms are not authorized for travel or for wear off military installations, except in transit between an individual's quarters and duty station. The commander may authorize food service personnel to wear these uniforms off post when providing support for activities in the civilian community, such as parades or ceremonies. (See para 2–6c for other exceptions to this policy.) These uniforms are worn only in garrison and are not authorized for wear in the field.

## 11–4. Insignia and accouterments
The following insignia are authorized for wear on the food service uniforms.

  *a.* Grade insignia, non-subdued (paras 28–5, 28–6, and 28–7).

  *b.* Headgear insignia (para 28–3).

  *c.* Nameplate (para 28–24c).

  *d.* Organizational flash (para 28–31a).

## 11–5. General guidelines
  *a.* The food handler's apron and the food handler's cap (CTA 50–970) are authorized for wear only within the immediate vicinity of the dining facility. No insignia is worn on the food handler's cap. The optional purchase, white unisex cardigan is authorized for wear as an outer garment with the food service utility uniform while on duty. However, soldiers may not wear the white cardigan when serving or preparing food. Soldiers may wear the white unisex cardigan buttoned or unbuttoned while indoors; when outdoors, with the exception of pregnant soldiers, they will wear the cardigan buttoned. Soldiers will wear the collar of the smock outside the sweater so rank is visible. Soldiers may wear the black all-weather coat and cold-weather camouflage coat (field jacket) as outer garments with these uniforms. When the cold-weather coat or other authorized cold-weather outer garments are worn, personnel may wear the olive green scarf and the black leather shell gloves, but they are not required to do so. Soldiers may wear the optional purchase, black windbreaker (para 27–30), except in formation.

  *b.* Black oxford shoes or combat boots are worn with the food service uniforms, unless other footwear is authorized by CTA 50–900. Soldiers will wear either black socks or sheer stockings with the black oxfords, with the pantsuit, or with the tunic with slacks. Sheer stockings are worn with the food service uniform dresses. The slacks are not bloused when wearing boots.

  *c.* The black beret became the basic headgear for this uniform on 14 June 2001 (see para 3–5 for wear policy). Soldiers may wear the food handler's cap only while in the dining facility.

  *d.* The food service supervisor may wear the white blouse, black slacks or skirt, black oxford shoes, and the beret, when authorized by the commander. The black windbreaker, black pullover sweater, black unisex cardigan, and black all-weather coat are authorized for wear with this uniform. Food service supervisors may wear the black cardigan buttoned or unbuttoned while indoors; outdoors, with the exception of pregnant soldiers, they must button the sweater. The food inspector's smock is authorized for wear with the food service supervisor uniform only while in the dining facility.

  *e.* The black scarf, black dress gloves, and the AG 489 cold-weather service cap are authorized for wear with the black all weather-coat with the food service uniforms. Females may carry handbags with these uniforms, except when in formation.

  *f.* The issuance of the food service maternity uniform to female personnel has no bearing on the issuance of the Army green maternity service uniform (chap 17), or the maternity work uniform (chap 4).

  *g.* Figure 11–1 shows the food service uniform for females.


# Chapter 12
# Flight Uniforms

## 12–1. Authorization for wear
The Army flight uniform is authorized for year-round wear by flight crews, when prescribed by CTA 50–900 and the commander. (See fig 12–1.)

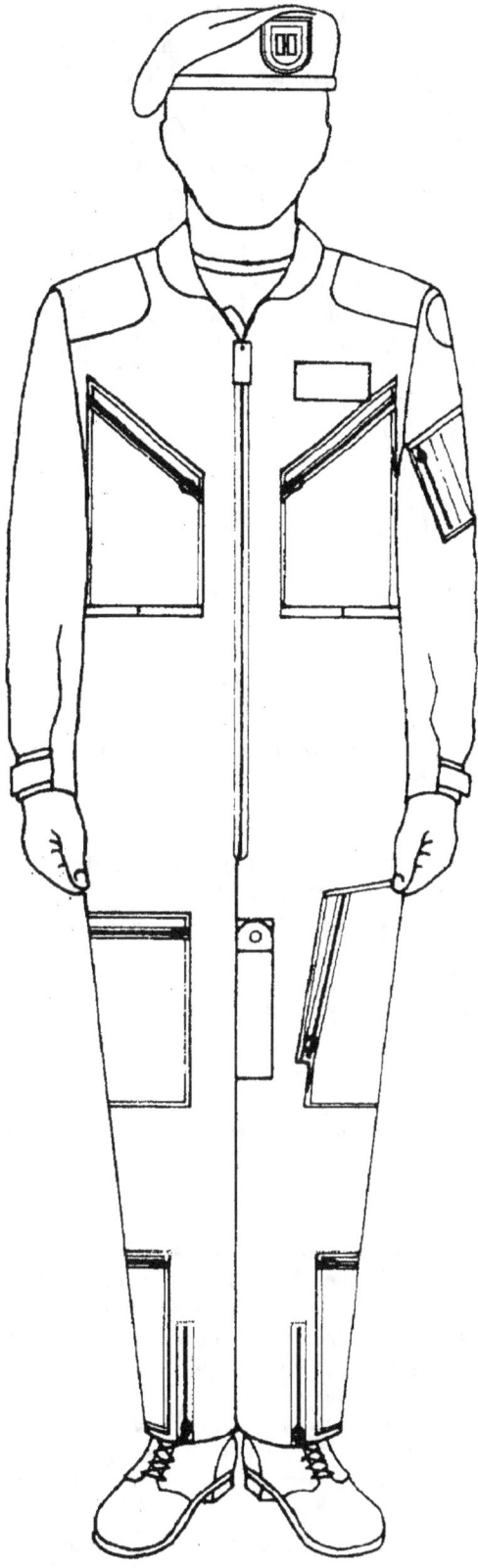

Figure 12–1. Flight uniform, with beret

## 12–2. Composition and classification

*a.* Material composition. The flight coverall fabric is a blend of 92 percent NOMEX, 5 percent Kevlar, and 3 percent static dissipative fiber, plain weave, sage green and tan 380 in color.

*b.* Uniform composition. The flight uniform comprises the following items:

(1) One-piece organizational flight coverall. The coveralls are unlined, with a slide-fastener front closure, hook-and-pile fastener tape adjustments for the waist and sleeves, and a slide fastener on the bottom of each leg. There are two breast patch pockets, a combination utility and pencil pocket on the left sleeve, two thigh patch pockets, a knife pocket with lanyard on the left thigh, two lower-leg patch pockets, and a multiple pencil compartment pocket on the right lower-leg pocket. Except for the knife pocket, all pockets have slide-fastener closures.

(2) Gloves, flight. The gloves are of the four-finger and thumb type. The front of the hand and fingers are leather. An elastic take-up tab is used on the front of the wrist.

(3) Jacket, flight. The jacket has knitted cuffs and waistband, a front slide-fastener closure with an inside protective flap, a collar with a hook-and-pile tab closure, and diagonal side pockets with flaps. The left sleeve has a utility/pencil pocket. The jacket is fully lined.

*c.* Accessories. The following accessories are normally worn with the flight uniform.

(1) Boots, combat leather, black (para 27–3).

(2) Headgear.

*(a)* Beret (para 3–2*b*(1)).

*(b)* Cap, patrol (formerly BDU) (para 3–2*b*(2)).

*(c)* Helmet, aviator.

(3) Socks, black, cushion sole (para 27–24*a*).

(4) Undergarments (para 27–28).

(5) Undershirt, brown (para 27–28*e*).

(6) Organizational clothing and equipment, as determined by the commander in accordance with CTA 50–900.

(7) Gloves, flyer's, LIN J67052.

*d.* Classification. The flight uniform is an organizational issue uniform. The beret is an organizational issue item. DA Pam 710–2–1 governs turn-in and reissue of the beret.

## 12–3. Occasions for wear

The flight uniform is worn on duty when flying, on standby awaiting flight, or as directed by the commander. The flight uniform is not authorized for travel or for wear off military installations, except in transit between an individual's quarters and duty station. (See para 2–6*c* for exceptions to this policy.)

## 12–4. Insignia and accouterments

The following insignia are authorized for wear on the flight uniform.

*a.* Grade insignia (para 12–5*b*).

*b.* Headgear insignia (para 28–3).

*c.* Nameplate (para 12–5*b*).

*d.* Subdued shoulder sleeve insignia (SSI), current organization (para 28–16*e*(2)).

*e.* Organizational flash (para 28–31*a*).

## 12–5. General guidelines

*a.* Flight coverall. The organizational flight uniform is for use by flight crews as prescribed in CTA 50–900. Alterations to the uniform are not authorized. The black leather combat boots and the flyer's insulated boots (when authorized according to CTA 50–900) are the authorized footwear for the flight uniform. Personnel will not tuck the flight coverall into the boots. Soldiers will keep the sleeves down on the flight uniform during flight operations. The flight uniform is not intended for wear as an all-purpose uniform when other uniforms are more appropriate. Flight jackets are worn only with the organizational flight uniform. The black beret became the basic headgear for this uniform on 14 June 2001. Soldiers will wear the beret when not performing flight duties, unless the commander has prescribed wear of the patrol cap, as described in chapter 3 of this regulation. (See para 3–5 for wear policy of the beret and the patrol cap.) Commanders may authorize other uniforms for wear during administrative flights.

*b.* Insignia and accouterments.

(1) A 2-inch by 4-inch leather nameplate is attached to the 2-inch by 4-inch Velcro attachments affixed to the flight suit and jacket. This nameplate consists of ¼-inch block style lettering in silver, with the appropriate crewmember's

badge on the first line, full name (first, middle initial, and last name) on the second line, and abbreviated rank and the words "U.S. Army" on the third line. The nameplate is provided at no expense to the soldier.

(2) The SSI is worn ½ inch below the shoulder seam. Officer personnel will wear subdued embroidered insignia of grade on the shoulder of the organizational flight suit and flight jacket. The insignia is centered ⅝ inch in from the shoulder seam. Chest insignia patches are not authorized.

(3) Local commanders may authorize all aviation personnel who are not authorized flight clothing to remove pin-on metal insignia from the work uniforms while engaged in maintenance activities near the aircraft.

(4) Local commanders may authorize the wear of solid baseball caps (when authorized in accordance with CTA 50–900) by aircraft and ground crewmembers as a safety and identification measure, while on the flight line or in the base operations area. Personnel will wear standard headgear outside this area. Soldiers will wear grade insignia on organizational baseball caps, in accordance with para 28–3f. Commanders will provide the caps to soldiers at no expense.

*c.* Commanders may authorize the use of a camouflage personal hydration system only in the following situations: in a field environment, in high-heat areas, or on work details. Soldiers will not carry hydration systems in a garrison environment, unless the commander has authorized it for one of the situations described above. Soldiers will not let the drinking tube hang from their mouths when the device is not in use.


## Chapter 13
## Combat Vehicle Crewman Uniform

### 13–1. Authorization for wear
The combat vehicle crewman (CVC) uniform is authorized for year-round wear by combat vehicle crewmen, when issued in accordance with CTA 50–900 and prescribed by the commander. (See fig 13–1.)

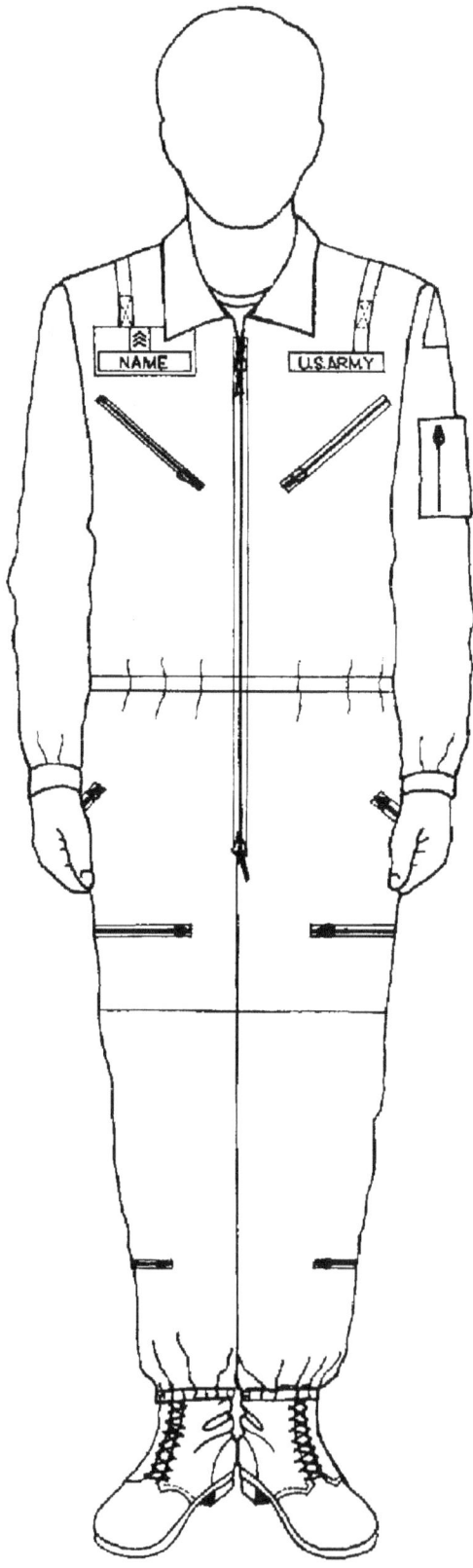

Figure 13–1. Combat vehicle crewman's uniform

## 13–2. Composition and classification

*a.* Material composition. The fabric is high-temperature resistant, anti-static treated, non-melting aramid blend, plain weave, OG-106 and tan 380 in color.

*b.* Uniform composition.

(1) Coverall. The coverall is a one-piece design that has a front entry zippered closure, a drop seat, an extraction strap located at the upper back, and pockets located on the left sleeve, chest, right and left sides, right-left front hips, right-left upper thigh, and right-left lower legs. All pockets have slide-fastener closures. This is the only component produced in the tan 380, but it may be worn with OG-106 components.

(2) Jacket, cold weather. The jacket is single-breasted with a front slide-fastener closure, and an inside protective flap. The back has a yoke-and-retrieval strap opening with a hook-and-pile closure. The left sleeve has a utility and pencil pocket, and the sleeves have elbow patches. The cuffs and waistband are rib knit. The jacket is fully lined with quilted, flame-resistant batting material. (See fig 13–2.)

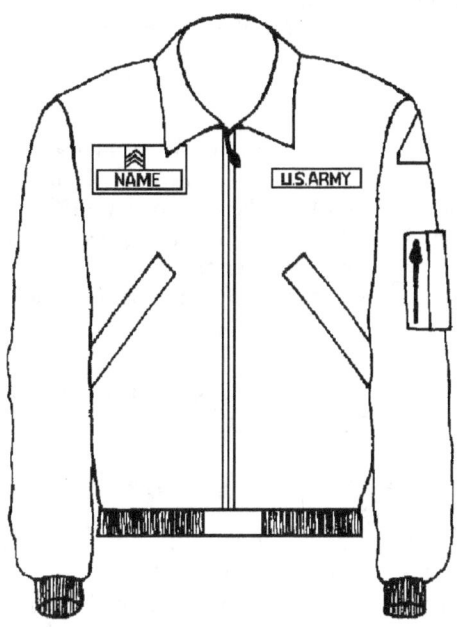

**Figure 13–2. Jacket, cold weather**

*c.* Accessories. The following accessories are normally worn with these uniforms.

(1) Balaclava hood, CVC, LIN H46881, CTA 50–900.

(2) Bib, overalls, LIN P37820.

(3) Body armor, ballistic undergarment, LIN 80592N.

(4) Boots, combat, leather, black (para 27–3).

(5) Gloves, CVC, cold weather, LIN C67081.

(6) Gloves, CVC, summer, LIN G70780.

(7) Headgear.

*(a)* Beret (para 3–2*b*(1)).

*(b)* Cap, patrol (formerly BDU) (para 3–2*b*(2)).

*(c)* Helmet, CVC.

(8) Socks, black, cushion sole (para 27–24*a*).

(9) Undergarments (para 27–28).

(10) Undershirt, brown (para 27–28*e*).

(11) Organizational clothing and equipment, as determined by the commander, in accordance with CTA 50–900.

*d.* Classification. The CVC uniform is an organizational issue uniform. The beret is an organizational issue item. DA Pam 710–2–1 governs turn-in and reissue of the beret.

## 13–3. Occasions for wear

The CVC uniform is worn on duty when directed by the commander. It is not authorized for travel or for wear off military installations, except in transit between an individual's quarters and duty station. (See para 2–6*c* for exceptions to this policy.) These uniforms are not intended for wear as all-purpose uniforms when other uniforms are more appropriate.

## 13–4. Insignia and accouterments

The following insignia and accouterments are authorized for wear on these uniforms.

*a.* Grade insignia (paras 28–5, 28–6, and 28–7); attachment (para 13–5*b*).

*b.* Headgear insignia (para 28–3).

*c.* Nametape (para 28–24*b*); attachment (para 13–5*b*).

*d.* U.S. Army tape (para 28–24*a*); attachment (para 13–5*b*).

*e.* Subdued shoulder sleeve insignia, current organization (para 28–16*e*(2)).

*f.* Organizational flash (para 28–31*a*).

## 13–5. General guidelines

*a.* Basic uniform. When issued, all combat vehicle crewmen wear the CVC uniform whenever they are operating their vehicles. Alterations to the uniform are not authorized. The black leather combat boot is the authorized footwear for wear with the CVC uniform. Soldiers will not tuck the uniform into the boots. The only outer garment authorized for wear with the CVC uniform is the cold-weather jacket. The black beret became the basic headgear for this uniform on 14 June 2001. The beret will be worn when the CVC helmet is not worn, unless the commander has prescribed wear of the patrol cap, as described in chapter 3 of this regulation. (See para 3–5 for wear policy of the beret and the patrol cap.)

*b.* Wear of insignia.

(1) The U.S. Army tape is worn horizontal to the ground, approximately ½ inch up from the outside zipper seam on the left breast. The nametape is worn on the right side, in line with the U.S. Army tape. The subdued sew-on grade insignia is worn centered ¼ inch above the nametape.

(2) On the cold-weather jacket, the nametape and U.S. Army tape are worn horizontal to the ground, approximately 1½ inches above the top of the pocket flaps.

(3) Commanders will provide, and have attached, the subdued sew-on grade insignia, nametape, U.S. Army tape, and shoulder sleeve insignia, without cost to enlisted personnel.

*c.* Commanders may authorize the use of a camouflage personal hydration system only in the following situations: in a field environment, in high-heat areas, or on work details. Soldiers will not carry hydration systems in a garrison environment, unless the commander has authorized it for one of the situations described above. Soldiers will not let the drinking tube hang from their mouths when the device is not in use.

*d.* Figures 13–1 and 13–2 show the basic uniform and the cold-weather jacket.

## Chapter 14
## Physical Fitness Uniform

## 14–1. Authorization for wear

The physical fitness uniform (PFU) is authorized for year-round wear by all personnel, when prescribed by the commander. The improved PFU (IPFU) replaces the PFU. Soldiers may wear the PFU until 30 Sep 2003; mandatory possession for the IPFU is 1 Oct 2003. (See fig 14–1 for authorized variations of the IPFU and figure 14–2 for the PFU.)

Figure 14–1. Improved physical fitness uniform variations

Figure 14–1. Improved physical fitness uniform variations—Continued

Figure 14–2. Physical fitness uniform

## 14–2. Composition and classification

*a.* The PFU consists of the following components.

(1) T-shirt, athletic, gray.

(2) Trunks, general purpose, gray.

(3) Sweatpants, gray.

(4) Sweatshirt, hooded, gray, with zipper.

(5) Cap, knit, black.

*b.* The IPFU consists of the following components.

(1) Jacket, running, gray and black.

(2) Pants, running, black.

(3) Trunks, running, black, moisture-wicking.

(4) T-shirt, gray, short sleeve, moisture-wicking.

(5) T-shirt, gray, long sleeve, moisture-wicking.

(6) Cap, knit, black.

## 14–3. Accessories

*a.* Commanders may authorize the wear of commercial running shoes, calf-length or ankle-length, plain white socks with no logos, gloves, reflective belts or vests, long underwear, and other items appropriate to the weather conditions and type of activity. If soldiers wear long underwear or other similar items, they must conceal them from view with the hooded sweatshirt and sweat pants when wearing the PFU, or the running jacket and pants if wearing the IPFU.

*b.* Soldiers are authorized to wear commercially purchased gray or black spandex shorts under the PFU or IPFU shorts. The length of the shorts must end above the knee or higher. The commercial shorts must be plain, with no logos, patterns, or obtrusive markings. Soldiers are not required to buy the spandex shorts.

## 14–4. Occasions for wear

The PFU and the IPFU are authorized for wear on and off duty, on and off the installation, when authorized by the commander. Soldiers may wear all or part of the PFU or IPFU with civilian attire off the installation, when authorized by the commander.

## 14–5. Insignia

The only insignia authorized for wear on the PFU or IPFU is the physical fitness badge. When the physical fitness badge is worn, it is sewn on the upper left front side of the PFU and IPFU T-shirt, and the PFU sweatshirt. On the IPFU running jacket, the insignia is sewn centered ½ inch above the word "Army." See AR 600–8–22 for criteria for wear of the physical fitness badge.

## 14–6. General guidelines

*a.* Soldiers may not mix or match PFU and IPFU items. When soldiers wear either the PFU or IPFU as a complete uniform, they will keep the sleeves down on the sweatshirt or jacket, the legs down on the pants, and they will tuck the T-shirt inside the trunks. Soldiers may not roll or push up the sleeves of the PFU sweatshirt or the IPFU jacket. Soldiers may wear the sleeves of the PFU sweatshirt cuffed or uncuffed; they may not cuff the IPFU jacket sleeves. Soldiers will wear the black knit cap pulled down snugly on the head, with the bottom edge of the cap folded up; soldiers will not roll the edge of the cap. A similar, commercially designed black knit cap is authorized for wear. There are no restrictions on the combination of IPFU items worn, unless the commander has prescribed a particular combination for formation. Standards of wear and appearance specified in paragraphs 1–7 and 1–8 of this regulation apply at all times.

*b.* The PFU and the IPFU are clothing bag items. Each element of the PFU and IPFU is identified with a national stock number (NSN) and a Defense Logistics Agency (DLA) contract number printed on a label and sewn into the garment. If the label does not contain this information, the garment is not the authorized garment.

*c.* Commanders should expect both uniforms (PFU and IPFU) in their formations until all soldiers acquire the IPFU by the mandatory possession date.

*d.* Pregnant soldiers will wear the PFU or IPFU until the uniform becomes too small or uncomfortable. Pregnant soldiers are authorized to wear the T-shirt outside the trunks. At no time will commanders require pregnant soldiers to purchase a larger PFU or IPFU in order to accommodate the pregnancy. When the uniform becomes too small or uncomfortable, pregnant soldiers may wear equivalent civilian workout clothes.

**Part Three**
**Service Uniforms**

## Chapter 15
## Army Green Service Uniform—Male

### 15–1. Authorization for wear
The class A and B Army green uniforms are authorized for year-round wear by all male personnel. The class A service uniform is an optional dress uniform for all male enlisted personnel when worn with the white shirt and bow tie. The Army green dress uniform, with white shirt and bow tie, is equivalent to the Army blue and white uniforms. (For the officer Army green service uniform, see fig 15–1; for officer and enlisted berets, see fig 15–2 and 15–3; for garrison cap, officer, see fig 15–4 ; for Army green uniform, enlisted, see fig 15–5; for garrison cap, officer, see fig 15–5, for garrison cap, enlisted, see fig 15–6; and for shirt and tie options with class B Army green uniforms, see fig 15–7, 15–8, and 15–9.)

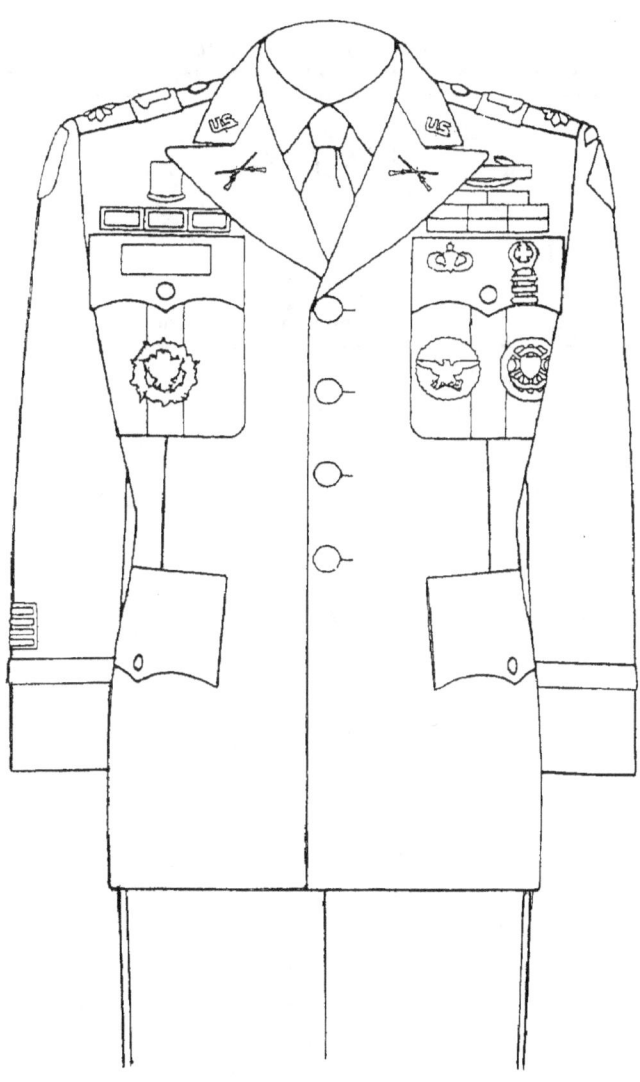

**Figure 15–1. Army green service uniform, officer**

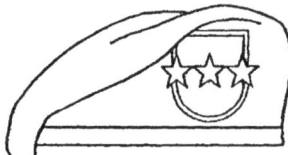

Figure 15–2. Beret, officer

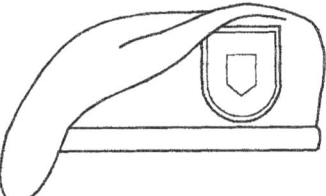

Figure 15–3. Beret, enlisted

Figure 15–4. Garrison cap, officers

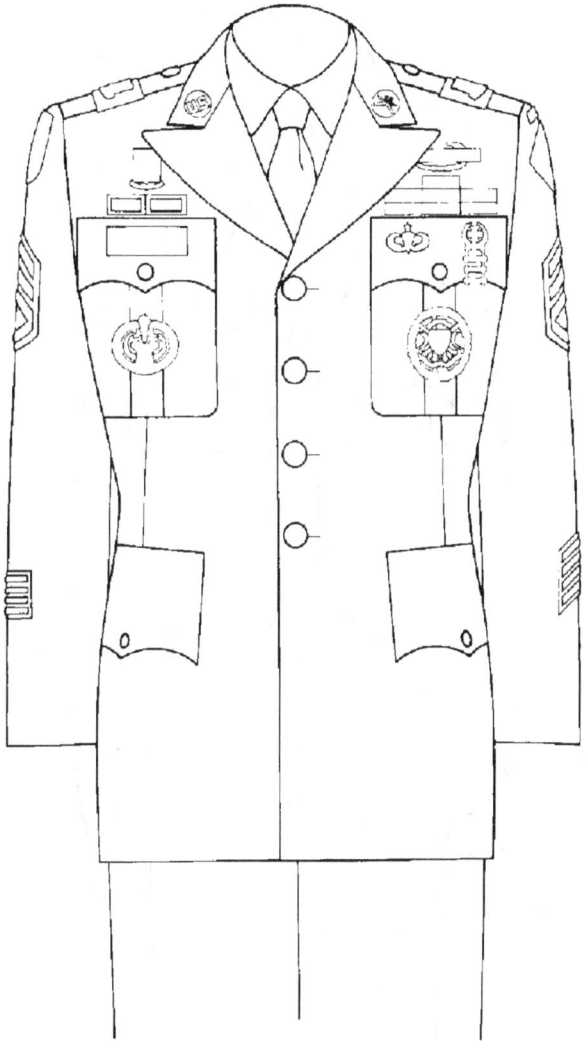

Figure 15–5. Army green uniform, enlisted

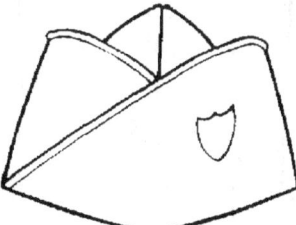

Figure 15–6. Garrison cap, enlisted

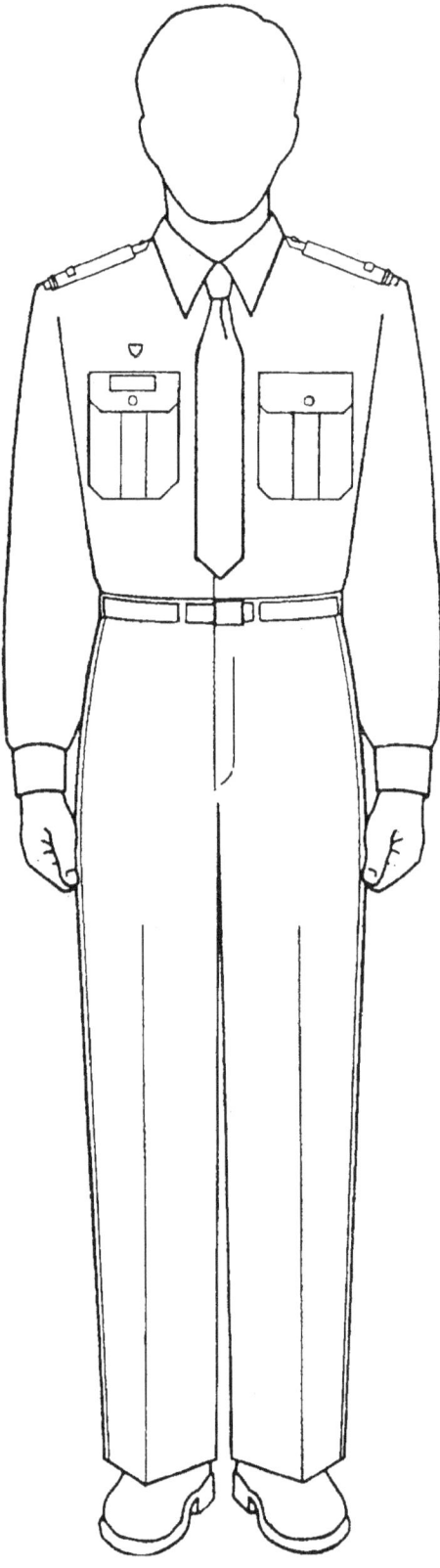

Figure 15–7. Class B Army green uniform, long-sleeved shirt and tie

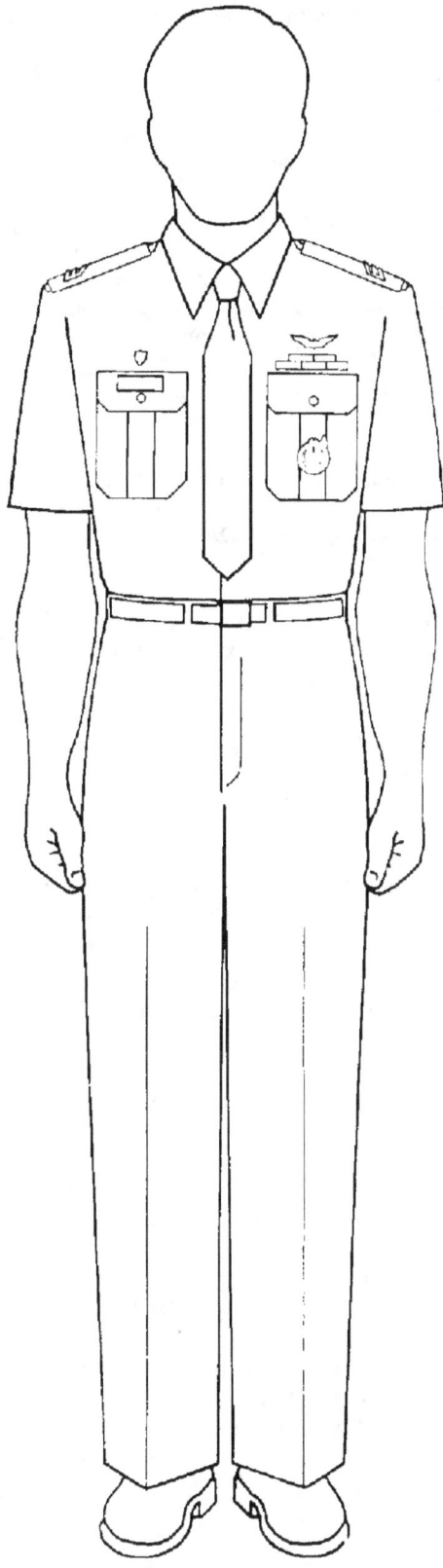

Figure 15–8. Class B Army green uniform, short-sleeved shirt and tie

## 15–2. Composition

*a.* The class A green service uniform comprises the Army green coat and trousers, an Army green (AG) shade 415 short- or long-sleeved shirt, and a black four-in-hand necktie. (For accessories and other items authorized for wear on the class A green service uniform, see para 15–10.)

*b.* The class B green uniform comprises the Army green trousers and AG shade 415 short- or long-sleeved shirt. Soldiers will wear a four-in-hand necktie with the long-sleeved AG shade 415 shirt when it is worn without the class A coat, as an outer garment. (See para 15–10 for accessories and other items authorized for wear with the class B uniform.)

*c.* The Army green dress uniform (authorized for enlisted personnel only) comprises the Army green coat and trousers, a commercial long-sleeved white shirt, and a black four-in-hand tie (before retreat) or a black bow tie (after retreat). The black beret is authorized for wear with this uniform. When the enlisted Army green dress uniform is worn for evening social occasions (after retreat), headgear is not required. Combat boots and organizational items, such as brassards and military police (MP) accessories, are not authorized for wear with the Army green dress uniform. All other accessories and insignia that are authorized for wear with the class A service uniform are authorized for wear on the Army green dress uniform (see para 15–10).

## 15–3. Classification

The Army green service uniform is a clothing bag issue item. The Army green dress uniform is an optional dress uniform for enlisted personnel when worn with a white shirt and black four-in-hand tie (before retreat) or black bow tie (after retreat). The beret is an organizational issue item. DA Pam 710–2–1 governs turn-in and reissue of the beret.

## 15–4. Occasions for wear

*a.* The Army green service uniform (class A) and authorized variations (class B) are authorized for wear by all male personnel when on duty, off duty, or during travel. These uniforms also are acceptable for informal social functions after retreat, unless the host prescribes other uniforms.

*b.* The following are appropriate occasions for enlisted personnel to wear the Army green dress uniform.

(1) At social functions of a private or official nature, either before or after retreat, and while in transit to and from such functions. Otherwise, it is not authorized for travel.

(2) When designated by the host.

## 15–5. Materials

*a.* Coat and trousers. The coat and trousers will be made of the same material and shade.

(1) Polyester/wool serge, 11.8 ounce (standard issue fabric), AG shade 489.

(2) Polyester/wool gabardine, 10.6 ounce (optional purchase fabric), AG shade 489.

(3) Texturized woven polyester, 10.1 ounce (optional purchase fabric), AG shade 491.

(4) Polyester/wool elastique, 16.0 ounce (optional purchase fabric), AG shade 489.

*b.* Headgear.

(1) Beret (para 3–2*b*(1)).

(2) Garrison cap, male personnel. The material may be any of the materials listed for the coat and trousers in 15–5a, above.

## 15–6. Coat, Army green

*a.* Design. The coat will be made from an approved specification or pattern.

*b.* General description. The coat is a single-breasted, peak-lapel, four-button coat extending below the crotch, fitting easily over the chest and shoulders, with a slight draped effect in the front and back. The coat is fitted slightly at the waist, conforming to body shape without tightness and with no prominent flare.

*c.* Coat sleeve ornamentation.

(1) General officers. The sleeve has a band of black mohair, polyester, or mercerized cotton braid 1½ inches wide, sewn on each sleeve with the lower edge parallel to, and 3 inches above the bottom edge of each sleeve.

(2) Other officers. The sleeve has a band of black mohair, polyester, or mercerized cotton braid ¾ inch wide, sewn on each sleeve with the lower edge parallel to, and 3 inches above the bottom edge of each sleeve.

(3) Enlisted personnel. The sleeve is plain.

## 15–7. Trousers, Army green

*a.* Design. The trousers will be made from an approved specification or pattern.

*b.* General description. The trousers are straight legged without cuffs, and with side and hip pockets. The left hip pocket has a buttonhole tab and button.

*c.* Trouser leg ornamentation. Ornamental braid is sewn on each outside seam of the trouser leg, from the bottom of the waistband to the bottom of the trouser leg, as follows.

(1) General officers. Each trouser leg has two ½-inch wide black mohair, polyester, or mercerized cotton braids sewn ½ inch apart.

(2) Other officers. Each leg has one braid, 1½ inches in width, made of black mohair, polyester, or mercerized cotton braid.

(3) Enlisted personnel. The trouser leg is plain.

## 15–8. Shirt, long- and short-sleeved

*a.* The clothing bag (issue) shirt is a pre-cured durable press, 65/35 polyester and cotton broadcloth shirt, AG shade 415, in short- and long-sleeved versions. (See figs 15–7, 15–8, and 15–9.) The shirt is a dress type with shoulder loops, a seven-button front, and two pleated pockets with button-down flaps.

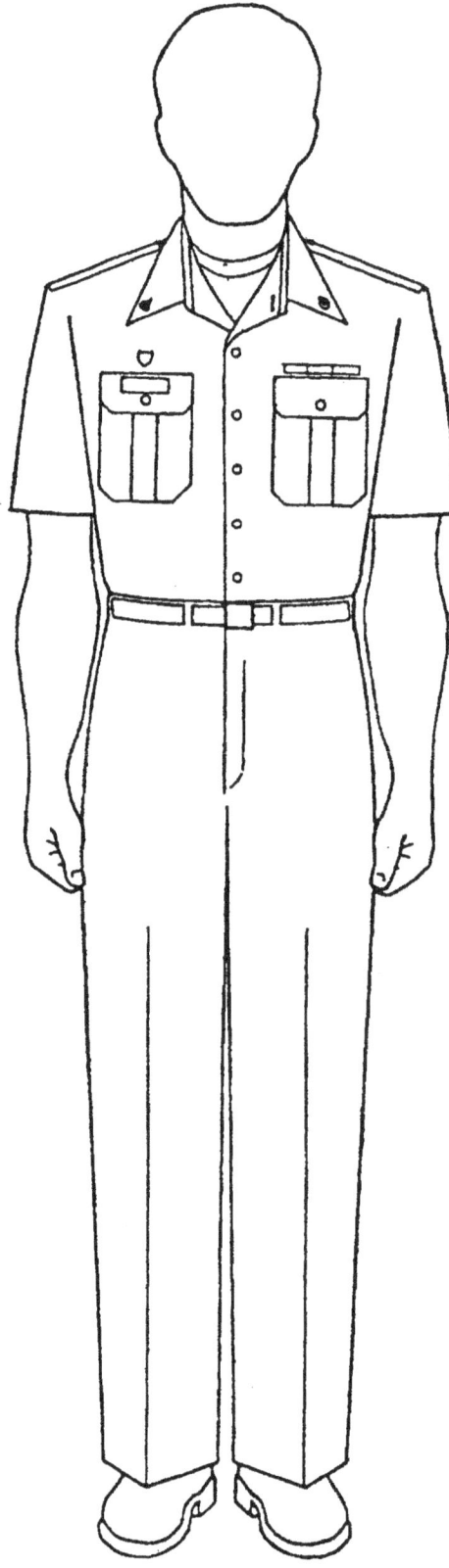

Figure 15–9. Class B Army green uniform, short-sleeved shirt without tie

*b.* Soldiers are authorized to wear the optional purchase polyester/wool short-sleeved (AG shade 469) and long-sleeved (AG shade 428) shirts. In accordance with care instructions provided on the shirts, soldiers may not starch or bleach the AG shades 415, 428, or 469 shirts.

*c.* Soldiers are authorized to wear the short- and long-sleeved shirts with the class A coat, black unisex pullover and cardigan sweaters, and the windbreaker.

(1) Soldiers must wear a black four-in-hand necktie when wearing the short- or long-sleeved shirt with the class A coat, or when wearing the long-sleeved shirt as an outer garment without the class A coat. They have the option of wearing a tie when the short-sleeved shirt is worn as an outer garment.

(2) Soldiers have the option of wearing a tie when they wear the short- or long-sleeved shirts with the pullover sweater or cardigan sweaters. If a tie is worn with the pullover or cardigan sweaters, soldiers will wear the collar of the shirt inside the sweater. If no tie is worn with the pullover sweater, the collar is worn outside. If no tie is worn with the cardigan sweater, soldiers may wear the collar inside or outside the sweater. Soldiers may wear the cardigan sweater buttoned or unbuttoned while indoors, but they must button it when outdoors.

## 15–9. Headgear

*a.* Beret (para 3–2*b*(1)). (See figs 15–2 and 15–3.)

*b.* Garrison cap, Army green. (See figs 15–4 and 15–6.)

(1) Design. The cap will be made from an approved specification or pattern.

(2) Ornamental braid. Garrison cap braid refers to the piping that is secured to the tip edge of the curtain of the garrison cap, and that is used for additional identification purposes. For junior and senior ROTC cadets, the cap has a cord edge braid of the same material as the cap, in AG shade 489 or 491.

(3) Wear. The beret became the standard headgear for class A and B Army green service uniforms, and the enlisted Army green dress uniform, on 14 June 2001.

(4) Proper wear position.

*(a)* See para 3–5 for wear policy on the beret.

*(b)* The garrison cap is worn with the front vertical crease of the cap centered on the forehead in a straight line with the nose, with the front lower portion of the cap approximately 1 inch above the eyebrows (approximately the width of the first two fingers). The cap is placed on the head in such a manner that the front and rear vertical creases and the top edge of the crown form unbroken lines in silhouette, and so the ridge of the cap is parallel to the ground while standing at attention. Personnel will not crush or shape the crown of the cap to form peaks at the top front or top rear of the cap.

## 15–10. Items normally worn with the Army green uniform

*a.* Accessories. The following accessories are worn with the Army green uniform:

(1) Belt, black web, with brass tip (para 27–2*b*).

(2) Boots, combat, leather, black (only when bloused trousers are authorized; not authorized with the enlisted Army green dress uniform) (para 27–3).

(3) Buckle, solid brass (para 27–2*d*).

(4) Buttons (para 27–4).

(5) Cap, cold-weather, AG shade 489 (only when wearing the black all-weather coat or black windbreaker) (para 27–5).

(6) Chaplain's apparel (para 27–7).

(7) Coat, black all-weather (para 27–8).

(8) Gloves, black, leather, unisex, dress (only when worn with the class A, Army enlisted green dress uniform, black all-weather coat, or windbreaker) (para 27–12*b*).

(9) Hat, drill sergeant (not authorized with the enlisted Army green dress uniform) (para 27–14*b*).

(10) Judge's apparel (para 27–15).

(11) Military police accessories (not authorized with the enlisted Army green dress uniform) (para 27–16).

(12) Neckties.

*(a)* Black, bow (only with the enlisted Army green dress uniform) (para 27–19*a*).

*(b)* Black, four-in-hand (para 27–19*c*).

(13) Scarf, black (only with black all-weather coat or windbreaker) (para 27–21*a*).

(14) Shirt, white (only with the enlisted Army green dress uniform) (para 27–22*c*).

(15) Shoes, oxford, black, and overshoes (paras 27–23*c* and 27–20).

(16) Socks.

*(a)* Black, cushion sole (worn with boots only) (para 27–24*a*).

*(b)* Black, dress (para 27–24*b*).

(17) Sweater, unisex cardigan, black (para 27–26a).

(18) Sweater, pullover, black (para 27–26c).

(19) Undershirt, white (para 27–28f).

(20) Windbreaker, black (only with class B uniform) (para 27–30).

b. Insignia, awards, badges, and accouterments worn on the Army green uniform (class A and B) and the enlisted Army green dress uniform. Note the following exceptions:

(1) Aiguillette, service (officers only) (not authorized on the class B uniform) (para 28–25).

(2) Brassards (not authorized on the enlisted Army green dress uniform) (para 28–29).

(3) Branch of service scarves (not authorized on the enlisted Army green dress uniform) (para 28–20).

(4) Fourragere/lanyards (not authorized on the class B uniform) (para 29–11).

(5) Distinctive items for infantry personnel (para 28–30).

(6) Branch insignia (not authorized on the class B uniform) (paras 28–10 and 28–12a).

(7) U.S. insignia (not authorized on the class B uniform) (para 28–4).

(8) Insignia of grade (paras 28–5, 28–6, and 28–7).

(9) Headgear insignia (para 28–3).

(10) Distinctive unit insignia (DUI) (not authorized on the enlisted Army green dress uniform and the class B uniform) (para 28–22).

(11) Regimental distinctive insignia (RDI) (para 28–23).

(12) Combat leaders identification (not authorized on the class B uniform or enlisted Army green dress uniform) (para 28–21).

(13) OCS/WOC insignia (paras 28–14 and 28–15).

(14) Shoulder sleeve insignia, current organization, full color (not authorized on the class B uniform) (para 28–16).

(15) Shoulder sleeve insignia, former wartime service, full color (not authorized on the class B uniform) (para 28–17).

(16) Nameplate (para 28–24c).

(17) Organizational flash (para 28–31a).

(18) Airborne background trimming (para 28–31b).

(19) Overseas service bars (not authorized on the class B uniform) (para 28–28).

(20) Service stripes (enlisted personnel only; not authorized on the class B uniform) (para 28–27).

(21) Decorations and service medal ribbons (soldiers may not wear miniature medals on the enlisted Army green dress uniform; they may wear full-size or miniature medals on the class B uniform) (paras 29–7, 29–8, and 29–9).

(22) Unit awards (para 29–11).

(23) U.S. badges (identification, marksmanship, combat, and special skill) (cloth special skill and marksmanship badges and tabs are not authorized on the class B uniform; full, miniature, and dress miniature badges are authorized on the class B uniform) (paras 29–13, 29–16, and 29–18).

(24) Foreign badges (para 29–19).

c. Insignia authorized for wear with the class B uniform.

(1) Same as paragraph 15–10b, except that the distinctive unit insignia (DUI), branch and U.S. insignia, sew-on insignia, and combat leaders identification are not authorized for wear.

(2) The DUI is authorized for wear on the black pullover sweater. If no DUI is authorized, then the RDI is worn (para 28–23b(1)). Recruiters will wear the recruiting badge in lieu of the DUI or RDI.

## 15–11. General guidelines

a. The Army green service uniforms are intended for wear during most duty, non-field, or utility occasions, and for travel and off-duty purposes. While both the class A and B uniforms are authorized for year-round wear, the appropriate uniform is worn based on weather conditions, duties, and the formality of the occasion. When a specific service uniform is not prescribed for formations or other occasions when uniformity in appearance is not required, soldiers may wear the class A or any of the variations of the class B uniform, with the accessories authorized for these uniforms.

b. Soldiers will not wear those awards and decorations on the AG shade 415 shirt that they cannot wear properly because of size or configuration. Commanders will not require the wear of optional items, such as windbreakers or sweaters, unless such items are provided to the soldier without cost.

c. Soldiers may purchase and wear the Army green service uniform in any of the authorized fabrics listed in paragraph 15–5. However, individuals who purchase uniforms or uniform items from commercial sources are responsible for ensuring that the items conform to military specifications, or are manufactured in accordance with the procedures prescribed by the uniform quality control program (see chap 2 for details). Only those alterations authorized by AR 700–84 and TM 10–227 are authorized. General fitting instructions for these uniforms are provided in chapter 1 of this regulation. Soldiers will wear these uniforms with the shirt tucked into the trousers so that the shirt edge is aligned with the front fly opening, so the outside edge of the belt buckle forms a straight "gig line." Only soldiers authorized to wear the tan, green, or maroon berets, those assigned to Air Assault coded positions, and MPs performing MP duties may wear bloused (tucked-in or by the use of blousing rubbers/bands) trousers with black leather combat boots. Figures 15–1 through 15–9 show the class A and B Army green service uniforms and authorized headgear.

# Chapter 16
# Army Green Service Uniform—Female

## 16–1. Authorization for wear
The class A and B Army green uniforms are authorized for year-round wear by all female personnel. The class A service uniform is an optional dress uniform for all female enlisted personnel when worn with the skirt, a white shirt, and the neck tab. The Army green dress uniform, with white shirt and neck tab, is equivalent to the Army blue and white uniforms. (For the Army green uniform with slacks, officer, see fig 16–1; for the garrison cap, officer, see fig 16–2; for the beret, officer, see fig 16–3; for the beret, enlisted, see fig 16–4; for the Army green uniform with skirt, enlisted, see fig 16–5; for the garrison cap, enlisted, see fig 16–6; and for the class B variations of the Army green uniform, female, see fig 16–7.)

Figure 16–1. Army green uniform with slacks, officer

AR 670–1 • 3 February 2005

Figure 16–2. Garrison cap, officer

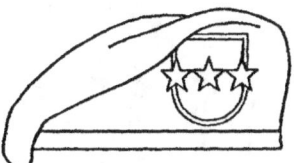

Figure 16–3. Berets, officer

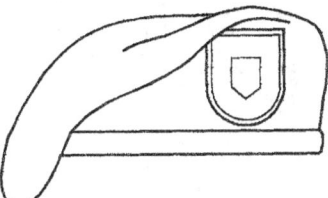

Figure 16–4. Beret, enlisted

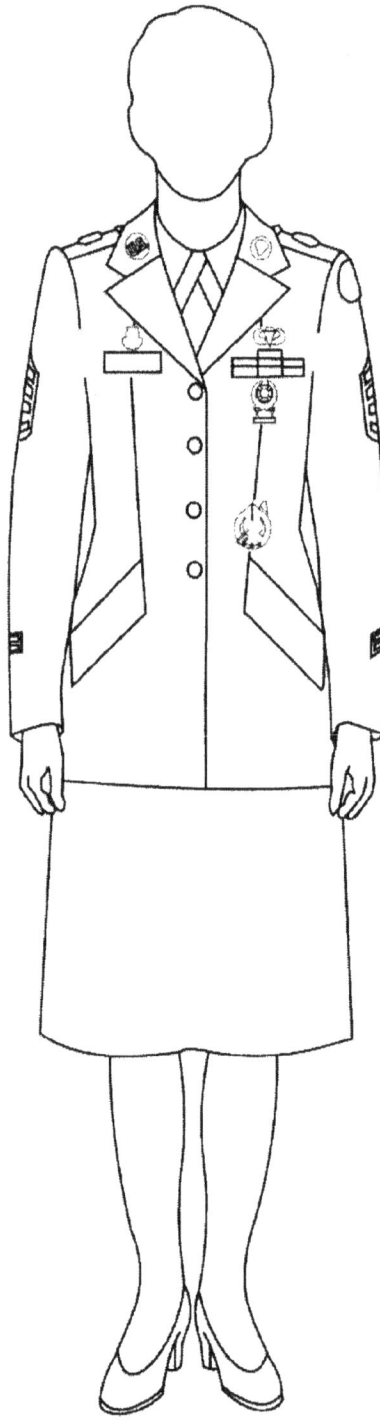

Figure 16–5. Army green uniform with skirt, enlisted

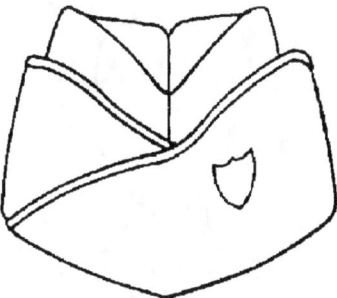

Figure 16–6. Garrison cap, enlisted

Long sleeve shirt (tucked in)
and neck tab with slacks

Short sleeve shirt (tucked in)
and neck tab with skirt

Short sleeve shirt (tucked in),
open, with skirt

Figure 16–7. Class B variations of the Army green uniform, female

**Long sleeve shirt and neck tab with skirt**

**Short sleeve shirt and neck tab with slacks**

**Short sleeve shirt open, with skirt**

Figure 16–7. Class B variations of the Army green uniform, female—Continued

### 16–2. Composition

*a.* The class A green service uniform consists of the Army green coat, skirt or slacks, an AG shade 415 short- or long-sleeved tuck-in shirt, and a black neck tab. (For accessories and other items authorized for wear on the class A green service uniform see para 16–11.)

*b.* The class B green uniform consists of the Army green skirt or slacks and an AG shade 415 long- or short-sleeved tuck-in shirt. Soldiers will wear a black neck tab with the long-sleeved AG shade 415 shirt when it is worn without the class A coat, as an outer garment. (See para 16–11 for accessories and other items authorized for wear with the class B uniform.)

*c.* The Army green dress uniform (authorized for enlisted personnel only) consists of the Army green coat and skirt, white shirt with black neck tab, and black service pumps. The black beret is authorized for wear with this uniform. When the enlisted Army green dress uniform is worn for evening social occasions (after retreat), headgear is not required. Combat boots, oxford shoes, and organizational items, such as brassards and MP accessories, are not authorized for wear with the enlisted Army green dress uniform. All other accessories and insignia that are authorized for wear with the class A service uniform are authorized for wear with the enlisted Army green dress uniform (see para 16–11 below).

### 16–3. Classification

The Army green service uniform is a clothing bag issue item. The Army green dress uniform is an optional dress uniform for enlisted personnel when worn with the skirt and white shirt with black neck tab. The beret is an organizational issue item. DA Pam 710–2–1 governs turn-in and reissue of the beret.

### 16–4. Occasions for wear

*a.* The Army green service uniform (class A) and authorized variations (class B) are authorized for wear by all female personnel when on duty, off duty, or during travel. These uniforms also are acceptable for informal social functions after retreat, unless the host prescribes other uniforms.

*b.* The following are appropriate occasions for enlisted personnel to wear the Army green dress uniform.

(1) At social functions of a private or official nature either before or after retreat, and while in transit to and from such functions. Otherwise, it is not authorized for travel.

(2) When designated by the host.

### 16–5. Materials

*a.* The mandatory date for possession of the materials described in paragraph 16–5*b*, below, is extended until 1 Oct 2003. Until that time, females are authorized to wear the green service uniform components in AG shades 344 (poly/wool) and 434 (polyester).

*b.* Coat, slacks, and skirt. The coat, slacks, and skirt will be made of the same material and shade.

(1) Polyester/wool serge, 11.8 ounce (standard-issue fabric), AG shade 489.

(2) Polyester/wool gabardine, 10.6 ounce (optional purchase fabric), AG shade 489.

(3) Texturized woven polyester, 10.1 ounce (optional purchase fabric), AG shade 491.

(4) Polyester/wool elastique, 16.0 ounce (optional purchase fabric), AG shade 489.

*c.* Headgear.

(1) Beret (para 3–2*b*(1)).

(2) Garrison cap, female personnel. The material may be any of the materials listed for the coat, slacks, and skirt in paragraph 16–5*a*, above.

### 16–6. Coat, Army green

*a.* Design. The coat will be made from an approved specification or pattern.

*b.* General description. The coat is a single-breasted, four-button, hip-length coat, with two slanted, flap front pockets, button-down shoulder loops, a notched collar, and side-body construction.

*c.* Coat sleeve ornamentation.

(1) General officers. The sleeve has a band of black mohair, polyester, or mercerized cotton braid 1½ inches wide, sewn on each sleeve with the lower edge parallel to, and 3 inches above the bottom edge of each sleeve.

(2) Other officers. The sleeve has a band of black mohair, polyester, or mercerized cotton braid ½ inch wide, sewn on each sleeve with the lower edge parallel to, and 3 inches above the bottom edge of each sleeve.

(3) Enlisted personnel. The sleeve is plain.

## 16–7. Slacks, Army green

*a.* Design. The slacks will be made from an approved specification or pattern.

*b.* General description.

(1) The slacks are straight legged, have a zipper front closure on the center front with a button fly tab, and two side pockets. These slacks are authorized for wear until 30 September 2003.

(2) Newly designed slacks replace the older style as of 1 October 2003. The newer design incorporates belt loops and a non-slip waistband. When wearing the slacks with belt loops with the tuck-in versions of the AG shade 415 blouse, personnel will wear a 1-inch black web belt with brass tip, and a 1⅛ inch yellow brass buckle. Soldiers are not required to wear a belt when wearing the new style slacks with the overblouse version of the AG shade 415 blouse.

*c.* Slack leg ornamentation. Ornamental braid is sewn on each outside seam of the slack leg, from the bottom of the waistband to the bottom of the slack leg, as follows:

(1) General officers. Each slack leg has two ½-inch-wide black mohair, polyester, or mercerized cotton braids sewn ½ inch apart.

(2) Other officers. Each leg has one braid, 1 inch wide, made of black mohair, polyester, or mercerized cotton braid.

(3) Enlisted personnel. The slack leg is plain.

## 16–8. Skirt, Army green

*a.* Design. The skirt will be made from an approved specification or pattern.

*b.* General description.

(1) The skirt is knee length, slightly flared, with a waistband and zipper closure on the left side. This skirt is authorized for wear until 30 September 2003.

(2) A newly designed skirt replaces the older style, as of 1 October 2003. The new design skirt is tapered and incorporates a non-slip waistband, back zipper closure, back open (kick) pleat, two darts each in the front and back; it is fully lined.

## 16–9. Shirts, long- and short-sleeved

*a.* The clothing bag (issue) shirt is a pre-cured, durable press, 65/35 polyester and cotton broadcloth shirt, AG shade 415, in short- and long-sleeved versions. The shirt is a tuck-in design with front princess seams, a convertible collar, and shoulder loops. The collar and shoulder loops have fusible interlinings, and the collar has stays.

*b.* Optional purchase shirts. Soldiers are authorized to wear the optional purchase polyester/wool (AG shade 469) and polyester/cotton (AG shade 415) short- and long-sleeved overblouse shirts. This shirt is a semi-fitted, hip-length, overblouse style shirt with front princess seams, and a three-piece back. The shirt has shoulder loops, a convertible collar, and a six-button front. The collar and shoulder loops have fusible interlinings and the collar has stays. In accordance with care instructions provided on the shirts, soldiers may not starch or bleach the AG shades 415 or 469 shirts.

*c.* Soldiers are authorized to wear the short- and long-sleeved shirts with the class A coat, black unisex pullover and cardigan sweaters, and the windbreaker.

(1) Soldiers must wear the black neck tab when wearing the short- or long-sleeved shirt with the class A coat, or when wearing the long-sleeved shirt as an outer garment (without the class A coat). Soldiers have the option of wearing the neck tab with the short-sleeved shirt when it is worn as an outer garment.

(2) Soldiers have the option of wearing a neck tab when they wear the short- or long-sleeved shirts with the pullover sweater or cardigan sweaters. If a neck tab is worn with the pullover or cardigan sweaters, soldiers will wear the collar of the shirt inside the sweater. If no neck tab is worn with the pullover sweater, the collar is worn outside. If no neck tab is worn with the cardigan sweater, soldiers may wear the collar inside or outside the sweater. Soldiers may wear the cardigan sweater buttoned or unbuttoned while indoors, but they must button it when outdoors.

## 16–10. Headgear

*a.* Beret (para 3–2*b*(1)). (See figs 16–3 and 16–4.)

*b.* Garrison cap, Army green. (See figs 16–2 and 16–6.)

(1) Design. The cap will be made from an approved specification or pattern.

(2) Ornamental braid. Garrison cap braid refers to the piping that is secured to the tip edge of the curtain of the garrison cap and that is used for additional identification purposes. For junior and senior ROTC cadets, the cap has a cord edge braid of the same material as the cap, in AG shade 489 or 491.

(3) Wear. The beret became the standard headgear for class A and B Army green service uniforms, and the enlisted Army green dress uniform, on 14 June 2001.

(4) Proper wear position.

*(a)* See para 3–5 for wear policy on the beret.

*(b)* The garrison cap is worn with the front vertical crease of the cap centered on the forehead, with the front lower portion of the cap approximately 1 inch above the eyebrows (approximately the width of the first two fingers). The top

of the cap is opened to cover the crown of the head. The bottom of the rear vertical crease will fit snugly to the back of the head. Hair will not be visible on the forehead below the front bottom edge of the cap.

## 16–11. Items normally worn with the Army green uniform

*a.* Accessories. The following accessories are worn with the Army green uniform.

(1) Belt, black web, 1-inch, with brass tip (para 27–2*b*).

(2) Boots, combat, leather, black (only when bloused slacks are authorized; not authorized with the enlisted Army green dress uniform) (para 27–3).

(3) Buckle, solid brass, 1⅛ inch (para 27–2*d*).

(4) Buttons (para 27–4).

(5) Cap, service, cold weather, AG shade 489 (only when wearing the black all-weather coat or black windbreaker) (para 27–5).

(6) Chaplain's apparel (para 27–7).

(7) Coat, black, all weather (para 27–8).

(8) Gloves, black, leather, unisex, dress (only when worn with the class A, enlisted Army green dress uniform, black all-weather coat, or windbreaker) (para 27–12*b*).

(9) Handbags.

*(a)* Black, clutch type, optional purchase (para 27–13*a*).

*(b)* Black, shoulder (para 27–13*d*).

(10) Hat, drill sergeant (not authorized with Army green dress uniform) (para 27–14*a*).

(11) Judge's apparel (para 27–15).

(12) Military police accessories (not authorized with the enlisted Army green dress uniform) (para 27–16).

(13) Scarf, black (only with black all-weather coat or windbreaker) (para 27–21*a*)

(14) Shirt, white (only with enlisted Army green dress uniform) para 27–22*a*).

(15) Shoes.

*(a)* Oxford, black (not authorized with the enlisted Army green dress uniform) (para 27–23*a*).

*(b)* Pumps, black (para 27–23*f*).

(16) Socks.

*(a)* Black, cushion sole (worn with boots only) (para 27–24*a*).

*(b)* Black, dress (authorized only with the slacks) (para 27–24*b*).

(17) Stockings, sheer (para 27–24*d*).

(18) Sweater, unisex cardigan, black (para 27–26*a*).

(19) Sweater, pullover, black (para 27–26*c*).

(20) Umbrella, black (para 27–27).

(21) Undergarments (para 27–29).

(22) Windbreaker, black (only with class B uniform) (para 27–30).

*b.* Insignia, awards, badges, and accouterments worn on the Army green uniforms (class A and B) and the enlisted Army green dress uniform; note exceptions.

(1) Aiguillette, service (officers only) (not authorized on the class B uniform) (para 28–25).

(2) Brassards (not authorized on the enlisted Army green dress uniform) (para 28–29).

(3) Branch of service scarves (not authorized on the enlisted Army green dress uniform) (para 28–20).

(4) Fourragere/lanyard (not authorized on the class B uniform) (para 29–11).

(5) Branch insignia (not authorized on the class B uniform) (paras 28–10 and 28–12*a*).

(6) U.S. insignia (not authorized on the class B uniform) (para 28–4).

(7) Insignia of grade (paras 28–5, 28–6, and 28–7).

(8) Headgear insignia (para 28–3).

(9) Distinctive unit insignia (DUI) (not authorized on the enlisted Army green dress uniform and the class B uniform) (para 28–22).

(10) Regimental distinctive insignia (RDI) (para 28–23).

(11) Combat leaders identification (not authorized on the class B uniform or the enlisted Army green dress uniform (para 28–21).

(12) OCS/WOC insignia (paras 28–14 and 28–15).

(13) Shoulder sleeve insignia, current organization, full color (not authorized on the class B uniform) (para 28–16).

(14) Shoulder sleeve insignia, former wartime service, full color (not authorized on the class B uniform) (para 28–17).

(15) Nameplate (para 28–24*c*).

(16) Organizational flash (para 28–31*a*).

(17) Airborne background trimming (para 28–31*b*).

(18) Overseas service bars (not authorized on the class B uniform) (para 28–28).

(19) Service stripes (enlisted personnel only; not authorized on the class B uniform) (para 28–27).

(20) Decorations and service medal ribbons (soldiers may not wear miniature medals on the enlisted Army green dress uniform; they may wear full-size or miniature medals on the class B uniform) (paras 29–7, 29–8, and 29–9).

(21) Unit awards (para 29–11).

(22) U.S. badges (identification, marksmanship, combat, and special skill) (cloth special skill and marksmanship badges and tabs are not authorized on the class B uniform; full, miniature, and dress miniature badges are authorized on the class B uniform) (paras 29–13, 29–16, 29–17, and 29–18).

(23) Foreign badges (para 29–19).

*c.* Insignia authorized for wear with the class B uniform.

(1) Same as paragraph 16–11*b*, except that the DUI, branch and U.S. insignia, sew-on insignia, and combat leaders identification are not authorized for wear.

(2) The DUI is authorized for wear on the black pullover sweater. If no DUI is authorized, then the RDI is worn (para 28–23*b*(2)). Recruiters will wear the recruiting badge in lieu of the DUI or RDI.

## 16–12. General guidelines

*a.* The Army green service uniforms are intended for wear during most duty, non-field, or utility occasions, and for travel and off-duty purposes. While both the class A and B uniforms are authorized for year-round wear, the appropriate uniform is worn based on weather conditions, duties, and the formality of the occasion. When a specific service uniform is not prescribed for formations or other occasions when uniformity in appearance is not required, soldiers may wear the class A or any of the variations of the class B uniform, with the accessories authorized for these uniforms.

*b.* Soldiers will not wear those awards and decorations on the AG shade 415 shirt that they cannot wear properly because of size or configuration. Commanders will not require the wear of optional items, such as windbreakers or sweaters, unless such items are provided to the soldier without cost.

*c.* Soldiers may purchase and wear the Army green service uniform in any of the authorized fabrics listed in paragraph 16–5. However, individuals who purchase uniforms or uniform items from commercial sources are responsible for ensuring that the items conform to military specifications, or are manufactured in accordance with the procedures prescribed by the uniform quality control program (see chapter 2 for details). Only those alterations authorized by AR 700–84 and TM 10–227 are authorized. General fitting instructions for these uniforms are provided in chapter 1 of this regulation.

*d.* When soldiers wear these uniforms with the tuck-in version of the shirt, they will tuck the shirt into the slacks or skirt. When tucked into the slacks, the shirt edge is aligned with the front fly opening, so the outside edge of the belt buckle forms a straight "gig line." The overblouse version of the shirt is worn outside the slacks or skirt. Only soldiers authorized to wear the tan, green, or maroon berets, those assigned to Air Assault coded positions, and MPs performing MP duties may wear bloused slacks with black leather combat boots.

## Chapter 17
## Green Maternity Service Uniform

### 17–1. Authorization for wear

The Army green maternity uniform is authorized for year-round wear by pregnant soldiers as a service or dress uniform, when prescribed for wear by CTA 50–900, AR 700–84, and the commander. (See fig 17–1 for the Army green maternity service uniform, class A; see fig 17–2 for the Army green maternity service uniform, class B.)

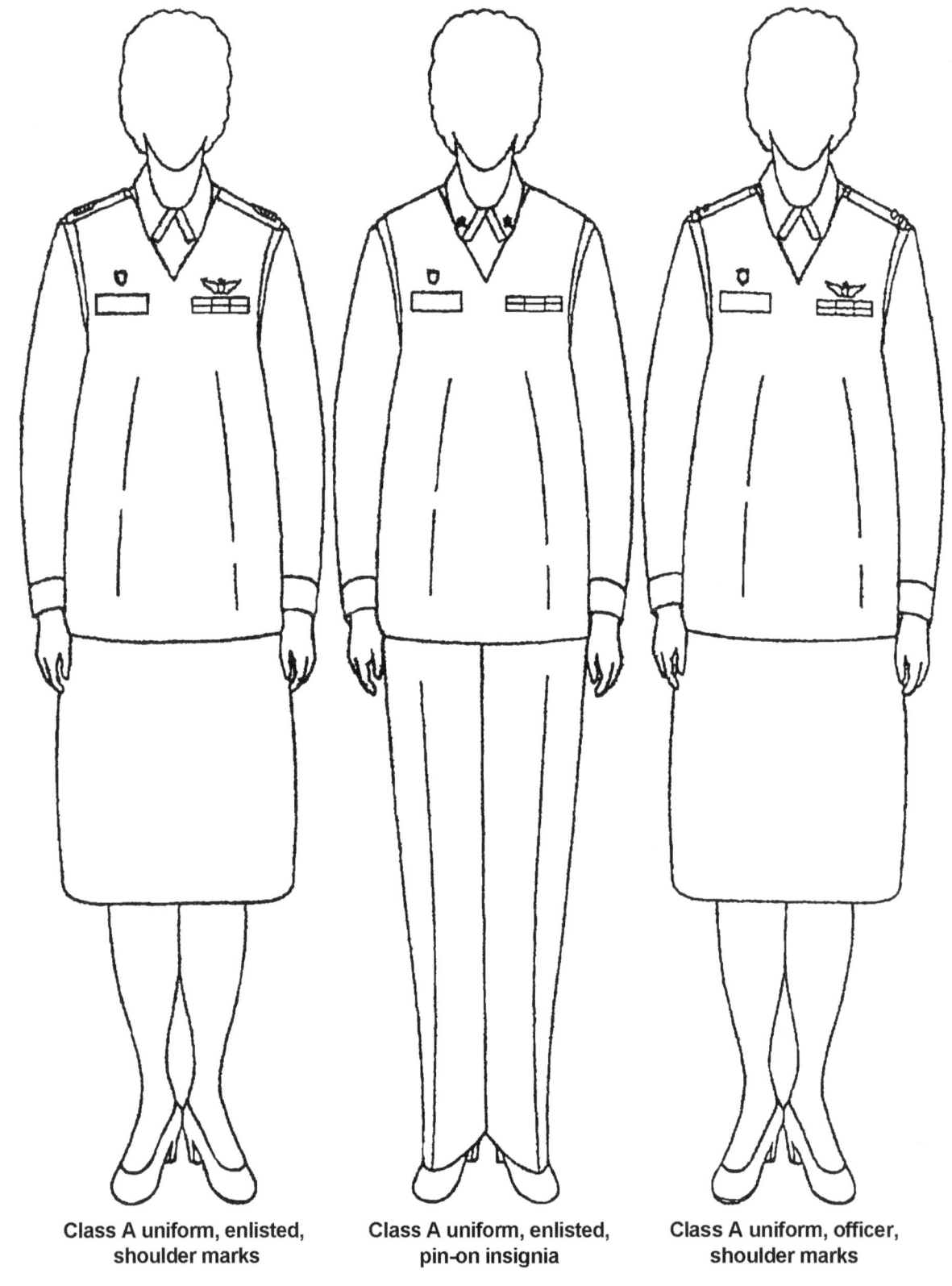

Class A uniform, enlisted,
shoulder marks

Class A uniform, enlisted,
pin-on insignia

Class A uniform, officer,
shoulder marks

Figure 17–1. Army green maternity service uniform, class A

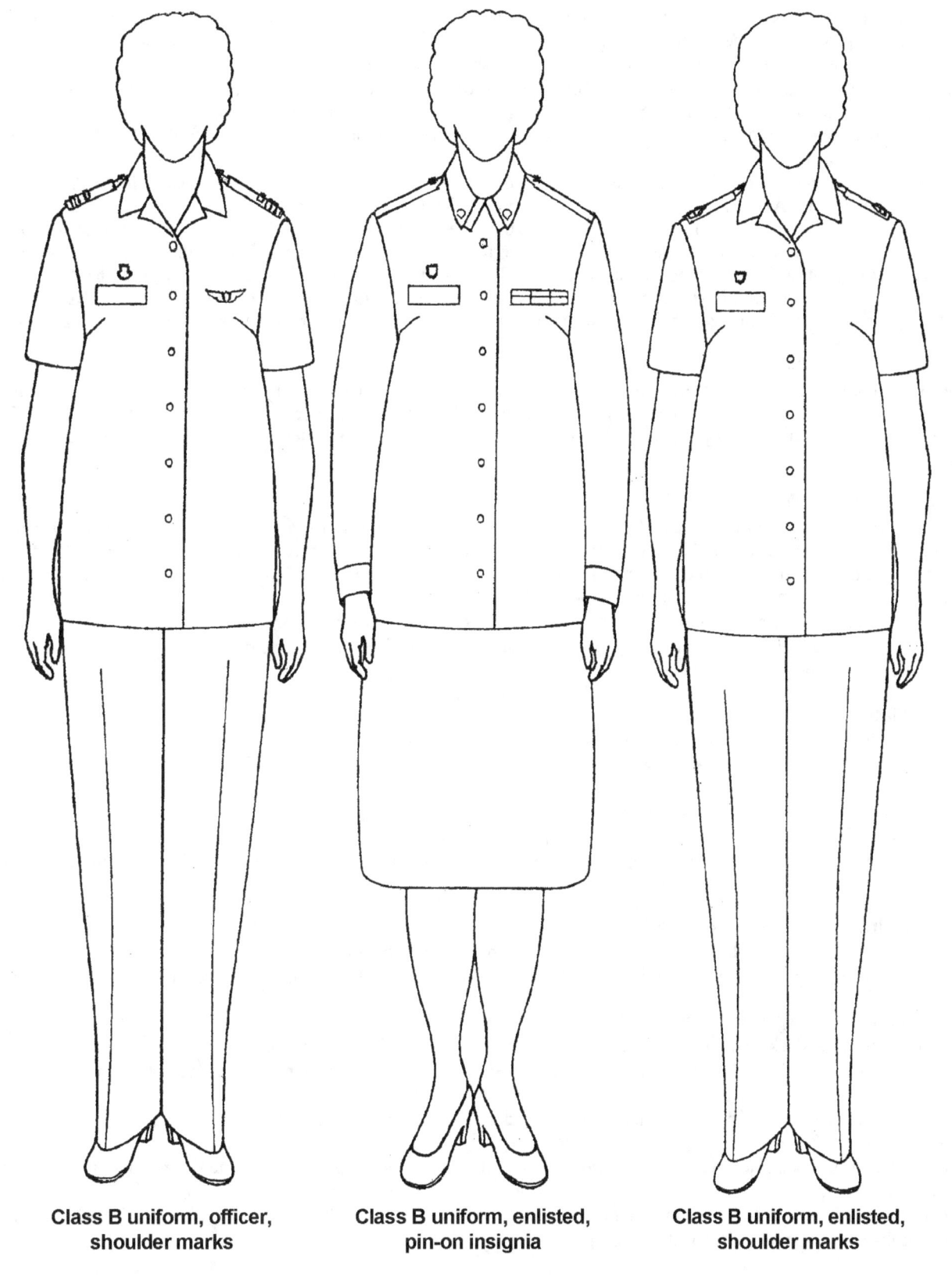

**Class B uniform, officer, shoulder marks**

**Class B uniform, enlisted, pin-on insignia**

**Class B uniform, enlisted, shoulder marks**

Figure 17–2. Army green maternity service uniform, class B

### 17–2. Composition

*a.* The class A Army green maternity uniform consists of the Army green maternity skirt or slacks, tunic, the AG shade 415 long- or short-sleeved maternity shirt, and black neck tab. For accessories and other items authorized for wear on the class A Army green maternity uniform, see paragraph 17–11.

*b.* The class B Army green maternity uniform consists of the Army green maternity skirt or slacks, and the AG shade 415 long- or short-sleeved shirt. Soldiers will wear the neck tab with the long-sleeved shirt when it is worn with or without the tunic. (See para 17–11 for accessories and other items authorized for wear with the class B Army green maternity uniform.)

*c.* The Army green maternity dress uniform (authorized for all pregnant soldiers) consists of the Army green maternity skirt, tunic, AG shade 415 long- or short-sleeved shirt, and black neck tab. The black beret is authorized for wear with this uniform. When the Army green maternity dress uniform is worn for evening social occasions (after retreat), headgear is not required. The Army green maternity dress uniform is equivalent to the Army blue and white uniforms. Organizational items, such as brassards and MP accessories, are not authorized for wear with the Army green maternity dress uniform. All other accessories and insignia that are authorized for wear with the class A Army green maternity uniform are authorized for wear with the Army green maternity dress uniform (see para 17–11 below).

### 17–3. Classification

The Army green maternity service uniform is provided as a supplemental issue uniform to enlisted soldiers, according to CTA 50–900 and AR 700–84. The Army green maternity service uniform is classified as an optional dress uniform for all female personnel during pregnancy. The beret is an organizational issue item. DA Pam 710–2–1 governs turn-in and reissue of the beret.

### 17–4. Occasions for wear

*a.* All pregnant soldiers may wear the Army green maternity service uniform (class A) and authorized variations (class B maternity uniform) when on duty, off duty, or during travel. These uniforms also are acceptable for formal and informal social functions after retreat. Pregnant soldiers may wear appropriate civilian maternity attire in lieu of the uniform for social functions, in accordance with paragraphs 1–7 and 1–8.

*b.* The following are appropriate occasions for pregnant soldiers to wear the Army green maternity dress uniform.

(1) At social functions of a private or official nature, either before or after retreat.

(2) When designated by the host.

### 17–5. Materials

*a.* The skirt, slacks, and tunic are all made of 100 percent, texturized polyester, AG shade 491.

*b.* For headgear material, see paragraph 16–5c of this regulation.

### 17–6. Tunic, Army green, maternity

*a.* Design. The tunic will be made from an approved specification or pattern.

*b.* General description. The tunic is hip length with a V-neck design, pockets at the side seams, and pleats that form below the bustline.

### 17–7. Skirt, Army green, maternity

*a.* Design. The skirt will be made from an approved specification or pattern.

*b.* General description. The skirt is knee length, with an elastic waistband and a nylon-knitted, stretch-front panel.

### 17–8. Slacks, Army green, maternity

*a.* Design. The slacks will be made from an approved specification or pattern.

*b.* General description. The slacks are straight legged, with an elastic waistband and nylon-knitted, stretch-front panel.

*c.* Slack leg ornamentation. Ornamental braid is sewn on each outside seam of the slack leg, from the bottom of the waistband to the bottom of the slack leg, as follows:

(1) General officers. Each slack leg has two ½-inch-wide black mohair, polyester, or mercerized cotton braids sewn ½ inch apart.

(2) Other officers. Each leg has one braid, 1-inch wide, made of black mohair, polyester, or mercerized cotton braid.

(3) Enlisted personnel. The slack leg is plain.

## 17–9. Shirts, long- and short-sleeved, maternity

*a.* Pre-cured, durable-press, 65/35 polyester and cotton broadcloth, AG shade 415, in long- and short-sleeved versions. The shirt has an eight-button front, a straight-cut bottom, and turndown-style collars with shoulder loops.

*b.* Personnel may wear the short-sleeved shirt with or without the black neck tab. Soldiers will wear the long-sleeved shirt with a black neck tab when it is worn with or without the tunic. Soldiers may not starch or bleach the AG shade 415 shirts.

*c.* Soldiers have the option of wearing a neck tab when they wear the short- or long-sleeved shirts with the cardigan sweater. If a neck tab is worn, soldiers will wear the collar of the shirt inside the sweater. If no neck tab is worn, soldiers may wear the collar inside or outside the sweater. Soldiers may wear the cardigan sweater buttoned or unbuttoned while indoors; outdoors, pregnant soldiers may wear the cardigan unbuttoned.

## 17–10. Headgear

See paragraphs 3–5 and 16–10 for the description and wear of authorized headgear.

## 17–11. Items normally worn with the Army green maternity uniform

*a.* Accessories. The following accessories are worn with the Army green maternity service and dress uniforms; note exceptions:

(1) Boots, combat, leather, black (only when bloused slacks are authorized; not authorized with the Army green maternity dress uniform) (para 27–3).

(2) Cap, service, cold weather, AG shade 489 (only when wearing the black all-weather coat or black windbreaker) (para 27–5).

(3) Chaplain's apparel (para 27–7).

(4) Coat, black, all weather (para 27–8).

(5) Gloves, black, leather, unisex, dress (only with Army green maternity service and dress uniforms, black all-weather coat, or windbreaker) (para 27–12*b*).

(6) Handbags.

*(a)* Black, clutch type, optional purchase (para 27–13*a*).

*(b)* Black, shoulder (para 27–13*d*).

(7) Hat, drill sergeant (not authorized with Army green maternity dress uniform) (para 27–14*a*).

(8) Judge's apparel (para 27–15).

(9) Military Police accessories (not authorized with the Army green maternity dress uniform) (para 27–16).

(10) Scarf, black (only with black all-weather coat or windbreaker) (para 27–21*a*).

(11) Shoes.

*(a)* Oxford, black (not authorized with the Army green maternity dress uniform) (para 27–23*a*).

*(b)* Pumps, black (para 27–23*f*).

(12) Socks.

*(a)* Black, cushion sole (worn with boots only) (para 27–24*a*).

*(b)* Black (authorized only with the slacks) (para 27–24*b*).

(13) Stockings, sheer (para 27–24*d*).

(14) Sweater, unisex cardigan, black (para 27–26*a*).

(15) Umbrella, black (para 27–27).

(16) Undergarments (para 27–28).

*b.* The following insignia, awards, badges, and accouterments are worn on the Army green maternity service and dress uniforms; note exceptions.

(1) Aiguillette, service (officers only) (not authorized on the class B uniform) (para 28–25).

(2) Brassards (not authorized on the Army green maternity dress uniform) (para 28–29).

(3) Branch of service scarves (not authorized on Army green maternity dress uniform) (para 28–20).

(4) Fouragerre/lanyards (not authorized on the class B uniform) (para 29–11).

(5) Insignia of grade (paras 28–5, 28–6, and 28–7).

(6) Headgear insignia (para 28–3).

(7) Distinctive unit insignia (DUI) (not authorized on the Army green maternity dress uniform) (para 28–22).

(8) Regimental distinctive insignia (RDI) (para 28–23).

(9) Nameplate (para 28–24*c*).

(10) Organizational flash (worn on berets; not authorized on the Army green maternity dress uniform) (para 28–31*a*).

(11) Airborne background trimming (para 28–31*b*).

(12) Decoration and service medal ribbons, (only full-size medals may be worn on the Army green maternity dress uniform) (paras 29–7, 29–8, and 29–9).

(13) Unit awards (para 29–11).

(14) U.S. badges (identification, marksmanship, combat, and special skill badges) (cloth special skill and marksmanship badges and tabs are not authorized on the class B Army green maternity uniform; full, miniature, and dress miniature badges are authorized on the class B Army green maternity uniform (paras 29–13, 29–16, 29–17, and 29–18).

(15) Foreign badges (para 29–19).

*c.* Insignia authorized for wear with the class B Army green maternity uniform. Same as paragraph 17–11*b*, except that the DUI, branch and U.S. insignias, sew-on insignia, and combat leaders identification are not authorized for wear.

### 17–12. General guidelines

*a.* The Army green maternity service uniform is intended for wear during most duty, non-field occasions, and for travel and off-duty purposes. While both the class A and B Army green maternity uniforms are authorized for year-round wear, the appropriate uniform is worn based on weather conditions, duties, and the formality of the occasion. When a specific service uniform is not prescribed for formations or other occasions when uniformity in appearance is required, soldiers may wear the class A or any of the variations of the class B uniform, with the accessories authorized for these uniforms. Those awards and decorations that cannot be worn properly because of size or configuration will not be worn on the AG shade 415 shirt. Commanders will not require the wear of optional items, such as cardigan sweaters, unless such items are provided to the soldier without cost.

*b.* This uniform is worn with the maternity shirt left outside the skirt and slacks, with or without the maternity tunic. Pregnant soldiers may wear the black all-weather coat unbuttoned, if necessary. Only soldiers authorized to wear the tan, green, or maroon berets, those assigned to Air Assault coded positions, and MPs performing MP duties may wear bloused slacks with black leather combat boots. Figures 17–1 and 17–2 show the class A and B Army green maternity uniform.

## Part Four
## Dress Uniforms

## Chapter 18
## Army White Uniform—Male

### 18–1. Authorization for wear

The Army white uniform is authorized for wear by all male personnel as an optional dress uniform. Personnel normally wear this uniform from April to October, except in clothing zones I and II, where they may wear it year-round (see CTA 50–900). (For Army white uniform, officer, see fig 18–1; for service cap, white, general and field grade officers, see fig 18–2; for service cap, white, company grade officers, see fig 18–3; for service cap, white, warrant officers, see fig 18–4; for Army white uniform, enlisted, see fig 18–5; and for service cap, white, enlisted, see fig 18–6.)

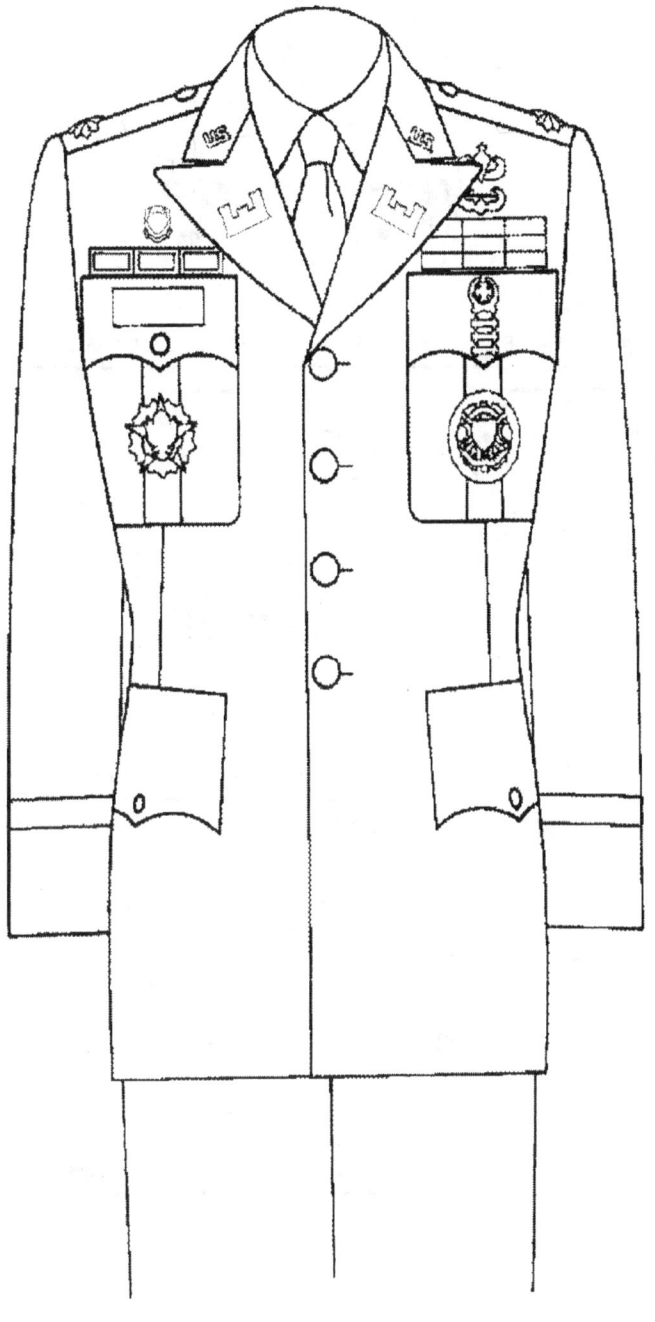

Figure 18–1. Army white uniform, officer

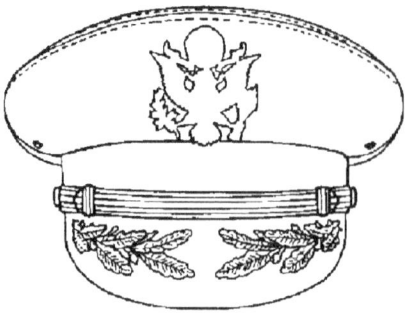

Figure 18–2. Service cap, white, general and field grade officers

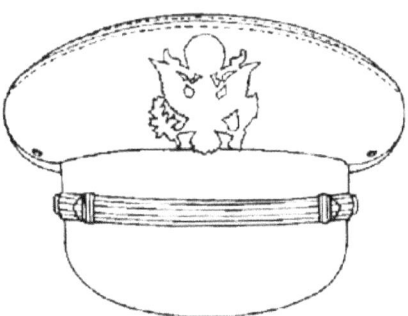

Figure 18–3. Service cap, white, company grade officers

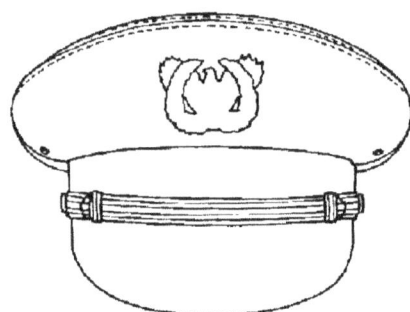

Figure 18–4. Service cap, white, warrant officers

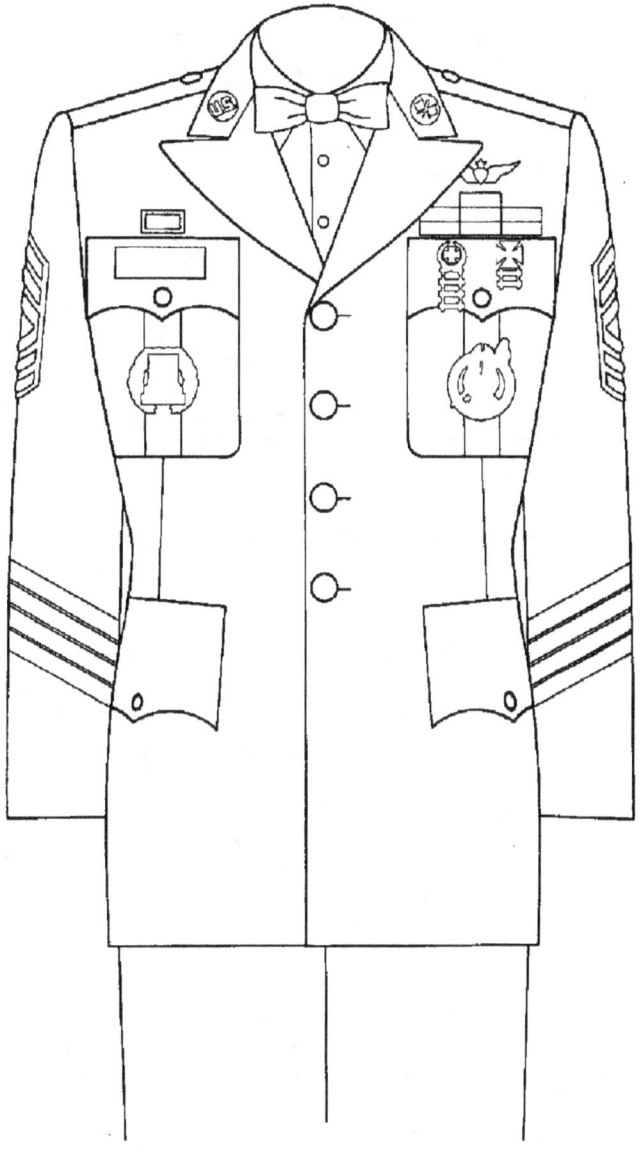

Figure 18–5. Army white uniform, enlisted

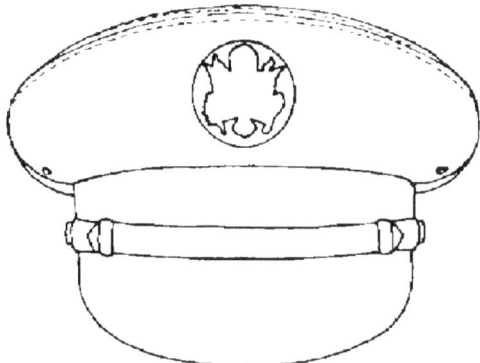

Figure 18–6. Service cap, white, enlisted

## 18–2. Composition

The Army white uniform comprises the Army white coat and trousers, white shirt, and black bow tie or black four-in-hand necktie.

## 18–3. Occasions for wear

*a.* The following are appropriate occasions for personnel to wear the Army white uniform.

(1) On duty in all areas, when appropriate and authorized by the local commander.

(2) Off duty, for social occasions.

*b.* Personnel may wear the Army white uniform with either the black bow tie or the black four-in-hand tie. When worn with a black bow tie, the Army white uniform constitutes a dress uniform and corresponds to a civilian summer tuxedo. When worn with a black four-in-hand tie, the Army white uniform is an informal uniform.

## 18–4. Materials

The material for this uniform is white polyester and texturized woven serge, 6.5–ounce weight.

## 18–5. Coat, Army white

*a.* Design. The coat will be made from an approved specification or pattern.

*b.* General description. The coat is a single-breasted, peak-lapel, four-button coat extending below the crotch, fitting easily over the chest and shoulders, with a slight draped effect in the front and back. The coat is fitted slightly at the waist, conforming to body shape without tightness and with no prominent flare.

*c.* Coat sleeve ornamentation.

(1) General officers. The sleeve has a band of white mohair or white mercerized cotton braid 1½ inches wide sewn on each sleeve, with the lower edge parallel to, and 3 inches above the bottom edge of each sleeve.

(2) Other officers. The sleeve has a band of white mohair or white mercerized cotton braid ½ inch wide sewn on each sleeve, with the lower edge parallel to, and 3 inches above the bottom edge of each sleeve.

(3) Enlisted personnel. The sleeve is plain.

## 18–6. Trousers, Army white

*a.* Design. The trousers will be made from an approved specification or pattern.

*b.* General description. The trousers are straight legged without cuffs, and with front and hip pockets that are cut in a civilian style. Trousers that are made from 100 percent polyester should be lined. There is no ornamentation on the Army white trousers.

## 18–7. Shirt, white

A commercial, long-sleeved white shirt with barrel or French cuffs, and standard turndown collar is worn with the Army white uniform. (See para 27–22c for a complete description.)

## 18–8. Service cap, Army white

*a.* Design. The cap will be made from an approved specification or pattern, in a standard Army design. Officers have the option of wearing the cap frame with a removable cover made of the same material as the rest of the uniform.

*b.* Visor and visor ornamentation. The visor is plain black leather, or poromeric with a leather finish. The visor ornamentation is as follows.

(1) General and field grade officers. The top of the visor is black cloth with two arcs of oak leaves in groups of two, embroidered in gold bullion, synthetic metallic gold-colored yarn, or manufactured from anodized aluminum in 24–karat gold color.

(2) Company grade officers, warrant officers, and enlisted personnel. The top of the visor is plain black shell cordovan or shell cordovan-finish leather, resin treated, with a waterproof edge.

*c.* Chinstrap and chinstrap ornamentation. The chinstrap consists of two straps, each ½ inch in width by 10 inches in length, with one end of each strap forming a slide, and the other end of each strap fastened to the cap at each end of the visor. The chinstrap ornamentation is as follows.

(1) Officers. The chinstrap is natural or light brown, full-grain pigskin or sheepskin, non-bleeding, with pointed ends covered with two-vellum gold wire lace, synthetic metallic gold-colored lace, or a one-piece strap manufactured from anodized aluminum in 24–karat gold color.

(2) Enlisted personnel. The chinstrap is plain black leather matching the visor in appearance, with rounded ends. Poromeric with a leather finish is authorized.

*d.* Hatband. All personnel will wear a white mercerized cotton braid or white mohair braid hatband, 1¾ inches in width, around the entire outside rim of the cap, with the bottom edge of the hatband covered with black cloth.

*e.* Cap insignia. Insignia is worn on the Army white service cap secured through the front eyelet. The service cap insignia is described in paragraph 28–3*b.*

*f.* Wear.

(1) All male personnel will wear the Army white service cap with the Army white uniform and the white mess and the white evening mess uniforms.

(2) Personnel are not required to wear headgear when wearing the Army white uniform to evening social functions (after retreat). However, on all other occasions, personnel will wear headgear with this uniform.

*g.* Proper wear position. The service cap is worn straight on the head so that the white hatband on the cap creates a straight line around the head, parallel to the ground. Such positioning automatically positions the visor correctly, so that it does not interfere with vision or ride up on the forehead. Personnel will not alter the shape of the service cap in any manner.

## 18–9. Cape, Army blue

As an option, all officers are authorized to wear the Army blue cape instead of the black all-weather coat, when wearing the Army white uniform after duty hours. Enlisted personnel may not wear the cape. (See para 27–6 for design and wear policy.)

## 18–10. Items normally worn with the Army white uniform

*a.* Accessories.

(1) Belt and buckle/suspenders (paras 27–2*b* and *d*, and 27–25).

(2) Buttons (para 27–4).

(3) Cape (officers only) (para 27–6*c*).

(4) Chaplain's apparel (para 27–7).

(5) Coat, black, all-weather (para 27–8).

(6) Cuff links and studs, gold (para 27–10).

(7) Gloves.

*(a)* Black, leather, unisex, dress (only when the black all-weather coat is worn) (para 27–12*b*).

*(b)* White, dress (para 27–12*c*).

(8) Neckties.

*(a)* Black, bow (worn after retreat) (para 27–19*a*).

*(b)* Black, four-in-hand (worn on duty) (para 27–19*c*).

(9) Scarf, black (only with black all-weather coat) (para 27–21*a*).

(10) Shoes, oxford, black (para 27–23*c*).

(11) Socks, black (para 27–24*b*).

(12) Undergarments, white (para 27–28).

*b.* Insignia, awards, badges, and accouterments worn on the Army white uniform.

(1) Aiguillettes (officers only).

*(a)* Service (para 28–25).

*(b)* Dress (para 28–26).

(2) Fourragere/lanyards (para 29–11*c*(3)).

(3) Distinctive items authorized for Infantry personnel (para 28–30).

(4) Branch insignia (para 28–10 and 28–12a).

(5) U.S. insignia (para 28–4).

(6) Grade insignia (paras 28–5, 28–6, and 28–7).

(7) Headgear insignia (para 28–3).

(8) Regimental distinctive insignia (para 28–23).

(9) OCS/WOC insignia (paras 28–14 and 28–15).

(10) Nameplate (para 28–24c).

(11) Service stripes (enlisted personnel only) (para 28–27).

(12) Decoration and service medal ribbons (full-size or miniature medals may be worn after retreat) (paras 29–7, 29–8, and 29–9).

(13) Unit awards (para 29–11).

(14) U.S. badges (identification, marksmanship, combat and special skill, full-size and miniature); dress miniature combat and special skill badges will be worn when miniature medals are worn (paras 29–13, 29–16, 29–17, and 29–18).

(15) Foreign badges (para 29–19).

## 18–11. General guidelines

General fitting instructions for this uniform are provided in chapter 1 of this regulation. When the Army white uniform is worn to social functions, soldiers may wear gold or gold-colored cuff links and studs. The black all-weather coat is authorized for wear. Personnel may wear white gloves with the basic uniform. Black oxford shoes with black socks are the only authorized footwear.

# Chapter 19
# Army White Uniform—Female

## 19–1. Authorization for wear

a. The Army white uniform is authorized for wear by all female personnel as an optional dress uniform. Personnel normally wear this uniform from April to October, except in clothing zones I and II where they may wear it year-round (see CTA 50–900). (See fig 19–1 for the Army white uniform, female.)

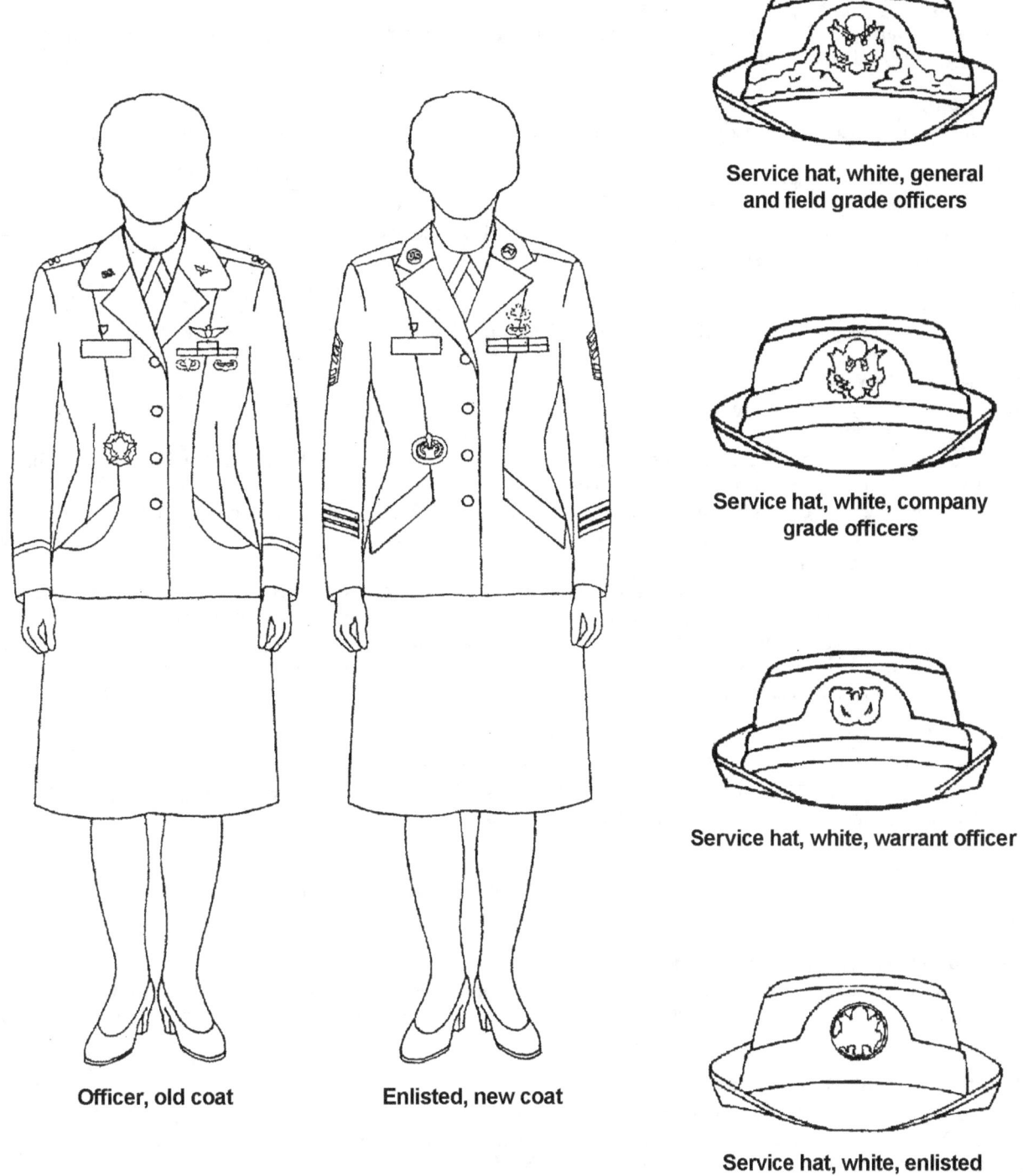

Service hat, white, general and field grade officers

Service hat, white, company grade officers

Service hat, white, warrant officer

Service hat, white, enlisted

Officer, old coat

Enlisted, new coat

Figure 19–1. Army white uniform, female

*b.* There are two versions of the Army white coat that officer and enlisted females may wear. The older version was designed prior to 10 August 1992 and is described in paragraph 19–5*b*(1), below. The military specification for the Army white coat was changed on 10 August 1992 to the same pattern as the Army green coat. The new version is described in paragraph 19–5*b*(2), below. Soldiers may continue to wear the older version of the coat (with rounded collars) as long as the uniform is in serviceable condition.

## 19–2. Composition
The Army white uniform comprises the Army white coat, skirt, and a white short-sleeved shirt with black neck tab.

## 19–3. Occasions for wear
The following are appropriate occasions for personnel to wear the Army white uniform.

*a.* On duty in all areas, when appropriate and authorized by the local commander.

*b.* Off duty, for social occasions.

## 19–4. Materials
The material for this uniform is white polyester and texturized woven serge, 6.5–ounce weight.

## 19–5. Coat, Army white
*a.* Design. The coat will be made from an approved specification or pattern.

*b.* General description.

(1) Old version. The coat is a single-breasted, four-button, hip-length coat with two slanted front pockets, button-down shoulder loops, and an easy-fitting open collar and lapels.

(2) New version. The coat is a single-breasted, four-button, hip-length coat, with two slanted flap front pockets, button-down shoulder loops, a notched collar, and side-body construction.

*c.* Coat sleeve ornamentation.

(1) General officers. The sleeve has a band of white mohair or white mercerized cotton braid 1½ inches wide sewn on each sleeve, with the lower edge parallel to, and 3 inches above the bottom edge of each sleeve.

(2) Other officers. The sleeve has a band of white mohair or white mercerized cotton braid ½ inch wide sewn on each sleeve, with the lower edge parallel to, and 3 inches above the bottom edge of each sleeve.

(3) Enlisted personnel. The sleeve is plain.

## 19–6. Skirt, Army white
*a.* Design. The skirt will be made from an approved specification or pattern.

*b.* General description. The skirt is knee length, with a three-piece front and three-piece back, slightly flared, with a waistband and a zipper closure on the left side.

## 19–7. Shirt, white
A short-sleeved white shirt with black neck tab is worn with the Army white uniform. (See para 27–22*a* for a complete description.)

## 19–8. Capes, Army blue and black
As an option, all female officers are authorized to wear the Army blue or the Army black cape instead of the black all-weather coat, when wearing the Army white uniform after duty hours. Enlisted personnel may not wear the cape. (See paragraph 27–6 for a complete description.)

## 19–9. Service hat, Army white
*a.* Design. The hat will be made from an approved specification or pattern.

*b.* General description. The hat has an oval-shaped crown and a detachable hatband for placement of insignia. Hat insignia is worn centered and secured through the hatband. (See para 28–3 for a description of insignia wear.)

*c.* Hatband. The detachable hatband has three rows of stitching of matching thread at the top of the band, and ornamentation as follows.

(1) General and field grade officers. The hat has two arcs of laurel leaves grouped in twos, embroidered in gold bullion, synthetic metallic gold-colored braid, or gold-colored nylon or rayon braid.

(2) Company grade officers and warrant officers. The hat has a band of ½-inch, two-vellum gold, gold-colored synthetic metallic braid, or gold-colored nylon or rayon braid, placed on the bottom edge of the hatband.

(3) Enlisted personnel. There is no ornamentation on the hatband.

*d.* Wear. All female personnel may wear the Army white service hat with the Army white uniform. Personnel are not required to wear headgear when wearing the Army white uniform to evening social functions (after retreat). However, on all other occasions, personnel will wear headgear with this uniform.

*e.* Proper wear position. The service hat is worn straight on the head so that the hatband creates a straight line around the head, parallel to the ground. Hair will not be visible below the front brim of the hat, and there should be ½ to 1 inch distance between the eyebrow and the brim of the hat.

## 19–10. Items normally worn with the Army white uniform

*a.* Accessories.

(1) Buttons (para 27–4).

(2) Capes (officers only).

*(a)* Black (para 27–6*a*).

*(b)* Blue (para 27–6*b*).

(3) Chaplain's apparel (para 27–7).

(4) Coat, black, all weather (para 27–8).

(5) Gloves.

*(a)* Black, leather, unisex, dress (only when the black all-weather coat is worn) (para 27–12*b*).

*(b)* White, dress (para 27–12*c*).

(6) Handbag, white dress (para 27–13*c*).

(7) Scarf, black (only with black all-weather coat or windbreaker) (para 27–21*a*).

(8) Shirt, white, short-sleeved (para 27–22*a*).

(9) Shoes, white, pump (paras 27–23*f* and *g*).

(10) Stockings, sheer (para 27–24*d*).

(11) Umbrella, black (para 27–27).

(12) Undergarments, white (para 27–28).

*b.* Insignia, awards, badges and accouterments worn on the Army white uniform.

(1) Aiguillettes (officers only).

*(a)* Service (para 28–25).

*(b)* Dress (para 28–26).

(2) Fourragere/lanyards (para 28–11*c*(3)).

(3) Branch insignia (para 28–10 and 28–12*a*).

(4) U.S. insignia (para 28–4).

(5) Grade insignia (paras 28–5, 28–6, and 28–7).

(6) Headgear insignia (para 28–3).

(7) Regimental distinctive insignia (para 28–23).

(8) OCS/WOC insignia (paras 28–14 and 28–15).

(9) Nameplate (para 28–24*c*).

(10) Service stripes (enlisted personnel only) (para 28–27).

(11) Decoration and service medal ribbons (full size or miniature medals may be worn after retreat) (paras 29–7, 29–8, and 29–9)).

(12) Unit awards (para 29–11).

(13) U.S. badges (identification, marksmanship, combat and special skill, full size and miniature); dress miniature combat and special skill badges will be worn when miniature medals are worn (paras 29–13, 29–16, 29–17, and 29–18).

(14) Foreign badges (para 29–19).

## 19–11. General guidelines

*a.* The skirt is worn no longer than 1 inch above, or 2 inches below the crease in the back of the knee. The black all-weather coat is authorized for wear with this uniform. Personnel may wear white gloves with the basic uniform. Females may carry the white leather handbag during duty or after duty hours; they may carry the white fabric handbag only after duty hours, however. White pumps and sheer stockings are the authorized footwear for this uniform. After duty hours, personnel may wear white fabric pumps with this uniform.

*b.* Soldiers who possess the old version of the Army white coat will wear one branch and one U.S. insignia on the collar. Those who possess the new version of the Army white coat will wear their insignia as they do on the Army green coat (see paras 28–4 and 28–12).

# Chapter 20
# Army Blue Uniform—Male

## 20–1. Authorization for wear

*a.* The Army blue uniform is authorized for year-round wear by all male personnel.

*b.* All active duty officers are required to own the Army blue uniform for wear on appropriate occasions. The only exception to this policy applies to officers who are on active duty for 6 months or less, who have the option of purchasing the Army blue uniform.

*c.* The Army blue uniform is authorized for optional wear for enlisted personnel.

*d.* When prescribed by CTA 50–900, the Army blue uniform is worn as an organizational uniform.

## 20–2. Composition

The Army blue uniform comprises a dark-blue coat, dark-blue or light-blue trousers, a white turndown-collar shirt, and a black bow tie or black four-in-hand necktie. When worn with a black bow tie, the Army blue uniform constitutes a formal uniform and corresponds to a civilian tuxedo. When worn with a black four-in-hand necktie, the Army blue uniform is an informal uniform. (For the Army blue uniform, officer, see fig 20–1; for the service cap, blue, general officers, see fig 20–2; for the service cap, blue, field grade officers, see fig 20–3; for the service cap, blue, company grade officers, see fig 20–4; for the service cap, blue, warrant officers, see fig 20–5; for the Army blue uniform, enlisted, see fig 20–6; for the service cap, blue, enlisted, see fig 20–7.)

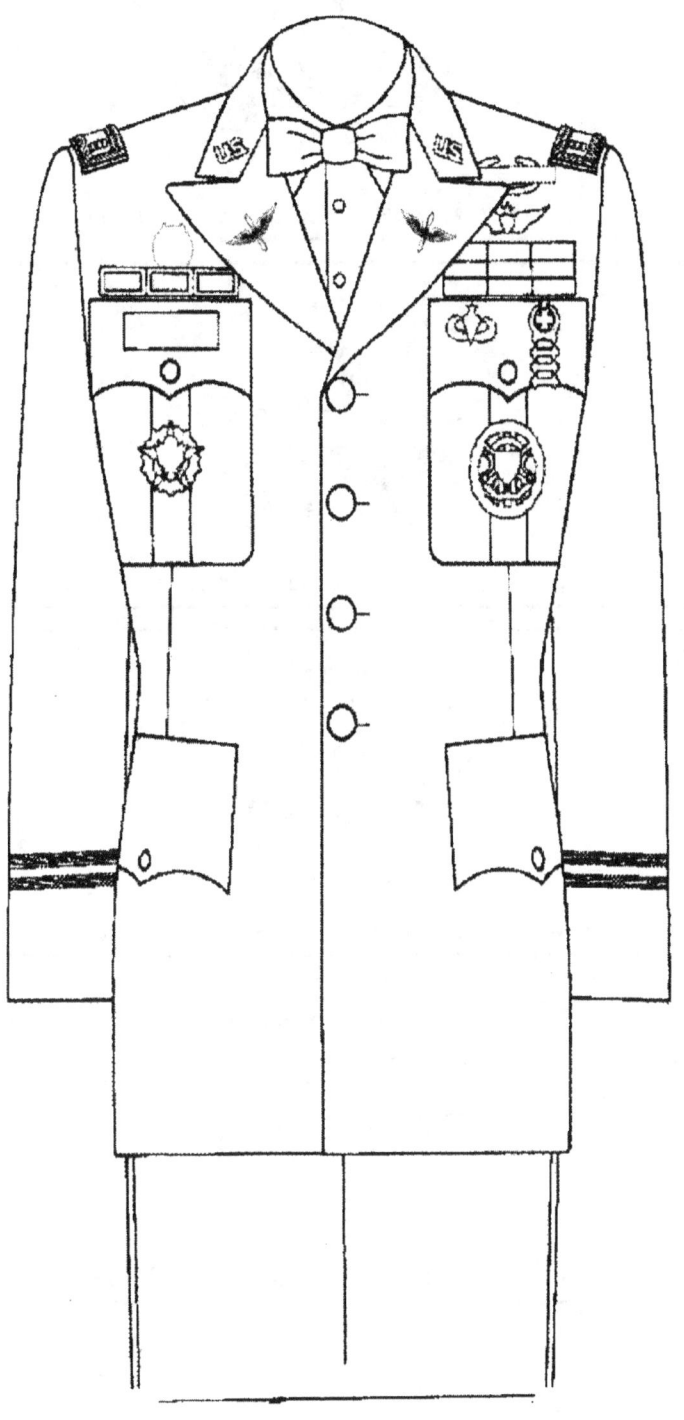

**Figure 20–1. Army blue uniform, officer**

Figure 20–2. Service cap, blue, general officers

Figure 20–3. Service cap, blue, field grade officers

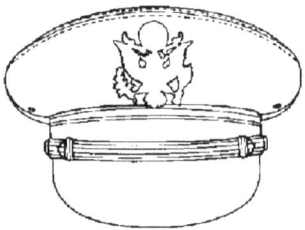

Figure 20–4. Service cap, blue, company grade officers

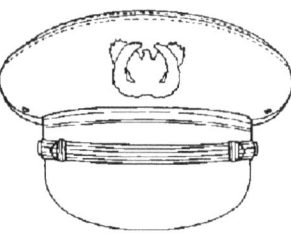

Figure 20–5. Service cap, blue, warrant officers

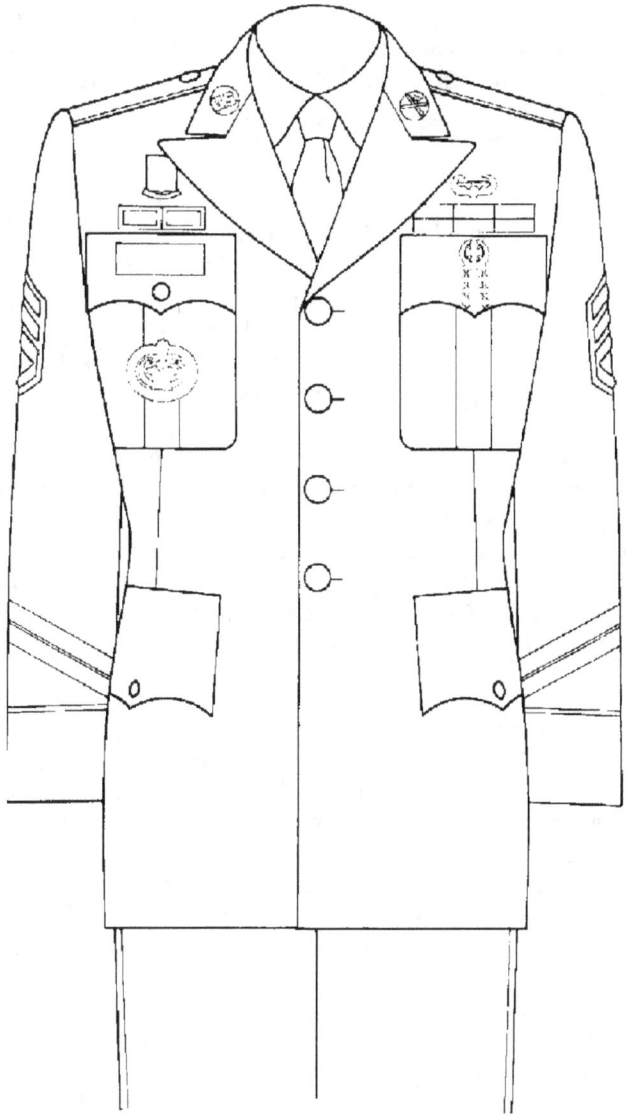

Figure 20–6. Army blue uniform, enlisted

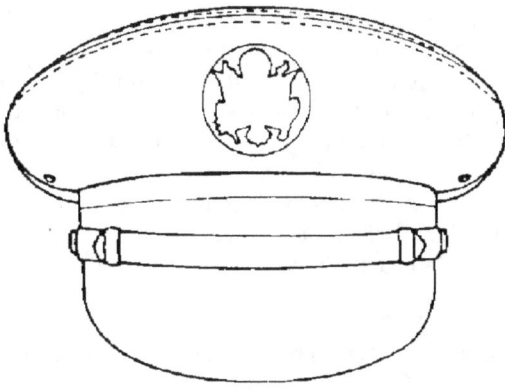

Figure 20–7. Service cap, blue, enlisted

## 20-3. Occasions for wear

The following are appropriate occasions for personnel to wear the Army blue uniform.

*a.* On duty, as prescribed by the local commander.

*b.* For social functions of a general or official nature, before or after retreat.

*c.* On other appropriate occasions, as desired by the individual.

## 20-4. Materials

*a.* Coat

(1) Wool barathea, 14-ounce weight, dark blue, Army shade 150.

(2) Wool gabardine, 11- or 14.5-ounce weight, dark blue, Army shade 150.

(3) Wool elastique, 16-ounce weight, dark blue, Army shade 150.

(4) Wool tropical, 10.5-ounce weight, dark blue, Army shade 150.

(5) Polyester and wool-blend fabric in twill weave, 9.5-ounce weight, dark blue, Army shade 450.

(6) Polyester and wool-blend fabric in plain weave, 9.5-ounce weight, dark blue, Army shade 450.

*b.* Trousers.

(1) General officers. The coat and trousers will be made in the same material and shade.

(2) Other officers and enlisted personnel. The trousers are made in the same material as the coat, except the color will be light blue, in Army shade 151 or 451.

*c.* Headgear, service cap. The service cap will be made in the same material and shade as the coat, except that officers also are authorized to wear the service cap in fur felt, 9-ounce weight, dark blue, Army shade 250.

*d.* Braid. Nylon gold-colored braid or synthetic metallic gold braid is more suitable than gold bullion when attached to lightweight fabrics (11 ounces or less).

## 20-5. Coat, Army blue

*a.* Design. The coat will be made from an approved specification or pattern.

*b.* General description. The Army blue coat is a single-breasted, peak-lapel, four-button coat extending below the crotch, fitting easily over the chest and shoulders, with a slight draped effect in front and back. The coat is fitted slightly at the waist, conforming to the body shape without tightness and with no prominent flare.

*c.* Shoulder buttons.

(1) Officers authorized to wear an aiguillette will attach a 20-ligne button on the left or right outside shoulder seam of the Army blue coat, depending upon the position in which the aiguillette is worn.

(2) Officers authorized to wear a fourragere will attach a 20-ligne button on the left shoulder seam, ½ inch outside the collar edge.

*d.* Shoulder ornamentation and insignia.

(1) Shoulder straps for officers. (See para 28-8*b* for ornamentation and insignia.)

(2) Shoulder loops for enlisted personnel.

*(a)* A shoulder loop of the same material as the coat is used and attached on each shoulder.

*(b)* The loop is 2½ inches wide at the outside shoulder edge, 1½ inches wide at the inside collar edge, and piped all around with gold-colored nylon or rayon cord edge braid, ⅛ inch wide. The braid is inserted in the joining seams so it is completely visible around each loop. The loop is sewn on the outside shoulder seam and extends to a point approximately ½ inch from the inside collar seam. The loop has a buttonhole ⅜ inch from the inside edge of the braid, which is buttoned to the shoulder with a 25-ligne button.

*e.* Coat sleeve ornamentation. Ornamental braid is worn on both sleeves of the Army blue coat. Gold bullion, synthetic metallic gold, or gold-colored nylon or rayon braid is authorized for officers. Gold-colored nylon or rayon braid is authorized for enlisted personnel. The braid on the trouser legs and the coat sleeve will be of the same material. The bottom of the braid is positioned parallel to, and 3 inches above the bottom of each sleeve as follows.

(1) General officers have one 1½ inch gold braid on each sleeve.

(2) For all other officers, each sleeve has a ¾-inch braid consisting of two, ¼-inch gold braids placed ¼ inch apart on silk material, of the first-named color of their basic branch.

(3) Enlisted personnel have a ⅛-inch soutache braid of gold-colored nylon or rayon on each sleeve.

## 20-6. Trousers, Army blue

*a.* Design. The trousers will be made from an approved specification or pattern.

*b.* General description.

(1) Low-waisted. The low-waisted blue trousers are straight-legged without cuffs, with side and hip pockets. The left hip pocket has a buttonhole tab and button.

(2) High-waisted. The high-waisted blue trousers are authorized for wear with the Army blue uniform instead of low-waisted trousers. The high-waisted trousers are required for wear with the Army blue mess and evening mess uniforms. High-waisted trousers are cut along the lines of civilian dress trousers, with a high waist, and without pleats, cuffs, or hip pockets.

(3) Trouser leg ornamentation. Ornamental braid is worn on each outside seam of the trouser leg, from the bottom of the waistband to the bottom of the trouser leg, as follows:

(a) General officers have two, ½-inch, two-vellum gold, synthetic metallic gold, or gold-colored nylon or rayon braids, spaced ½ inch apart.

(b) All other officers have one, 1½ inch, two-vellum gold, synthetic metallic gold, or gold-colored nylon or rayon braid.

(c) Enlisted personnel have one 1½ inch gold-colored nylon or rayon braid.

## 20–7. Shirt, white
A commercial long-sleeved white shirt with barrel or French cuffs and a standard turndown collar is worn with the Army blue uniform. (See para 27–22c for a complete description.)

## 20–8. Service cap, Army blue
a. Design. The cap will be made from an approved specification or pattern, in a standard Army design. Officers have the option of wearing the cap frame with a removable cover made of the same material as the rest of the uniform.

b. Visor and visor ornamentation. The visor is plain black leather, or poromeric with a leather finish. The visor ornamentation is as follows:

(1) General and field grade officers. The top of the visor is black cloth with two arcs of oak leaves in groups of two, embroidered in gold bullion, synthetic metallic gold-colored yarn, or manufactured from anodized aluminum in 24–karat gold color.

(2) Company grade officers, warrant officers, and enlisted personnel. The top of the visor is plain black shell cordovan or shell cordovan-finish leather, resin treated, with a waterproof edge.

c. Chinstrap and chinstrap ornamentation. The chinstrap consists of two straps, each ½ inch in width by 10 inches in length, with one end of each strap forming a slide, and the other end of each strap fastened to the cap at each end of the visor. The chinstrap ornamentation is as follows.

(1) Officers. The chinstrap is natural or light brown, full-grain pigskin or sheepskin, non-bleeding, with pointed ends covered with two-vellum gold wire lace, synthetic metallic gold-colored lace, or a one-piece strap manufactured from anodized aluminum in 24–karat gold color.

(2) Enlisted personnel. The chinstrap is plain black leather matching the visor in appearance, with rounded ends. Poromeric with a leather finish is authorized.

d. Hatband. All personnel will wear an outside hatband, 1¾ inches in width, around the entire outside rim of the cap. The hatband ornamentation follows.

(1) General officers. The band is blue-black velvet with two arcs of oak leaves in groups of two, 1 inch long and ¾ inch wide, embroidered in gold, synthetic metallic gold-colored braid, or gold-colored nylon or rayon.

(2) All other officers. The band is grosgrain silk of the first-named color of the officer's basic branch, with a band of ½ inch, two-vellum gold, synthetic metallic gold, or gold-colored nylon or rayon braid, placed at the top and bottom of the hatband. If the officer's branch has two colors, ⅛-inch piping of the second color is placed on the inside edges of the gold braid.

(3) Enlisted personnel. The band is basket-weave mohair braid matching the shade of the cap material, with a ½-inch band of two-vellum gold-colored nylon, rayon, or polyester braid placed at the top part of the hatband.

e. Cap insignia. Insignia is worn on the Army blue service cap secured through the front eyelet. The service cap insignia is described in paragraph 28–3b.

f. Wear.

(1) All male personnel will wear the Army blue service cap with the Army blue, blue mess, and blue evening mess uniforms.

(2) Personnel are not required to wear headgear when wearing the Army blue uniform to evening social functions (after retreat). However, on all other occasions, personnel will wear headgear with this uniform.

g. Proper wear position. The service cap is worn straight on the head so that the braid hatband on the service cap creates a straight line around the head, parallel to the ground. Such positioning automatically positions the visor correctly, so that it does not interfere with vision or ride up on the forehead. Personnel will not alter the shape of the service cap in any manner.

## 20–9. Cape, Army blue
As an option, all officers are authorized to wear the Army blue cape instead of the black all-weather coat, when

wearing the Army blue uniform after duty hours. Enlisted personnel may not wear the cape. (See para 27–6 for design and wear policy.)

## 20–10. Items normally worn with the Army blue uniform

*a.* Accessories.

(1) Belt with buckle/suspenders (paras 27–2*b* and *d*, and 27–25).

(2) Buttons (para 27–4).

(3) Cape (officers only) (para 27–6*c*).

(4) Chaplain's apparel (para 27–7).

(5) Coat, black, all weather (para 27–8).

(6) Cuff links and studs, gold (para 27–10).

(7) Gloves.

*(a)* Black, leather, unisex, dress (only when the black all-weather coat is worn) (para 27–12*b*).

*(b)* White, dress (para 27–12*c*).

(8) Headgear, cap, service, cold weather, AG 489 (para 27–5).

(9) Neckties.

*(a)* Black, bow (worn after retreat) (para 27–19*a*).

*(b)* Black, four-in-hand (worn on duty) (para 27–19*c*).

(10) Scarf, black (para 27–21*a*).

(11) Shirt, white, long sleeve (para 27–22*c*).

(12) Shoes, oxford, black (para 27–23*c*).

(13) Socks, black (para 27–24*b*).

(14) Undergarments, white (para 27–28).

*b.* Insignia, awards, badges, and accouterments worn on the Army blue uniform.

(1) Aiguillettes (officers only).

*(a)* Service (para 28–25).

*(b)* Dress (para 28–26).

(2) Fourragere/lanyards (para 28–11).

(3) Distinctive items authorized for Infantry personnel (para 28–30).

(4) Branch insignia (paras 28–10 and 28–12*a*).

(5) U.S. insignia (para 28–4).

(6) Grade insignia (paras 28–5, 28–6, and 28–7).

(7) Headgear insignia (para 28–3).

(8) Regimental distinctive insignia (para 28–23).

(9) OCS/WOC insignia (paras 28–14 and 28–15).

(10) Nameplate (para 28–24*c*).

(11) Service stripes (enlisted personnel only) (para 28–27).

(12) Decoration and service medal ribbons (full size or miniature medals may be worn after retreat) (paras 29–7, 29–8, and 29–9).

(13) Unit awards (para 29–11).

(14) U.S. badges (identification, marksmanship, combat and special skill, full size and miniature); dress miniature combat and special skill badges will be worn when miniature medals are worn (paras 29–13, 29–16, 29–17, and 29–18).

(15) Foreign badges (para 29–19).

## 20–11. General guidelines

*a.* General fitting instructions for this uniform are provided in chapter 1 of this regulation. Suspenders are authorized for wear with this uniform. Personnel may wear optional purchase gold or gold-colored cuff links and studs with this uniform at social functions. The black scarf and black leather dress gloves are authorized for wear with the black all-weather coat. Soldiers may wear white gloves with the basic uniform. When weather conditions warrant, the AG 489 cold-weather cap is authorized for wear with the black all-weather coat or the cape. Black oxford shoes with black socks are the only authorized footwear for this uniform. (See para 28–10*e* for information on color ornamentation and branch insignia for detailed officers.)

*b.* Enlisted personnel assigned to units authorized by CTA 50–900 to wear the Army blue uniform as an organizational uniform, such as table of organization and equipment (TOE) bands, selected honor guards, and other ceremonial units, may wear distinctive unit insignia (DUI), military police accessories, and other items authorized by CTA 50–900, when prescribed by the commander.

## Chapter 21
## Army Blue Uniform—Female

### 21–1. Authorization for wear

*a.* The Army blue uniform is authorized for year-round wear by all female personnel. (Fig 21–1 shows the Army blue uniform with the old and new version coats, and authorized headgear.)

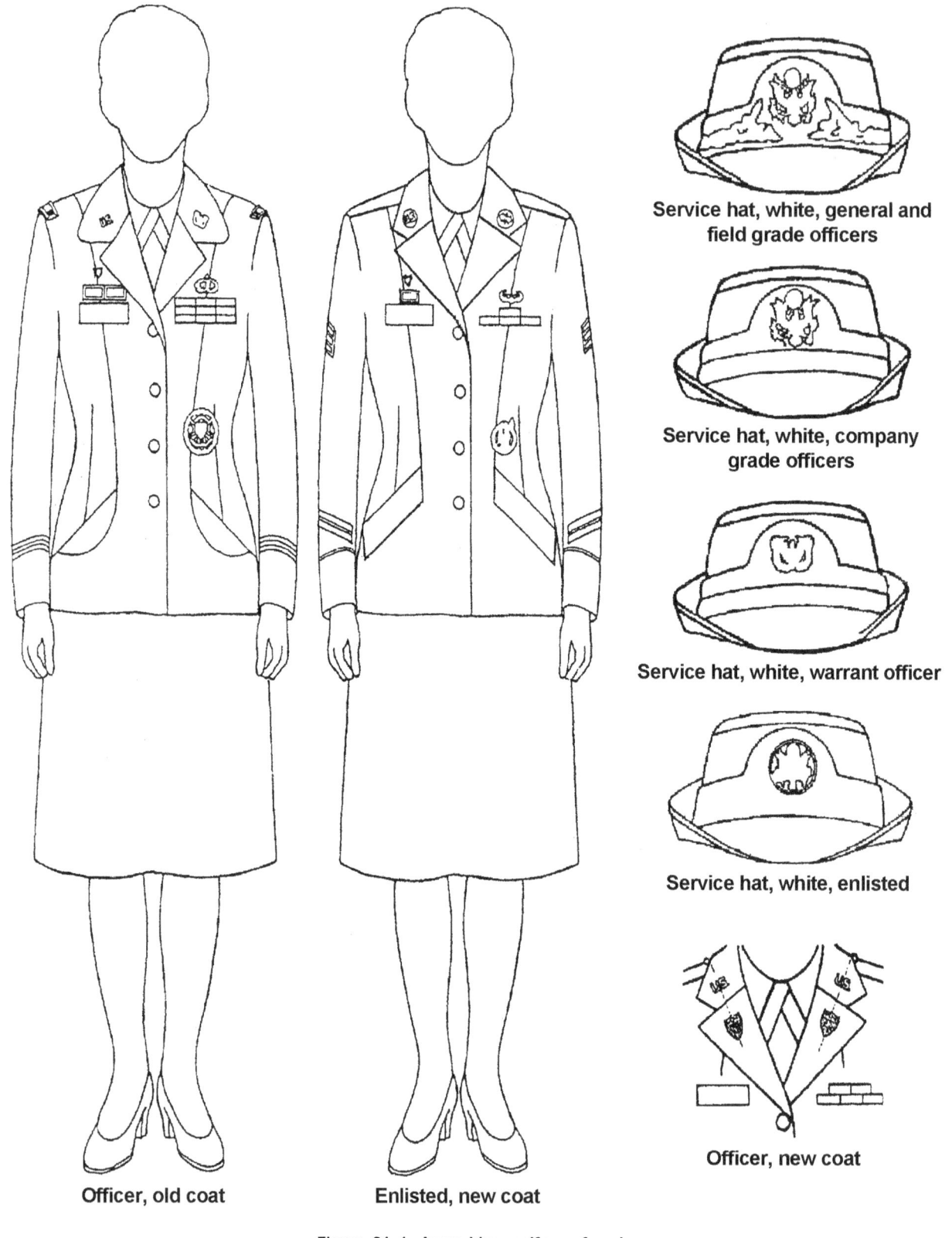

Service hat, white, general and field grade officers

Service hat, white, company grade officers

Service hat, white, warrant officer

Service hat, white, enlisted

Officer, new coat

Officer, old coat

Enlisted, new coat

Figure 21–1. Army blue uniform, female

*b.* All active duty officers are required to own the Army blue uniform for wear on appropriate occasions. The only exception to this policy applies to officers who are on active duty for 6 months or less, who have the option of purchasing the Army blue uniform.

*c.* The Army blue uniform is authorized for optional wear for enlisted personnel.

*d.* When prescribed by CTA 50–900, the Army blue uniform is worn as an organizational uniform.

*e.* There are two versions of the Army blue coat that officer and enlisted personnel may wear. The older version was designed prior to 10 August 1992 and is described in paragraph 21–5*b*(1), below. The military specification for the Army blue coat was changed on 10 August 1992 to the same pattern as the Army green coat. The new version is described in paragraph 21–5*b*(2), below. Soldiers may continue to wear the older version of the coat (with the rounded collars) as long as the uniform is in serviceable condition.

## 21–2. Composition
The Army blue uniform comprises an Army blue coat, slacks, skirt, and a white short-sleeved shirt with a black neck tab.

## 21–3. Occasions for wear
The following are appropriate occasions for personnel to wear the Army blue uniform.

*a.* On duty, as prescribed by the local commander.

*b.* For social functions of a general or official nature, before or after retreat.

*c.* On other appropriate occasions, as desired by the individual.

## 21–4. Materials
*a.* Coat, skirt, slacks, and service hat.

(1) Wool barathea, 12– or 14–ounce weight, Army blue shade 150.

(2) Wool gabardine, 11– or 14.5–ounce weight, Army blue shade 150.

(3) Wool elastique, 16–ounce weight, Army blue shade 150.

(4) Wool tropical, 10.5–ounce weight, Army blue shade 150.

(5) Polyester and wool blend fabric in gabardine, 9.5–ounce weight, Army blue shade 450.

(6) Polyester and wool blend fabric in tropical 9.5–ounce weight, Army blue shade 450.

*b.* Braid. Nylon gold-colored braid or synthetic metallic gold braid is more suitable than gold bullion when attached to lightweight fabrics (11 ounces or less).

## 21–5. Coat, Army blue
*a.* Design. The coat will be made from an approved specification or pattern.

*b.* General description.

(1) Old version. The Army blue coat is a single-breasted, four-button, hip-length coat with two slanted front pockets, long sleeves, and an easy-fitting, open collar.

(2) New version. The coat is a single-breasted, four-button, hip-length coat, with two slanted flap front pockets, button-down shoulder loops, notched collar, and side-body construction.

*c.* Shoulder buttons.

(1) Officers authorized to wear an aiguillette will attach a 21-ligne button on the left or right outside shoulder seam of the Army blue coat, depending upon the position in which the aiguillette is worn.

(2) Officers authorized to wear a fourragere will attach a 21-ligne button on the left shoulder seam, ½ inch outside the collar edge.

*d.* Shoulder ornamentation and insignia.

(1) Shoulder straps for officers. (See para 28–8*b* for ornamentation and insignia.

(2) Shoulder loops for enlisted personnel.

*(a)* A shoulder loop of the same material as is used for the coat is attached to each shoulder.

*(b)* The loop is 2½ inches wide at the outside shoulder edge, 1½ inches wide at the inside collar edge, and piped all around with gold-colored nylon or rayon cord edge braid, ⅛ inch wide. The braid is inserted in the joining seams so it is completely visible around each loop. The loop is sewn on the outside shoulder seam and extends to a point approximately ½ inch from the inside collar seam. The loop has a buttonhole ⅜ inch from the inside edge of the braid, which is buttoned to the shoulder with a 25-ligne button.

*e.* Coat sleeve ornamentation. Ornamental braid is worn on both sleeves of the Army blue coat. Gold bullion, synthetic metallic gold, or gold-colored nylon or rayon braid is authorized for officers. Gold-colored nylon or rayon braid is authorized for enlisted personnel. The braid on the slacks and the coat sleeve will be of the same material. The bottom of the braid is positioned parallel to, and 3 inches above the bottom of each sleeve as follows.

(1) General officers have one 1½ inch gold braid on each sleeve.

(2) For all other officers, each sleeve has a ¾-inch braid consisting of two ¼-inch gold braids placed ¼ inch apart on silk material, of the first-named color of their basic branch.

(3) Enlisted personnel have a ⅛-inch soutache braid of gold-colored nylon or rayon on each sleeve.

## 21–6. Skirt, Army blue

*a.* Design. The skirt will be made from an approved specification or pattern.

*b.* General description. The skirt is knee length, with a three-piece front and three-piece back, slightly flared, with a waistband and a zipper closure on the left side.

## 21–7. Slacks, Army blue

*a.* Design. The slacks will be made from an approved specification or pattern.

*b.* General description. The slacks are straight-legged with slightly flared bottoms and a zipper front closure on the center front. The slacks have two side pockets.

*c.* Slack leg ornamentation. Ornamental braid is worn on each outside seam of the slack leg, from the bottom of the waistband to the bottom of slack leg, as follows:

(1) General officers have two ½-inch two-vellum gold, synthetic metallic gold, or gold-colored nylon or rayon braids, spaced ½ inch apart.

(2) All other officers have one 1-inch two-vellum gold, synthetic metallic gold, or gold-colored nylon or rayon braid.

(3) Enlisted personnel have one 1-inch gold-colored nylon or rayon braid.

*d.* Personnel will not wear the Army blue slacks for social functions. They are approved for wear by selected females (such as, but not limited to, band, honor guard, and female chaplains), in the performance of their daily duties where the Army blue uniform slacks are more appropriate than the Army blue skirt.

## 21–8. Shirt, white

A short-sleeved white shirt with black neck tab is worn with the Army blue uniform. (See para 27–22*a* for a complete description.)

## 21–9. Capes, Army blue and black

As an option, all female officers are authorized to wear the Army blue or Army black cape instead of the black all-weather coat when wearing the Army blue uniform after duty hours. Enlisted personnel may not wear the cape. (See para 27–6 of this regulation for a complete description of cape wear.)

## 21–10. Service hat, Army blue

*a.* Design. The hat will be made from an approved specification or pattern.

*b.* General description. The hat has an oval-shaped crown and a detachable hatband for placement of insignia. Hat insignia is worn centered and secured through the hatband. (See para 28–3 for a description of insignia wear.)

*c.* Hatband. The detachable hatband has three rows of stitching of matching thread at the top of the band and ornamentation, as follows:

(1) General and field grade officers. The hat has two arcs of laurel leaves grouped in twos, embroidered in gold bullion, synthetic metallic gold-colored braid, or gold-colored nylon or rayon braid.

(2) Company grade officers and warrant officers. The hat has a band of ½–inch, two-vellum gold, gold-colored synthetic metallic braid, or gold-colored nylon or rayon braid, placed on the bottom edge of the hatband.

(3) Enlisted personnel. There is no ornamentation on the hatband.

*d.* Wear. All female personnel may wear the Army blue service hat with the Army blue uniform. Personnel are not required to wear headgear when wearing the Army blue uniform to evening social functions (after retreat). However, on all other occasions personnel will wear headgear with this uniform.

*e.* Proper wear position. The service hat is worn straight on the head so that the hatband creates a straight line around the head, parallel to the ground. Hair will not be visible below the front brim of the hat, and there should be ½- to 1-inch distance between the eyebrow and the brim of the hat.

## 21–11. Items normally worn with the Army blue uniform

*a.* Accessories.

(1) Buttons (para 27–4).

(2) Capes (officers only).

*(a)* Black (para 27–6*a*).

(b) Blue (para 27–6b).

(3) Chaplain's apparel (para 27–7).

(4) Coat, black, all weather (para 27–8).

(5) Gloves.

(a) Black, leather, unisex, dress (only when the black all-weather coat is worn) (para 27–12b).

(b) White, dress (para 27–12c).

(6) Handbags, black.

(a) Fabric or leather (para 27–13b).

(b) Black, shoulder (para 27–13d).

(7) Headgear, cap, cold weather, AG 489 (para 27–5).

(8) Scarf, black (para 27–21a).

(9) Shirt, white, short-sleeved (para 27–22a).

(10) Shoes, black, pump (paras 27–23f and g).

(11) Stockings, sheer (para 27–24d).

(12) Umbrella, black (para 27–27).

(13) Undergarments, white (para 27–28).

b. Insignia, awards, badges and accouterments worn on the Army blue uniform.

(1) Aiguillettes (officers only).

(a) Service (para 28–25).

(b) Dress (para 28–26).

(2) Fourragere/lanyards (para 28–11).

(3) Branch insignia (para 28–10 and 28–12a).

(4) U.S. insignia (para 28–4).

(5) Grade insignia (paras 28–5, 28–6, and 28–7).

(6) Headgear insignia (para 28–3).

(7) Regimental distinctive insignia (para 28–23).

(8) OCS/WOC insignia (paras 28–14 and 28–15).

(9) Nameplate (para 28–24c).

(10) Service stripes (enlisted personnel only) (para 28–27).

(11) Decoration and service medal ribbons (full-size or miniature medals may be worn after retreat) (paras 29–7, 29–8, and 29–9).

(12) Unit awards (para 29–11).

(13) U.S. badges (identification, marksmanship, combat and special skill, full size and miniature); dress miniature combat and special skill badges will be worn when miniature medals are worn (paras 29–13, 29–16, 29–17, and 29–18).

(14) Foreign badges (para 29–19).

## 21–12. General guidelines

a. The skirt is worn no longer than 1 inch above, or 2 inches below the crease in the back of the knee. The black scarf and the black leather dress gloves are authorized for wear with the black all-weather coat. Personnel may wear white gloves with the basic uniform. Females may carry the black leather handbag during duty or after duty hours; they may carry the black fabric handbag only after duty hours, however. When weather conditions warrant, the AG 489 cold-weather cap is authorized for wear with the black all-weather coat or the capes. Black pumps and sheer stockings are the authorized footwear for this uniform. After duty hours, personnel may wear the black fabric pumps with this uniform. (See para 28–10e for information on color ornamentation and branch insignia for detailed officers.)

b. Enlisted personnel assigned to units authorized by CTA 50–900 to wear the Army blue uniform as an organizational uniform, such as table of organization and equipment (TOE) bands, selected honor guards, and other ceremonial units, may wear distinctive unit insignia (DUI), Military Police accessories, and other items authorized by CTA 50–900, when prescribed by the commander.

c. Soldiers who possess the old version of the Army blue coat will wear one branch and one U.S. insignia on the collar. Those who possess the new version of the Army blue coat will wear their insignia as they do on the Army green coat (see paras 28–4 and 28–12 of this regulation).

# Chapter 22
## Army White Mess and Evening Mess Uniforms—Male

### 22–1. Authorization for wear

The Army white mess and Army white evening mess uniforms are authorized for optional wear by all male personnel. Personnel normally wear these uniforms from April to October, except in clothing zones I and II, where they may wear them year-round (see CTA 50–900). (See fig 22–1 for Army white mess uniform, general officers; see fig 22–2 for Army white mess uniform, other officers; see fig 22–3 for Army white mess uniform, enlisted.)

**Figure 22–1. Army white mess uniform, general officers**

Figure 22–2. Army white mess uniform, other officers

Figure 22-3. Army white mess uniform, enlisted

## 22–2. Composition

*a.* The Army white mess uniform comprises the Army white jacket, black high-waisted trousers, white semiformal dress shirt with a turndown collar, black bow tie, and black cummerbund (see figs 22–1 and 22–3).

*b.* The Army white evening mess uniform comprises the Army white jacket, black high-waisted trousers, white formal dress shirt with a wing collar, white vest, and white bow tie (see fig 22–2).

## 22–3. Occasions for wear

The following are appropriate occasions for personnel to wear the Army white mess and white evening mess uniforms.

*a.* Social functions of a general or official nature, held after retreat.

*b.* Private, formal dinners or other private, formal social functions held after retreat.

## 22–4. Materials

*a.* White jacket and vest.

(1) Cotton twill, 8.2–ounce weight, white.

(2) Polyester and wool blend fabric in plain weave, 9–ounce tropical weight, white.

(3) Polyester and wool blend fabric in gabardine, 10.5-ounce weight, white.

(4) Polyester texturized woven serge, 6.5–ounce weight, white.

*b.* Trousers. Commercial, black, of a tuxedo-type lightweight material.

## 22–5. Jacket, Army white

*a.* Design. The jacket will be made from an approved specification or pattern.

*b.* General description. The jacket, which is cut on the lines of an evening dress coat, descends to the point of the hips and is slightly curved to a peak in back and in front. Two 25-ligne buttons, joined by a small gold or gold-colored chain about 1½ inches long, are worn in the upper buttonholes. The shoulders have a device for the attachment of shoulder knots on officer uniforms.

*c.* Shoulder knots. (See para 24–5*d* and fig 22–11.)

**Figure 22–11. Shoulder knot**

*d.* Jacket sleeve ornamentation.

(1) General officers wear a cuff of white mohair or mercerized cotton braid 4 inches in width, positioned ⅛ inch from the bottom edge of each sleeve. General officer grade insignia is centered on the outside of the sleeves, 1 inch above the upper edge of the cuff braid. When general officers wear their branch insignia, it is centered on the outside of the sleeves, 1 inch above the upper edge of the cuff braid. Grade insignia is positioned 1 inch above the branch insignia. If branch insignia is worn, general officers will wear the non-subdued, metal pin-on insignia. Grade insignia is embroidered white cloth or silver bullion. General officer stars are 1 inch in diameter and are worn with one point facing upward. The following describes general officer stars:

(a) General insignia is four stars, with 1¼ inches between the midpoints, centered horizontally on the outside of the sleeves (see fig 22–4).

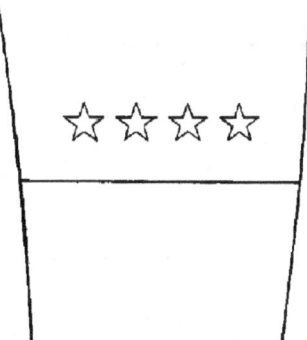

**Figure 22–4. Sleeve ornamentation, white mess, general**

*(b)* Lieutenant general insignia is three stars, with 1⅜ inches between the midpoints, with the middle star centered horizontally on the outside of the sleeves (see fig 22–5).

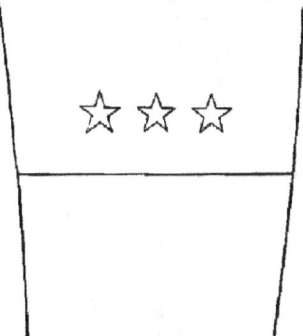

**Figure 22–5. Sleeve ornamentation, white mess, lieutenant general**

*(c)* Major general insignia is two stars, with 2 inches between the midpoints, centered horizontally on the outside of the sleeves (see fig 22–6).

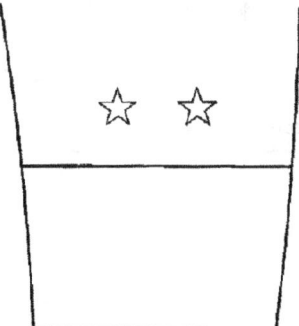

**Figure 22–6. Sleeve ornamentation, white mess, major general**

*(d)* Brigadier general insignia is one star centered horizontally on the outside of the sleeves (see fig 22–7).

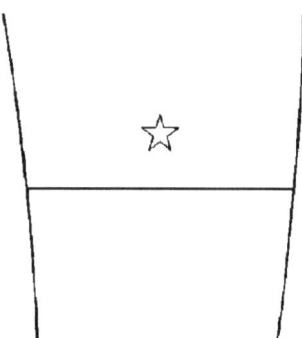

Figure 22–7. Sleeve ornamentation, white mess, brigadier general

(2) Other commissioned and warrant officers wear a band of white mohair or mercerized cotton braid sewn on each sleeve, ½ inch wide, with the lower edge parallel to, and 3 inches above the bottom edge of each sleeve. A trefoil is attached to the upper edge of the braid on each sleeve. It consists of a knot composed of three loops, one large upper loop and two small lower loops of ¼-inch white soutache braid, interlaced at the points of crossing, with the ends of the knots resting on the sleeve braid. Officer grade insignia (non-subdued pin-on or embroidered white cloth) is worn vertically in the center of the space formed by the lower curves of the knot and the upper edge of the braid (see figs 22–8 and 22–9).

Figure 22–8. Sleeve ornamentation, white mess, field and company grade officers

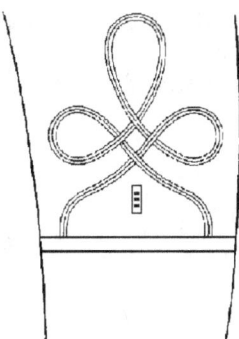

**Figure 22–9. Sleeve ornamentation, white mess, warrant officers**

(3) Previously authorized sleeve ornamentation, which consists of the sleeve band, the branch insignia centered in the space formed by the lower curves of the trefoil and the upper edge of the sleeve band, and the number of trefoils appropriate to the specific grade of the wearer, is authorized for wear for the life of the jacket. This option is for commissioned officers only, and it applies only to jackets purchased prior to 11 August 1975. This ornamentation is not authorized for jackets purchased after 11 August 1975.

(4) Enlisted personnel wear a ⅛-inch soutache braid of gold-colored nylon or rayon, 3 inches above the bottom of each sleeve (see fig 22–10).

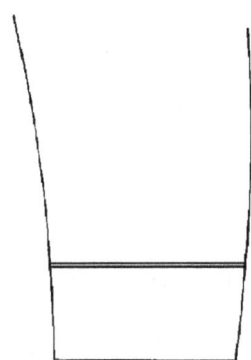

**Figure 22–10. Sleeve ornamentation, white mess, enlisted**

## 22–6. Trousers, black
*a.* Design. The trousers will be made from an approved specification or pattern.

*b.* General description. The black trousers are cut along the lines of civilian dress trousers, with a high waist and without pleats, cuffs, or hip pockets.

*c.* Trouser leg ornamentation. The trouser leg ornamentation consists of a black silk or satin braid, no less than ¾ inch wide, or more than 1 inch wide, sewn on the outside seam of the trouser leg, from the bottom of the waistband to the bottom of the trouser leg.

## 22–7. Shirts, white dress
*a.* Semiformal. A commercial, white, long-sleeved semiformal dress shirt with a soft bosom, French cuffs, and a standard turndown collar is worn with the Army white mess uniform when it is worn with the black cummerbund and black bow tie.

*b.* Formal. A commercial, white, long-sleeved formal dress shirt with a stiff bosom, French cuffs, and a wing-type collar is worn with the Army white evening mess uniform when it is worn with the white vest and white bow tie.

## 22–8. Headgear

*a.* The Army white service cap is the authorized headgear for wear with the Army white mess and white evening mess uniforms. (See para 18–8 of this regulation for a complete description of the wear of the cap.)

*b.* Personnel are not required to wear headgear with the Army white mess and white evening mess uniforms to evening social events.

## 22–9. Cape, Army blue

As an option, all officers are authorized to wear the Army blue cape instead of the black all-weather coat, when wearing the Army white mess and white evening mess uniforms after duty hours. Enlisted personnel may not wear the cape. (See para 27–6*c* for design and wear policy.)

## 22–10. Cummerbund, black

*a.* Design. The cummerbund will be made from a commercial design. It is made of silk or satin material, with four or five pleats running the entire length of the cummerbund.

*b.* Wear. All male personnel are authorized to wear the black cummerbund with the Army white mess uniform. The cummerbund will be made of the same material as the bow tie, and is worn with the pleats facing down.

## 22–11. Vest, white

*a.* Design. The vest will be made from an approved specification or pattern.

*b.* General description. The white vest is single breasted, cut low, with a rolling collar and pointed bottom, and fastened with three detachable, extra small white buttons.

*c.* How worn. The white vest is worn with the white bow tie and white formal dress shirt with a wing collar, as part of the white evening mess uniform.

## 22–12. Items normally worn with the Army white mess and evening mess uniforms

*a.* Accessories
(1) Buttons (para 27–4).
(2) Cape (officers only) (para 27–6*c*).
(3) Coat, black, all weather (para 27–8).
(4) Cuff links and studs.
*(a)* Gold (white mess only) (para 27–10*b*(2)).
*(b)* White (white evening mess only) (para 27–10*b*(1)).
(5) Gloves.
*(a)* Black, leather, unisex, dress (only when the black all-weather coat is worn) (para 27–12*b*).
*(b)* White, dress (para 27–12*c*).
(6) Headgear, cap, service white (para 18–8).
(7) Neckties.
*(a)* Black, bow (white mess only) (para 27–19*a*).
*(b)* White, bow (evening white mess only) (para 27–19*b*).
(8) Shirts, white.
*(a)* Semiformal, dress (para 27–22*d*).
*(b)* Formal (para 27–22*e*).
(9) Shoes, oxford, black (para 27–23*c*).
(10) Socks, black (para 27–24*b*).
(11) Suspenders (para 27–25).
(12) Undergarments, white (para 27–28).

*b.* Insignia, awards, badges, and accouterments worn on the Army white mess and evening mess uniforms.
(1) Aiguillette, dress (officers only) (para 28–26).
(2) Insignia.
*(a)* Branch insignia (paras 28–10 and 28–12). Branch insignia is worn as prescribed in paras 22–5*d*(1) and (3).
*(b)* Grade insignia (paras 28–5 through 28–8). Grade insignia is worn as prescribed in paras 22–5*d*(1) and (2).
*(c)* Regimental distinctive insignia (para 28–23).
*(d)* Headgear insignia, cap, service, white (para 28–3*c*).
(3) Service stripes (enlisted personnel only) (para 28–27).
(4) Decorations and service medals, miniature (para 29–9).
(5) U.S. badges (combat and special skill, dress miniature, and identification) (paras 29–17*c* and 29–18*c*).

## 22–13. General guidelines

Personnel may wear the black dress gloves when wearing the black all-weather coat with these uniforms. Personnel may wear the white gloves with the basic uniform. The black oxford shoes with black socks are the only authorized footwear for these uniforms.

# Chapter 23
# Army White Mess, All-White Mess, and Evening White Mess Uniforms—Female

## 23–1. Authorization for wear

*a.* The Army white mess, all-white mess, and evening white mess uniforms are authorized for wear by all female personnel. Personnel normally wear these uniforms from April to October, except in clothing zones I and II, where they may wear them year-round (see CTA 50–900).

*b.* There are two versions of the Army white jacket. The older version of the jacket is authorized for wear by officers only. The newer version of the jacket is authorized for wear by all females. Officers may continue to wear the older version jacket as long as it is serviceable.

## 23–2. Composition

There are three variations to the Army white mess uniform.

*a.* The Army white mess uniform comprises the Army white jacket, the Army black knee-length skirt, the black cummerbund, and the formal white blouse with black dress neck tab (see fig 23–1).

Figure 23–1. Army white mess uniform, other officers (new version jacket)

*b.* The Army all-white mess uniform comprises the Army white jacket, the Army white knee-length mess skirt, white cummerbund, and the formal white blouse with black dress neck tab (see fig 23–2).

*c.* The Army white evening mess uniform comprises the Army white jacket, Army black full-length skirt, black cummerbund, and formal white blouse with black dress neck tab (see fig 23–3).

*d.* Figure 23–3 shows the Army white evening mess uniform with the old version of the white mess jacket.

Figure 23–2. Army all-white mess uniform, enlisted (new version jacket)

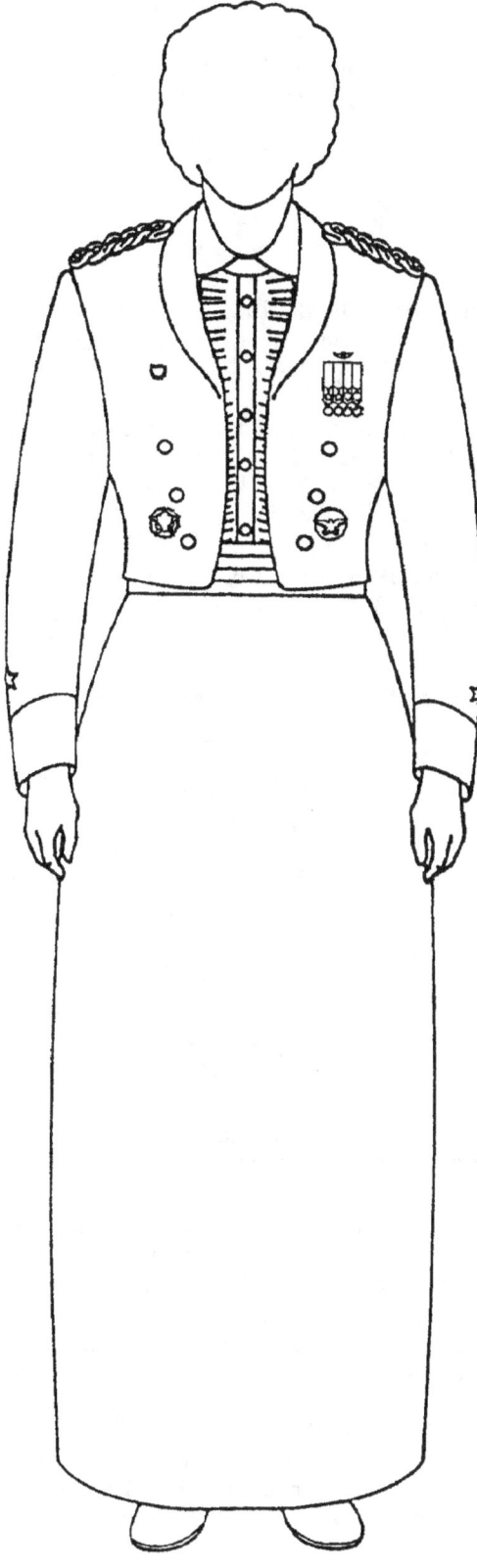

Figure 23–3. Army white evening mess uniform, general officer (old version jacket)

### 23–3. Occasions for wear

The following are appropriate occasions for personnel to wear the Army white, all-white, and evening white mess uniforms.

*a.* Social functions of a general or official nature, held after retreat.

*b.* Private, formal dinners or other private, formal social functions held after retreat.

### 23–4. Materials

*a.* White jacket and skirt.

(1) Polyester and rayon blend fabric in gabardine weave, 6– or 8–ounce weight, Army white.

(2) Texturized polyester serge, 6.5–ounce weight, Army white.

*b.* Black skirt, knee and full length.

(1) Wool tropical, 8.5–ounce weight, Army black shade 149.

(2) Polyester and wool blend fabric in tropical weave, 10–ounce weight, Army black shade 332.

### 23–5. Jacket, Army white mess

*a.* Old version. The jacket is single breasted with a natural-waist length and a shawl-type collar. It has a two-piece front, and a two-panel back. The front pieces have three 20-ligne buttons on each side, and the shoulders have two loops for the attachment of shoulder boards. Each sleeve has a band of white braid, ½ inch in width, with the lower edge of the band 3 inches from the bottom of the sleeve.

(1) Shoulder ornamentation and insignia, old version jacket (officers only).

*(a)* General officers. Detachable shoulder knots are worn on each shoulder. A description of shoulder knots is provided in paragraph 25–5*d*(1). (See fig 23–11.)

**Figure 23–11. Shoulder knot**

*(b)* Other officers. Detachable shoulder boards are worn on each shoulder, snapped to the jacket through the shoulder loops, with the square end of the shoulder board positioned on the outside shoulder seam. A general description of shoulder boards is in paragraph 28–8*c* of this regulation.

(2) Jacket sleeve ornamentation and insignia, old version jacket.

*(a)* General officers wear a cuff of white mohair or mercerized cotton braid 4 inches in width, positioned ⅛ inch from the bottom edge of each sleeve. General officer grade insignia is centered on the outside sleeves, 1 inch above the upper edge of the cuff braid. When general officers wear their branch insignia, it is centered on the outside of the sleeves, 1 inch above the upper edge of the cuff braid. Grade insignia is positioned 1 inch above the branch insignia. If branch insignia is worn, general officers will wear the non-subdued metal pin-on insignia. Grade insignia is embroidered white cloth or silver bullion. General officer stars are 1 inch in diameter, with one point facing upward. (See para 22–5*d*(1) and figs 23–4 through 23–7 for size and position of stars.)

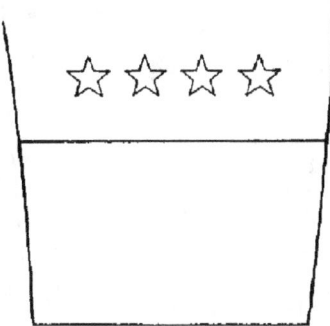

Figure 23–4. Sleeve ornamentation, white mess, general

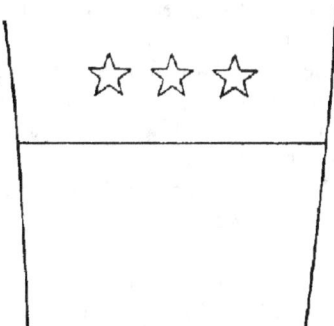

Figure 23–5. Sleeve ornamentation, white mess, lieutenant general

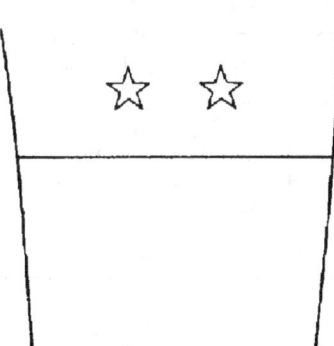

Figure 23–6. Sleeve ornamentation, white mess, major general

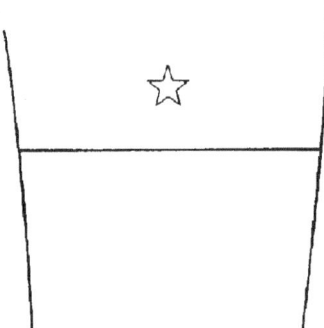

Figure 23–7. Sleeve ornamentation, white mess, brigadier general

*(b)* Other officers wear a band of white mohair or mercerized cotton braid, ½ inch wide, with the lower edge parallel to, and 3 inches above the bottom edge of each sleeve.

*b.* New version. The jacket is cut along the natural waistline and is slightly curved to a peak in back and in front. The coat has a shawl collar with white, self-fabric facing, and is fully lined with an inside vertical pocket on the right side. The coat front has six gold 20-ligne buttons. Two 20-ligne buttons, joined by a gold or gold-colored chain about 1½ inches long, are worn in the upper buttonholes.

(1) Shoulder ornamentation. Officer's jackets have a device for the attachment of shoulder knots. A description of the shoulder knots is provided in paragraph 25–5*d*(1) (see fig 23–11).

(2) Sleeve ornamentation.

*(a)* General officers wear a cuff of white mohair or mercerized cotton braid 4 inches in width, positioned ⅛ inch from the bottom edge of each sleeve. General officer grade insignia is centered on the outside of the sleeves, 1 inch above the upper edge of the cuff braid. When general officers wear their branch insignia, it is centered on the outside of the sleeves, 1 inch above the upper edge of the cuff braid. Grade insignia is positioned 1 inch above the branch insignia. If branch insignia is worn, general officers will wear the non-subdued metal pin-on insignia. Grade insignia is embroidered white cloth or silver bullion. General officer stars are 1 inch in diameter and are worn with one point facing upward. (See para 22–5*d*(1) and figs 23–4 through 23–7 for size and position of stars.)

*(b)* Other commissioned and warrant officers wear a band of white mohair or white mercerized cotton braid sewn on each sleeve, ½–inch wide, with the lower edge parallel to, and 3 inches above the bottom edge of the braid on each sleeve. A trefoil is attached to the upper edge of the braid on each sleeve. It consists of a knot composed of three loops, one large upper loop and two small lower loops of ¼–inch white soutache braid, interlaced at the points of crossing, with the ends of the knots resting on the sleeve braid. Officer grade insignia (non-subdued pin-on or embroidered white cloth) is worn vertically in the center of the space formed by the lower curves of the knot and the upper edge of the braid (see figs 23–8 and 23–9).

Figure 23–8. Sleeve ornamentation, white mess, field and company grade officers

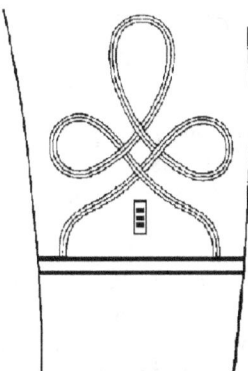

**Figure 23–9. Sleeve ornamentation, white mess, warrant officers**

*(c)* Previously authorized sleeve ornamentation, which consists of the sleeve band, the branch insignia centered in the space formed by the lower curves of the trefoil and the upper edge of the sleeve band, and the number of trefoils appropriate to the specific grade of the wearer, is authorized for wear for the life of the jacket. This option is for commissioned officers only, and it applies only to jackets purchased prior to 11 August 1975. This ornamentation is not authorized for jackets purchased after 11 August 1975.

*(d)* Enlisted personnel wear a ⅛–inch soutache braid of gold-colored nylon or rayon 3 inches above the bottom of each sleeve (see fig 23–10).

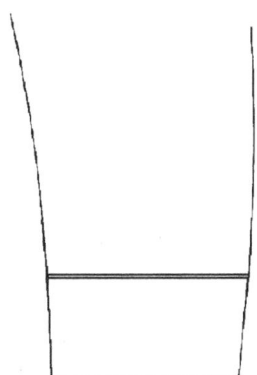

**Figure 23–10. Sleeve ornamentation, white mess, enlisted**

## 23–6. Skirts
*a.* The all-white mess uniform skirt is a white knee-length skirt, with a one-panel front and four-panel back of straight design, with a waistband and a zipper closure on the left side.

*b.* The white mess skirt is a black knee-length skirt, with a one-panel front and a four-panel back of straight design, with a waistband and a zipper closure on the left side.

*c.* The white evening mess skirt is a black full-length skirt, with a one-panel front and four-panel back of straight design, with a waistband, a zipper closure on the left side, and an overlapped center back pleat.

## 23–7. Blouse, white formal
The blouse is a tuck-in style made of polyester and cotton fabric, with a front closure containing seven removable dome-shaped buttons. On each side of the front opening, there are three vertical rows of ruffles. The blouse has short sleeves and a rounded collar.

## 23–8. Neck tab, black, dress
The material is polyester and cotton broadcloth, in Army shade 305. It is a quarter-moon neck tab, which fits under the collar of the white formal blouse.

## 23–9. Capes, Army black and blue
As an option, all female officers are authorized to wear the Army blue or the Army black cape instead of the black all-weather coat, when wearing the Army white uniform after duty hours. Enlisted personnel may not wear the cape. (See paras 27–6a and b for a complete description of the wear of the cape.)

## 23–10. Cummerbunds, black and white
a. The cummerbund will be made from a commercial design. It is made in either black or white silk or satin material, with four or five pleats running the entire length of the cummerbund.

b. Wear. The black cummerbund is worn with the white mess and white evening mess uniforms. The white cummerbund is worn with the all-white mess uniform. The cummerbund is worn with the pleats facing down.

c. Females who possess cummerbunds made from previously authorized materials may continue to wear them for as long as they are serviceable.

## 23–11. Headgear
No headgear is authorized for wear by female personnel with the Army white mess, all-white mess, or white evening mess uniforms.

## 23–12. Items normally worn with the Army white mess, all-white mess, and evening white mess uniforms
a. Accessories.

(1) Buttons (para 27–4).

(2) Capes (officers only).

(a) Black (para 27–6a).

(b) Blue (para 27–6b).

(2) Coat, black all weather (para 27–8).

(3) Gloves.

(a) Black, leather, unisex, dress (only when the black all-weather coat is worn) (para 27–12b).

(b) White, dress (para 27–12c).

(4) Handbags.

(a) Black, dress (carried with white mess and evening mess only) (para 27–13b).

(b) White, dress (carried with all-white mess only) (para 27–13c).

(5) Shoes.

(a) Pumps, black (worn with white mess and evening white mess only) (paras 27–23f and g).

(b) Pumps, white (worn with all-white mess only) (paras 27–23f and g).

(6) Stockings, sheer (para 27–24d).

(7) Umbrella, black (para 27–27).

(8) Undergarments (para 27–28).

b. Insignia, awards, badges, and accouterments worn on the Army white mess, all-white mess, and evening mess uniforms.

(1) Aiguillette, dress (officers only) (para 28–26).

(2) Insignia.

(a) Branch insignia (paras 28–10 and 28–12a). Branch insignia is worn as prescribed in paras 23–5a(2) and 23–5b(2).

(b) Grade insignia (paras 28–5 through 28–8). Grade insignia is worn as prescribed in paras 23–5a(2) and 23–5b(2).

(c) Regimental distinctive insignia (para 28–23).

(3) Service stripes (enlisted personnel only) (para 28–27).

(4) Decorations and service medals, miniature (para 29–9).

(5) U.S. badges (combat and special skill, dress miniature, and identification) (paras 29–17c and 29–18c).

## 23–13. General guidelines
Personnel will wear knee-length mess skirts no longer than 1 inch above or 2 inches below the crease in the back of the knee. The black evening mess skirt is worn full length. Personnel may wear the black dress gloves when wearing the black all-weather coat. Personnel may wear white gloves with all uniforms. The black pumps with sheer stockings

are the only authorized footwear for the white mess and white evening mess uniforms. The white pumps with sheer stockings are the only authorized footwear for the all-white mess uniform.

## Chapter 24
## Army Blue Mess and Evening Mess Uniforms—Male

### 24–1. Authorization for wear
The Army blue mess and blue evening mess uniforms are authorized for year-round wear by all male personnel.

### 24–2. Composition
*a.* The Army blue mess uniform comprises the Army blue jacket, dark- or light-blue high-waisted trousers, white semiformal dress shirt with a turndown collar, black bow tie, and black cummerbund (see figs 24–1, 24–2, and 24–3).

Figure 24–1. Army blue mess uniform, general officers

Figure 24–2. Army blue evening mess uniform, other officers

Figure 24–3. Army blue mess uniform, enlisted

*b.* The Army blue evening mess uniform comprises the Army blue jacket, dark- or light-blue high-waisted trousers, white formal dress shirt with a wing collar, white vest, and white bow tie (see fig 24–2).

### 24–3. Occasions for wear

The blue mess uniform is worn for black tie functions and corresponds to a civilian tuxedo. The blue evening mess uniform is the most formal uniform worn by Army personnel and corresponds to the civilian "white tie and tails." The following are appropriate occasions for personnel to wear the Army blue mess and blue evening mess uniforms:

*a.* Social functions of a general or official nature, held after retreat.

*b.* All private, formal social functions held after retreat.

### 24–4. Materials

*a.* Jacket.

(1) Wool barathea, dark blue, 14–ounce weight, Army shade 150.

(2) Wool gabardine, dark blue, 11– or 14.5–ounce weight Army shade 150.

(3) Wool elastique, dark blue, 15–ounce weight, Army shade 150.

(4) Wool tropical, dark blue, 9–ounce weight, Army shade 150.

(5) Polyester and wool blend gabardine, dark blue, 9.5–ounce weight, Army shade 450.

(6) Polyester and wool blend fabric in plain weave, dark blue, 9.5–ounce tropical weight, Army shade 450.

*b.* Trousers.

(1) General officers. The trousers will be made in the same material and shade (dark blue) as the jacket.

(2) Other officers and enlisted personnel. The trousers will be made in the same material as the jacket, except the color will be light blue, Army shade 151 or 451.

(3) Braid. Nylon gold-colored braid or synthetic metallic gold braid is more suitable than gold bullion when attached to lightweight fabrics (11 ounces or less).

### 24–5. Jacket, Army blue mess

*a.* Design. The jacket will be made from an approved specification or pattern.

*b.* General description. The jacket, which is cut on the lines of an evening dress coat, descends to the point of the hips and is slightly curved to a peak in back and in front. Two 25-ligne buttons, joined by a small gold or gold-colored chain about 1½ inches long, are worn in the upper buttonholes. The shoulders have a device for the attachment of shoulder knots on officer uniforms.

*c.* Lapels. The lapels of the Army blue jacket are rayon, acetate, or other synthetic fabric with a satin face in the following colors:

(1) General officers, except chaplains: dark blue.

(2) All chaplains: black.

(3) All other officers: the first-named color of their basic branch of service. (See para 28–19.)

(4) Enlisted personnel: dark blue.

*d.* Shoulder knots (officers only). (See fig 24–11.)

**Figure 24–11. Shoulder knot**

(1) General description. The shoulder knot is made from ¼–inch diameter cord, of gold bullion, synthetic metallic gold, or gold-colored nylon or rayon. The shoulder knot is formed of four plaits composed of three cords interlaced as one, and rounded at the top with a gold 20-ligne button positioned in the upper end of the knot. The knot is no more than 5½ inches in length and 2½ inches in width, conforming to the shoulder, and stiffened on the underside with a flexible backing, covered with dark blue or black cloth. The flexible backing has an attachment that is suitable for fastening it to the shoulders of the jacket (see fig 24–11).

(2) How worn. Officers wear the shoulder knots attached to the shoulders of the Army blue jacket.

*e.* Sleeve ornamentation.

(1) General officers wear a cuff of blue-black velvet braid 4 inches in width, positioned ⅛ inch from the bottom edge of each sleeve. A band of oak leaves in groups of two, 1 inch in width, are embroidered on each cuff of braid, 1 inch below the upper edge, in gold bullion, synthetic metallic gold, or gold-colored nylon or rayon. General officer grade insignia is centered on the outside sleeve 1 inch above the upper edge of the cuff braid. When general officers wear their branch insignia, it is centered on the outside of the sleeves, 1 inch above the upper edge of the cuff braid. Grade insignia is positioned 1 inch above the branch insignia. If branch insignia is worn, general officers will wear the non-subdued, metal pin-on insignia. Grade insignia is embroidered silver bullion. General officer stars are 1 inch in diameter and are worn with one point facing upward. The following describes general officer stars.

*(a)* General insignia is four stars, with 1¼ inches between the midpoints, and with the stars centered horizontally on the outside of the sleeves (see fig 24–4).

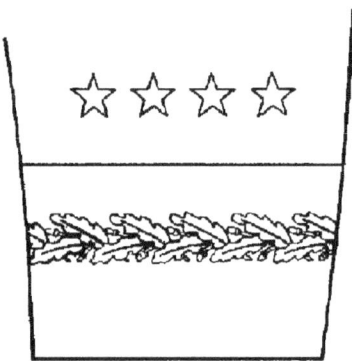

**Figure 24–4. Sleeve ornamentation, blue mess, general**

*(b)* Lieutenant general insignia is three stars, with 1⅜ inches between the midpoints, and with the middle star centered horizontally on the outside of the sleeves (see fig 24–5).

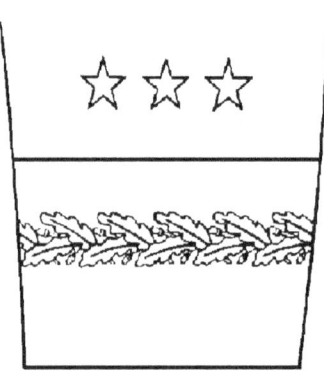

**Figure 24–5. Sleeve ornamentation, blue mess, lieutenant general**

*(c)* Major general insignia is two stars, with 2 inches between the midpoints and with the stars centered horizontally on the outside of the sleeves (see fig 24–6).

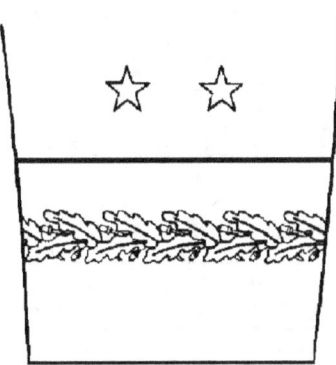

**Figure 24–6. Sleeve ornamentation, blue mess, major general**

*(d)* Brigadier general insignia is one star centered horizontally on the outside sleeves (see fig 24–7).

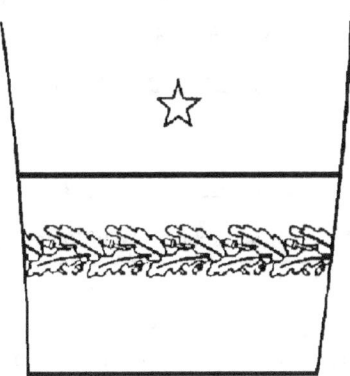

**Figure 24–7. Sleeve ornamentation, blue mess, brigadier general**

(2) Other commissioned and warrant officers wear a ¾–inch braid consisting of two ¼–inch, two-vellum gold, synthetic metallic gold, or gold-colored nylon or rayon braids, placed on each sleeve ¼ inch apart on a silk stripe of the first-named color of their basic branch. The bottom of the braid is positioned parallel to, and 3 inches above the bottom edge of each sleeve. A trefoil is attached to the upper edge of the braid on each sleeve. It consists of a knot composed of three loops, one large upper loop and two small lower loops of ¼ inch gold, synthetic metallic gold, or gold-colored braid, interlaced at the points of crossing, with the ends of the knots resting on the sleeve braid. Officer grade insignia (non-subdued pin-on or embroidered silver bullion) is worn vertically in the center of the space formed by the lower curves of the knot and the upper edge of the braid (see figs 24–8 and 24–9).

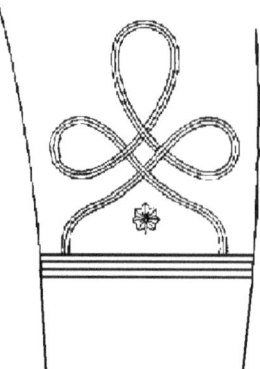

Figure 24–8. Sleeve ornamentation, blue mess, field and company grade officers

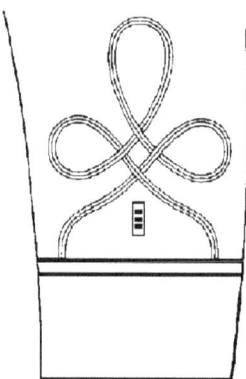

Figure 24–9. Sleeve ornamentation, blue mess, warrant officers

(3) Previously authorized sleeve ornamentation, which consists of the sleeve band, the branch insignia centered in the space formed by the lower curves of the trefoil and the upper edge of the sleeve band, and the number of trefoils appropriate to the specific grade of the wearer, is authorized for wear for the life of the jacket. This option is for commissioned officers only, and it applies only to jackets purchased prior to 11 August 1975. This ornamentation is not authorized for jackets purchased after 11 August 1975.

(4) Enlisted personnel wear a ⅛–inch soutache braid of gold-colored nylon or rayon, 3 inches above the bottom of each sleeve (see fig 24–10).

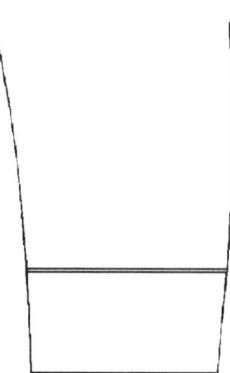

Figure 24–10. Sleeve ornamentation, blue mess, enlisted

## 24–6. Trousers, Army blue

*a.* Design. The trousers will be made from an approved specification or pattern.

*b.* General description. The blue trousers are cut along the lines of civilian dress trousers, with a high waist and without pleats, cuffs, or hip pockets. Personnel will wear only the high-waisted trousers with these uniforms. Suspenders are authorized for wear, but they may not be visible when worn. (See para 24–4*b*, above, for additional information on the trousers.)

*c.* Trouser leg ornamentation. The trouser leg ornamentation consists of an ornamental braid worn on the outside seam of the trouser leg, from the bottom of the waistband to the bottom of the trouser leg, as follows:

(1) General officers have two ½–inch, two-vellum gold, synthetic metallic gold, or gold-colored nylon or rayon braids, spaced ½ inch apart.

(2) All other officers and enlisted personnel have one 1½ inch, two-vellum gold, synthetic metallic gold, or gold-colored nylon or rayon braid.

## 24–7. Shirts, white dress

*a.* Semiformal. A commercial, white, long-sleeved semiformal dress shirt with a soft bosom, French cuffs, and a standard turndown collar is worn with the Army blue mess uniform.

*b.* Formal. A commercial, white, long-sleeved formal dress shirt with a stiff bosom, French cuffs, and a wing-type collar is worn with the Army blue evening mess uniform.

## 24–8. Headgear

*a.* The Army blue service cap is the authorized headgear for wear with the Army blue mess and evening mess uniforms. (See para 20–8 for a complete description.)

*b.* Personnel are not required to wear headgear with the Army blue mess and evening mess uniforms to evening social events.

## 24–9. Cape, Army blue

As an option, all officers are authorized to wear the Army blue cape instead of the black all-weather coat when wearing the Army blue mess and blue evening mess uniforms after duty hours. Enlisted personnel may not wear the cape. (See para 27–6*c* for design and wear policy.)

## 24–10. Cummerbund, black

*a.* Design. The cummerbund will be made from a commercial design. It is made of silk or satin material, with four or five pleats running the entire length of the cummerbund.

*b.* Wear. All male personnel are authorized to wear the black cummerbund with the Army blue mess uniform. The cummerbund will be made of the same material as the bow tie, and it is worn with the pleats facing down.

## 24–11. Vest, white

*a.* Design. The vest will be made from an approved specification or pattern.

*b.* General description. The white vest is single breasted, cut low, with a rolling collar and pointed bottom, and fastened with three detachable, extra small white buttons.

*c.* Wear. The white vest is worn with the Army blue evening mess uniform.

## 24–12. Items normally worn with the Army blue mess and evening mess uniforms

*a.* Accessories.

(1) Buttons (para 27–4).

(2) Cape (officers only) (para 27–6*c*).

(3) Coat, black, all-weather (para 27–8).

(4) Cuff links and studs.

*(a)* Gold (blue mess only) (para 27–10*b*(2)).

*(b)* White (blue evening mess only) (para 27–10*b*(1)).

(5) Gloves.

*(a)* Black, leather, unisex, dress (only when the black all-weather coat is worn) (para 27–12*b*).

*(b)* White, dress (para 27–12*c*).

(6) Headgear.

*(a)* Cap, service, blue (para 20–8).

*(b)* Cap, cold weather, AG 489 (para 27–5).

(7) Neckties.

*(a)* Black, bow (blue mess only) (para 27–19*a*).

*(b)* White, bow (blue evening mess only) (para 27–19*b*).

(8) Scarf, black (para 27–21*a*)

(9) Shirts, white.

*(a)* Semiformal, dress (para 27–22*d*).

*(b)* Formal (para 27–22*e*).

(10) Shoes, oxford, black (para 27–23*c*).

(11) Socks, black (para 27–24*b*).

(12) Suspenders (para 27–25).

(13) Undergarments, white (para 27–28).

*b.* Insignia, awards, badges, and accouterments worn on the Army blue mess and evening mess uniforms.

(1) Aiguillette, dress (officers only) (para 28–26).

(2) Insignia.

*(a)* Branch insignia (paras 28–10 and 28–12*a*). Officers wear branch insignia as prescribed in para 24–5*e*(1) and (3).

*(b)* Grade insignia (paras 28–5 through 28–8). Officers wear grade insignia as prescribed in para 24–5*e*(1) and (2).

*(c)* Regimental distinctive insignia (para 28–23).

*(d)* Headgear insignia, cap, service, white (para 28–3*c*).

(3) Service stripes (enlisted personnel only) (para 28–27).

(4) Decorations and service medals, miniature (para 29–9).

(5) U.S. badges (combat and special skill, dress miniature, and identification) (paras 29–17*c* and 29–18*c*).

## 24–13. General guidelines

Personnel may wear the black dress gloves, black scarf, and the AG 489 cold-weather cap when wearing the black all-weather coat. Personnel may wear white gloves with the basic uniforms. The black oxford shoes with black socks are the only authorized footwear for these uniforms. (See paras 28–10*d* and 28–19 for information on lapel facing. See para 28–10*e* for information on color of ornamentation and branch insignia for detailed officers.)

## Chapter 25
## Army Blue Mess and Evening Mess Uniforms—Female

### 25–1. Authorization for wear

The Army blue mess and blue evening mess uniforms are authorized for year-round wear by all female personnel.

### 25–2. Composition

*a.* The Army blue mess uniform comprises the Army blue jacket, the Army blue knee-length skirt, the formal white blouse with black dress neck tab, and the black cummerbund (see figs 25–1 and 25–2).

Figure 25–1. Army blue mess uniform, general officers

Figure 25–2. Army blue mess uniform, enlisted

*b.* The Army blue evening mess uniform comprises the Army blue jacket, the Army blue full-length skirt, the formal white blouse with black dress neck tab, and the black cummerbund (see fig 25–3).

Figure 25–3. Army blue evening mess uniform, other officers

## 25–3. Occasions for wear

The following are appropriate occasions for personnel to wear the Army blue mess and blue evening mess uniforms.

*a.* Social functions of a general or official nature, held after retreat.

*b.* All private, formal social functions held after retreat.

*c.* The Army blue mess evening mess uniform is the most formal uniform worn by Army female personnel.

## 25–4. Materials

*a.* Wool barathea, dark blue, 14–ounce weight, Army shade 150 or 450.

*b.* Wool gabardine, dark blue, 11– or 14.5–ounce weight, Army shade 150 or 450.

*c.* Wool elastique, dark blue, 15–ounce weight, Army shade 150 or 450.

*d.* Wool tropical, dark blue, 9–ounce weight, Army shade 150 or 450.

*e.* Polyester and wool blend gabardine, dark blue, 9.5–ounce weight, Army shade 450.

*f.* Polyester and wool blend fabric in plain weave, dark blue, 9.5–ounce tropical weight, Army shade 450.

## 25–5. Jacket, Army blue mess

*a.* Design. The jacket will be made from an approved specification or pattern.

*b.* General description. The jacket is cut along the lines of an evening dress coat, descending to the point of the hips and slightly curved to a peak in back and in front. The coat has a notched collar with a branch of service colored lapel insert and is fully lined, with an inside vertical pocket on the right side. The coat front has six gold 20-ligne buttons. Two 20-ligne buttons, joined by a gold or gold-colored chain about 1½ inches long, are worn in the upper buttonholes. The shoulders have a device for the attachment of shoulder knots on officer uniforms.

*c.* Lapels. The lapels of the Army blue jacket are rayon, acetate, or other synthetic fabric with a satin face in the following colors.

(1) General officers, except chaplains: dark blue.

(2) All chaplains: black.

(3) All other officers: the first named color of their basic branch of service. (See para 28–19.)

(4) Enlisted personnel: dark blue.

*d.* Shoulder knots (officers only). (See fig 25–11.)

**Figure 25–11. Shoulder knot**

(1) General description. The shoulder knot is made from ¼–inch diameter cord of gold bullion, synthetic metallic gold, or gold-colored nylon or rayon. The shoulder knot is formed of four plaits, composed of three cords interlaced as one, and rounded at the top with a gold 20-ligne button positioned in the upper end of the knot. The knot is no more than 4½ inches in length and 1⅞ inches in width, conforming to the shoulder and stiffened on the underside with a flexible backing, covered with dark blue or black cloth. The flexible backing has an attachment that is suitable for fastening it to the shoulders of the jacket.

(2) How worn. Officers wear the shoulder knots attached to the shoulders of the Army blue jacket.

*e.* Sleeve ornamentation.

(1) General officers wear a cuff of blue-black velvet braid, 4 inches in width, positioned ⅛ inch from the bottom edge of each sleeve. A band of oak leaves in groups of two, 1 inch in width, are embroidered on each cuff of braid, 1 inch below the upper edge, in gold bullion, synthetic metallic gold, or gold-colored nylon or rayon. General officer grade insignia is centered on the outside of the sleeve, 1 inch above the upper edge of the cuff braid. When general officers wear their branch insignia, it is centered on the outside of the sleeves 1 inch above the upper edge of the cuff braid. Grade insignia is positioned 1 inch above the branch insignia. If branch insignia is worn, general officers will wear the non-subdued, metal pin-on insignia. Grade insignia is embroidered silver bullion. General officer stars are 1 inch in diameter and are worn with one point facing upward. The following describes general officer stars:

*(a)* General insignia is four stars, with 1¼ inches between the midpoints, centered horizontally on the outside of the sleeves (see fig 25–4).

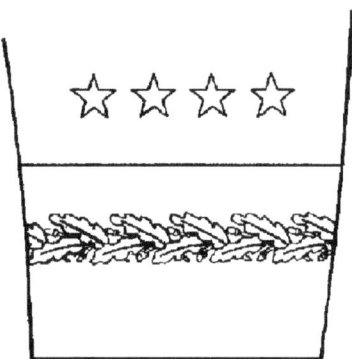

**Figure 25–4. Sleeve ornamentation, blue mess, general**

*(b)* Lieutenant general insignia is three stars, with 1⅜ inches between the midpoints, with the middle star centered horizontally on the outside of the sleeves (see fig 25–5).

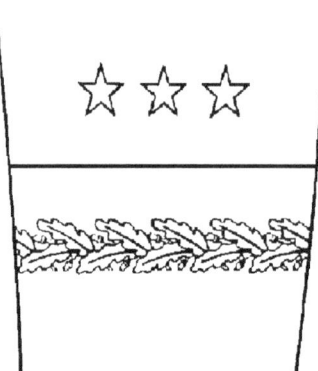

**Figure 25–5. Sleeve ornamentation, blue mess, lieutenant general**

*(c)* Major general insignia is two stars, with 2 inches between the midpoints and centered horizontally on the outside of the sleeves (see fig 25–6).

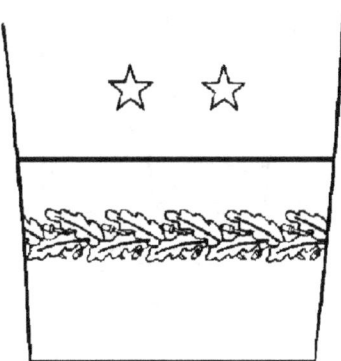

**Figure 25–6. Sleeve ornamentation, blue mess, major general**

*(d)* Brigadier general insignia is one star centered horizontally on the outside of the sleeves (see fig 25–7).

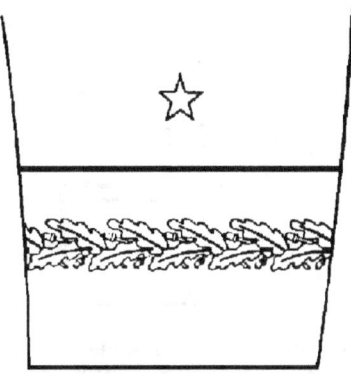

**Figure 25–7. Sleeve ornamentation, blue mess, brigadier general**

(2) Other commissioned and warrant officers wear a ¾–inch braid consisting of two ¼–inch two-vellum gold, synthetic metallic gold, or gold-colored nylon or rayon braids, placed on each sleeve ¼ inch apart on a silk stripe of the first-named color of their basic branch. The bottom of the braid is positioned parallel to, and 3 inches above the bottom edge of each sleeve. A trefoil is attached to the upper edge of the braid on each sleeve. It consists of a knot composed of three loops, one large upper loop and two small lower loops of ¼ inch gold, synthetic metallic gold, or gold-colored braid, interlaced at the points of crossing, with the ends of the knots resting on the sleeve braid. Officer grade insignia (non-subdued pin-on or embroidered silver bullion) is worn vertically in the center of the space formed by the lower curves of the knot and the upper edge of the braid (see figs 25–8 and 25–9).

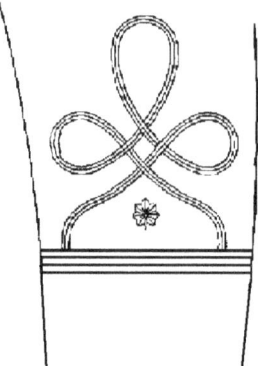

Figure 25–8. Sleeve ornamentation, blue mess, field and company grade officers

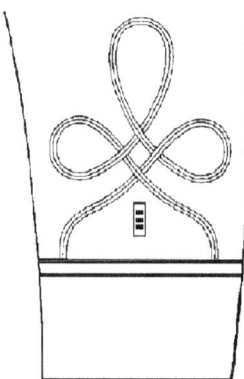

Figure 25–9. Sleeve ornamentation, blue mess, warrant officers

(3) Previously authorized sleeve ornamentation, which consists of the sleeve band, the branch insignia centered in the space formed by the lower curves of the trefoil and the upper edge of the sleeve band, and the number of trefoils appropriate to the specific grade of the wearer, is authorized for wear for the life of the jacket. This option is for commissioned officers only, and applies only to jackets purchased prior to 11 August 1975. This ornamentation is not authorized for jackets purchased after 11 August 1975.

(4) Enlisted personnel wear a ⅛–inch soutache braid of gold-colored nylon or rayon, 3 inches above the bottom of each sleeve (see fig 25–10).

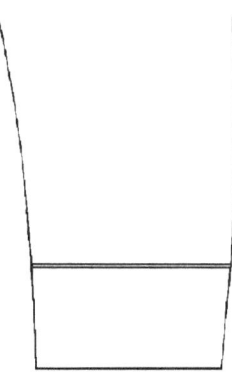

Figure 25–10. Sleeve ornamentation, blue mess, enlisted

### 25–6. Skirts

*a.* The Army blue mess skirt is knee length, with a one-piece front with waist darts (one on each side), a four-piece back, a slide-fastener closure on the left side, and a sewn-on waistband that is closed with three hooks and eyes. The skirt is fully lined.

*b.* The Army blue evening mess skirt is full length, with a one-piece front with waist darts (one on each side), a four-piece back, a slide-fastener closure on the left side, a sewn-on waistband that is closed with three hooks and eyes, and an overlapped center back pleat. The skirt is fully lined.

### 25–7. Blouse, white formal

The blouse is a tuck-in style made of polyester and cotton fabric with a front closure containing seven removable dome-shaped buttons. On each side of the front opening, there are three vertical rows of ruffles. The blouse has short sleeves and a rounded collar.

### 25–8. Neck tab, black, dress

The material is polyester and cotton broadcloth, in Army shade 305. It is a quarter-moon neck tab, which fits under the collar of the white formal blouse.

### 25–9. Capes, Army black and blue

As an option, all female officers are authorized to wear the Army blue or the Army black cape, instead of the black all-weather coat, when wearing the Army blue uniform after duty hours. Enlisted personnel may not wear the cape. (See paras 27–6*a* and *b* for a complete description.)

### 25–10. Cummerbund, black

The cummerbund will be made from a commercial design. It is made of silk or satin material, with four or five pleats running the entire length of the cummerbund. The black cummerbund is worn with the pleats facing down.

### 25–11. Headgear

No headgear is authorized for wear by female personnel with the Army blue mess or blue evening mess uniforms.

### 25–12. Items normally worn with the Army blue mess and blue evening mess uniforms

*a.* Accessories.

(1) Buttons (para 27–4).

(2) Capes.

*(a)* Black (para 27–6*a*).

*(b)* Blue (para 27–6*b*).

(3) Coat, black all weather (para 27–8).

(4) Gloves.

*(a)* Black, leather, unisex, dress (only when the black all-weather coat is worn) (para 27–12*b*).

*(b)* White, dress (para 27–12*c*).

(5) Handbag, black, dress fabric (para 27–13*b*).

(6) Scarf, black (para 27–21*a*).

(7) Shoes, pumps, black (paras 27–23*f* and *g*).

(8) Stockings, sheer (para 27–24*d*).

(9) Umbrella, black (para 27–27).

(10) Undergarments (para 27–28).

*b.* Insignia, awards, badges, and accouterments worn on the Army blue mess and evening mess uniforms.

(1) Aiguillette, dress (officers only) (para 28–26).

(2) Insignia.

*(a)* Branch (paras 28–10 and 28–12*a*). Officers wear branch insignia as prescribed in para 25–5*e*(1) and (3).

*(b)* Grade (paras 28–5 through 28–8). Officers wear grade insignia as prescribed in para 25–5*e*(1) and (2).

*(c)* Regimental distinctive insignia (para 28–23).

(3) Service stripes (enlisted personnel only) (para 28–27).

(4) Decorations and service medals, miniature (para 29–9).

(5) U.S. badges (combat and special skill, dress miniature, and identification) (paras 29–17*c* and 29–18*c*).

## 25–13. General guidelines

Personnel will wear knee-length mess skirts no longer than 1 inch above or 2 inches below the crease in the back of the knee. The blue evening mess skirt is worn full length. Personnel may wear the black dress gloves and black scarf when wearing the black all-weather coat. Personnel may wear white gloves with all uniforms. The black pumps or the black fabric pumps with sheer stockings are the authorized footwear for the blue mess and blue evening mess uniforms. (See paras 28–10*d* and 28–19 for information on lapel facings. (See para 28–10*e* for information on color of ornamentation and branch insignia for detailed officers.)

## Chapter 26
## Army Black Mess and Evening Mess Uniforms—Female

### 26–1. Authorization for wear

The Army black mess and black evening mess uniforms are authorized for year-round wear by all female officers. The Army blue mess and blue evening mess uniforms replaced the Army black mess and evening mess uniforms. The wear-out date for the Army black mess and evening mess uniforms is 30 September 2003. Effective 1 October 2003, only the blue mess and evening mess uniforms may be worn for the occasions listed in para 26–3, below. Enlisted females are not authorized to wear the black mess uniforms.

### 26–2. Composition

*a.* The Army black mess uniform comprises the Army black jacket, the Army black knee-length skirt, the formal white blouse with black dress neck tab, and the black cummerbund (see fig 26–1).

Figure 26–1. Army black mess uniform, other officers

*b*. The Army black evening mess uniform comprises the Army black jacket, the Army black full-length skirt, the formal white blouse with black dress neck tab, and the black cummerbund (see fig 26–2).

Figure 26-2. Army black evening mess uniform, general officers

## 26–3. Occasions for wear

The following are appropriate occasions for personnel to wear the Army black mess and black evening mess uniforms:

  *a.* Social functions of a general or official nature, held after retreat.

  *b.* All private, formal social functions held after retreat.

## 26–4. Materials

  *a.* Wool tropical, 8.5-ounce weight, black, Army shade 149.

  *b.* Polyester and wool blend fabric in tropical 10-ounce weight, black, Army shade 332.

## 26–5. Jacket, Army black mess

  *a.* Design. The jacket is made from an approved specification or pattern.

  *b.* General description. The jacket is single-breasted with a natural-waist length and a shawl-type collar. It has a two-piece front on each side, and a two-panel back. The front pieces have three 20-ligne buttons on each side, and the shoulders have two loops for the attachment of shoulder boards or shoulder knots.

  *c.* Shoulder ornamentation and insignia.

  (1) General officers. Detachable shoulder knots are worn on each shoulder, fastened to the shoulder loops and positioned with the button on the inside shoulder seam nearest the collar. A description of shoulder knots is provided in para 25–5*d*(1). All general officers will wear the shoulder knots attached to the shoulders of the Army black mess jacket.

  (2) Other commissioned and warrant officers. Detachable shoulder boards are worn on each shoulder snapped to the jacket through the shoulder loops, with the square end of the shoulder board positioned on the outside shoulder seam. (See para 28–8*c* for a general description of shoulder boards.)

  *d.* Sleeve ornamentation.

  (1) General officers wear a cuff of blue-black velvet braid, 4 inches in width, positioned ⅛ inch from the bottom edge of each sleeve. A band of oak leaves in groups of two, 1 inch in width, are embroidered on each cuff of braid, 1 inch below the upper edge, in gold bullion, synthetic metallic gold, or gold-colored nylon or rayon. General officer grade insignia is centered on the outside of the sleeve, 1 inch above the upper edge of the cuff braid. When general officers wear their branch insignia, it is centered on the outside of the sleeves 1 inch above the upper edge of the cuff braid. Grade insignia is positioned 1 inch above the branch insignia. If branch insignia is worn, general officers will wear the non-subdued, metal pin-on insignia. Grade insignia is embroidered silver bullion. General officer stars are 1 inch in diameter and are worn with one point facing upward. The following describes general officer stars:

  *(a)* General insignia is four stars, with 1¼ inches between the midpoints, centered horizontally on the outside of the sleeves (see fig 25–4).

  *(b)* Lieutenant general insignia is three stars, with 1⅜ inches between the midpoints, with the middle star centered horizontally on the outside of the sleeves (see fig 25–5).

  *(c)* Major general insignia is two stars, with 2 inches between the midpoints, centered horizontally on the outside of the sleeves (see fig 25–6).

  *(d)* Brigadier general insignia is one star centered horizontally on the outside of the sleeves (see fig 25–7).

  (2) Other commissioned and warrant officers wear a band of black mohair braid or black mercerized cotton braid, ½ inch wide, sewn on each sleeve, with the lower edge parallel to, and 3 inches above the bottom edge of each sleeve. Detachable shoulder boards are worn on each shoulder, snapped to the jacket through the shoulder loops, with the square end of the shoulder board positioned on the outside shoulder seam. (See para 28–8*c* for a description of shoulder boards.)

## 26–6. Skirts

  *a.* The Army black mess skirt is the same skirt worn with the white mess uniform. It is a black knee-length skirt, with a one-panel front and four-panel back of straight design, with a waistband and a zipper closure on the left side.

  *b.* The Army black evening mess skirt is a black full-length skirt, with one-panel front and four-panel back of straight design, with a waistband, a zipper closure on the left side, and an overlapped center back pleat.

## 26–7. Blouse, white formal

The blouse is a tuck-in style made of polyester and cotton fabric, with a front closure containing seven removable dome-shaped buttons. On each side of the front opening, there are three vertical rows of ruffles. The blouse has short sleeves and a rounded collar.

## 26–8. Neck tab, black, dress

The material is polyester and cotton broadcloth, in Army shade 305. It is a quarter-moon neck tab, which fits under the collar of the white formal blouse.

## 26–9. Capes, Army black and blue

As an option, all female officers are authorized to wear the Army blue or the Army black cape instead of the black all-weather coat, when wearing the Army black uniform after duty hours. (See paras 27–6*a* and *b* for a complete description.)

## 26–10. Cummerbund, black

The cummerbund will be made from a commercial design. It is made of silk or satin material, with four or five pleats running the entire length of the cummerbund. The black cummerbund is worn with the pleats facing down.

## 26–11. Headgear

No headgear is authorized for wear with the Army black mess or black evening mess uniforms.

## 26–12. Items normally worn with the Army black mess and black evening mess uniforms

*a.* Accessories.

(1) Buttons (para 27–4).

(2) Capes.

*(a)* Black (para 27–6*a*).

*(b)* Blue (para 27–6*b*).

(3) Coat, black all weather (para 27–8).

(4) Gloves.

*(a)* Black, leather, unisex, dress (only when the black all-weather coat is worn) (para 27–12*b*).

*(b)* White, dress (para 27–12*c*).

(5) Handbag, black, dress fabric (para 27–13*b*).

(6) Scarf, black (para 27–21*a*).

(7) Shoes, pumps, black (paras 27–23*f* and *g*).

(8) Stockings, sheer (para 27–24*d*).

(9) Umbrella, black (para 27–27).

(10) Undergarments (para 27–28).

*b.* Insignia, awards, badges, and accouterments worn on the Army black mess and evening mess uniforms.

(1) Aiguillette, dress (officers only) (para 28–26).

(2) Insignia.

*(a)* Branch insignia (paras 28–10 and 28–12*a*). Officers wear branch insignia as prescribed in para 26–5*d*(1).

*(b)* Grade insignia (paras 28–5 through 28–8). Officers wear grade insignia as prescribed in para 26–5*d*(1) and (2).

*(c)* Regimental distinctive insignia (para 28–23).

(3) Decorations and service medals, miniature (para 29–9).

(4) U.S. badges (combat and special skill, dress miniature, and identification) (paras 29–17*c* and 29–18*c*).

## 26–13. General guidelines

Personnel will wear knee-length mess skirts no longer than 1 inch above or 2 inches below the crease in the back of the knee. The black evening mess skirt is worn full length. Personnel may wear the black dress gloves and black scarf when wearing the black all-weather coat. Personnel may wear white gloves with all uniforms. The black fabric pumps with sheer stockings are the only authorized footwear for these uniforms.

# Part Five
# Accessories, Decorations, and Insignia

# Chapter 27
# Uniform Accessories

## 27–1. General

This chapter lists, in alphabetical order, most uniform accessories referenced in the individual uniform chapters.

## 27–2. Belts, web waist and buckles

*a.* Belt, web waist, black tip.

(1) Type. The black tip belt is a clothing bag issue item.

(2) Description. The belt is black cotton web or black woven elastic, with a black tip, and is 1¼ inches wide.

(3) How worn.

*(a)* The black tip belt is worn with the black, open-faced buckle. It is worn so that the tipped end passes through the buckle to the wearer's left; the tipped end will not extend more than 2 inches beyond the edge of the buckle. The plain end of the belt may extend beyond the keeper portion of the inside of the buckle, as long as it is not visible when worn.

*(b)* All personnel will wear the black tip belt and black, open-faced buckle with utility uniforms that have belt loops.

*b.* Belt, web waist, brass tip.

(1) Type. The brass tip belt is a clothing bag issue item.

(2) Description. The belt is black cotton web or black woven elastic, with a brass tip. The men's belt is 1¼ inches wide, and the women's belt is 1 inch wide.

(3) How worn.

*(a)* The brass tip belt is worn only with the brass buckle. The belt is worn so that the tipped end passes through the buckle to the wearer's left for males, and the wearer's right for females. The tipped end will extend beyond the end of the buckle so that only the brass tip is visible, and no fabric portion of the belt can be seen beyond the buckle. The plain end (no tip) of the belt may extend beyond the keeper portion of the inside of the buckle, as long as it is not visible when worn.

*(b)* Males wear the 1¼-inch brass tip belt and brass buckle with service and dress uniforms. Males may wear suspenders of a commercial design with dress uniforms, as long as they are not visible.

*(c)* Females wear the 1-inch brass tip belt with the service uniform when wearing slacks with the tuck-in version of the AG 415 shirt. Females are not required to wear a belt when wearing the overblouse with the slacks.

*c.* Buckle, belt, black, open-faced.

(1) Type. The buckle is a clothing bag issue item.

(2) Description. A black, opened-faced brass buckle, 1–11/16 inches long and 1⅝ inches wide (see fig 27–1).

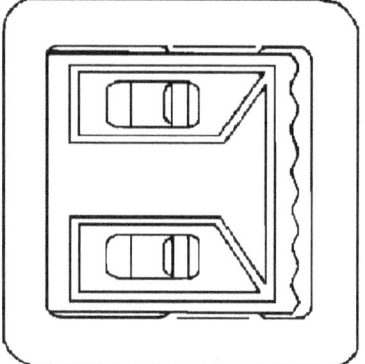

**Figure 27–1. Black buckle**

(3) How worn. The buckle is attached to the end of the black web belt with the black tip, and is worn only with utility uniforms.

*d.* Buckle, belt, brass.

(1) Type. The buckle is a clothing bag issue item.

(2) Description. A brass buckle, 1–11/16 inches long and 1⅝ inches wide for males; 1⅛ inches by 2 inches for females (see fig 27–2).

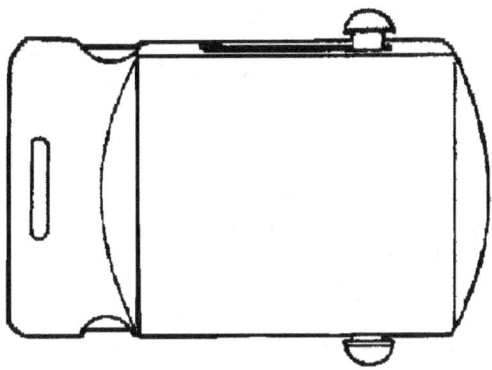

Figure 27–2. Brass buckle

(3) How worn. The buckle is attached to the end of the black web belt with the brass tip and is worn with service and dress uniforms.

### 27–3. Boots, combat, leather, black

*a.* Type. The combat boots are clothing bag issue items.

*b.* Description. The issue boot is made of black leather with a deep lug tread sole made of vulcanized rubber, a removable cushioned insert, a closed-loop speed lace system, and a leather padded collar. Soldiers are required to possess two pairs of issue (specification) boots.

*c.* How worn.

(1) The boots are laced diagonally with black laces, with the excess lace tucked into the top of the boot under the bloused trousers or slacks, or wrapped around the top of the boot. Metal cleats and side tabs are not authorized for wear except by honor guards and ceremonial units in the performance of ceremonial duties. When metal cleats and side tabs are authorized for wear, commanders will furnish them to soldiers at no cost. Sewn-in or laced-in zipper inserts are not authorized.

(2) A vulcanized rubber sole is the only outsole material that currently meets the need for durability and traction on surfaces. Other materials (that may be of a lighter weight) may have significant problems in these areas.

(3) Only soldiers authorized to wear the tan, green, or maroon berets, those assigned to Air Assault coded positions, and MPs performing MP duties may wear bloused (tucked-in or by the use of blousing rubbers/bands) trousers or slacks with black leather combat boots. When trousers or slacks are bloused, personnel will not wrap them around the leg so tightly so as to present a pegged appearance. When the trousers or slacks are bloused properly, the bloused portion of the trousers or slacks should not extend below the third eyelet from the top of the boot. Soldiers will not blouse boots so that the bloused portion extends down to the ankle area of the boot.

*d.* Optional boots.

(1) As an option, soldiers may wear commercial boots of a design similar to that of the standard issue combat boot, 8 to 10 inches in height. The boots must be made of black leather, with a plain or capped toe, and have a black, vulcanized rubber outsole. Boots made of either patent leather or poromeric are not authorized. Soldiers may wear optional boots in lieu of the standard issue black combat boot; however, they do not replace issue boots as a mandatory possession item.

(2) Personnel are authorized to wear the green or black Army jungle boot in lieu of the standard issue black combat boot. No other canvas and leather boot is authorized for wear. The green jungle boot is no longer available for purchase; therefore, personnel may wear this boot only as long as it is serviceable. Personnel may not wear the black or green jungle boot in formation, unless authorized by the commander. A vulcanized rubber sole is the only outsole material that currently meets the need for durability and traction on surfaces. Other materials (that may be of a lighter weight) may have significant problems in these areas.

(3) Optional boots are not authorized for wear when the commander issues and prescribes standard organizational footwear for safety or environmental reasons (such as insulated boots or safety shoes). Personnel may wear specialty boots authorized for wear by specific groups of soldiers, such as the tanker boot, only if the commander authorizes such wear. Soldiers may not wear optional boots in formation when uniformity in appearance is required.

(4) Soldiers are not authorized to wear any boot with the brand name "Hi-Tech," or any other boot deemed to have

a sneaker-type construction, unless they were authorized an exception to policy by Headquarters, Department of the Army.

*e.* Organizational boots. When prescribed and issued by the commander according to CTA 50–900, personnel may wear, instead of the combat boot, such organizational boots as flyer or safety boots with field and utility uniforms.

## 27–4. Buttons

*a.* Regular Army

(1) Type. The buttons are clothing bag issue items.

(2) Description. Regular Army buttons are yellow-gold plated with the coat of arms of the United States superimposed. Buttons are available in sizes 20-ligne, 25-ligne, 30-ligne, and 36-ligne; there are 40-ligne to an inch. The previously optional white gold anodized aluminum buttons are no longer authorized for wear (see fig 27–3).

**Figure 27–3. Regular Army button**

(3) How worn. Regular Army buttons are worn on the coats and jackets of service, dress, and mess uniforms, except as provided below.

*b.* Corps of Engineers.

(1) Type. The buttons are optional purchase items.

(2) Description. The buttons are yellow-gold plated and have an eagle holding a scroll in its beak inscribed with the word "Essayons." In the distance is a bastion with embrasures surrounded by water, with the sun rising over the top of the water. The buttons are available in sizes 20-ligne, 25-ligne, 30-ligne, and 36-ligne. The previously optional white gold anodized aluminum buttons are no longer authorized for wear (see fig 27–4).

**Figure 27–4. Corps of Engineers button**

(3) How worn. The buttons are worn on the coats and jackets of service, dress, and mess uniforms by commissioned officers of the Corps of Engineers and all warrant officers with a Corps of Engineers primary specialty.

## 27–5. Cap, cold weather, AG shade 489

*a.* Type. The cold-weather cap is an optional purchase item.

*b.* Description. The cap is made of AG shade 489 fabric with a black synthetic fur visor and side flaps. Snap fasteners are attached to hold the visor and flaps in the up position. An eyelet in the center of the front visor is provided to center and attach headgear insignia. Because of the thickness of the fur pile, headgear insignia worn on the cap must have a center post and screw. Therefore, all soldiers will wear the male headgear insignia on the cold-weather cap (see para 28–3 and fig 27–5).

**Figure 27–5. Cold-weather service cap, AG 489**

*c.* How worn. The cap is worn straight on the head so that the headgear insignia is centered on the forehead. No hair will be visible on the forehead. The side flaps are fastened under the chin when the flaps are worn down. The cap is authorized for wear when wearing the black windbreaker with the class B uniform and with the black all-weather coat with service, dress, mess, hospital duty, and food service uniforms. It is not authorized for wear when the black pullover or cardigan sweaters are worn as outer garments with the class B uniform.

## 27–6. Capes

*a.* Cape, black, female (officers only).

(1) Type. The cape is an optional purchase item.

(2) Description. The black cape will be made from an approved specification or pattern. The material is wool gabardine, black, in Army shade 149. The cape is fully lined with white rayon satin. The cape has fitted shoulders with front and back darts, a high, rounded soft collar, and Army slits, and it is devoid of visible stitching. The black cape is approximately knee length and will extend at least 1 inch below the skirt hem of the Army mess uniform short skirts (see fig 27–6).

Figure 27–6. Black cape, female officers

(3) How worn. The cape may be worn with the Army blue and white dress uniforms, and with the Army blue, black, white, and all-white mess and evening mess uniforms.

b. Cape, blue, female (officers only).

(1) Type. The cape is an optional purchase item.

(2) Description. The blue cape will be made from an approved specification or pattern. The materials are wool elastique, dark blue, in Army shade 150; wool gabardine, dark blue, in Army shade 150; wool tropical, dark blue, in Army shade 150; polyester-wool tropical, dark blue, in Army shade 450; or polyester-wool gabardine, dark blue, in Army shade 450. The blue cape is finger-tip length, with fitted shoulders and a high neck closure secured with a hook and eye fastener (see fig 27–7). The female blue cape is lined with rayon twill or satin, in one of the following colors.

Figure 27–7. Blue cape, female officers

*(a)* General officers: dark blue.

*(b)* All other officers: the first-named color of the basic branch.

(3) How worn. Officers may wear the cape with the Army blue and white dress uniforms, and with the Army blue, black, white, and all-white mess and evening mess uniforms. Enlisted personnel are not authorized to wear the cape.

*c.* Cape, blue, male (officers only).

(1) Type. The cape is an optional purchase item.

(2) Description. The blue cape will be made from an approved specification or pattern. The materials are cloth, wool, and broadcloth, dark blue, in Army shade 150; cloth, wool, and gabardine, dark blue, in Army shade 150; cloth, wool, and elastique, dark blue, in Army shade 150. The cape will reach to at least the midpoint of the knee, but it will be no lower than 2 inches below the knee (see fig 27–8). The lining of the Army blue cape is rayon, acetate, or another synthetic fabric, with a satin face and wool nap back, in one of the following colors:

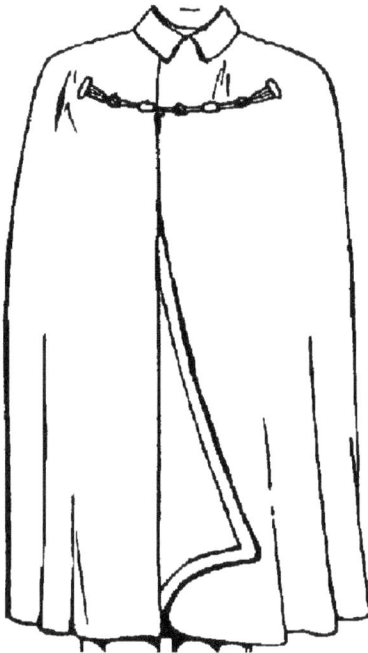

**Figure 27–8. Blue cape, male officers**

*(a)* General officers: dark blue.

*(b)* All other officers: the first-named color of the basic branch.

(3) How worn. Officers may wear the cape with Army white and blue dress, mess, and evening mess uniforms. Enlisted personnel are not authorized to wear the cape.

## 27–7. Chaplain's apparel

*a.* Scarves.

(1) Type. The scarves are organizational issue items.

(2) Description.

*(a)* Christian faith. A scarf of standard Army ecclesiastical pattern, of suitable black material, 9 feet long. On each end, in gold-colored machine embroidery, the scarf is embroidered with the coat of arms of the United States, 3 inches high, with the Christian chaplain's insignia, 4 inches high, spaced ½ inch below the coat of arms. The bottom edge of the Christian insignia is 6½ inches from the end of the scarf.

*(b)* Jewish faith. A scarf of standard Army ecclesiastical pattern, of suitable white or black material, 9 feet long. On each end, in gold-colored machine embroidery, the scarf is embroidered with the coat of arms of the United States, 3 inches high, with the Jewish chaplain's insignia, 4 inches high, spaced ½ inch below the coat of arms. The bottom edge of the Jewish insignia is 6½ inches from the end of the scarf.

*(c)* Muslim faith. A scarf of standard Army ecclesiastical pattern, of suitable white or black material, 9 feet long. On each end, in gold-colored machine embroidery, the scarf is embroidered with the coat of arms of the United States, 3 inches high, with the Muslim chaplain's insignia, 4 inches high, spaced ½ inch below the coat of arms. The bottom edge of the Muslim insignia is 6½ inches from the end of the scarf.

*b.* Vestments. Chaplains are authorized to wear the military uniform, vestments, or other appropriate attire prescribed by ecclesiastical law or denominational practice, when conducting religious services.

*c.* Chaplain candidates will wear a distinctive nameplate, as prescribed, and the staff specialist branch insignia, in accordance with AR 165–1.

*d.* How worn. Chaplains may wear the chaplain's scarf or stole with the uniform, vestments, or other appropriate attire when conducting religious services.

## 27–8. Coats, black, all weather (male and female)

*a.* Type. The black all-weather coat is a clothing bag issue item.

*b.* Description. The black all-weather coat is made of polyester/cotton (65/35) in Army shade 385. The coat is a six-button, double-breasted model with a belt, convertible collar that buttons at the neck, gun flap, shoulder loops, adjustable sleeve straps, welt pockets with two inside hanging pockets, and zip-out liner. The back of the coat has a yoke and center vent. The coat is one-quarter lined with basic material; the sleeve lining is made of nylon taffeta (see fig 27–9). There is no wear-out date for the interim version of the double-breasted coat made from polyester/cotton (50/50).

**Figure 27–9. Army black all-weather coat**

*c.* How worn. Personnel may wear the all-weather coat with or without the liner. They will wear the coat buttoned, except for the neck closure, which personnel may wear open or closed (see paras 4–5*d* and 17–12*b* for exceptions). Male and female coats are buttoned and belted from opposite directions. The black scarf is authorized for wear with the all-weather coat. Personnel may wear the coat with the service, dress, mess, hospital duty, and food service uniforms. The black all-weather coat is authorized for wear with utility uniforms only in a garrison environment when personnel have not been issued organizational rain gear. Only non-subdued pin-on grade insignia is worn on this coat. When the grade insignia is removed from the coat, personnel may wear the coat with civilian clothing.

## 27–9. Cover, cap, rain
*a.* Type. The cap cover is an optional purchase item.

*b.* Description. The cover is made of transparent plastic with a visor protector. There is elastic webbing around the peripheral opening of the crown cover and the edge of the visor cover.

*c.* How worn. Males may wear the cover when wearing the blue or white service caps. The cover will completely cover the crown and visor.

## 27–10. Cuff links and studs
*a.* Type. Cuff links and studs are optional purchase items.

*b.* Description. Males may wear the cuff links and studs with the following uniforms.

(1) The Army blue evening mess uniform. Personnel may wear plain white studs or cuff links (such as white mother-of-pearl), with or without rims of platinum or white gold.

(2) The Army blue and white mess uniforms. Personnel may wear gold or gold-colored metal studs or cuff links with a round, plain face. The cuff links may be post or link type, ½ to ¾ inch in diameter; studs may be ¼ to ⅜ inch in diameter.

(3) The Army blue and white dress uniforms. If worn, the cuff links will be plain gold or gold-colored metal, as described in paragraph 27–10b(2), above.

## 27–11. Cummerbunds

*a.* Cummerbund, black, female and male.

(1) Type. The cummerbund is an optional purchase item.

(2) Description. The cummerbund is black, made of a commercial design, in silk or satin material, with four or five pleats running the entire length of the cummerbund.

(3) How worn. The cummerbund is worn with the pleats facing down. Females wear the black cummerbund with the black, blue, and white mess and evening mess uniforms; males wear it with the white and blue mess uniforms. The male bow tie and cummerbund must be made of the same material.

*b.* Cummerbund, white, female.

(1) Type. The cummerbund is an optional purchase item.

(2) Description. The cummerbund is white, made of a commercial design, in silk or satin material, with four or five pleats running the entire length of the cummerbund.

(3) How worn. The white cummerbund is worn with the pleats facing down. Females wear the white cummerbund with the all-white mess uniform.

## 27–12. Gloves

*a.* Gloves, black, with inserts, unisex, leather shell.

(1) Type. The gloves are clothing bag issue items.

(2) Description. The gloves are a five-finger design in a slip-on style. An adjustable strap and buckle is provided on the back of the gloves. The inserts are black wool and are worn inside the black leather shell gloves. There is no wear-out date for the green wool inserts, which may be worn until stocks are exhausted or until unserviceable.

(3) How worn. These gloves are authorized for wear with or without cold-weather outer garments (to include the DBDU parka). Soldiers may wear the black leather shell gloves with utility uniforms without cold-weather outer garments, provided sleeves are rolled down. Personnel may not wear the inserts without the leather shell gloves when worn with utility uniforms and cold weather outer garments.

*b.* Gloves, black, leather, unisex, dress.

(1) Type. The gloves are clothing bag issue items.

(2) Description. The gloves are black leather in an approved specification or pattern, or of a similar commercial design.

(3) How worn. The gloves are authorized for wear with the class A service, Army green dress, and Army green maternity dress uniforms, and when wearing the black all-weather coat, windbreaker, or capes.

*c.* Gloves, white dress.

(1) Type. The gloves are optional purchase items.

(2) Description. The gloves are made of cotton, kid, doeskin, silk, or other material of appropriate commercial design.

(3) How worn. The gloves are authorized for year-round wear with the Army blue and white dress uniforms, and the Army blue, white, and black mess and evening mess uniforms. When prescribed by the commander, military police may wear white gloves with service uniforms.

## 27–13. Handbags

*a.* Handbag, clutch-type, leather, polyurethane, or vinyl.

(1) Type. The handbag is an optional purchase item.

(2) Description. The handbag is black and is made of leather, polyurethane, or vinyl, in a commercial design with a zipper, snap, or envelope-type closure. The handbag may have a wrist strap, but not a shoulder strap.

(3) How worn. Females may carry the clutch-type handbag with the female service uniforms, and with the utility uniforms while in a garrison (non-field) environment. The leather version of this handbag is authorized for use with the female Army blue uniform, during and after duty hours.

*b.* Handbag, fabric or leather, black, dress.

(1) Type. The handbag is an optional purchase item.

(2) Description. The handbag is untrimmed, in black leather or fabric, of a commercial design, envelope or clutch style, with or without a chain or strap.

(3) Wear.

*(a)* Females may carry the black leather handbag with the Army blue uniform, during and after duty hours.

*(b)* Females may carry the black fabric handbag with the black, white, and blue mess and evening mess uniforms. It is also authorized for use with the Army blue uniform, after duty hours.

*c.* Handbag, fabric or leather, white, dress.

(1) Type. The handbag is an optional purchase item.

(2) Description. The handbag is untrimmed, in white leather or fabric, of a commercial design, envelope or clutch style, with or without a chain or strap.

(3) Wear.

(a) Females may carry the white leather handbag when wearing the Army white dress uniform, during or after duty hours.

(b) The white fabric handbag is authorized for use with the Army all-white mess uniform. Females also may carry the handbag when wearing the Army white dress uniform, after duty hours.

(4) The handbag and shoes must be made of the same or similar material.

d. Handbag, shoulder, black.

(1) Type. The handbag is a one-time cash allowance item as part of the initial clothing bag allowance.

(2) Description. The handbag is a commercial design, black, in polyurethane or leather, with a shoulder strap attached.

(3) How worn. Females may carry this handbag with the service and Army blue uniforms, and with utility uniforms while in a garrison (non-field) environment. Females may carry the bag in the hand or wear it over one shoulder. Soldiers may not wear the shoulder bag in such a manner that the strap is draped diagonally across the body, with the purse resting on the hip opposite the shoulder holding the strap.

## 27–14. Hat, drill sergeant

a. Female.

(1) Type. The hat is an organizational issue item.

(2) Description. The hat is made from an approved specification or pattern.

(3) How worn.

(a) The hat is worn with the utility and service uniforms by female drill sergeants assigned to valid drill sergeant positions. Noncommissioned officer (NCO) faculty members of a drill sergeant school who have graduated from drill sergeant school and are actively engaged in drill sergeant instruction will wear this hat. Upon release from this assignment, NCOs are no longer authorized to wear the drill sergeant hat.

(b) The hat is worn straight on the head with no hair visible on the forehead below the front brim of the hat. Personnel will wear the hat so as to retain its original design and will not crush, flatten, dent, or otherwise reshape the hat. Personnel will wear the hat with the left side of the brim snapped, and the right side parallel to the ground. The chinstrap is worn with the chinstrap keeper pushed up under the chin. The headgear insignia worn on the drill sergeant hat is described in paragraph 28–3c (see fig 27–10).

Figure 27–10. Hat, drill sergeant, female

*b.* Males.

(1) Type. The hat is an organizational issue item.

(2) Description. The hat is made from an approved specification or pattern.

(3) How worn.

*(a)* The hat is worn with the service and utility uniforms by male drill sergeants assigned to valid drill sergeant positions. Noncommissioned officer faculty members of a drill sergeant school, who have graduated from drill sergeant school and are actively engaged in drill sergeant instruction, will wear this hat. Upon release from this assignment, NCOs are no longer authorized to wear the drill sergeant hat.

*(b)* The black leather strap, issued with the hat, is worn threaded through the appropriate eyelets in the brim of the hat, so that the strap goes around the front of the hat, and the buckle is fastened and centered at the back of the wearer's head. The running end of the strap will be to the wearer's left. Personnel will wear the hat without noticeable tilt to the front, rear, or either side, so the brim of the hat is as nearly level in all directions as is possible. No modifications in the shape of the hat are authorized. The headgear insignia worn on the drill sergeant hat is prescribed in paragraph 28–3*b* (see fig 27–11).

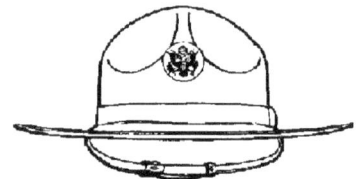

**Figure 27–11. Hat, drill sergeant, male**

### 27–15. Judge's apparel

*a.* Type. Judicial robes are organizational issue items.

*b.* Description. The judicial robes are of the type customarily worn in the U.S. Court of Appeals for the Armed Forces.

*c.* How worn. Judicial robes are worn by officers designated as military judges and appellate military judges when participating in trials by court-martial, hearings by a court of military review, and other judicial proceedings. When a judicial robe is worn, personnel will wear a service uniform underneath the robe.

### 27–16. Military Police accessories

*a.* Type. MP accessories are organizational issue items.

*b.* Description.

(1) Badge, Military Police.

(2) Belt, black leather, 2¼ inches wide, with a buckle.

(3) Brassards, dark blue or black, non-subdued; olive green, subdued.

(4) Carrier, club ring.

(5) Case, ammunition magazine, black leather.

(6) Case, first aid, black leather.

(7) Case, handcuffs, black leather.

(8) Club, policeman's, with leather thong.

(9) Duty jacket.

(10) Gloves, white cotton.

(11) Flashlight.

(12) Flashlight, carrier ring.

(13) Handcuffs, ratchet type, double lock.

(14) Hat, service, with cover, female; cap, service, white, MP, male.

(15) Helmet liner, MP.

(16) Holster, black leather.

(17) Lanyard, pistol, olive-drab (OD) nylon cord.

(18) Lanyard, pistol, white nylon cord.

(19) Whistle, patrolman, brass.

(20) Whistle, patrolman, OD.

*c.* How worn. The articles listed in b, above, are authorized for wear with the class A, B, and utility uniforms by MP personnel, while performing MP duties. When wearing combat boots with service uniform trousers or slacks, personnel will blouse the trousers or slacks. Wear of the Military Police badge is determined by local policy. The Military Police badge is not authorized for wear on the utility uniforms, but it may be worn suspended from a fob device on the class B uniform (see figs 27–12 and 27–13).

Figure 27–12. MP accessories, male

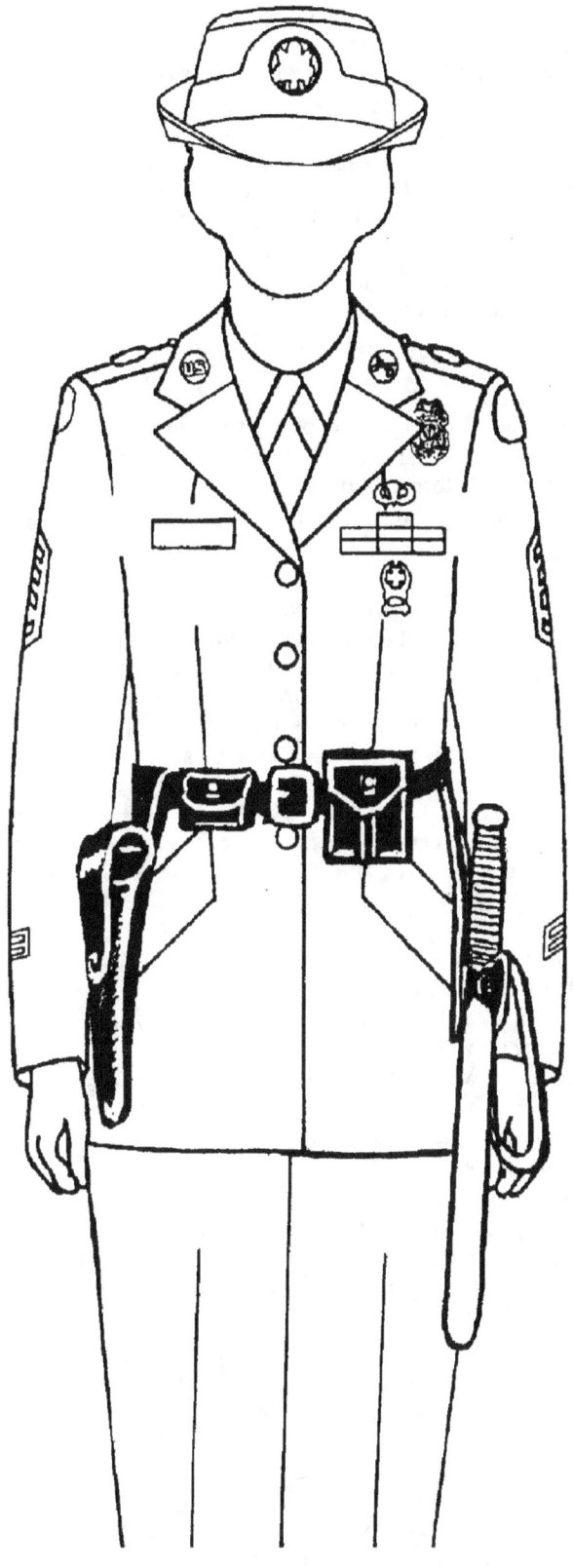

Figure 27-13. MP accessories, female

## 27–17. Neckgaiter

*a.* Type. The neckgaiter is an optional purchase item.

*b.* Description. The neckgaiter is a dark brown or tan knitted cylindrical tube of approximately 10x15 inches, consisting of 90 percent polypropylene and 10 percent Lycra. The neckgaiter is camouflage compatible; one size fits all soldiers.

*c.* How worn.

(1) The neckgaiter is authorized for optional wear with the temperate, hot-weather, enhanced hot-weather, and maternity BDUs; with the extended cold-weather clothing system (ECWCS), and other cold-weather uniforms. It may be worn as a neck warmer, hood, balaclava, ear band, or hat in cold, windy, or dusty environments.

(2) Commanders cannot require soldiers to purchase or wear the neckgaiter on an individual basis. However, if the unit purchases the neckgaiter per the Federal Acquisition Regulation (FAR) from within current available operating funds, the commander can require the unit to wear the neckgaiter.

## 27–18. Neck tabs, female

*a.* Black, dress.

(1) Type. The black dress neck tab is an optional purchase item.

(2) Description. The material is polyester and cotton broadcloth, in Army shade 305. It is a quarter-moon neck tab, which fits under the collar of the white formal blouse.

(3) How worn. The black dress neck tab is worn with the white formal blouse, with the mess and the evening mess uniforms.

*b.* Black, service.

(1) Type. The black service neck tab is a clothing bag issue item.

(2) Description. The material is polyester and cotton, pre-cured durable press, plain-weave poplin, in an inverted V-shape, in Army shade 305. The neck tab wraps around the neck under the collar of the female AG shade 415 (poly/cotton) and AG shade 469 (poly/wool) long- and short-sleeved, tuck-in and overblouse shirts, and fastens to itself with a Velcro hook-and-pile fastener. The neck tab design is one of overlapping tabs forming an angle.

(3) How worn. The neck tab is worn with the class A uniform, and with the AG shade 415 (poly/cotton) and AG shade 469 (poly/wool) long- and short-sleeved shirts, in the tuck-in and overblouse styles. The neck tab is required for wear when the long-sleeved shirt is worn without the class A coat. It is also required for wear when the long-sleeved and short-sleeved shirts are worn with the class A coat. The neck tab is optional when the short-sleeved and long-sleeved shirts are worn with the black pullover and cardigan sweaters.

## 27–19. Neckties, male

*a.* Necktie, bow, black, dress or mess.

(1) Type. The bow tie is an optional purchase item.

(2) Description. The material is black silk or satin of a commercial design, without stripes or figures. The bow has square ends not more than 2½ inches wide.

(3) How worn. The black bow tie is worn with the Army green dress uniform, the white and blue mess uniforms, and the Army blue and white uniforms, after retreat. Enlisted males may wear the black bow tie with the Army green dress uniform with the white shirt at social functions.

*b.* Necktie, bow, white, evening mess.

(1) Type. The white bow tie is an optional purchase item.

(2) Description. The material is plain white silk or satin, or of the same material as the shirt, without stripes or figures, in a conventional, civilian full-dress style, not more than 2½ inches wide.

(3) How worn. The white bow tie is worn with the Army blue evening mess uniform, or, as an option, males may wear it with the Army white evening mess uniform.

*c.* Necktie, four-in-hand, black, service.

(1) Type. The four-in-hand necktie is a clothing bag issue item.

(2) Description. The material is polyester, wool, tropical, or a similar type of woven fabric; a knitted fabric necktie also is authorized. The necktie will be two-fold, four-in-hand, with pointed ends. As an option, a pre-tied, snap-on necktie is authorized for wear.

(3) How worn.

*(a)* Personnel may wear the tie in a Windsor, half-Windsor, or four-in-hand knot. Use of a conservative tie tack or tie clasp is authorized. The necktie is tied so it is no shorter than 2 inches above the top of the belt buckle, and so it does not extend past the bottom of the belt buckle.

*(b)* The black four-in-hand necktie is worn with the class A uniform, and with the AG shade 415 (poly/cotton) or

the AG shade 469 (poly/wool) long-sleeved and short-sleeved shirts. The necktie is required for wear when the long-sleeved shirt is worn without the class A coat, and when the long- and short-sleeved shirts are worn with the class A coat. It is optional when the short-sleeved and long-sleeved shirts are worn with the black pullover and cardigan sweaters. The necktie is worn with the Army green dress, white, and blue uniforms before retreat or on duty. Personnel may wear the four-in-hand tie with the Army blue or white uniform after retreat, when the dress code is "military informal."

## 27–20. Overshoes, black

*a.* Type. The overshoes are optional purchase items.

*b.* Description. The material is rubber or synthetic, of a commercial design.

*c.* How worn. The overshoes are for optional wear with oxford shoes by male personnel during inclement weather, when not in formation. They are worn with service, dress, and mess uniforms.

## 27–21. Scarves

*a.* Dress, black.

(1) Type. Scarves are optional purchase items.

(2) Description. The material is wool, silk, or rayon, of a commercial design, approximately 12 by 52 inches.

(3) How worn. The scarf is authorized for wear by all personnel with the Army black all-weather coat and the windbreaker. The scarf is worn folded in half lengthwise, with the lengths crossed left over right at the neck, and the ends of the scarf tucked neatly into the neckline of the outer garment. When worn properly, the folded portion of the scarf may be slightly visible above the collar of the outer garment.

*b.* Utility, OG 208.

(1) Type. The scarves are organizational issue items.

(2) Description. The material is wool, flat-jersey knit, in OG shade 208, in a tubular, seamless-type style with reinforced ends, 51½ to 55½ inches long, by 8½ to 9½ inches wide.

(3) How worn. The scarf is authorized for wear with the cold-weather utility coats (field jackets and parkas). The scarf is worn with the lengths folded in half lengthwise and crossed left over right at the neck, with the ends of the scarf tucked neatly into the neckline of the outer garment. When worn properly, the folded portion of the scarf may be slightly visible above the collar of the outer garment.

## 27–22. Shirts

*a.* Shirt, white, short-sleeved with black neck tab, female.

(1) Type. The shirt is an optional purchase item.

(2) Description. The material is white polyester and cotton broadcloth. The shirt has short sleeves and a pointed collar. The black neck tab that is worn with the AG shade 415 shirt is worn with the short-sleeved white shirt.

(3) How worn. Enlisted females wear the shirt when they wear the Army green service uniform as a dress uniform. All females wear the shirt with the Army blue and white dress uniforms.

*b.* Shirt, white, formal, female mess.

(1) Type. The shirt is an optional purchase item.

(2) Description. The shirt is a tuck-in style made of polyester and cotton fabric, with a front closure containing seven removable, dome-shaped, pearl-like buttons. On each side of the front opening, there are three vertical rows of ruffles. The shirt has short sleeves and a rounded collar.

(3) How worn. The shirt is worn with mess and evening mess uniforms.

*c.* Shirt, white, long-sleeved, male.

(1) Type. The shirt is an optional purchase item.

(2) Description. The material is a plain polyester and cotton broadcloth, of a commercial design. The shirt has long sleeves, regular or French cuffs, and a standard turndown collar with tapered points, approximately 2⅝ inches long. Button-down or snap tab collars are not authorized.

(3) How worn. Enlisted males wear the shirt with the Army green uniform when they wear it as a dress uniform. All males wear the shirt with the Army blue and white uniforms.

*d.* Shirt, white, semiformal, dress, male mess.

(1) Type. The shirt is an optional purchase item.

(2) Description. The shirt is a white, semiformal dress shirt with long sleeves, a soft bosom, French cuffs, and a standard turndown collar.

(3) How worn. The shirt is worn with the blue and white mess uniforms.

*e.* Shirt, white, formal, male evening mess.

(1) Type. The shirt is an optional purchase item.

(2) Description. The shirt is a white, formal dress shirt with long sleeves, a stiff bosom, French cuffs, and a wing collar.

(3) How worn. The shirt is worn with the evening mess uniforms.

## 27–23. Shoes

*a.* Shoes, oxford, black, female.

(1) Type. The shoes are clothing bag issue items.

(2) Description.

*(a)* The shoes are made from an approved specification or pattern, or from a similar commercial design and are made of leather, poromeric, or patent leather. The shoe is a dress tie-oxford style, with at least three eyelets and a closed toe and heel, with the heel no higher than 2 inches. The shoe is plain, with no designs in the shoe material.

*(b)* As an option, females may wear an ankle-high boot, similar to a jodhpur (riding) boot, when wearing slacks. If worn, the boot must be plain, without straps or buckles, with a non-contrasting heel and sole, and a heel no higher than 2 inches. An inconspicuously placed zipper is authorized.

(3) How worn. The oxford shoe is worn with the service, hospital duty, and food service uniforms.

*b.* Optional footwear, inclement weather, female.

(1) Type. The footwear is an optional purchase item.

(2) Description. The footwear is a commercially designed, over-the-foot boot in black leather, rubber, or other synthetic material. The boot must be plain and untrimmed, with heels no higher than 3 inches. The boots may have an inconspicuously placed zipper or snap-type closure.

(3) How worn. Females may wear these commercial boots with service uniforms while going to or from duty in inclement weather. They also may wear these boots with the dress and mess uniforms in inclement weather, while in transit. Personnel will exchange the boots for standard footgear when indoors.

*c.* Shoes, oxford, black, male.

(1) Type. The shoes are clothing bag issue items.

(2) Description.

*(a)* The shoes are made from an approved specification or pattern or from a similar commercial design, and are made of leather, poromeric, or patent leather. The shoe is dress tie-oxford style, with at least three eyelets, and a closed toe and heel. The shoe is plain, with no designs in the shoe material.

*(b)* As an option, males may wear an ankle-high boot, similar to a jodhpur or chukka (riding) boot. If worn, the boot must be plain, without straps or buckles, with a non-contrasting heel and sole, and a heel no higher than 2 inches. An inconspicuously placed zipper is authorized.

(3) How worn. The oxford shoes are authorized for wear with service, dress, mess, evening mess, hospital duty, and food service uniforms.

*d.* Shoes, oxford, white, female.

(1) Type. The shoes are optional purchase items.

(2) Description. The shoes are made from an approved specification or pattern, or of a similar commercial design in white leather, poromeric, or patent leather. The shoe style is dress tie oxford. If worn, the shoe must be plain and untrimmed, with no designs in the material. The shoe must have at least two eyelets, a closed toe and heel, a non-contrasting heel and sole, with the heel no higher than 2 inches.

(3) How worn. The shoes are worn with the hospital duty uniforms.

*e.* Shoes, oxford, white, male.

(1) Type. The shoes are optional purchase items.

(2) Description. The shoes are made from an approved specification or pattern, or of a similar commercial design in white leather, poromeric, or patent leather. The shoe style is dress tie oxford. If worn, the shoe must be plain and untrimmed, with at least two eyelets, a closed toe and heel, and a non-contrasting heel and sole.

(3) How worn. The shoes are worn with the hospital duty uniforms.

*f.* Shoes, pumps, black or white, female.

(1) Type. Black service pumps are a one-time cash allowance item as part of the initial clothing bag allowance. White service pumps are optional purchase items.

(2) Description. The pumps are of a commercial design in fine grain leather, poromeric, or patent leather. Suede pumps are not authorized. The pumps are untrimmed, with a closed toe and heel. The heel must be at least ½ inch, but no more than 3 inches. The sole thickness will not exceed ½ inch.

(3) Wear.

*(a)* Black service pumps are authorized for wear by all female personnel with the service, dress, and mess uniforms, and the Army green uniform when worn as a dress uniform. The black service pumps are required for all female personnel.

*(b)* White service pumps are authorized for wear by all female personnel with the Army white dress and all-white mess uniforms.

*g.* Shoes, dress, pumps, black or white, fabric.

(1) Type. The shoes are optional purchase items.

(2) Description. The pumps are of a commercial design in black or white fabric. The pumps are untrimmed, with a closed toe and heel. The heel must be at least ½ inch but no more than 3 inches. The sole thickness will not exceed ½ inch. When a handbag is carried, the shoes and handbag must be made of the same material.

(3) Wear.

(a) Black dress fabric pumps are authorized for wear with the blue, black, and white mess uniforms; with all evening mess uniforms; and with the Army blue uniform after duty hours.

(b) White dress fabric pumps are authorized for wear with the all-white mess uniform, and with the Army white uniform after duty hours.

## 27–24. Socks

a. Socks, black, cushion sole.

(1) Type. The socks are clothing bag issue items.

(2) Description. The socks are black nylon and wool blend, stretch type, calf-length with a cushion sole.

(3) How worn. The black, cushion sole socks are worn by all personnel when wearing combat or organizationally issued boots. They can also be worn as a two-sock system with the standard liner sock (also called the black dress sock) for additional foot protection.

b. Socks, dress black, and sock, boot liner.

(1) Type. The socks are clothing bag issue items for male personnel and optional purchase items for females.

(2) Description. The socks are made from an approved specification or commercial design. They are calf-length, black polyester and nylon.

(3) How worn. Black socks are worn with black oxford shoes.

c. Socks, white, service.

(1) Type. The socks are optional purchase items.

(2) Description. The socks are of an approved specification or commercial design. They are white cotton, or cotton and nylon, plain, ribbed, stretch type, or with an elastic top.

(3) How worn. Males wear the white socks with the white oxford shoes. Females may wear the white socks instead of white stockings when wearing the hospital duty pantsuit with the white oxford shoes.

d. Stockings, sheer.

(1) Type. The stockings are a one-time cash allowance as part of the initial clothing bag allowance.

(2) Description. The stockings are sheer or semi-sheer, without seams, and of tones complementary to the wearer's skin tone and to the uniform. No patterned or pastel stockings are authorized while in uniform.

(3) How worn. The stockings are worn with the service, dress, and mess uniforms. As an option when wearing slacks, females may wear black socks with the black oxford shoe or the optional ankle boots. The socks must be calf length, plain, black cotton, or cotton and nylon (see para 27–24a, above).

e. Stockings, white.

(1) Type. The stockings are optional purchase items.

(2) Description. They are sheer or semi-sheer, without seams.

(3) How worn. Females wear the white stockings with the hospital duty uniforms, when wearing the white oxford shoes. Females may wear white socks instead of white stockings when wearing the hospital duty pantsuit.

## 27–25. Suspenders

a. Type. Suspenders are optional purchase items.

b. Description. They are of commercial design.

c. How worn. Males may wear suspenders with the dress, mess, and evening mess uniforms, as long as they are not visible when worn.

## 27–26. Sweaters

a. Cardigan, black, unisex.

(1) Type. The black cardigan is an optional purchase item.

(2) Description. The black cardigan is 50/50 acrylic and wool, in a long-sleeved coat style, with five buttons, and shoulder epaulets (see fig 27–14).

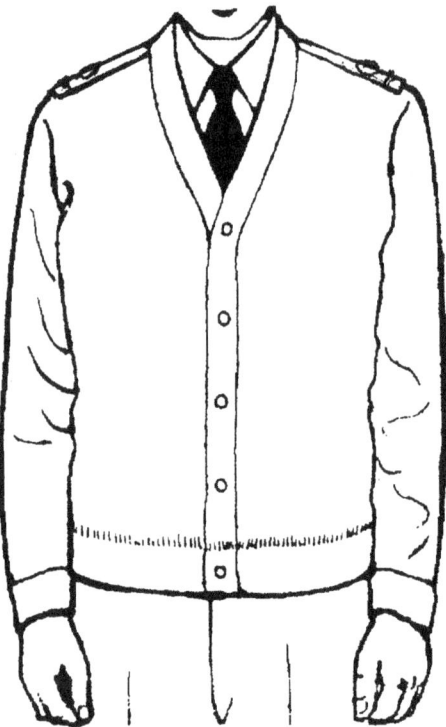

**Figure 27–14. Black unisex cardigan**

(3) How worn.

*(a)* The black unisex cardigan sweater is authorized for wear by all personnel with the class B uniform, and by food service supervisors with the food service supervisor uniform. Personnel may wear the cardigan indoors or outdoors. When worn indoors, personnel may wear the cardigan buttoned or unbuttoned; when outdoors, personnel, except for pregnant soldiers, must button all five buttons.

*(b)* When the black cardigan is worn with the long- or short-sleeved AG shade 415 shirts, personnel have the option of wearing a necktie or necktab. Personnel may wear the collar of the shirts inside or outside the cardigan. Personnel may cuff the sleeves of the cardigan, but they may not roll or push up the sleeves.

*(c)* Officers and enlisted personnel in the rank of corporal or higher will wear shoulder marks on the epaulets of the black cardigan. Personnel will not wear the nameplate, distinctive unit insignia (DUI), or regimental distinctive insignia (RDI) on the cardigan. Personnel may wear the cardigan without rank insignia when wearing civilian clothes.

*(d)* Hospital and food service personnel may no longer wear the black unisex cardigan with the hospital and food service uniforms. (See para *b*, below.)

*b.* Cardigan, white, unisex.

(1) Type. The white cardigan is an optional purchase item.

(2) Description. The white cardigan is 100-percent acrylic in a long-sleeved coat style, with six buttons and two pockets (see fig 27–15).

**Figure 27–15. White unisex cardigan**

(3) How worn.

*(a)* The white unisex cardigan sweater is authorized for wear with the hospital and food service uniforms, indoors or outdoors, by hospital and food service personnel. When worn indoors, personnel may wear the cardigan buttoned or unbuttoned; when outdoors, personnel, except for pregnant soldiers, must button all six buttons.

*(b)* Personnel will wear the collars of the hospital and food service uniforms outside the cardigan, so rank insignia is visible. Personnel may cuff the sleeves of the cardigan, but they may not roll or push up the sleeves. Personnel will not wear rank insignia, nameplate, distinctive unit insignia (DUI), or regimental distinctive insignia (RDI) on the cardigan. Personnel may wear the cardigan when wearing civilian clothes. Food service personnel will not wear the white cardigan when preparing food.

*c.* Pullover, black, unisex.

(1) Type. The black pullover is an optional purchase item.

(2) Description. The black pullover is available in either 100–percent wool or 100–percent acrylic, in a V-neck style, with shoulder, elbow, and chest patches made in a polyester and cotton fabric (see fig 27–16).

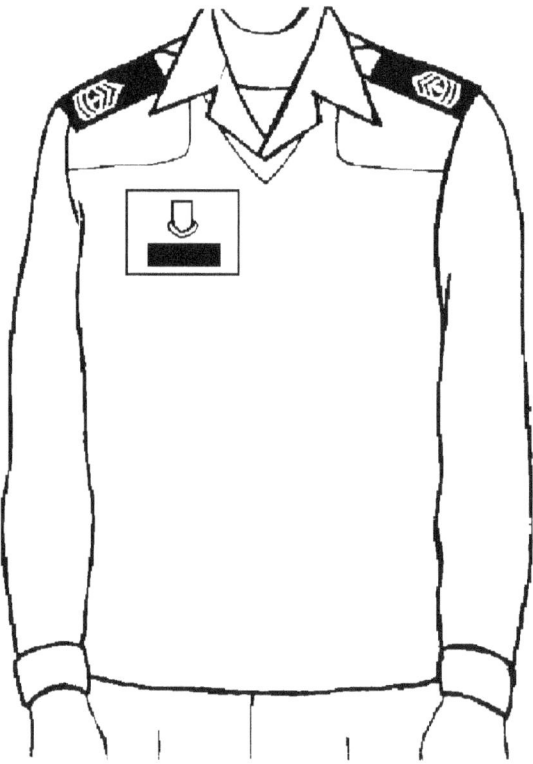

Figure 27–16. Black unisex pullover sweater

(3) How worn.

(a) The black pullover sweater is authorized for wear by all personnel with the class B uniform, and by food service supervisors with the food service supervisor uniform.

(b) When the black pullover is worn with the long- or short-sleeved AG shade 415 shirts, personnel have the option of wearing a necktie or necktab. Personnel will wear the collar of the shirts outside the pullover if they do not wear a necktie or necktab. Personnel may cuff the sleeves of the pullover, but they may not roll or push up the sleeves.

(c) Officers and enlisted personnel in the rank of corporal or higher will wear shoulder marks on the epaulets of the black pullover. The nameplate is worn centered ¼ inch above the bottom of the chest patch, and the distinctive unit insignia (DUI) is worn centered from left to right and from top to bottom on the chest patch, above the nameplate. Soldiers not authorized a DUI will wear the regimental distinctive insignia (RDI) instead of a DUI. Chaplains will wear their branch insignia. Personnel may adjust the placement of the nameplate and DUI or RDI up or down on the patch, to allow for larger size DUI or RDI, or to adjust to body configuration.

(d) Personnel may wear the black pullover under the black all-weather coat and black windbreaker. When worn under the windbreaker, the pullover must not be visible below the windbreaker. Personnel may wear the pullover without insignia when wearing civilian clothes.

## 27–27. Umbrella

a. Type. The umbrella is an optional purchase item.

b. Description. The umbrella is black, plain, with no logos or designs, and is of a commercial design.

c. How worn. Females may carry and use an umbrella, only during inclement weather, when wearing the service (class A and B), dress, and mess uniforms. Umbrellas are not authorized in formations or when wearing field or utility uniforms.

## 27–28. Undergarments

a. Brassieres and underpants.

(1) Type. Brassieres and underpants are a one-time cash allowance purchase as part of the initial clothing bag allowance.

(2) Description. Brassieres and underpants may be of a commercial design, in white, black, or other neutral colors that are not readily apparent when worn under the uniform. The category of brassieres also includes sports bras.

(3) How worn. Females will wear brassieres and underpants with all uniforms.

*b. Camisole.*

(1) Type. The camisole is an optional purchase item.

(2) Description. The camisole is of a commercial design in white, black, or other neutral colors not readily apparent under the uniform.

(3) How worn.

*(a)* Females are authorized to wear the camisole with all uniforms. The camisole is not a substitute for the brown undershirt when the brown undershirt is normally part of the uniform (such as the BDU, flight uniform, cold-weather uniform, and so forth).

*(b)* The camisole is not a substitute for brassieres. Females will ensure that uniforms fit properly when wearing the camisole.

*c. Drawers.*

(1) Type. Drawers are clothing bag issue items.

(2) Description. The drawers are brown, in brief length.

(3) How worn. All males will wear drawers with all uniforms. Either the brief or boxer style drawers are authorized for wear. Males also may wear commercially purchased brief or boxer versions of drawers, in white, brown, or other neutral colors.

*d. Slips.*

(1) Type. Slips are a one-time cash allowance purchase as part of the initial clothing bag allowance.

(2) Description. Slips will be of a commercial design, in white, black, or other neutral colors not readily apparent under the uniform.

(3) How worn. Females will wear slips with the service, dress, and mess skirts, and with the hospital duty and food service dresses.

*e.* Undershirt, brown, AG shade 436.

(1) Type. The undershirt is a clothing bag issue item.

(2) Description. The material is cotton knitted cloth, with quarter-length sleeves and a crew neck, or is of a similar commercial design.

(3) How worn. All personnel will wear the undershirt with all utility uniforms, except for hospital duty and food service uniforms.

*f.* Undershirt, white, crew neck.

(1) Type. The crew neck undershirt is a clothing bag issue item for males.

(2) Description. The white undershirt is of a commercial design, short-sleeved, in a crew neck style.

(3) How worn.

*(a)* Males may wear the white crewneck undershirt with the service, dress, mess, hospital duty, and food service uniforms.

*(b)* Personnel are not authorized to wear the white undershirt with the BDU, flight uniforms, combat vehicle crewman uniforms, or other utility or field uniforms that require wear of the brown undershirt.

*g.* Undershirt, white, V-neck.

(1) Type. The V-neck undershirt is an optional purchase item for all soldiers.

(2) Description. The white V-neck undershirt is of a commercial design, short-sleeved, in a V-neck style.

(3) How worn.

*(a)* Soldiers may wear the V-neck undershirt with the service, dress, mess, hospital duty, and food service uniforms. Females may not substitute the V-neck undershirt for brassieres, and they must ensure uniforms fit properly when wearing the V-neck undershirt.

*(b)* Personnel are not authorized to wear the white V-neck undershirt with the BDU, flight uniforms, combat vehicle crewman uniforms, or other utility or field uniforms that require wear of the brown undershirt.

## 27–29. Vest, white, male

*a.* Type. The vest is an optional purchase item.

*b.* Description. The materials are cotton twill, white; polyester and wool-blended fabrics in tropical, white; polyester and wool-blended fabrics in twill weave, white; or polyester-textured woven serge, white. The white vest is single-breasted, cut low with a rolling collar and pointed bottom, and fastened with three detachable, small white buttons.

*c.* How worn. Male personnel will wear the white vest when wearing the Army white evening mess uniform with formal accessories, and with the Army blue evening mess uniform.

### 27–30. Windbreaker, black

*a.* Type. The windbreaker is an optional purchase item.

*b.* Description. The black windbreaker is made of polyester and wool (65/35), in Army shade 458, and has a Velcro-in liner. The officer windbreaker has a knit collar, cuffs, and waist. The enlisted windbreaker has a standard collar, knit cuffs and waist. Female windbreakers have bust darts. Females are authorized to wear the female or male windbreakers (see fig 27–17).

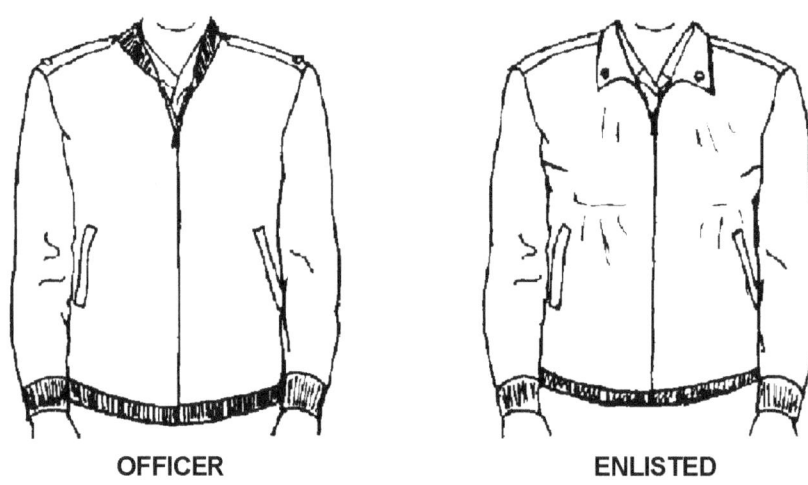

OFFICER  ENLISTED

**Figure 27–17. Windbreakers**

*c.* How worn. All personnel may wear the windbreaker with the class B, hospital duty, and food service uniforms. Personnel will not wear the windbreaker in formations unless authorized by the commander. Personnel will wear the windbreaker zipped to at least the second button down from the top of the shirt. Only non-subdued, pin-on grade insignia is worn on the windbreaker. Personnel may wear the windbreaker without insignia when wearing civilian clothing.

## Chapter 28
## Wear of Insignia and Accouterments

### 28–1. General

*a.* This regulation, CTA 50–900, and special authorization by HQDA specify the only items of insignia that personnel may wear on any of the U.S. Army uniforms.

*b.* The insignia worn by military personnel designates grade, branch, organization, duty assignments, and prior Army service.

*c.* When authorized by the commander, members of honor guards, color guards, and similar details will wear the prescribed uniform with authorized accouterments and those accessories authorized in CTA 50–900 (see para 2–6e).

*d.* Personnel will submit all requests for insignia designs to The Institute of Heraldry, U.S. Army, 9325 Gunston Road, Room S112, Fort Belvoir, VA 22060–5579.

### 28–2. General description

*a.* Material. Insignia will meet the approved military specifications and conform to proper color designation (gold, silver, or subdued). Officers may wear embroidered insignia in lieu of non-subdued metal insignia on mess and evening mess uniforms. All personnel may wear either subdued embroidered cloth insignia or subdued metal insignia on utility uniforms; they may not mix the two. Subdued embroidered insignia is on a cloth backing and will not be embroidered directly on the uniform. Personnel may not wear embroidered, sew-on subdued insignia on organizational items, unless otherwise specified in this regulation. Subdued, embroidered insignia for woodland camouflage uniforms is black block lettering or appropriate design, on olive-green cloth backing. For desert camouflage uniforms, it is spice-brown block lettering, or appropriate design, on khaki cloth backing.

*b.* Attachment. Personnel will attach insignia on the uniform so that it rests firmly without turning. Soldiers will ensure that embroidered cloth insignia is sewn on the uniform so the stitching blends inconspicuously with the background material.

## 28–3. Headgear insignia

*a.* Garrison cap, Army green, male and female.

(1) Officers wear non-subdued grade insignia on the garrison cap, centered vertically on the left curtain, 1 inch from the front crease (see fig 28–1).

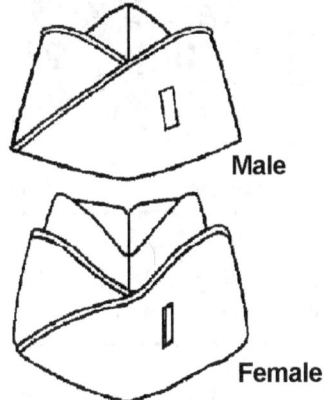

**Figure 28–1. Garrison cap, officer insignia**

(2) Enlisted personnel wear their DUI on the garrison cap, centered vertically on the left curtain, 1 inch from the front crease (see fig 28–2).

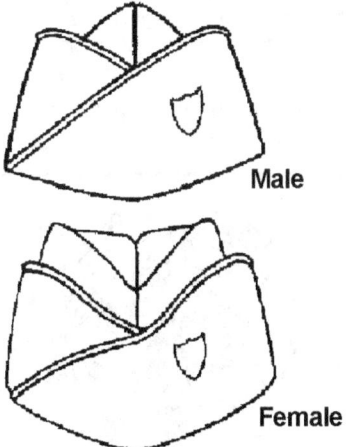

**Figure 28–2. Garrison cap, enlisted, DUI**

*b.* Service cap, Army blue and white; and drill sergeant hat, male personnel. Male personnel wear the following insignia, secured through the front eyelet, on the service caps and drill sergeant hat.

(1) Commissioned officers. The insignia is the coat of arms of the United States, 2⅜ inches in height, in gold-colored metal (see fig 28–3).

**Figure 28–3. Service cap insignia, commissioned officer, male**

(2) Warrant officers. The insignia is an eagle rising with wings displayed, standing on a bundle of two arrows, enclosed in a wreath. The insignia is 1½ inches in height, in gold-colored metal (see fig 28–4).

**Figure 28–4. Service cap insignia, warrant officer, male**

(3) Sergeant Major of the Army. The insignia is the coat of arms of the United States within a wreath, 1–15/16 inches in height, in gold-colored metal (see fig 28–5).

**Figure 28–5. Service cap insignia, sergeant major of the Army**

(4) Enlisted personnel. The insignia is a plain, gold-colored disk, 1½ inches in diameter, with a gold-colored metal coat of arms of the United States attached to the disk (see fig 28–7).

**Figure 28–7. Service cap insignia, enlisted, male**

*c.* Service hat, Army blue, and white; and drill sergeant hat, female personnel. Female personnel wear the headgear insignia centered on the hatband of the service hat. On the drill sergeant hat, the insignia is worn centered between the top of the hat and the hatband.

(1) Commissioned officers. The insignia is the coat of arms of the United States, 1⅝ inches in height, in gold-colored metal (see fig 28–6).

**Figure 28–6. Service cap insignia, commissioned officer, female**

(2) Warrant officers. The insignia is an eagle rising with wings displayed, standing on a bundle of two arrows, enclosed in a wreath. The insignia is 1½ inches in height, in gold-colored metal (see fig 28–4).

(3) Enlisted personnel. The insignia is the coat of arms of the United States, within a ring that is 1¾ inches in diameter, in gold-colored metal (see fig 28–8).

**Figure 28–8. Service cap insignia, enlisted female**

*d.* Cold-weather cap, AG 489. Because of the thickness of the fur pile, headgear insignia worn on the cap must have a center post and screw. Therefore, all soldiers will wear the male headgear insignia on the cold-weather cap (see fig 27–3).

*e.* Beret, black/tan/green/maroon. Personnel will wear the following insignia on berets:

(1) Airborne, Ranger, and Special Forces soldiers wear their distinctive flashes on their berets. All other soldiers wear the Army flash on the black beret, unless authorization for another flash was granted before implementation of the black beret as the standard Army headgear (see para 3–5*a*(3)). The flash is sewn centered on the stiffener of the beret, with non-contrasting thread (see fig 28–9).

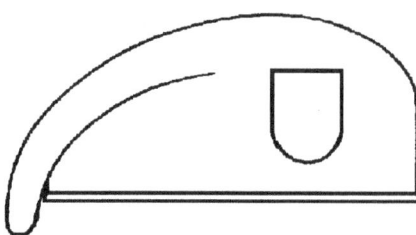

Figure 28–9. Beret with flash

(2) Officers wear non-subdued grade insignia centered on the flash; chaplains wear their branch insignia (see fig 28–10).

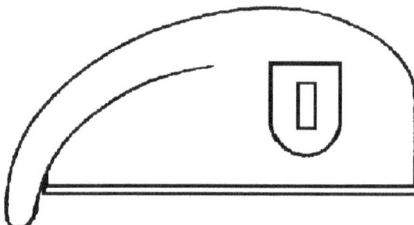

Figure 28–10. Beret with flash, officer

(3) Enlisted personnel wear their DUI centered on the flash. Soldiers assigned to units without a DUI wear the regimental distinctive insignia (RDI) on the flash. (see fig 28–11).

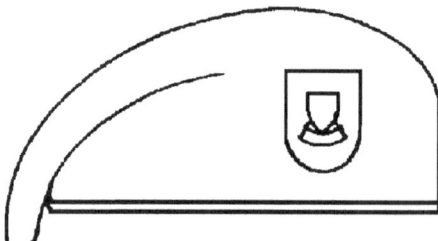

Figure 28–11. Beret with flash, enlisted

*f.* Cap, organizational, baseball-style. Personnel will wear non-subdued grade insignia on the front of the cap, centered left to right and top to bottom (see fig 28–12).

**Figure 28–12. Organizational baseball cap, enlisted**

*g.* Helmet liner and helmet camouflage cover. Only the insignia prescribed below is authorized for wear on the helmet liner or helmet camouflage cover, as indicated. Personnel will not alter the color of the helmet except for safety or training requirements.

(1) All personnel, except chaplains, wear their subdued grade insignia centered on the front of the camouflage cover, approximately 2½ inches up from the bottom rim. Subdued pin-on or embroidered sew-on grade insignia is authorized for wear on the camouflage cover. Commanders may not require enlisted soldiers to attach embroidered grade insignia, unless it is issued and attached without cost to the soldier (see fig 28–13). Chaplains wear their subdued branch insignia, in lieu of grade insignia. Wear of nametapes or the use of other means to apply names to helmet bands is determined by the commander and is provided to soldiers at no cost.

**Figure 28–13. Helmet cover with rank insignia**

(2) Military Police (MP) personnel. Military Police may have the letters "MP" in white, centered on the front of the helmet liner, 1½ inches up from the bottom rim (see fig 28–14). On helmets with camouflage covers, MP personnel are authorized to have the letters "MP" in black, 1½ inches up from the rim. Personnel will center their grade insignia ½ inch above the white or black "MP" letters. Helmets also must have a painted stripe, 1¼ inches wide and 2 inches up from the bottom rim, parallel to the rim and following the contour of the helmet liner. As an option, MP personnel may wear the numerical designation of their unit and distinctive unit insignia over the left and right ears, respectively, centered on the painted stripe. Personnel will wear the following color stripes on the helmet liner.

Figure 28–14. Helmet insignia, MP

*(a)* Division units: a red stripe, 1¼ inches wide (see fig 28–15).

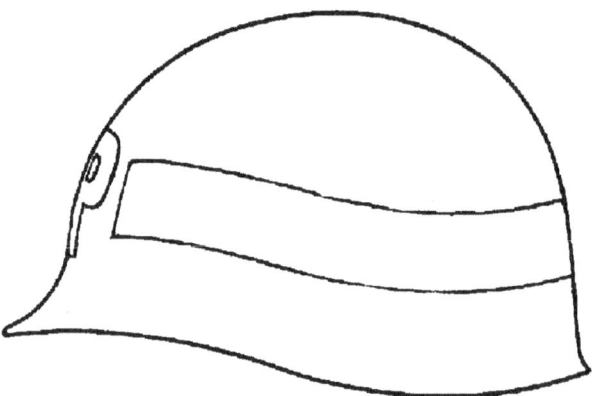

Figure 28–15. Helmet insignia, MP division unit

*(b)* Corps units: a blue stripe, ⅝-inch wide, above a ⅝-inch wide red stripe, (see fig 28–16).

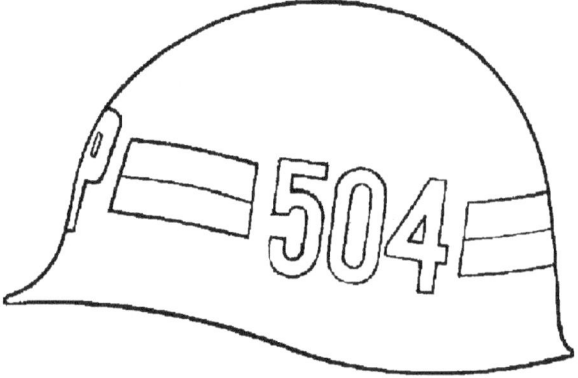

Figure 28–16. Helmet insignia, MP corps unit

*(c)* Army units: a white stripe, ⅝-inch wide, above a ⅝-inch wide red stripe (see fig 28–17).

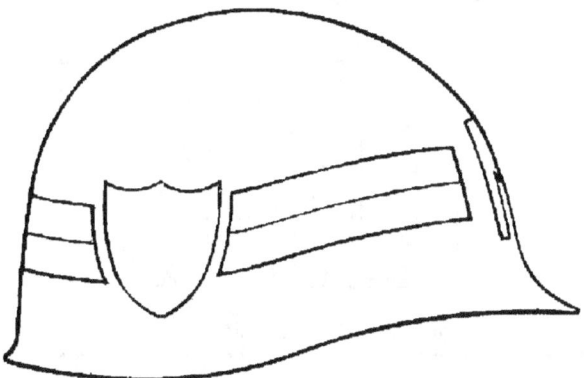

**Figure 28–17. Helmet insignia, MP Army unit**

*(d)* All other MP units: a white stripe, 1¼ inches wide (see fig 28–14).

*h.* Woodland and desert camouflage patrol (formerly the BDU and DBDU) caps, desert camouflage hat, and cold-weather utility caps.

(1) Enlisted personnel wear subdued grade insignia on the patrol caps, the desert patrol hat, and cold-weather utility caps. The grade insignia is centered on the front of the headgear left to right, and top to bottom (see fig 28–18). Officers will wear non-subdued grade insignia when in a garrison environment, and subdued insignia when in a field environment. Chaplains wear non-subdued branch insignia in a garrison environment, and subdued branch insignia in a field environment.

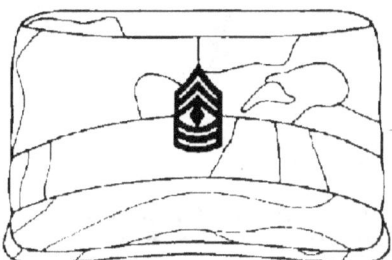

**Figure 28–18. Patrol cap insignia, enlisted**

(2) Grade insignia (branch insignia for chaplains) is centered on the front of the headgear left to right, and top to bottom; no other insignia is worn on the headgear listed above (see fig 28–19).

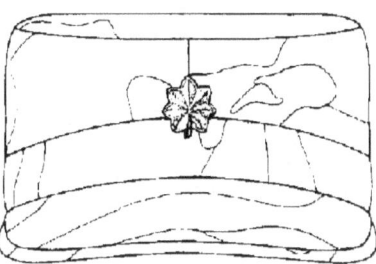

**Figure 28–19. Patrol cap insignia, officer**

## 28–4. U.S. insignia

*a.* All officers.

(1) Description. The U.S. insignia consists of the block letters, "U.S." in gold-colored metal, 7/16 inch in height, with each letter followed by a period (see fig 28–20).

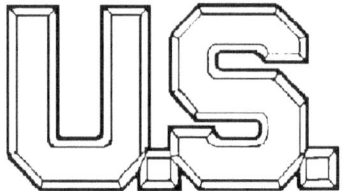

**Figure 28–20. U.S. insignia, officer**

(2) How worn.

*(a)* Male officers. On the Army green, white, and blue uniform coats, officers wear the U.S. insignia ⅝ inch above the notch on both collars, with the centerline of the insignia bisecting the notch, and parallel to the inside edge of the lapel (see fig 28–21).

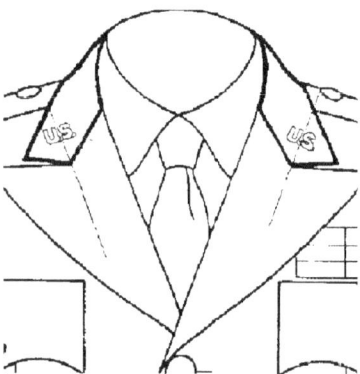

**Figure 28–21. Wear of U.S. insignia, officer, male**

*(b)* Female officers. There are two versions of the white and blue uniform coats: the old version produced prior to 10 August 1992, and the new version produced after that date. On the old version of the white and blue uniform coats, the U.S. insignia is centered 1 inch above the notch on the right collar, with the centerline of the insignia bisecting the notch, and parallel to the inside edge of the lapel (see fig 28–22). On the new version of the white and blue uniform coats, and on the Army green coat, the U.S. insignia is centered on both collars, approximately ⅝ inch up from the collar and lapel seam, with the centerline of the insignia parallel to the inside edge of the lapel (see fig 28–23).

**Figure 28–22. Wear of U.S. insignia, officer, female, old version Army blue and white uniforms**

**Figure 28–23. Wear of U.S. insignia, officer, female, Army green uniform and new version blue and white uniforms**

*b.* Enlisted personnel.

(1) Description. The enlisted U.S. insignia consists of the block letters "U.S." in gold-colored metal, 7/16 inch in height, with each letter followed by a period. The "U.S." is placed on a 1-inch diameter disk in gold-colored metal (see fig 28–24).

**Figure 28–24. U.S. insignia, enlisted**

*(2)* How worn.

*(a)* All male enlisted personnel except basic trainees. On the Army green, white, and blue uniform coats, the bottom of the U.S. insignia disk is placed approximately 1 inch above the notch, centered on the right collar, with the centerline of the insignia parallel to the inside edge of the lapel (see fig 28–25).

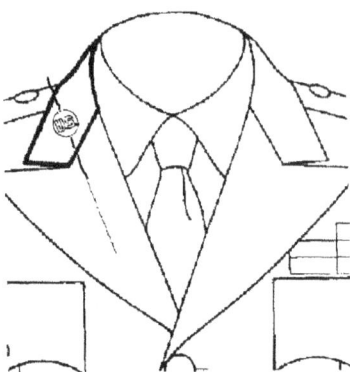

**Figure 28–25. Wear of U.S. insignia, male**

*(b)* All female enlisted personnel except basic trainees. There are two versions of the white and blue uniform coats: the old version produced prior to 10 August 1992, and the new version produced after that date. On the old version of the white and blue uniform coats, the bottom of the U.S. insignia disk is centered approximately 1 inch above the notch on the right collar, with the centerline of the insignia bisecting the notch, and parallel to the inside edge of the lapel (see fig 28–26). On the new versions of the white and blue uniform coats, and on the Army green coat, the bottom of the U.S. insignia disk is centered on the right collar, approximately ⅝ inch up from the collar and lapel seam, with the centerline of the insignia parallel to the inside edge of the lapel (see fig 28–27).

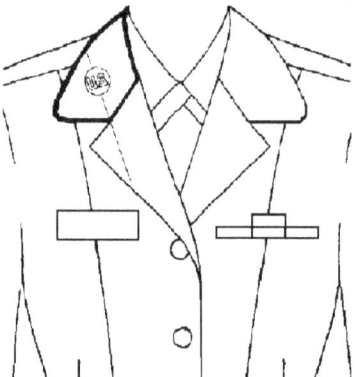

**Figure 28–26. Wear of U.S. insignia, enlisted, female, old version Army blue and white uniforms**

**Figure 28–27. Wear of U.S. insignia, enlisted, female, Army green uniform and new version blue and white**

*(c)* Basic trainee personnel. The U.S. insignia is worn on both collars in the same manner as described for enlisted male and female personnel above. Upon award of their primary military occupational specialty (PMOS), trainee personnel will wear the appropriate branch insignia on the left collar, in accordance with paragraphs 28–12*a*(2) and (4), below.

*c.* CID special agents. When wearing utility uniforms, special agents of the CID (MOS 95D and 311A) may wear the subdued U.S. insignia in lieu of insignia of rank, as directed by the Commanding General, U.S. Army Criminal Investigation Command.

(1) Description. The subdued U.S. insignia consists of the block letters "U.S." in black-colored metal, 7/16 inch in height, with each letter followed by a period.

(2) How worn.

*(a)* Utility shirts. The insignia is worn centered horizontally on the left and right collars, 1 inch up from the lower edge.

*(b)* Cold-weather coat. The insignia is worn centered on the shoulder loops, ⅝ inch from the outside shoulder seam, with the bottom edge of the insignia facing the shoulder seam.

*(c)* Patrol (formerly BDU) caps. The insignia is worn centered on the front of the cap, left to right, and top to bottom.

*(d)* Helmet camouflage covers. The insignia is worn centered on the front of the cover, approximately 2½ inches up from the bottom rim.

## 28–5. Grade insignia for general officers

*a.* Description. The grade insignia described below applies to male and female general officers.

(1) General. The non-subdued grade insignia has four silver-colored, five-pointed stars, each 1 inch in diameter. Medium silver-colored stars, ¾ inch in diameter, and miniature silver-colored stars, ⅝ inch in diameter, also are authorized. The subdued grade insignia is the same as above, except the color is black (see fig 28–28).

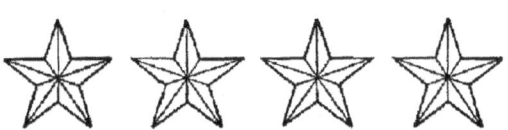

**Figure 28–28. Insignia of grade, general**

(2) Lieutenant general. The non-subdued grade insignia has three silver-colored, five-pointed stars, each 1 inch in diameter. Medium silver-colored stars, ¾ inch in diameter and miniature silver-colored stars, ⅝ inch in diameter, also are authorized. The subdued grade insignia is the same as above, except the color is black (see fig 28–29).

Figure 28–29. Insignia of grade, lieutenant general

(3) Major general. The non-subdued grade insignia has two silver-colored, five-pointed stars, each 1 inch in diameter. Medium silver-colored stars, ¾ inch in diameter, and miniature silver-colored stars, ⅝ inch in diameter, also are authorized. The subdued grade insignia is the same as above, except the color is black (see fig 28–30).

Figure 28–30. Insignia of grade, major general

(4) Brigadier general. The non-subdued grade insignia has one silver-colored, five-pointed star, 1 inch in diameter. Medium silver-colored stars, ¾ inch in diameter, and miniature silver-colored stars, ⅝ inch in diameter, also are authorized. The subdued grade insignia is the same as above, except the color is black (see fig 28–31).

Figure 28–31. Insignia of grade, brigadier general

*b.* How worn.

(1) Non-subdued.

*(a)* The appropriate number of stars is worn centered on the shoulder loops, equidistant between the outside edge of the shoulder loop and the outer edge of the shoulder loop button on the Army green and white uniform coats, black all-weather coat, and the windbreaker. Stars are worn "point to 'V'" on shoulder loops (see fig 28–32).

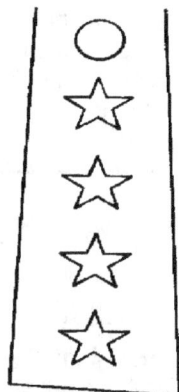

**Figure 28–32. Insignia of grade, general officers, on shoulder loop**

*(b)* Shoulder marks with the appropriate number of stars are worn on the AG shade 415 long- and short-sleeved shirts, the black unisex cardigan, and the black pullover sweater.

*(c)* The appropriate number of stars is worn centered on the beret flash, point-to-point (see fig 28–33).

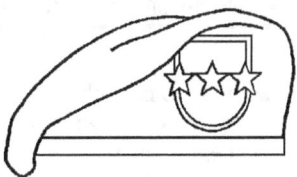

**Figure 28–33. Insignia of grade, general officers, on beret**

*(d)* General officers may wear medium or miniature stars in lieu of regular size stars. As an option, general officers may mount full-size, medium, or miniature stars on a bar for wear on coats, jackets, and the beret. When this option is chosen, the bar is worn centered on the shoulder loop or beret flash.

(2) Subdued. Subdued grade insignia is worn on all utility uniform shirts. The subdued insignia is worn centered with one point facing the neck and in a vertical line, with the end of the "V" 1 inch from the lower edge of the collar. General officers may wear branch insignia on the left collar in lieu of grade insignia (see fig 28–34). The grade insignia is worn on the shoulder loops of the cold-weather coats in the same manner as non-subdued grade insignia, covered above. The subdued grade insignia point-to-point stars are worn on the headgear as prescribed in paragraph 28–3, above (see fig 28–19).

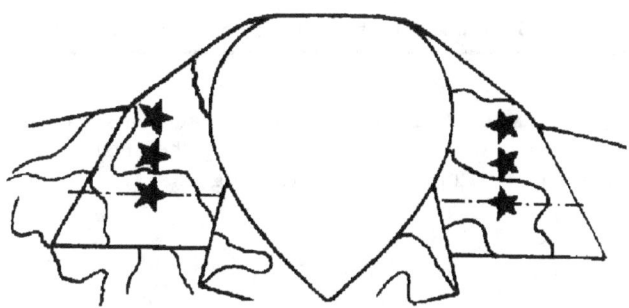

**Figure 28–34. Insignia of grade, general officers, on utility shirt collar**

**28–6. Grade insignia for other officers**

*a.* Description. The insignia described below applies to both male and female officers.

(1) Colonel. The non-subdued grade insignia is a silver-colored spread eagle, in a shiny finish, ¾ inch high, with 1½ inches between the tips of the wings. The head of the eagle faces to the wearer's right, or to the front. The subdued grade insignia is the same as above, except the color is black (see fig 28–35).

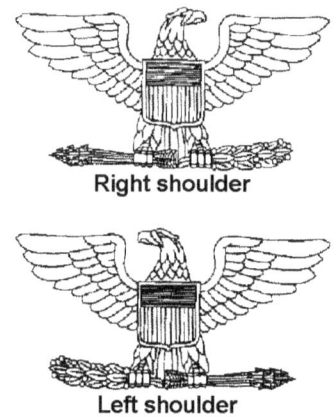

Right shoulder

Left shoulder

Figure 28–35. Insignia of grade, colonel

(2) Lieutenant colonel. The non-subdued grade insignia is a silver-colored oak leaf, in a satin finish with an irregular surface, 1⅛ inches high and 1 inch wide. The leaf is worn with the stem facing the outside shoulder seam. The subdued grade insignia is the same as above, except the color is black (see fig 28–36).

Figure 28–36. Insignia of grade, lieutenant colonel (silver)

(3) Major. The non-subdued grade insignia is a gold-colored oak leaf, in a satin finish with an irregular surface, 1⅛ inches high and 1 inch wide. The leaf is worn with the stem facing the outside shoulder seam. The subdued grade insignia is the same as above, except the color is brown (see fig 28–37).

**Figure 28–37. Insignia of grade, major (gold)**

(4) Captain. The non-subdued grade insignia is two silver-colored bars, each ⅜ inch in width and 1 inch in length, with a smooth surface. The bars are spaced ¼ inch apart and are worn lengthwise on shirt collars, parallel to the shoulder seam on shoulder loops. The subdued grade insignia is the same as above, except the color is black (see fig 28–38).

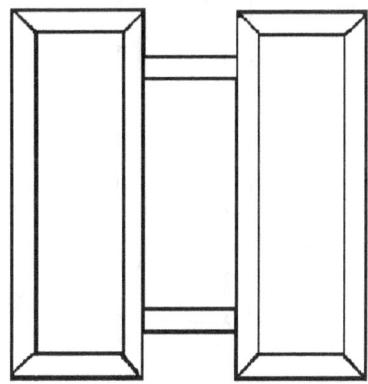

**Figure 28–38. Insignia of grade, captain**

(5) First lieutenant. The non-subdued grade insignia is one silver-colored bar, ⅜ inch in width and 1 inch in length, with a smooth surface. The bar is worn lengthwise on shirt collars, parallel to the shoulder seam on shoulder loops. The subdued grade insignia is the same as above, except the color is black (see fig 28–39).

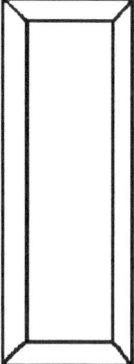

**Figure 28–39. Insignia of grade, first lieutenant (silver)**

(6) Second lieutenant. The non-subdued grade insignia is one gold-colored bar, ⅜ inch in width and 1 inch in length, with a smooth surface. The bar is worn lengthwise on shirt collars, parallel to the shoulder seam on shoulder loops. The subdued grade insignia is the same as above, except the color is brown (see fig 28–40).

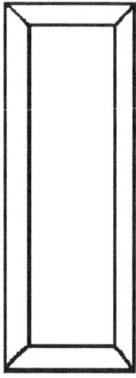

**Figure 28–40. Insignia of grade, second lieutenant (gold)**

(7) Chief warrant officer 5 (CW5). The non-subdued grade insignia is a silver-colored bar, ⅜ inch in width and 1⅛ inches in length, with a black line in the center of the bar.

**Figure 28–41. Insignia of grade, chief warrant officer 5**

(8) Chief warrant officer 4 (CW4). The non-subdued grade insignia is a silver-colored bar, ⅜ inch in width and 1⅛ inches in length, with four black enamel squares. The bar is worn lengthwise on shirt collars, parallel to the shoulder seam on shoulder loops. The subdued grade insignia is the same as above, except that the color is olive-drab with black squares (see fig 28–42).

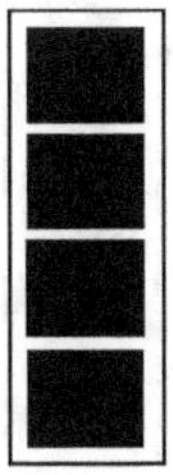

**Figure 28–42. Insignia of grade, chief warrant officer 4**

(9) Chief warrant officer 3 (CW3). The non-subdued grade insignia is a silver-colored bar, ⅜ inch in width and 1⅛ inches in length, with three black enamel squares. The bar is worn lengthwise on shirt collars, parallel to the shoulder seam on shoulder loops. The subdued grade insignia is the same as above, except that the color is olive-drab with black squares (see fig 28–43).

**Figure 28–43. Insignia of grade, chief warrant officer 3**

(10) Chief warrant officer 2 (CW2). The non-subdued grade insignia is a silver-colored bar, ⅜ inch in width and 1⅛ inches in length, with two black enamel squares. The bar is worn lengthwise on shirt collars, parallel to the shoulder seam on shoulder loops. The subdued grade insignia is the same as above, except that the color is olive-drab with black squares (see fig 28–44).

**Figure 28–44. Insignia of grade, chief warrant officer 2**

(11) Warrant officer 1 (WO1). The non-subdued grade insignia is a silver-colored bar, ⅜ inch in width and 1⅛ inches in length, with one black enamel square. The bar is worn lengthwise on shirt collars, parallel to the shoulder seam on shoulder loops. The subdued grade insignia is the same as above, except that the color is olive-drab with one black square (see fig 28–45).

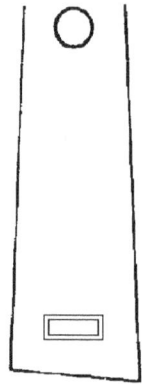

Figure 28–45. Insignia of grade, warrant officer 1

*b.* How worn.

(1) Non-subdued.

*(a)* On the Army green and white uniform coats, black all-weather coat, and the windbreaker, officer grade insignia is worn on the shoulder loops, ⅝ inch from the outside shoulder seam, and centered front to back (see fig 28–46).

Figure 28–46. Insignia of grade, other officers, on shoulder loops

*(b)* On the hospital duty uniform for male and female officers, the grade insignia is worn centered on the right collar, 1 inch from the lower edge of the collar, with the centerline of the insignia parallel to the lower edge of the collar.

*(c)* Headgear grade insignia is discussed in paragraph 28–3.

(2) Subdued.

*(a)* Officers wear subdued grade insignia on all utility uniforms, with the exception of the hospital duty uniform, as described above (see para 28–6*b*(1)(b)), and on the ECWCS (Gortex) parka.

*(b)* On utility uniforms, the subdued insignia is worn centered horizontally on the right collar, 1 inch from the lower edge of the collar, with the centerline of the insignia parallel to the lower edge of the collar (see fig 28–47). On cold-weather coats and flight uniforms, the subdued grade insignia is worn on the shoulder loops in the same manner as the non-subdued insignia described above. On the ECWCS (Gortex) parka, the subdued insignia is worn centered on the front tab. Wear of cloth rank insignia tab on the front tab of the ECWCS parka is authorized, as described in paragraph 28–8*d*, below. Only subdued pin-on grade insignia is worn on organizational clothing, unless otherwise specified in this regulation.

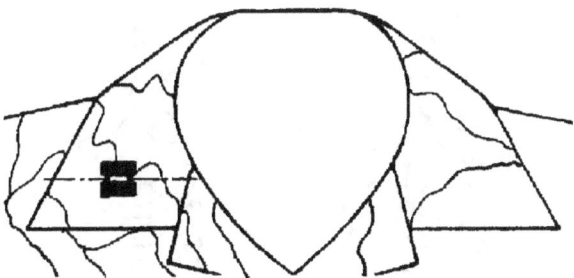

**Figure 28–47. Insignia of grade, subdued, other officers, on utility shirt collar**

*(c)* Officers may not mix pin-on and sew-on grade insignia on the uniform. However if they wear sew-on insignia on the shirts, they may wear pin-on insignia on the field jacket or headgear, or vice versa.

## 28–7. Grade insignia for enlisted personnel

*a.* Non-subdued, sew-on grade insignia for ranks other than specialist.

(1) Large insignia. The large, embroidered, sew-on grade insignia is goldenlite color. The width of each chevron and arc is 5/16 inch, with a 3/16-inch space between each chevron and each arc. The insignia has a background in Army green, blue, or white cloth, 3 inches wide, which provides a ⅛-inch edging around the entire insignia. The lowest chevron joins the topmost arc at each side of the insignia.

(2) Small insignia. The small, embroidered, sew-on grade insignia is goldenlite color. The width of each chevron and arc is ¼ inch with a 5/32–inch space between each chevron and each arc. The insignia has a background of Army green, blue, or white cloth, 2½ inches wide, which provides a ⅛-inch edging around the entire insignia. The lowest chevron joins the topmost arc at each side of the insignia. (Note: The old "female" size insignia is no longer authorized for wear.)

(3) Description. A description of enlisted grades follows.

*(a)* The Sergeant Major of the Army: three chevrons above three arcs, with the eagle from the Great Seal of the United States centered between two five-pointed stars centered horizontally between the chevrons and arcs (see fig 28–48).

Large          Small

**Figure 28–48. Insignia of grade, sergeant major of the Army**

*(b)* Command sergeant major: three chevrons above three arcs, with a five-pointed star within a wreath between the chevrons and arcs (see fig 28–49).

**Small**

**Large**

Figure 28–49. Insignia of grade, command sergeant major

*(c)* Sergeant major: three chevrons above three arcs, with a five-pointed star between the chevrons and arcs (see fig 28–50).

**Small**

**Large**

Figure 28–50. Insignia of grade, sergeant major

*(d)* First sergeant: three chevrons above three arcs, with a pierced lozenge between the chevrons and arcs (see fig 28–51).

**Small**

**Large**

Figure 28–51. Insignia of grade, first sergeant

*(e)* Master sergeant: three chevrons above three arcs (see fig 28–52).

**Large** **Small**

**Figure 28–52. Insignia of grade, master sergeant**

*(f)* Sergeant first class: three chevrons above two arcs (see fig 28–53).

**Large** **Small**

**Figure 28–53. Insignia of grade, sergeant first class**

*(g)* Staff sergeant: three chevrons above one arc (see fig 28–54).

**Large** **Small**

**Figure 28–54. Insignia of grade, staff sergeant**

*(h)* Sergeant: three chevrons (see fig 28–55).

Large   Small

**Figure 28–55. Insignia of grade, sergeant**

*(i)* Corporal: two chevrons (see fig 28–56).

Large   Small

**Figure 28–56. Insignia of grade, corporal**

*(j)* Private first class: one chevron above one arc (see fig 28–57).

Large   Small

**Figure 28–57. Insignia of grade, private first class**

*(k)* Private (E–2): one chevron (see fig 28–58).

Large   Small

**Figure 28–58. Insignia of grade, private, E–2**

*(l)* Private (E–1): no insignia.

*b.* Non-subdued, sew-on grade insignia for specialist.

(1) Large insignia. The large embroidered, sew-on grade insignia is goldenlite in color, shaped like an inverted chevron at the bottom, with an eagle device in the center. The insignia has a background of Army green, blue, or white cloth, 2⅞ inches wide, which provides a ⅛-inch edging around the entire insignia (see fig 28–59).

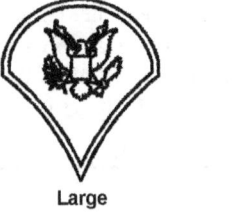 

Large　　　　Small

Figure 28–59. Insignia of grade, specialist

(2) Small insignia. The small embroidered, sew-on grade insignia is goldenlite, shaped like an inverted chevron at the bottom, with an eagle device in the center. The insignia has a background of Army green, blue, or white cloth, 2½ inches wide, which provides a ⅛-inch edging around the entire insignia (see fig 28–59).

*Note.* The old "female" size insignia is no longer authorized for wear.

*c.* Non-subdued pin-on grade insignia for enlisted personnel. Polished brass, pin-on grade insignia for all enlisted personnel is identical in design to the non-subdued grade insignia described above, except that the width of each chevron and arc is 3/32 inch, with a 1/16-inch open space between the chevrons and arcs (see fig 28–61).

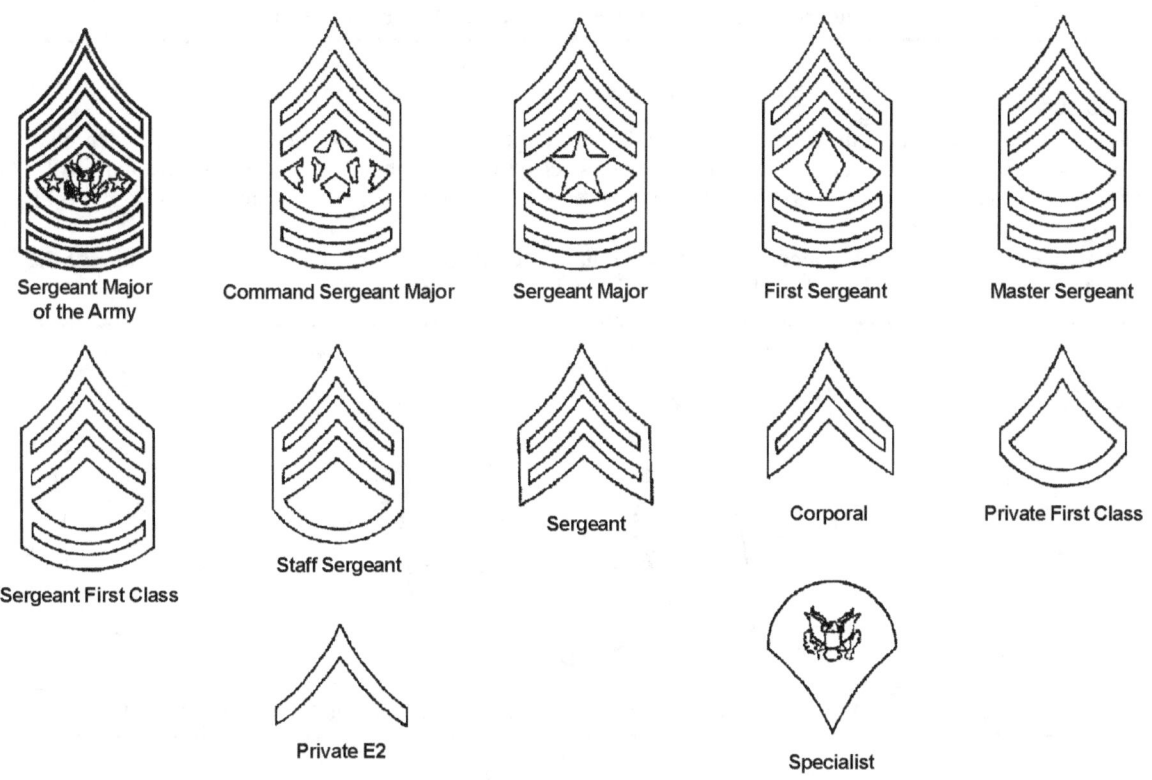

Figure 28–61. Pin-on insignia of grade, enlisted

*d.* Subdued pin-on grade insignia for enlisted personnel. Subdued metal pin-on grade insignia is identical to the non-subdued pin-on grade insignia described above, except the insignia has a dull, flat black finish.

*e.* How worn.

(1) Non-subdued grade insignia, sew-on.

*(a)* Enlisted non-subdued cloth grade insignia is sewn on each sleeve of the Army green, blue, and white uniform coats, and on each sleeve of the mess and evening mess jackets. Insignia with a green background is worn on the Army green uniform coat; insignia with a white background is worn on the white uniform coat, and on the white mess and white evening mess jackets. Insignia with a blue background is worn on the Army blue coat, and on the blue mess and blue evening mess jackets. Enlisted personnel may wear either the large- or small-size insignia.

*(b)* The insignia is worn centered between the shoulder seam and elbow on all uniform coats. When the position of the shoulder sleeve insignia (SSI) does not allow for proper placement of the grade insignia as stated above, the grade insignia is placed ½ inch below the SSI, on the left or right side of the coat, as applicable (see fig 28–60).

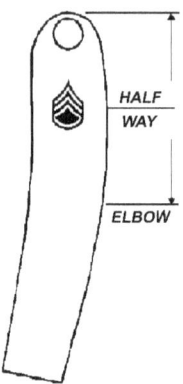

Figure 28–60. Wear of sew-on insignia of grade, enlisted

(2) Non-subdued grade insignia, pin-on.

*(a)* All enlisted personnel will wear non-subdued, pin-on grade insignia on the black all-weather coat and the windbreaker. All hospital and food service enlisted personnel will wear non-subdued, pin-on, insignia on the hospital duty and food service utility uniforms. All specialists and below will wear the non-subdued, pin-on grade insignia on the AG 415 shirt.

*(b)* Personnel will wear the non-subdued pin-on insignia centered on both collars, with the centerline of the insignia bisecting the points of the collar, 1 inch up from the collar point (see fig 28–62).

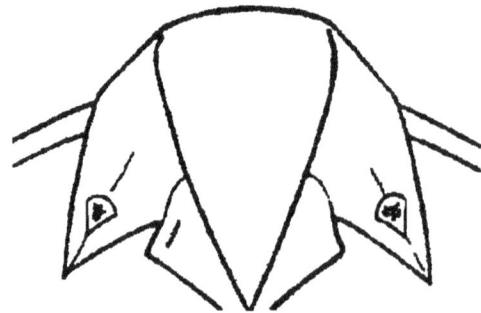

Figure 28–62. Wear of pin-on insignia of grade on collars, subdued and non-subdued

(3) Subdued grade insignia.

*(a)* All enlisted personnel will wear subdued grade insignia on utility uniforms, the cold-weather coat, and on the ECWCS (Gortex) parka. On utility uniforms and the cold-weather coat, the insignia is worn centered on the collar so that the centerline of the insignia bisects the points of the collar, and the bottom of the insignia (not the cloth backing, if sew-on insignia is worn) is positioned 1 inch up from the collar point. On the ECWCS parka, the subdued insignia is worn centered on the front tab of the parka. Wear of the cloth rank insignia tab on the front tab of the ECWCS parka is authorized, as described in paragraph 28–8*c*, below.

*(b)* Personnel may wear pin-on or sew-on, embroidered or woven, subdued grade insignia on the uniforms described above. Only subdued pin-on grade insignia is worn on organizational clothing unless otherwise specified in this regulation. Personnel may not mix pin-on and sew-on grade insignia on the uniform. However, if personnel wear sew-on insignia on the shirts, they may wear pin-on insignia on the field jacket or headgear, and vice versa (see fig 28–63).

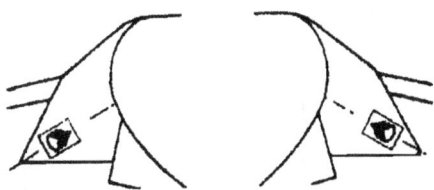

**Figure 28–63. Wear of embroidered insignia of grade on collars**

## 28–8. Other grade insignia

*a.* Shoulder marks.

(1) Officers. Shoulder marks for officers are black with a ⅛-inch yellow stripe below the embroidered grade insignia (see fig 28–64).

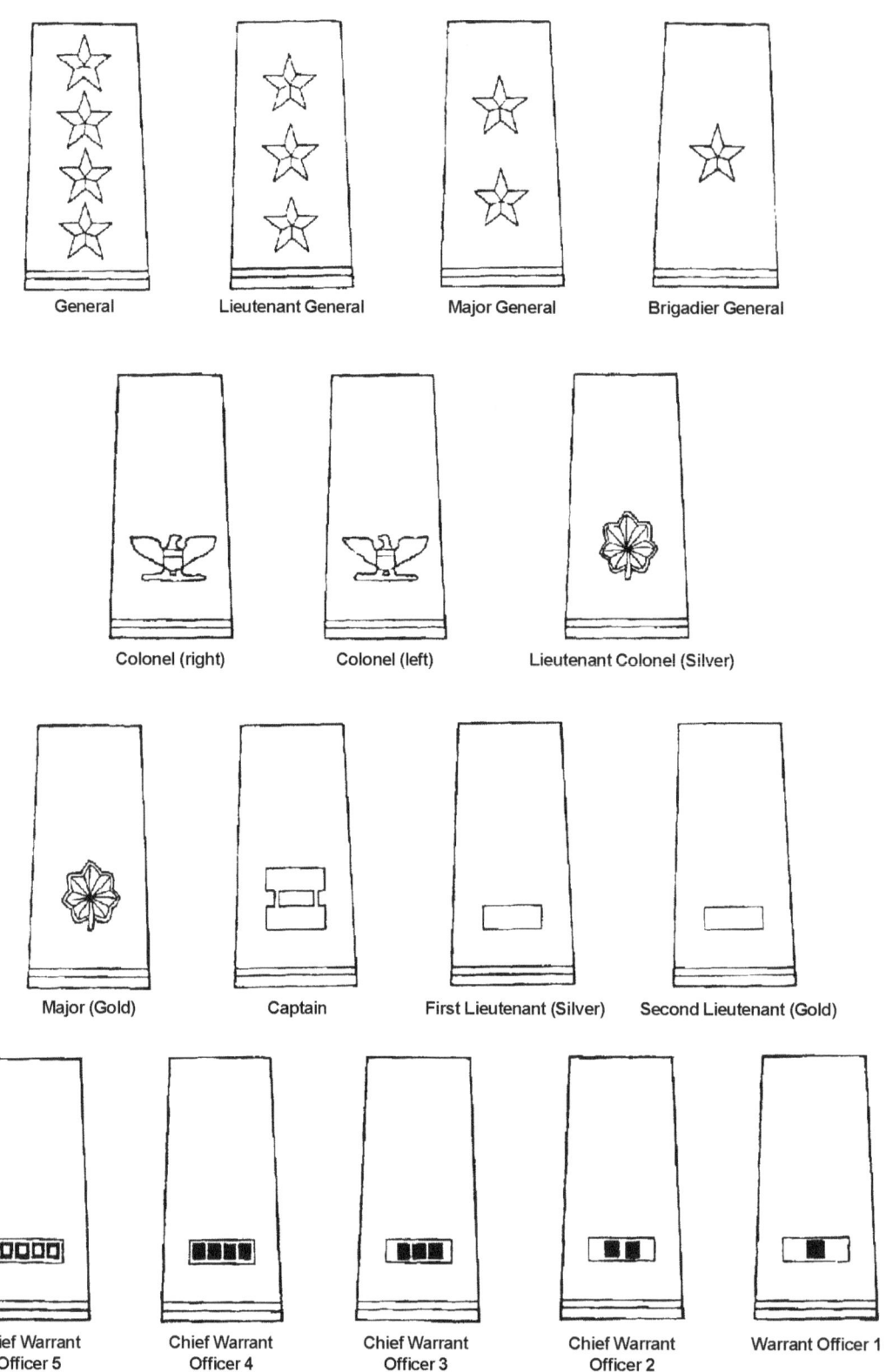

Figure 28–64. Shoulder marks, officer

(2) Enlisted personnel. Shoulder marks for enlisted personnel are black with grade insignia embroidered ⅝ inch from the lower end of the shoulder mark (see fig 28–65).

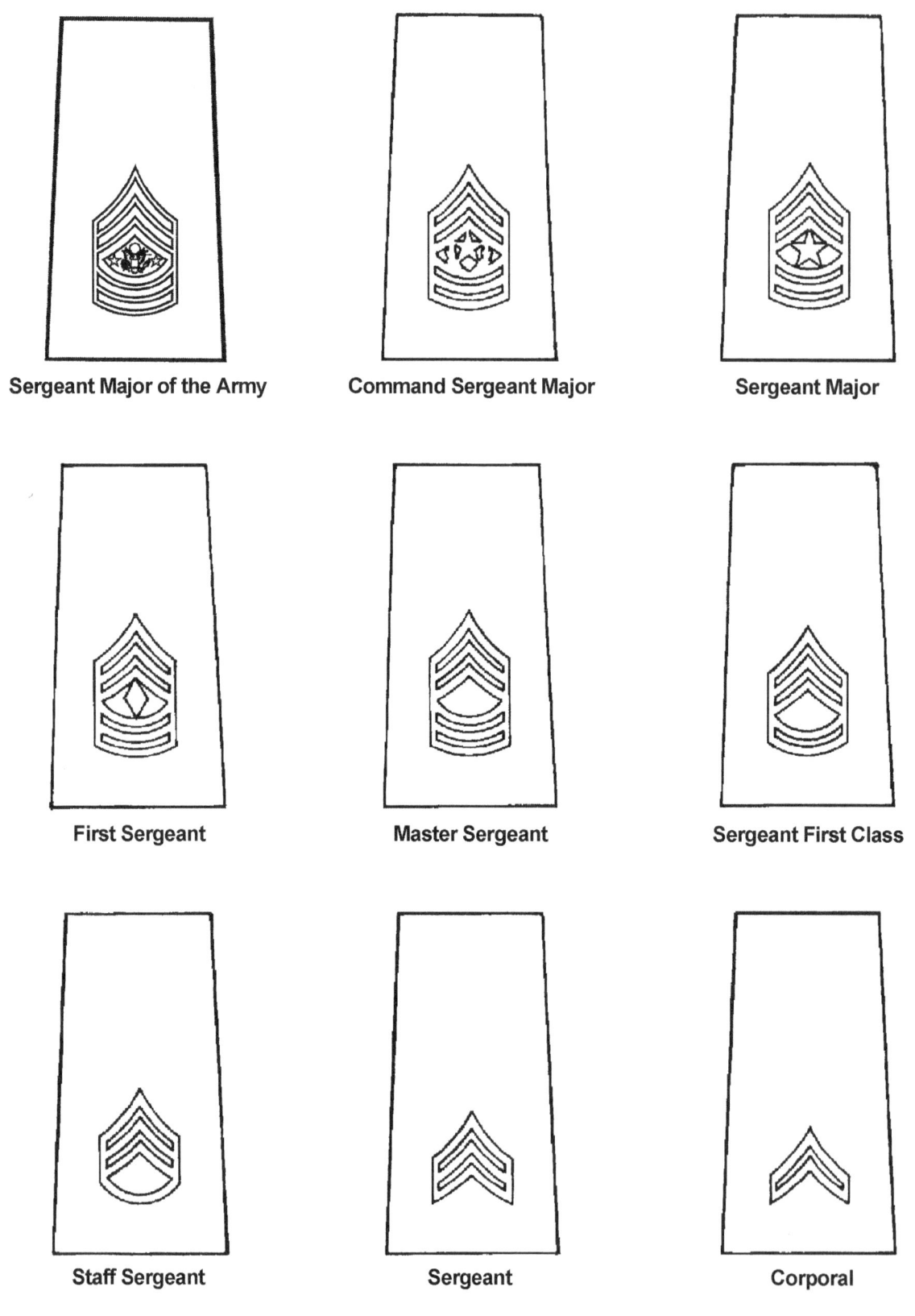

**Sergeant Major of the Army**    **Command Sergeant Major**    **Sergeant Major**

**First Sergeant**    **Master Sergeant**    **Sergeant First Class**

**Staff Sergeant**    **Sergeant**    **Corporal**

Figure 28–65. Shoulder marks, enlisted

(3) Sizes. Shoulder marks come in two sizes to accommodate differences in the manufacturing of shoulder loops on shirts and sweaters. All personnel may wear either size of the shoulder marks. The shoulder mark fits the shoulder loop properly when the Velcro attachments or buttons are completely exposed, enabling exact alignment of the Velcro hook and pile attachments, or fastening of buttons.

(a) Large. The large shoulder mark is 2⅛ inches wide at the base and 4¼ inches in length, tapering to 1¾ inches wide at the top.

(b) Small. The small shoulder mark is 2⅛ inches wide at the base and 3¼ inches in length, tapering to 1–25/32 inches wide at the top.

(4) How worn. Shoulder marks are worn by all personnel in the rank of corporal and above on the shoulder loops of the AG 415 shirt, the AG 415 maternity shirt, the black unisex cardigan, and the black pullover sweater. When the tunic is worn, pregnant soldiers will button the shoulder loop of the AG 415 maternity shirt over the top of the tunic shoulder piece, so the shoulder mark is visible.

b. Shoulder straps (officer personnel only).

(1) Sizes. Shoulder straps are made in large and small sizes.

(a) Male. The shoulder strap is 1⅝ inches wide and 4 inches long.

(b) Female. The shoulder strap is 1⅝ inches wide and 3½ inches long.

(2) Design. For general officers, the background is blue-black velvet. For all other officers, the background is a rayon-grosgrain ribbon of the first-named color of the officer's basic branch. The strap has an 11/32-inch gold-colored border, surrounded on the inside and outside by a single strand in gold jaceron. If the officer's branch has two colors, the second branch color is used as a ⅛-inch inside border, in lieu of gold jaceron. Insignia and borders are rayon embroidery or bullion and jaceron (see fig 28–66).

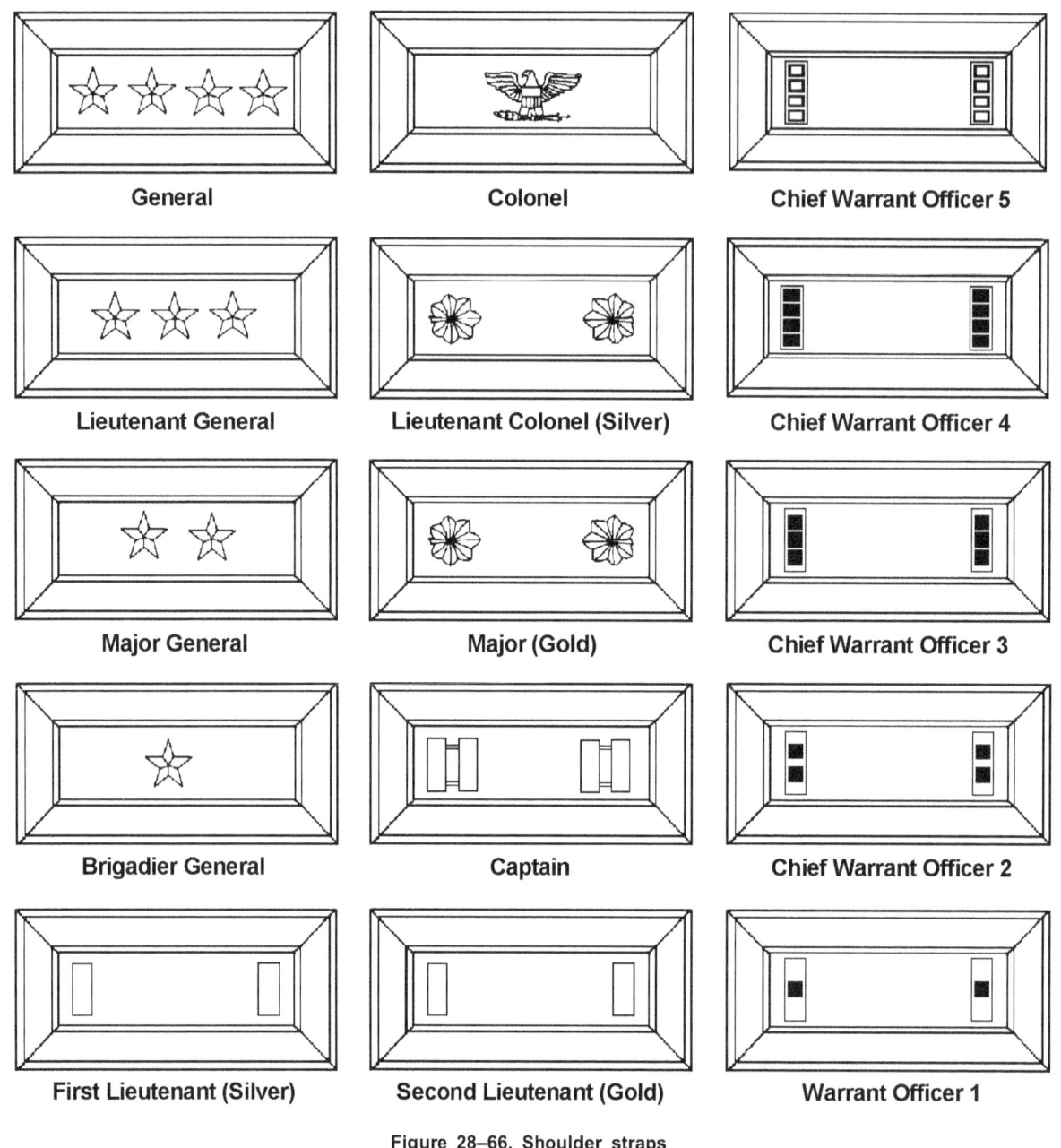

| | | |
|---|---|---|
| General | Colonel | Chief Warrant Officer 5 |
| Lieutenant General | Lieutenant Colonel (Silver) | Chief Warrant Officer 4 |
| Major General | Major (Gold) | Chief Warrant Officer 3 |
| Brigadier General | Captain | Chief Warrant Officer 2 |
| First Lieutenant (Silver) | Second Lieutenant (Gold) | Warrant Officer 1 |

Figure 28–66. Shoulder straps

(3) Insignia. Grade insignia for officers is embroidered on the shoulder straps in the following designs.

(a) General officers. The insignia is the appropriate number of silver-colored stars, each ⅝ inch in diameter. All stars are worn with one point facing the neck. Stars on the shoulder straps are placed point to point.

(b) Colonel. The insignia is a silver-colored spread eagle, ⅝ inch in height with 1¼ inches between the tips of the wings. Shoulder straps are made in pairs; on each strap, the eagle is centered with the head facing forward.

(c) Lieutenant colonel. The insignia is a silver-colored oak leaf, ⅝ inch in length and ⅝ inch in width, positioned on each end of the shoulder strap.

(d) Major. The insignia is a gold-colored oak leaf, ⅝ inch in length and ⅝ inch in width, positioned on each end of the shoulder strap.

(e) Captain. The insignia is two silver-colored bars, each ¼ inch in width and ⅝ inch in length, parallel to the ends of the strap, 3/16 of an inch apart and 3/16 of an inch from the inside border, positioned at each end of the shoulder strap.

*(f)* First lieutenant. The insignia is one silver-colored bar, ¼ inch in width and ⅝ inch in length, parallel to the ends of the strap and 3/16 of an inch from the inside border, positioned at each end of the shoulder strap.

*(g)* Second lieutenant. The insignia is one gold-colored bar, ¼ inch in width and ⅝ inch in length, parallel to the ends of the strap and 3/16 of an inch from the inside border, positioned at each end of the shoulder strap.

*(h)* Chief warrant officer 5 (CW5). The insignia is a silver-colored bar, ¼ inch in width and ¾ inch in length, with one black line in the center of the insignia.

*(i)* Chief warrant officer 4 (CW4). The insignia is a silver-colored bar, ¼ inch in width and ¾ inch in length, with four silver squares centered on the bar, positioned parallel to, and at each end of the shoulder strap.

*(j)* Chief warrant officer 3 (CW3). The insignia is a silver-colored bar, ¼ inch in width and ¾ inch in length, with three black squares centered on the bar, positioned parallel to, and at each end of the shoulder strap.

*(k)* Chief warrant officer 2 (CW2). The insignia is a silver-colored bar, ¼ inch in width and ¾ inch in length, with two black squares centered on the bar, positioned parallel to, and at each end of the shoulder strap.

*(l)* Warrant officer 1 (WO1). The insignia is a silver-colored bar, ¼ inch in width and ¾ inch in length, with one black square centered on the bar, positioned parallel to, and at each end of the shoulder strap.

(4) How worn. On each shoulder, the shoulder strap is sewn, snapped, or hooked to the coat of the Army blue uniform, centered lengthwise on the outside shoulder seam.

*c.* Shoulder boards (female officers). Shoulder boards are worn by female officers, in the ranks of colonel and below, on the black mess and the old version of the white mess uniform jackets. The shoulder board is 4–11/16 inches long and 2 inches wide at the outer end. The background is wool facing cloth, in silk or synthetic grosgrain, or in satin cloth of the first-named color of the officer's basic branch. The shoulder board has a gold or gold-colored nylon, rayon, or synthetic metallic gold band, ⅜ inch wide, placed 1/16 inch from the outer edge of each side of the board. If the officer's branch has two colors, the second-named color is used as a ⅛-inch border placed against the inside edge of each gold band. The grade insignia is embroidered in gold or silver bullion or synthetic metallic yarn and is centered ⅝ inch from the lower edge of the shoulder board. Detachable shoulder boards are worn on each shoulder with the square end of the shoulder board positioned on the outside shoulder seam (see fig 28–67). (Note: Enlisted females may not wear the black mess or older version of the white mess uniform.)

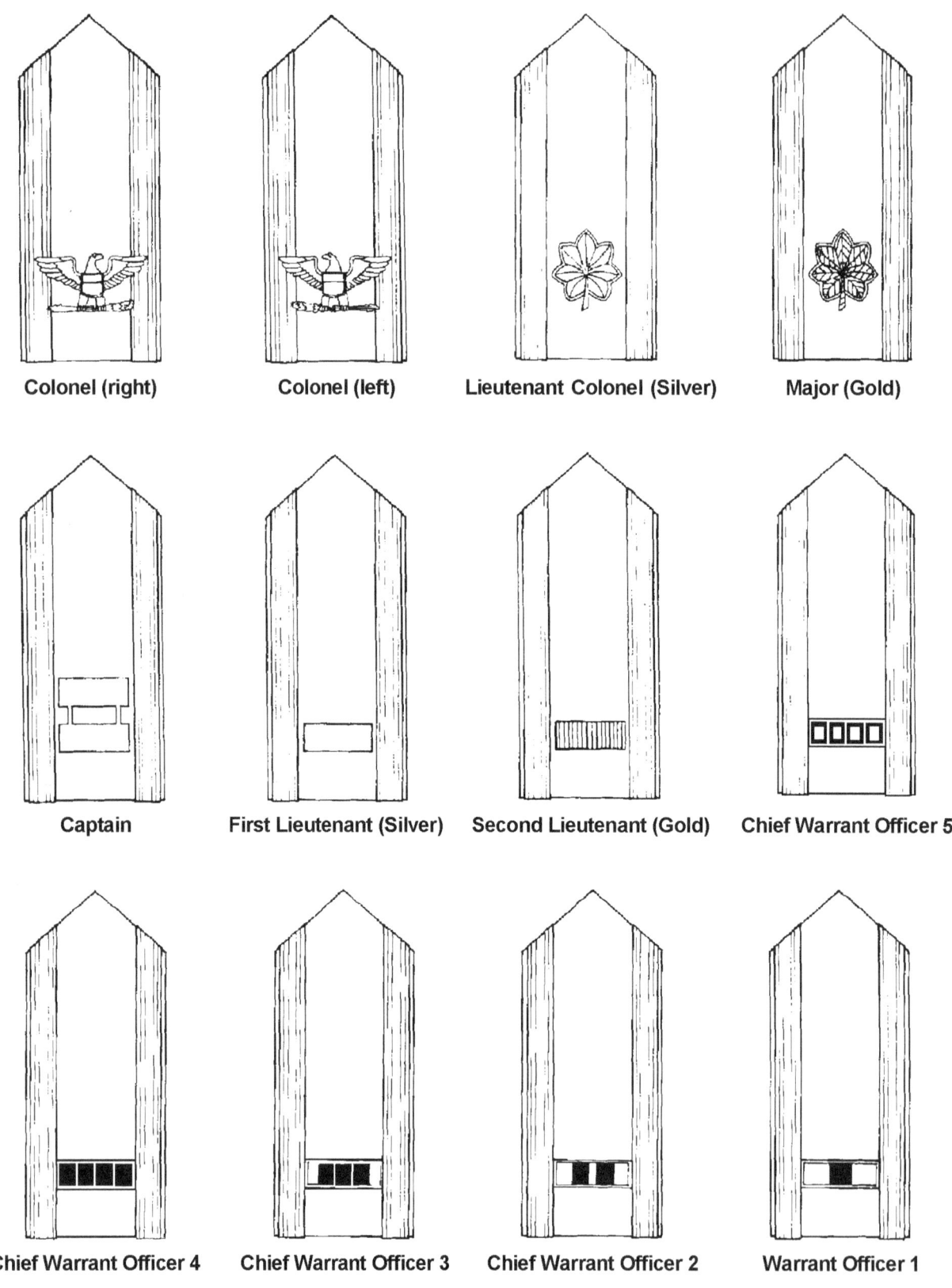

Colonel (right)    Colonel (left)    Lieutenant Colonel (Silver)    Major (Gold)

Captain    First Lieutenant (Silver)    Second Lieutenant (Gold)    Chief Warrant Officer 5

Chief Warrant Officer 4    Chief Warrant Officer 3    Chief Warrant Officer 2    Warrant Officer 1

Figure 28–67. Shoulder boards

*d.* Rank insignia tabs. Subdued cloth rank insignia tabs are optional purchase items for wear on the extended cold-weather clothing system (ECWCS) (Gortex) parka. Tabs are 1½ inches wide by 2 inches long and are sewn closed. The rank insignia tabs slip over the front tab of the parka.

## 28–9. Branch insignia—authority for

*a.* General officers.

(1) The Chief of Staff, former Chiefs of Staff, and generals of the Army (five star) may prescribe their branch insignia.

(2) All other general officers may wear branch insignia at their option. If they choose this option, general officers will wear the branch insignia for the position to which they are appointed, or for their duty assignment.

*b.* Other. All other commissioned and warrant officers serving on active duty will wear the insignia of their basic branch. When detailed to other branches, commissioned and warrant officers will wear the insignia of the branch to which they are detailed.

*c.* General staff. Warrant officers, and commissioned officers, other than general officers, will wear the general staff branch insignia as indicated below.

(1) When assigned to positions within the Office of the Secretary of the Army, the Under Secretary of the Army, or the Assistant Secretary of the Army, and when authorized by the Secretary of the Army to wear such insignia during their assignment in these offices.

(2) When detailed to duty on the Army General Staff (see AR 614–100).

(3) When detailed for general staff duty with troops (see AR 614–100).

(4) As directed by the Chief of Staff.

(5) When assigned to departmental or statutory tour table of distribution and allowance (TDA) positions in the National Guard Bureau.

(6) When assigned to the Army National Guard Command chief warrant officer positions within the office of the Adjutant General of each state, Puerto Rico, U.S. Virgin Islands, Guam, or the District of Columbia.

*d.* The Inspector General branch insignia is worn by the inspector general and those officers detailed as inspectors general, under the provisions of AR 614–100.

*e.* National Guard Bureau branch insignia is worn by those officers detailed to the National Guard Bureau for 180 days or longer, U.S. Property and Fiscal Office officers, and other Army National Guard (ARNG) tour officers, as prescribed by Chief, National Guard Bureau.

*f.* Officers assigned to the ARNG and the U.S. Army Reserve (USAR), and who are not on extended active duty, wear staff specialist branch insignia (see NGR 600–102 (ARNG) or AR 140–10).

*g.* Civil affairs (CA) reserve officers wear USAR branch insignia as follows:

(1) When assigned or detailed to the CA branch in accordance with AR 140–10, while serving in an inactive duty or active duty for training status.

(2) When assigned to a CA-USAR troop program unit that has mobilized.

(3) When serving on extended active duty with CA troop program units.

(4) When assigned to CA mobilization designation positions upon mobilization.

(5) Officers will wear the insignia of the branch in which they are detailed, unless they are on extended active duty with other than CA units.

*h.* Judge Advocate General's Corps officers detailed to the Judge Advocate General's Corps (JAGC), who are not yet admitted to practice law before a Federal court or the highest court of a state, will wear their basic branch insignia. They may wear JAGC insignia after they are admitted to practice.

*i.* Enlisted personnel. All enlisted personnel will wear the branch insignia of their PMOS, with the following exceptions.

(1) Basic trainees will wear the U.S. insignia on both collars; they will not wear branch insignia (see para 28–4*b*(2)(c)).

(2) Noncommissioned officers in authorized Inspector General MTOE or TDA positions will wear the Inspector General insignia.

(3) Command sergeants major will wear command sergeant major collar insignia in lieu of branch insignia.

(4) The Sergeant Major of the Army (SMA) will wear SMA insignia in lieu of branch insignia.

## 28–10. Branch insignia

*a.* Regimental collar insignia.

(1) Regimental collar insignia is the soldier's branch insignia on which the numerical designation of the regiment is affixed. Regimental collar insignia is worn in lieu of the branch insignia by officer and enlisted soldiers affiliated with

infantry, armor, field artillery, air defense artillery, cavalry, special forces, or aviation regiments. Soldiers affiliated with these regiments also will wear the regimental collar insignia when not assigned to the regiment, except as provided in paragraph 28–9, above. A soldier affiliated to a regiment but having a branch other than the currently assigned branch will wear the assigned branch insignia without a numeral. Soldiers will not wear numerals designating battalions on regimental collar insignia. Regimental collar insignia is locally procured and furnished as an organizational item to affiliated enlisted soldiers. Commanders will permit enlisted soldiers who are affiliated with the regiment to retain regimental collar insignia when reassigned from the affiliated regiment.

(2) The regimental number for the combat arms branches is positioned as shown in figure 28–176. For armor, cavalry, special forces, infantry, aviation and field artillery officer branches, personnel may wear the regimental number as a separate item, positioned in the same location as illustrated for the one-piece insignia.

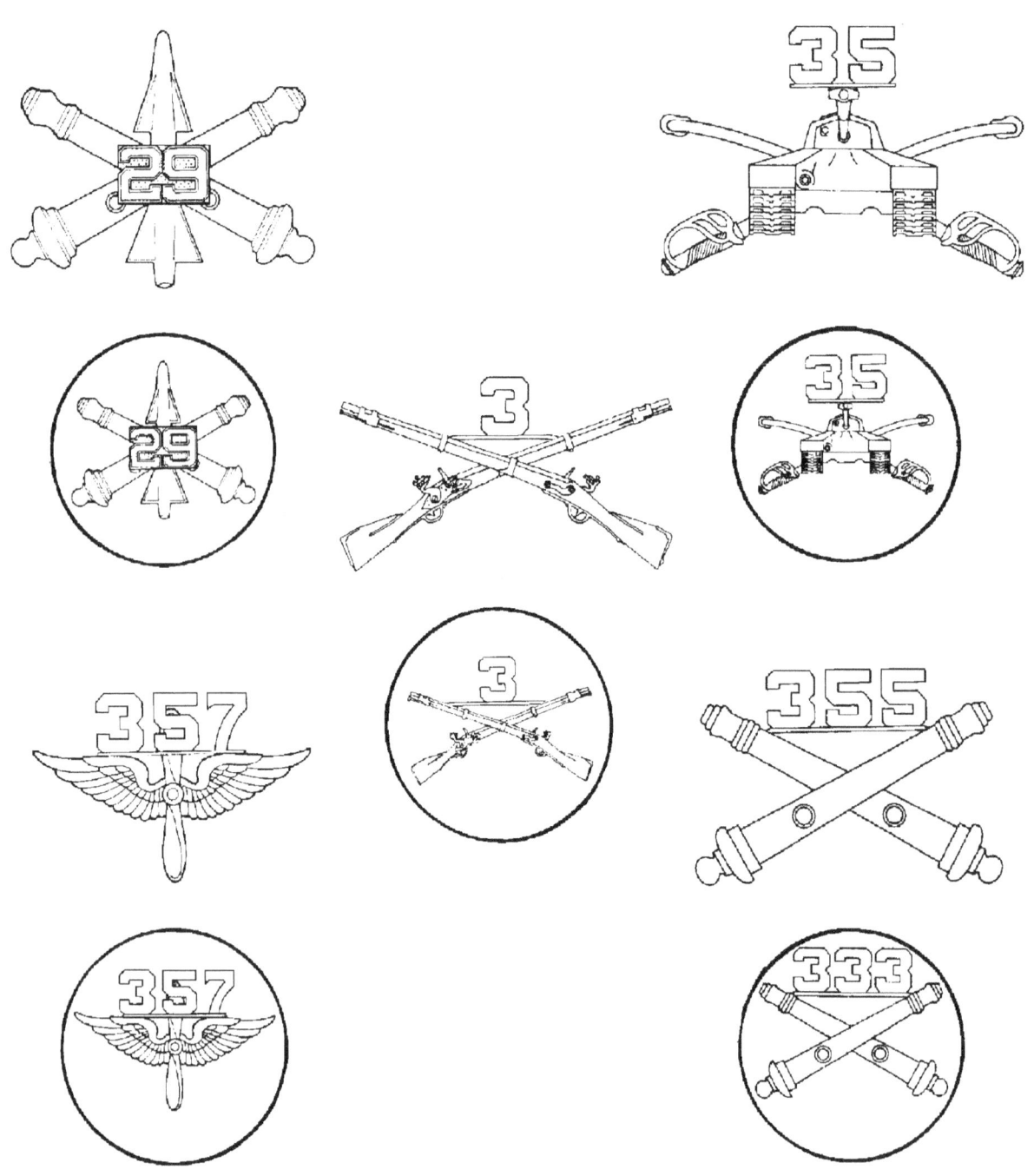

Figure 28–176. Regimental numbers attached to insignia

*b.* Branch insignia. Soldiers not affiliated with an infantry, armor, field artillery, air defense artillery, cavalry, special forces, or aviation regiment, except as provided for in paragraph 28–9, above, wear appropriate branch insignia. As an option, soldiers who are not affiliated with one of the above regiments, but who are assigned to a color-bearing regiment or separate TOE battalion of their branch, may wear the branch insignia with the numerical designation of the battalion or regiment affixed, when approved by the MACOM. Numerals are ¼ inch for officers and 3/16 inch for enlisted soldiers. All optional branch insignia are authorized for wear only while personnel are assigned to the designated unit. Soldiers will not purchase optional branch insignia using appropriated funds. Commanders will not require soldiers to purchase optional branch insignia. Listed below are the branch insignia authorized for wear:

(1) Adjutant General's Corps. The officer branch insignia is a silver-colored shield 1 inch in height, with a chief of blue upon which there are 1 large and 12 small silver stars, and 13 vertical stripes, 7 silver and 6 red. Enlisted personnel have the same design centered on a 1-inch disk in gold-colored metal (see fig 28–68).

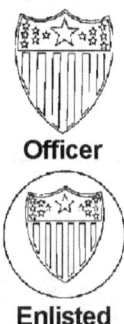

**Officer**

**Enlisted**

**Figure 28–68. Insignia of branch, Adjutant General's Corps**

(2) Air Defense Artillery. The officer branch insignia is a missile surmounting two crossed field guns, in gold-colored metal 1⅛ inches in height. Enlisted personnel have the same design centered on a 1-inch disk in gold-colored metal (see fig 28–69).

**Officer**

**Enlisted**

**Figure 28–69. Insignia of branch, Air Defense Artillery**

(3) Armor. The officer branch insignia is the front view of an M-26 tank gun, slightly raised and superimposed on two crossed cavalry sabers in scabbards with the cutting edge up, 13/16 inch in height overall, in gold-colored metal. Enlisted personnel have the same design centered on a 1-inch disk in gold-colored metal (see fig 28–70).

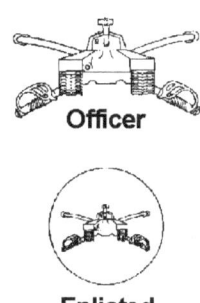

**Officer**

**Enlisted**

Figure 28-70. Insignia of branch, Armor

(4) Army Medical Specialist Corps (officers only). The branch insignia is a gold-colored metal caduceus, 1 inch in height, with a ⅜-inch monogram consisting of the letter "S" in black enamel, superimposed upon the caduceus (see fig 28-71).

Figure 28-71. Insignia of branch, Army Medical Specialist Corps, officer

(5) Army Nurse Corps (officers only). The branch insignia is a gold-colored metal caduceus, 1 inch in height, with a ⅜-inch monogram consisting of the letter "N" in black enamel, superimposed upon the caduceus (see fig 28-72).

Figure 28-72. Insignia of branch, Army Nurse Corps, officer

(6) Command Sergeant Major collar insignia (enlisted personnel only). The branch insignia is the coat of arms of the United States on a 1-inch disk, in gold-colored metal (see fig 28–73).

**Figure 28–73. Collar insignia, command sergeant major**

(7) Aviation branch. The officer branch insignia is a vertical silver propeller between two horizontal gold wings, 1⅛ inches in width. Enlisted personnel have the same design on a 1-inch disk in gold-colored metal (see fig 28–74).

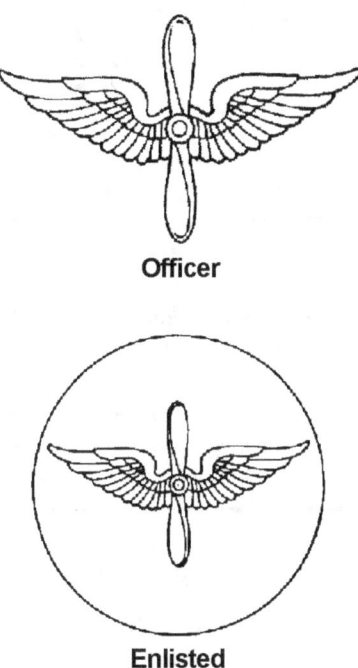

**Officer**

**Enlisted**

**Figure 28–74. Insignia of branch, Aviation**

(8) Cavalry collar insignia. Officers and enlisted personnel assigned to cavalry regiments, cavalry squadrons, or separate cavalry troops are authorized to wear cavalry insignia in lieu of the branch insignia, when approved by the MACOM commander. The officer collar insignia is two crossed sabers in scabbards with the cutting edge up, 11/16 inch in height, in gold-colored metal. The enlisted collar insignia is the same design on a 1-inch disk in gold-colored metal (see fig 28–75).

**Officer**

**Enlisted**

Figure 28–75. Insignia of branch, Cavalry

(9) Chaplains (see fig 28–76).

Figure 28–76. Insignia of branch, Chaplain, officer

*(a)* Christian faith (officers only). The insignia is a silver-colored Latin cross, 1 inch in height.

*(b)* Jewish faith (officers only). The insignia is a silver-colored double tablet bearing Hebrew numerals from I to X, surmounted by two interlaced, equilateral triangles, 1 inch in height.

*(c)* Buddhist faith (officers only). The insignia is a silver-colored dharma cakra (8–spoked wheel), 1 inch in height.

*(d)* Muslim faith (officers only). The insignia is a silver-colored crescent moon.

*(e)* Chaplain's assistant collar insignia (enlisted personnel only). The insignia is a gold-colored pair of stylized hands enclosing a chapel with the door open, on a 1-inch disk (see fig 28–77).

Figure 28–77. Collar insignia, chaplain assistant, enlisted

(10) Chemical Corps. The officer insignia is a benzene ring of cobalt blue enamel, superimposed in the center of crossed gold-colored retorts, ½ inch in height and 1–13/16 inch in width overall. Enlisted personnel have the same design on a 1-inch disk, in gold-colored metal (see fig 28–78).

**Figure 28–78. Insignia of branch, Chemical Corps**

(11) Civil Affairs. USAR. The officer branch insignia is a gold-colored globe, ⅝ inch in diameter, upon which is superimposed a torch of liberty, 1 inch in height, surmounted by a scroll and sword crossed in saltire. Enlisted personnel have the same design on a 1-inch disk, in gold-colored metal (see fig 28–79).

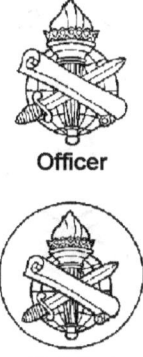

**Figure 28–79. Insignia of branch, Civil Affairs**

(12) Corps of Engineers. The officer branch insignia is a gold-colored, triple-turreted castle, 11/16 inch in height. Enlisted personnel have the same design on a 1-inch disk, in gold-colored metal (see fig 28–80).

Officer

Enlisted

**Figure 28–80. Insignia of branch, Corps of Engineers**

(13) Dental Corps (officers only). The insignia is a gold-colored metal caduceus, 1 inch in height, with a ⅜-inch monogram consisting of the letter "D" in black enamel, superimposed upon the caduceus (see fig 28–81).

**Figure 28–81. Insignia of branch, Dental Corps, officer**

(14) Field Artillery. The officer branch insignia is two crossed field guns in gold-colored metal, 13/16 inch in height. Enlisted personnel have the same design on a 1-inch disk, in gold-colored metal (see fig 28–82).

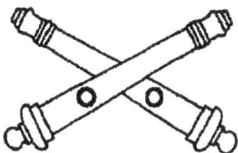

**Figure 28–82. Insignia of branch, Field Artillery**

(15) Finance Corps. The officer branch insignia is a gold-colored metal diamond, 1 inch by ¾ inch, with the short axis vertical. Enlisted personnel have the same design on a 1-inch disk, in gold-colored metal (see fig 28–83).

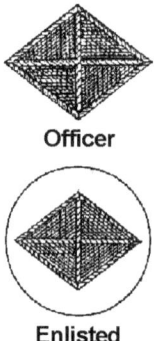

Officer

Enlisted

**Figure 28–83. Insignia of branch, Finance Corps**

(16) General Staff (commissioned and warrant officers only). The insignia is the coat of arms of the United States, 5/8 inch in height, in gold-colored metal, superimposed on a five-pointed, silver-colored star, 1 inch in diameter. The shield consists of enamel stripes of white and red, with a chief of blue, and a blue glory (see fig 28-84). The insignia is worn by officers and warrant officers as prescribed in para 28-9*c*(1) through (5).

**Figure 28–84. Insignia of branch, General Staff, officer**

(17) Infantry. The officer branch insignia is two gold-colored crossed muskets, ¾ inch in height. Enlisted personnel have the same design on a 1-inch disk, in gold-colored metal (see fig 28–85).

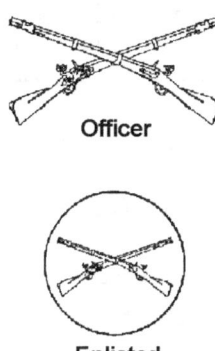

**Officer**

**Enlisted**

**Figure 28–85. Insignia of branch, Infantry**

(18) Inspector General. The officer branch insignia is a sword and fasces, ¾ inch in height, crossed and wreathed in gold-colored metal with the inscription "DROIT ET AVANT" (Right and Forward) in blue enamel, on the upper part of wreath. Enlisted personnel have the same design on a 1-inch disk, in gold-colored metal (see fig 28–86).

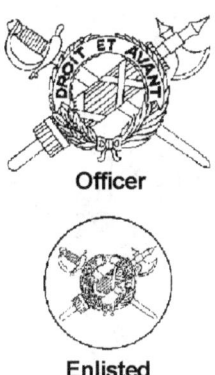

**Officer**

**Enlisted**

**Figure 28–86. Insignia of branch, Inspector General Corps**

(19) Judge Advocate General's Corps. The officer branch insignia is a gold-colored sword and pen, crossed and wreathed, 11/16 inch in height. Enlisted personnel have the same design on a 1-inch disk, in gold-colored metal (see fig 28–87).

**Officer**

**Enlisted**

Figure 28–87. Insignia of branch, Judge Advocate General's Corps

(20) Medical Corps. The officer branch insignia is a gold-colored caduceus, 1 inch in height. Enlisted personnel have the same design on a 1-inch disk, in gold-colored metal (see fig 28–88).

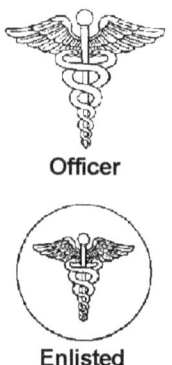

**Officer**

**Enlisted**

Figure 28–88. Insignia of branch, Medical Corps

(21) Medical Service Corps (officers only). The branch of insignia is a silver-colored caduceus, 1 inch in height, with a ⅜-inch monogram consisting of the letters "MS" in black enamel, superimposed upon the caduceus (see fig 28–89).

Figure 28–89. Insignia of branch, Medical Service Corps, officer

(22) Military Intelligence. The officer branch insignia is a gold-colored metal dagger, point up, 1¼ inches overall in height, upon which there is a gold-colored metal heraldic sun composed of four straight and four wavy alternating rays, surmounted by a gold heraldic rose with dark blue enamel petals. Enlisted personnel have the same design on a 1-inch disk, in gold-colored metal (see fig 28–90).

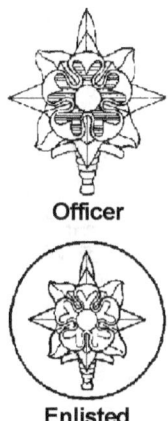

**Officer**

**Enlisted**

Figure 28–90. Insignia of branch, Military Intelligence

(23) Military Police Corps. The officer branch insignia is two crossed gold-colored metal pistols, ¾ inch in height. Enlisted personnel have the same design on a 1-inch disk, in gold-colored metal (see fig 28–91).

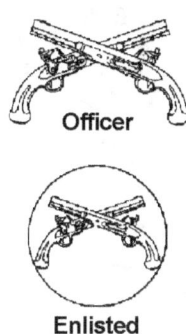

**Officer**

**Enlisted**

Figure 28–91. Insignia of branch, Military Police Corps

(24) National Guard Bureau (officers only). The branch insignia is two crossed gold-colored fasces superimposed on an eagle displayed with wings reversed, ¾ inch in height (see fig 28–92).

Figure 28–92. Insignia of branch, National Guard Bureau, officer

(25) Ordnance Corps. The officer branch insignia is a gold-colored shell and flame, 1 inch in height. Enlisted personnel have the same design on a 1-inch disk, in gold-colored metal (see fig 28–93).

**Officer**

**Enlisted**

**Figure 28–93. Insignia of branch, Ordnance Corps**

(26) Psychological Operations collar insignia (enlisted personnel only). The insignia is a Trojan horse with lightning bolts and two swords, on a 1-inch disk, in gold-colored metal (see fig 28–94).

**Figure 28–94. Insignia of branch, Psychological Operations, enlisted**

(27) Public Affairs collar insignia (enlisted personnel only). The insignia consists of a quill crossed with an electronic flash with a broadsword, on a 1-inch disk, in gold-colored metal (see fig 28–95).

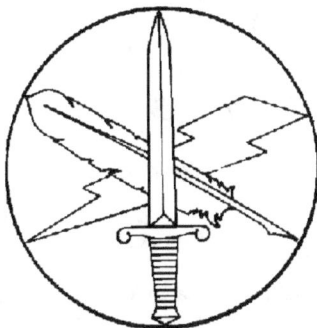

Figure 28–95. Insignia of branch, Public Affairs, enlisted

(28) Quartermaster Corps. The officer branch insignia is a gold-colored sword and key crossed on a wheel surmounted by a flying eagle, with the felloe of the wheel set with 13 stars, ¾ inch in height. The felloe of the wheel is blue enamel, and the hub center is red, edged with white. Enlisted personnel have the same design on a 1-inch disk, in gold-colored metal (see fig 28–96).

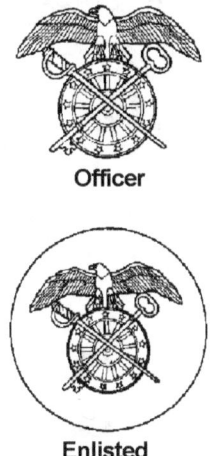

Officer

Enlisted

Figure 28–96. Insignia of branch, Quartermaster Corps

(29) Signal Corps. The officer branch insignia is two signal flags crossed, the dexter flag white with a red center, the other flag red with a white center, with staffs of gold and a flaming torch in gold-colored metal, upright at the center of the crossed flags, ⅞ inch in height. Enlisted personnel have the same design on a 1-inch disk, in gold-colored metal (see fig 28–97).

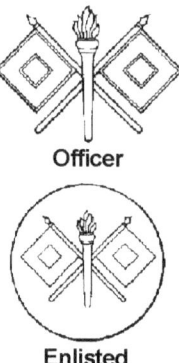

Officer

Enlisted

Figure 28–97. Insignia of branch, Signal Corps

(30) Staff Specialist, ARNG and USAR (officers only). The branch insignia is a sword, 1⅜ inches in length, laid horizontally across the upper part of an open book. Below the sword and across the lower corners of the book are two laurel branches crossed at the stems. The insignia is 13/16 inch in height, in gold-colored metal (see fig 28–98).

Figure 28–98. Insignia of branch, Staff Specialist, ARNG/USAR, officer

(31) Special Forces. The officer branch insignia is two crossed, gold-colored arrows, ¾ inch in height. Enlisted personnel have the same design on a 1-inch disk, in gold-colored metal (see fig 28–99).

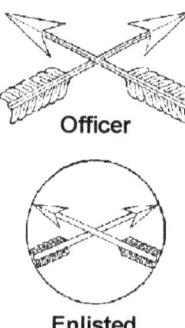

Officer

Enlisted

Figure 28–99. Insignia of branch, Special Forces

(32) The Sergeant Major of the Army collar insignia. The insignia is a gold-colored shield, ¾ inch in height, with the base divided diagonally from the upper left to the lower right. The upper part of the insignia is red and the lower part is white. The insignia consists of a silver five-pointed star surmounted by the coat of arms of the United States, in color, between two white five-pointed stars at the top, and two red five-pointed stars at the base. The shield is on a 1-inch disk, in gold-colored metal (see fig 28–100).

Figure 28–100. Collar insignia, Sergeant Major of the Army

(33) Transportation Corps. The officer branch insignia is a ship's steering wheel, upon which is superimposed a shield charged with a winged car wheel on a rail, all in gold-colored metal, 1 inch in height. Enlisted personnel have the same design on a 1-inch disk, in gold-colored metal (see fig 28–101).

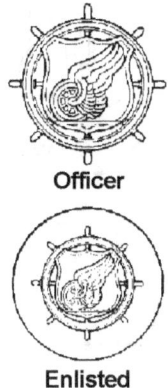

Officer

Enlisted

Figure 28–101. Insignia of branch, Transportation Corps

(34) Veterinary Corps (officers only). The branch insignia is a gold-colored metal caduceus, 1 inch in height, with a ⅜-inch monogram consisting of the letter "V" in black enamel, superimposed upon the caduceus (see fig 28–102).

Figure 28–102. Insignia of branch, Veterinary Corps, officer

(35) Warrant officer collar insignia. The insignia is an eagle rising with wings displayed, standing on a bundle of two arrows, all enclosed in a gold-colored wreath, in gold-colored metal, ¾ inch in height. Warrant officer candidates will wear the warrant officer "Eagle Rising" insignia beginning at the senior phase of warrant officer candidate school and continuing through their graduation from warrant officer basic course.

Figure 28–103. Insignia of branch, warrant officer

(36) Band collar insignia (enlisted personnel only). The band insignia is a music lyre on a 1-inch disk, in gold-colored metal (fig 28-177).

Figure 28–177. Collar insignia, band, enlisted

c. Subdued branch insignia.

(1) All subdued branch insignia is of the same design and size as the non-subdued insignia described above, except they are black-colored enamel, or black embroidery on green background cloth, with the exception of the following.

Note. Variations of spicebrown embroidery on khaki cloth are used for desert insignia.

(a) Army Medical Specialist Corps, Nurse Corps, Dental Corps, Medical Corps, Medical Service Corps, and Veterinary Corps. The embroidered caduceus is black and the superimposed letters are olive-drab.

(b) General Staff. The embroidered star is black and the eagle is olive drab.

(2) Enlisted personnel do not wear branch insignia on field or utility uniforms, therefore, subdued enlisted branch insignia is not authorized.

d. Branch insignia signified on the lapel of mess and evening mess uniforms. The lapels of the male and female Army blue mess and evening mess jackets are made from rayon, acetate, or other synthetic fabric with a satin face, in the following colors.

(1) General officers (except chaplains) and enlisted personnel: dark blue.

(2) All chaplains: black.

(3) All other officers: the first-named color of their basic branch.

e. Ornamentation and branch insignia for detailed officers. Detailed officers will wear shoulder straps, shoulder boards, and other colors of ornamentation (lapel facing, sleeve braid, cape lining; and blue service cap hatband for other than general officers) on the dress and mess uniforms in the colors of their basic branch. Detailed officers will wear the branch insignia for the branch to which they are detailed.

### 28–11. Insignia for aides

*a.* Non-subdued insignia for aides.

(1) Aides to the President of the United States. The insignia is a blue shield bearing a circle of 13 white stars, supporting a gold eagle displayed with wings inverted and displayed above the shield, 1¼ inches in height overall (see fig 28–104).

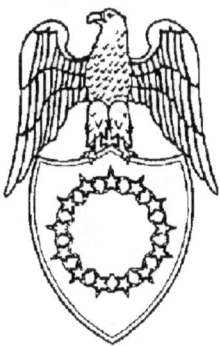

**Figure 28–104. Insignia for aides to the President of the United States**

(2) Aides to the Vice President of the United States. The insignia is a white shield bearing a circle of 13 blue stars, supporting a gold-colored eagle displayed with wings inverted above the shield, 1¼ inches in height overall (see fig 28–105).

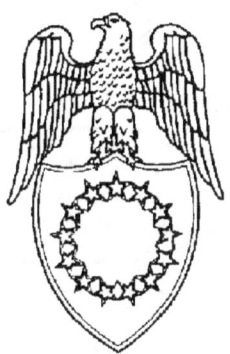

**Figure 28–105. Insignia for aides to the Vice President of the United States**

(3) Aides to the Secretary of Defense. The insignia is a blue shield, ¾ inch in height, bearing three gold-colored crossed arrows between four white enameled stars (two and two), supporting a gold-colored eagle displayed with wings reversed above the shield, ½-inch in height (see fig 28–106).

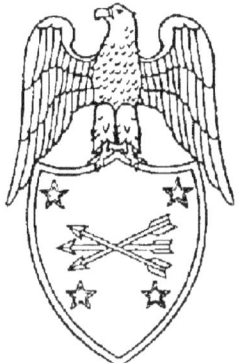

Figure 28–106. Insignia for aides to the Secretary of Defense

(4) Aides to the Secretary of the Army. The insignia is a red shield bearing the coat of arms of the United States in gold-colored metal, between four white enameled stars (two and two), supporting a gold-colored eagle displayed with wings reversed above the shield, 1¼ inches in height overall (see fig 28–107).

Figure 28–107. Insignia for aides to the Secretary of the Army

(5) Aides to the Under Secretary of the Army. The insignia is a white shield bearing the coat of arms of the United States in gold-colored metal, between four red enameled stars (two and two), supporting a gold-colored eagle displayed with wings reversed above the shield, 1¼ inches in height overall (see fig 28–108).

Figure 28–108. Insignia for aides to the Under Secretary of the Army

(6) Aides to the Chairman, Joint Chiefs of Staff. The insignia is a shield, ¾ inch in height, with the base divided diagonally from the upper left to the lower right. The upper part of the insignia is blue and the lower part is white. The shield bears a gold-colored eagle between two white five-pointed stars at the top and two blue five-pointed stars at the base. The shield supports a gold-colored eagle displayed with wings reversed above the shield, ½ inch in height (see fig 28–109).

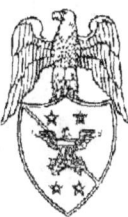

**Figure 28–109. Insignia for aides to the Chairman, Joint Chiefs of Staff**

(7) Aides to the Vice Chairman, Joint Chiefs of Staff. The insignia is a white shield, ¾ inch in height, bearing a gold-colored eagle between two five-pointed stars at the top and two five-pointed stars at the base (blue star on white, and white star on blue). The shield supports a gold-colored eagle displayed with wings reversed above the shield, ½ inch in height (see fig 28–110).

**Figure 28–110. Insignia for aides to the Vice Chairman, Joint Chiefs of Staff**

(8) Aides to the Chief of Staff of the Army. The insignia is a shield, ¾ inch in height, with the base divided diagonally from the lower left to the upper right. The upper part of the insignia is red and the lower part is white. The shield bears a silver, five-pointed star surmounted by the coat of arms of the United States in gold-colored metal, between two white five-pointed stars at the top, and two red five-pointed stars at the base. The shield supports a gold-colored eagle displayed with wings reversed above the shield, ½ inch in height (see fig 28–111).

**Figure 28–111. Insignia for aides to the Chief of Staff of the Army**

(9) Aides to the Vice Chief of Staff of the Army. The insignia is a shield, ¾ inch in height, with the base divided saltire-wise. The upper and lower parts of the shield are white, and each side is red. The shield bears a silver five-pointed star surmounted by the coat of arms of the United States in gold-colored metal, between two red five-pointed stars at the top and two red five-pointed stars at the base. The shield supports a gold-colored eagle displayed with wings reversed above the shield, ½ inch in height (see fig 28–112).

Figure 28–112. Insignia for aides to the Vice Chief of Staff of the Army

(10) Aides to general officers. The insignia is a shield, ¾ inch in height, with a blue chief and 13 vertical stripes (seven silver and six red). Above the chief is the applicable number of silver stars reflecting the grade of the general officer the aide is serving. The shield supports a gold-colored eagle displayed with wings reversed above the shield, ½ inch in height (see figs 28–113 through 28–117).

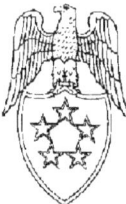

Figure 28–113. Insignia for aides to a general of the Army

Figure 28–114. Insignia for aides to a general

**Figure 28–115. Insignia for aides to a lieutenant general**

**Figure 28–116. Insignia for aides to a major general**

**Figure 28–117. Insignia for aides to a brigadier general**

*b.* Description of subdued branch insignia for aides.

(1) Aides to the President and Vice President of the United States. The insignia are the same designs and sizes as the full-color branch insignia covered in paragraph *a*, above, except the insignia are black-colored metal. For embroidered subdued insignia, the background of the shield is olive-drab and the eagle, stars, and outline of the shield are black.

*Note.* Variations of spicebrown embroidery on khaki cloth are used for desert insignia.

(2) Aides to the Secretary of Defense. The insignia is the same design and size as the full-color branch insignia covered in paragraph *a*, above, except the insignia is black-colored metal. For embroidered subdued insignia, the background of the shield is olive-drab and the eagle, stars, arrows, and outline of the shield are black.

(3) Aides to the Secretary of the Army. The insignia is the same design and size as the full-color branch insignia covered in paragraph *a*, above, except the insignia is black-colored metal. For embroidered subdued insignia, the background of the shield is olive-drab and the eagle, stars, device, and outline of the shield are black.

(4) Aides to the Under Secretary of the Army. The insignia is the same design and size as the full-color branch insignia covered in paragraph *a*, above, except the insignia is brown-colored metal. For embroidered subdued insignia, the background of the shield is olive drab and the eagle, stars, device, and outline of the shield are brown.

(5) Aides to the Chairman Joint Chiefs of Staff; aides to the Vice Chairman, Joint Chiefs of Staff; aides to the Chief of Staff of the Army, and aides to the Vice Chief of Staff of the Army. The insignia are the same designs and sizes as the full-color branch insignia covered in paragraph *a*, above, except the insignia are black-colored metal. For embroidered subdued insignia, the background of the shield is olive drab, and the charges, eagle, diagonal division line(s), and outline of the shield are black.

(6) Aides to general officers. The insignia is the same design and size as the full-color branch insignia covered in paragraph *a*, above, except the insignia is black-colored metal. For embroidered subdued insignia, the shield of

alternating stripes consists of olive-drab and black stripes. The background of the chief is olive-drab with black embroidered stars and eagles. The division line on the shield and the outline of the shield are black.

## 28–12. Branch insignia—how worn

As used in this paragraph, the word "collar" refers to that part of the coat or shirt (around the neck) that forms a neckband and turnover piece. Bold borders on figs 28–21 through 28–27 depict the collar area. The word "lapel" is used when referring to the fold of the front of the coat that is a continuation of the collar, and which usually is separated by a notch in the collar.

*a.* Non-subdued branch insignia.

(1) Male officers. On the Army green, blue, and white coats, male officers wear their branch insignia centered on both lapels, 1¼ inches below the U.S. insignia. The branch insignia is positioned so that the centerline of the insignia bisects the centerline of the U.S. insignia and is parallel to the inside edge of the lapel (see fig 28–118). On the hospital duty uniform, male officers wear their branch insignia centered between the inside edge and the outside edge on the left collar, 1 inch from the lower edge of the collar, with the centerline of the insignia parallel to the lower edge of the collar (see fig 28–119). Except for chaplains, male officers will not wear their branch insignia on the AG 415 long- or short-sleeved shirts. Chaplains wear their branch insignia centered immediately over the left breast pocket (see fig 28–120). On the black pullover sweater, chaplains will wear their branch insignia centered above the nameplate, in lieu of the distinctive unit insignia.

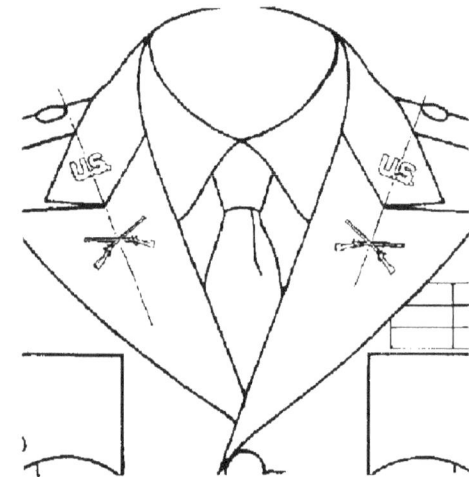

Figure 28–118. Wear of insignia of branch on the Army green, blue, and white uniforms, male officers

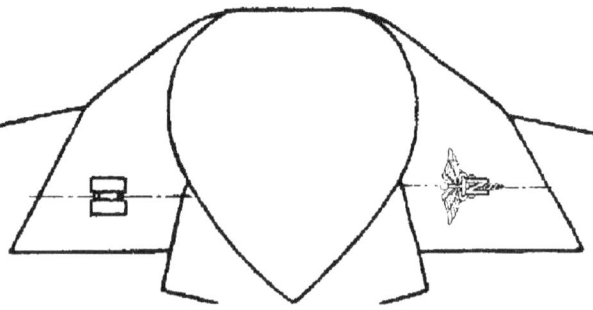

Figure 28–119. Wear of insignia of branch on the hospital duty uniform

Figure 28–120. Wear of chaplain insignia on the AG 415 shirt

(2) Male enlisted personnel. On the Army green, blue, and white coats, enlisted males wear their branch insignia centered on the left collar, with the bottom of the disk approximately 1 inch above the notch, with the centerline of the insignia parallel to the inside edge of the lapel (see fig 28–121).

Figure 28–121. Wear of insignia of branch on the Army green, blue, and white uniforms, male enlisted

(3) Female officers. On the old versions of the Army white and blue coats, female officers wear branch insignia on the left collar. The insignia is worn 1 inch above the notch, so the centerline of the insignia bisects the notch and is parallel to the inside edge of the collar (see fig 28–122). On the Army green coat and the new versions of the Army blue and white coats, female officers wear branch insignia on both lapels. The insignia is worn approximately 1¼ inches below the U.S. insignia, with the insignia bisecting the U.S. insignia and parallel to the inside edge of the lapel (see fig 28–123). On the hospital duty uniform, female officers wear the branch insignia centered on the left collar, 1 inch up from the lower edge of the collar, with the centerline of the insignia parallel to the lower edge of the collar. Except for chaplains, female officers will not wear branch insignia on the AG 415 short- or long-sleeved shirts. Female chaplains wear the branch insignia in a location similar to that described for male chaplains (see para 28–12a, above). On the black pullover sweater, chaplains wear their branch insignia centered above the nameplate, in lieu of the distinctive unit insignia.

Figure 28–122. Wear of insignia of branch, female officers, on the old version Army blue and white uniforms

Figure 28–123. Wear of insignia of branch, female officers, on the Army green uniform and the new version blue and white uniforms

(4) Female enlisted personnel. On the old versions of the Army blue and white coats, enlisted females wear branch insignia on the left collar. The insignia is worn 1 inch above the notch and centered, with the centerline of the insignia bisecting the notch, and parallel to the inside edge of the collar (see fig 28–124). On the Army green coat and the new versions of the Army blue and white coats, enlisted females wear their branch insignia on the left collar. The insignia is worn so the bottom of the disk is centered between the outside point and inside edge of the collar, approximately ⅝ inch up from the notch, with the centerline of the branch insignia parallel to the inside edge of the lapel (see fig 28–125).

**Figure 28–124. Wear of insignia of branch, enlisted female, on the old version Army blue and white uniforms**

**Figure 28–125. Wear of insignia of branch, enlisted female, on the Army green uniform and the new version blue and white uniforms**

*b.* Subdued branch insignia.

(1) On all field, utility, and select organizational uniforms, male and female officers wear subdued branch insignia centered on the left collar, 1 inch up from the lower edge of the collar with the centerline of the insignia parallel to the lower edge of the collar (see fig 28–119).

(2) Enlisted personnel are not authorized to wear subdued branch insignia on Army uniforms.

(3) Officers may wear metal pin-on or embroidered branch insignia on cloth backing. Officers may not mix materials used for the branch insignia and grade; both must be made from the same material.

## 28–13. Insignia for U.S. Military Academy (USMA) staff
The USMA non-subdued branch insignia is the USMA coat of arms, 1 inch in height. The coat of arms consists of the shield of the United States bearing a Greek sword surmounted by the helmet of Pallas. The shield supports an eagle displayed with scroll and USMA motto, in gold-colored metal. Permanent professors, registrars, and civilian instructors of the USMA wear this insignia in the same manner as prescribed in paragraph 28–12 for all other branch insignia (see fig 28–126).

Figure 28-126. U.S. Military Academy staff personnel insignia

## 28-14. Branch insignia—officer candidates

*a.* Description. The non-subdued OCS insignia consists of the block letters "O.C.S." in gold-colored metal, 7/16 inch in height, with each letter followed by a period. The subdued insignia is the same design as above, except it is black (see fig 28-127).

Figure 28-127. Officer candidate insignia

*b.* How worn.

(1) Non-subdued insignia. Officer candidates wear their insignia as follows.

*(a)* On service and dress uniform coats, male candidates wear the insignia on both collars, 1 inch above the notch, with the centerline of the insignia bisecting the notch, and parallel to the inside edge of the lapel. Female candidates wear the insignia in the same manner as the U.S. insignia (see fig 28-23). It is centered on both collars, approximately 5/8 inch up from the collar and lapel seam, with the centerline of the insignia parallel to the inside edge of the lapel. On the male and female AG 415 and 469 shirt collars, the insignia is worn on both collars, 1 inch above the lower edge of the collar, with the centerline of the insignia parallel to the lower edge of the collar (see figs 28-128 and 28-129).

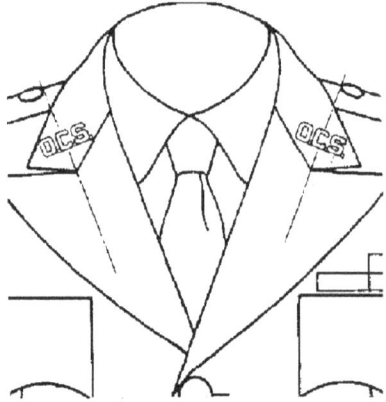

Figure 28-128. Wear of officer candidate insignia on coat lapels

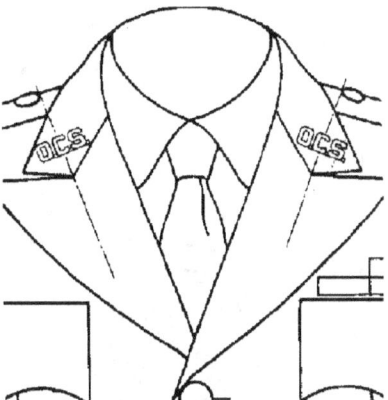

**Figure 28–129. Wear of officer candidate insignia on shirt collars**

*(b)* On the garrison cap, candidates wear the insignia centered on the left curtain, 1 inch from the front crease. Headgear insignia for service hats and caps are the same as prescribed for enlisted personnel (see paragraph 28–3 and fig 28–130).

**Figure 28–130. Wear of officer candidate insignia on garrison cap**

*(c)* On the helmet liner, candidates wear the O.C.S. decal in a prescribed color and size, centered on the front of the liner, 2½ inches from the bottom rim (see fig 28–131).

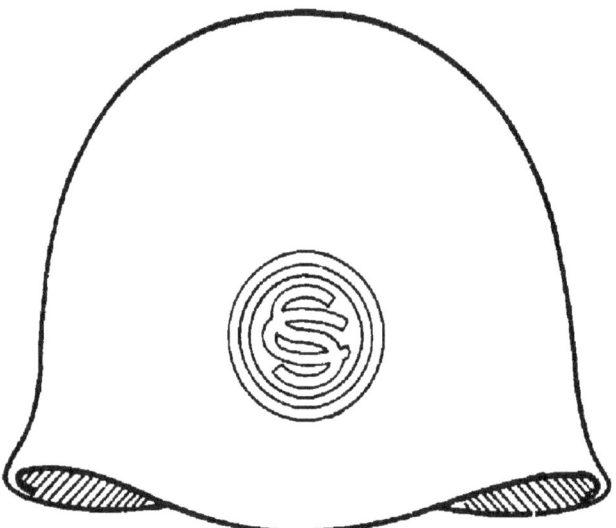

**Figure 28–131. Wear of officer candidate insignia on helmet liner**

*(d)* Senior candidates may wear the cloth O.C.S. design on the scarf (see fig 28–132).

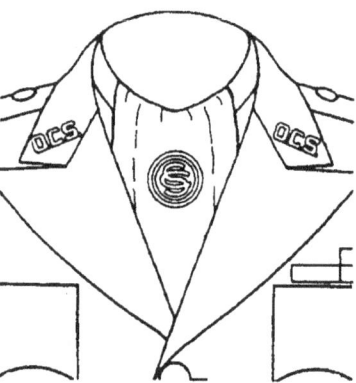

**Figure 28–132. Wear of officer candidate scarf**

(2) Subdued insignia. Candidates wear the subdued O.C.S. insignia on all utility shirts and cold-weather jackets in the same manner as the full-color insignia worn on shirt collars, as described above. All military personnel will wear this insignia while students at officer candidate schools.

## 28–15. Insignia for warrant officer candidates

*a.* Description. The non-subdued warrant officer candidate insignia consists of the block letters "W.O.C." in gold-colored metal, 7/16 inch in height, with each letter followed by a period. The subdued insignia is the same design as above, except it is black (see fig 28–133).

**Figure 28–133. Warrant officer candidate insignia**

*b.* How worn.

(1) Non-subdued insignia. Warrant officer candidates wear their insignia as follows.

*(a)* On service and dress uniform coats, candidates wear their insignia on both collars, in the same manner as described in para 28–14.

*(b)* On the garrison cap, candidates wear the insignia centered on the left curtain, 1 inch from the front crease. Headgear insignia for other service hats and caps are the same as prescribed for enlisted personnel (see para 28–3 and fig 28–130).

*(c)* On the helmet liner, candidates wear the W.O.C. decal painted on the front of the liner, in a prescribed color and size, 2½ inches from the bottom rim of the liner (see fig 28–131).

(2) Subdued insignia. Candidates wear subdued W.O.C. insignia on all utility shirts and cold-weather jackets in the same manner as the non-subdued insignia worn on shirt collars, as described above.

*c.* When worn. All active component personnel wear the insignia beginning on date of entry into the resident warrant officer entry course; all reserve component personnel wear the insignia beginning on date of board selection to enter WOC status. Both active component and reserve component WOC personnel will wear the insignia until appointed to the warrant officer category, or eliminated from WOC status.

## 28–16. Shoulder sleeve insignia-current organization

*a.* Authorization. Shoulder sleeve insignia (SSI) of a design approved by The Institute of Heraldry, U.S. Army, are authorized and prescribed for wear on the service and utility uniforms of the following echelons:

(1) MACOMs (as defined by AR 10–5).

(2) Armies.

(3) Corps.

(4) U.S. Army Reserve Command.

*(a)* Regional readiness commands.

*(b)* U.S. Army Reserve commands

(5) Divisions.

(6) Corps Support Command.

(7) Separate TOE brigades (not organic to divisions).

(8) Separate regiments (not organic to a group, brigade, or division), except training support regiments/battalions, which will wear the SSI of the training support division to which assigned.

(9) General officer commands, USAR.

(10) U.S. Army element of unified commands.

(11) DA field operating agencies based on the following:

*(a)* An identifiable command structure.

*(b)* A valid justification in terms of unit mission, improving unit morale, and degree of unit permanency.

*(c)* At least 250 military personnel assigned to the organization.

(12) Other organizations, except U.S. Army garrisons, meeting the following criteria.

*(a)* An identifiable command structure.

*(b)* A valid justification in terms of unit mission, improving unit morale, and degree of unit permanency.

*(c)* At least 500 military personnel assigned to the organization.

*b.* Approval of design. Units meeting the criteria established above will submit requests for authorization of SSI through command channels, with a copy of permanent orders activating the unit, to: Director, The Institute of Heraldry, U.S. Army, 9325 Gunston Road, Room S112, Fort Belvoir, VA 22060–5579.

*c.* Provisional units. The authorization of SSI will not be granted for provisional units.

*d.* By whom worn. Personnel assigned to units not authorized SSI will wear the SSI of the command to which the unit is assigned. As an exception, personnel assigned to training support regiments/battalions will wear the SSI of the training support division to which assigned or aligned.

(1) MACOM commanders are authorized to permit, on a case-by-case basis, the wear of corps or separate brigade SSI by members of units attached to specific corps or separate brigades on a permanent basis. The term "permanent" applies to those units that are, have been, or expect to be attached for an extended period of time. Units that are temporarily attached for activation, training, and deployment are not considered permanently attached.

(2) Enlisted personnel attached to Headquarters Company, U.S. Army, who are assigned to or performing duty with HQDA staff agencies and offices of the Department of Defense, will wear the Headquarters Company, U.S. Army, SSI.

(3) The DA staff support SSI is worn by personnel assigned to DA field operating agencies, unless the agency is authorized an SSI within its own right.

(4) Personnel assigned to corps artillery, division artillery, division brigades, and division support commands will wear the SSI of the corps or division.

(5) Army personnel assigned or attached for duty with advisors to foreign governments, except Army attachés, will wear the U.S. Army Mission SSI.

(6) Individuals being transferred from one organization to another may continue to wear the insignia of the former unit until they report for duty at the new organization.

(7) Officer personnel assigned, and ARNG Title 10 Long-Tour Program officers attached to HQDA, will not wear SSI on the left sleeve. There is no SSI authorized for wear by officer personnel assigned or attached to HQDA. (See para (2), above, for insignia worn by enlisted personnel assigned to HQDA.)

(8) Army personnel assigned to a joint command, DOD, or federal agencies will wear the SSI designated for joint or DOD agencies, unless agencies are entitled to an SSI within their own right.

(9) ROTC program. Army personnel, and ARNG and USAR active guard reserve (AGR) personnel assigned as ROTC instructors will wear the Cadet Command SSI.

(10) Army National Guard.

(a) Members of the ARNG not in active Federal service will wear the SSI of the division, separate brigade, or separate cavalry regiment to which assigned, including brigades integrated into active Army divisions.

(b) Members of the ARNG assigned to the State Area Command (STARC), and its detachments (troop command, recruiting and retention, medical detachment, training sites, and support units) will wear the STARC SSI designed for that state (state, commonwealth, territory, or district). However, members of the Selective Service System section will wear the Selective Service System SSI.

(c) Assigned and attached staff and faculty members of ARNG activities that are part of the Total Army School System (TASS) will wear the ARNG TASS SSI. These activities include TASS regional training institute, brigades, regiments, battalions or squadrons, companies, batteries and troops, NCO academies, special training sites, the National Guard professional education center, and the National Guard marksmanship training unit.

(d) Members of ARNG units not authorized a distinctive SSI, other than those indicated in paragraphs (a), (b), or (c) above, will wear the insignia of their STARC.

(e) Army National Guard Title 10, AGR Program. Army National Guard soldiers in this program will wear the SSI of the command, unit or agency to which attached, when one is authorized, except as indicated in paragraphs (7) or (8) above.

(11) United States Army Reserve.

(a) Units not authorized an organizational SSI that are assigned to a general officer command authorized an organizational SSI will wear the SSI of the general officer command, even though the general officer command may be assigned to a regional support command (RSC).

(b) Units not authorized an organizational SSI, but that are under the command of the U.S. Army Reserve Command, will wear the SSI of the U.S. Army Reserve Command.

(c) Units not authorized an SSI, but that are under the command of a general officer command that is authorized an SSI, will wear the insignia of the general officer command.

(d) Units assigned directly to a CONUS Army Headquarters and not authorized an SSI, or units under the command of a general officer command that is assigned directly to a CONUS Army Headquarters, will wear the insignia of the appropriate CONUS Army.

(e) Members of the individual ready reserve will wear the individual ready reserve SSI. Individual mobilization augmentees (IMAs) will wear the SSI of the organization to which designated. Personnel participating in the AGR or ROTC simultaneous membership programs will wear the SSI of commands, units, and agencies to which attached.

(12) Initial entry training soldiers who are in one of the following categories may wear organizational SSI:

(a) Army National Guard and USAR trainees will wear the insignia of their parent ARNG or USAR organization, as soon as they are issued uniforms. Their parent units will provide initial entry training soldiers their SSI before they enter initial entry training.

(b) Unit-of-choice trainees are authorized to wear the insignia of the specific unit for which they enlisted.

(13) Reserve component units with WARTRACE alignments may wear the SSI of the Active unit to which they are aligned, in lieu of their peacetime SSI, provided major RSC or state TAG, and MACOM commanders agree on such wear.

e. How worn.

(1) Non-subdued. All personnel will wear the non-subdued SSI of their current organization centered on the left sleeve, 1/2 inch below the top of the shoulder seam, on the coat of the Army green uniform. When the Sapper, Ranger, Special Forces, or President's Hundred tab is worn, the tab is placed 1/2 inch below the top of the shoulder seam. The SSI is worn 1/4 inch below special skill or marksmanship tabs. If there is simultaneous wear of two tabs or more, the SSI remains at 1/4 inch below the tabs. Tabs that are an integral part of SSI, such as airborne or mountain, are worn directly above the SSI with no space between the insignia and tab. Personnel will not wear non-subdued SSI on uniforms other than those specified above (see fig. 28-134).

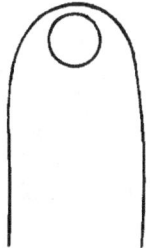

**Figure 28–134. Wear of shoulder sleeve insignia, current organization**

(2) Subdued. All personnel wear the subdued SSI on the temperate, hot-weather, enhanced hot-weather, aviation, and desert BDU; flight suit and flight jacket; combat vehicle crewman uniform; and the BDU field jacket. Personnel will not wear subdued SSI on hospital duty and food service uniforms. Positioning of the insignia is identical to the non-subdued insignia, covered above.

## 28–17. Shoulder sleeve insignia-former wartime service (SSI–FWTS)

*a.* General. Authorization to wear a shoulder sleeve insignia indicating former wartime service applies only to soldiers who are assigned to U.S. Army units that meet all the following criteria. Soldiers who were prior members of other Services that participated in operations that would otherwise meet the criteria below are not authorized to wear the SSI–FWTS. Wear is reserved for individuals who were members of U.S. Army units during the operations.

(1) The Secretary of the Army or higher must declare as a hostile environment the theater or area of operation to which the unit is assigned, or Congress must pass a Declaration of War.

(2) The units must have actively participated in, or supported ground combat operations against hostile forces in which they were exposed to the threat of enemy action or fire, either directly or indirectly.

(3) The military operation normally must have lasted for a period of thirty (30) days or longer. An exception may be made when U.S. Army forces are engaged with a hostile force for a shorter period of time, when they meet all other criteria, and a recommendation from the general or flag officer in command is forwarded to the Chief of Staff, Army.

(4) The Chief of Staff, Army, must approve the authorization for wear of the shoulder sleeve insignia for former wartime service.

*b.* Authorization. Authorization applies only to members of the Army who were assigned overseas with U.S. Army organizations during the following periods.

(1) World War II: between 7 December 1941 and 2 September 1946, both dates inclusive.

(2) Korea: between 27 June 1950 and 27 July 1954, both dates inclusive. Also from 1 April 1968 to 31 August 1973, for those personnel who were awarded the Purple Heart, Combat Infantryman badge, Combat Medical badge, or who qualified for at least one month's hostile fire pay for service in a hostile fire area in Korea.

(3) The Vietnam theater, including Thailand, Laos and Cambodia: from 1 July 1958 to 28 March 1973, both dates inclusive.

(4) The Dominican Republic: 29 April 1965 to 21 September 1966, both dates inclusive. Individuals are authorized to wear one of three organizational SSI: XVIII Airborne Corps, 82d Airborne Division, or 5th Logistical Command. Individuals previously attached, assigned, or under the operational control of these units will wear their respective insignia. A fourth organizational SSI (OEA-Spanish equivalent of Organization of American States) is authorized for individuals who were not in one of the three units listed above.

(5) Grenada, to include the Green and Carriacou Islands: between 24 October 1983 and 21 November 1983, both dates inclusive. Personnel are authorized to wear one of the following organizational SSI: XVIII Airborne Corps; 82d Airborne Division; 1st Special Operations Command (ABN); 1st Corps Support Command; 20th Engineer Brigade; 35th Signal Brigade; 16th Military Police Brigade; 44th Medical Brigade; 1st Battalion (Ranger), 75th Ranger Regiment; 2d Battalion (Ranger), 75th Ranger Regiment; and 101st Airborne Division (AASLT). Individuals attached to, or under the operational control of these units will wear their respective organizational SSI. Individuals attached to, or under the operational control of any unit whose parent organization is not authorized SSI, will wear the SSI of the unit to which attached or the unit that had operational control.

(6) Lebanon: from 6 August 1983 to 24 April 1984, for soldiers assigned to the Field Artillery School Target Acquisition Battery or the 214th Field Artillery Brigade, who were attached to the U.S. Marine Corps forces in and around Beirut, Lebanon, for the purpose of counterfire support.

(7) Korea: 23 November 1984, for soldiers who directly participated in the firefight with North Korean guards at the Joint Security Area (JSA), Panmunjom, Korea.

(8) Persian Gulf: from 27 July 1987 to 1 August 1990 for soldiers assigned or attached to, or under the operational control of a unit whose mission was direct support to Operation Earnest Will. Soldiers must have been eligible for the Armed Forces Expeditionary Medal and imminent danger pay.

(9) Panama: from 20 December 1989 to 31 January 1990 for soldiers assigned to the following units, and who participated in Operation Just Cause: XVIII Airborne Corps; U.S. Army Special Operations Command; U.S. Army South; 7th Infantry Division (Light); 82d Airborne Division; 5th Infantry Division (M); 1st Special Operations Command; 193d Infantry Brigade; 1stCorps Support Command; 16thMilitary Police Brigade; 18thAviation Brigade; 35th Signal Brigade; 7th Special Forces Group; 75th Ranger Regiment; 1st, 2d, and 3d Battalions, 75thRanger Regiment; 470thMilitary Intelligence Brigade; 525thMilitary Intelligence Brigade; 44th Medical Brigade; 1109th Signal Brigade; Military Surface Deployment and Distribution Command; and CIDC. Soldiers assigned to units not listed above will wear the shoulder sleeve insignia of the unit to which attached, or the unit that had operational control. Soldiers assigned to units not listed above and not attached to, or under the operational control of any of the units listed above, will wear the SSI of the U.S. Army South.

(10) The Persian Gulf: from 17 January 1991 to 31 August 1993, both dates inclusive, for soldiers participating in Operation Desert Storm. Soldiers must have been assigned or attached to, or under the operational control of a unit whose mission was direct support to Operation Desert Storm; they must have received imminent danger pay and been under the command and control of U.S. Army Element Central Command (USAE CENTCOM).

(11) El Salvador: from 1 January 1981 to 1 February 1992, both dates inclusive, for those personnel who participated in El Salvador operations.

(12) Somalia: from 5 December 1992 to 31 March 1995, both dates inclusive, for soldiers who participated in Operation Restore Hope/Continue Hope/United Shield. Exceptions are for Joint Task Forces: Patriot Defender, Elusive Concept, and Proven Force; those personnel are authorized to wear SSI–FWTS even though they were not under the command and control of USAE CENTCOM.

(13) Operation Enduring Freedom: from 19 September 2001 to a date to be determined, for soldiers assigned to Afghanistan, Pakistan, Tajikistan, Turkmenistan, and Uzbekistan; and from 31 July 2002 to a date to be determined, for soldiers deployed to the CENTCOM area of operations in support of Operation Enduring Freedom authorized combat zone tax exclusion as identified by CENTCOM CCJ1 AOR Danger Pay Entitlements. Soldiers who were deployed in the area of operations on training exercises or in support of operations other than Operation Enduring Freedom are not authorized the SSI-FWTS, unless those exercises or operations became combat or support missions to Operation Enduring Freedom.

(14) Operation Iraqi Freedom: from 19 March 2003 to a date to be determined, for soldiers assigned to units participating in Operation Iraqi Freedom. Soldiers must have been deployed in the CENTCOM area of operations, or participated in Operation Iraqi Freedom while deployed in Turkey, Israel, and Aegis cruisers. Soldiers who served with the 1st Marine Division from 19 March 2003 to 21 April 2003 during combat operations in support of Operation Iraqi Freedom are authorized to wear the 1st Marine Division shoulder sleeve insignia as their SSI-FWTS. Soldiers who were deployed in the area of operations on training exercises or in support of operations other than Iraqi Freedom are not authorized the SSI-FWTS, unless those exercises or operations became combat or support missions to Operation Iraqi Freedom.

*c.* How worn.

(1) Non-subdued. At the option of the wearer, individuals who were members of an Army unit during one of the operations listed above may wear the non-subdued U.S. Army organizational SSI of a wartime unit (para 28–17*b*) that was approved by HQDA on the right sleeve of the Army green uniform coat. The insignia is worn centered, ½ inch below the top of the right shoulder seam (see fig 28–136).

(2) Subdued. Authorized personnel may wear the subdued SSI–FWTS on the right sleeve of the temperate, hot-weather, enhanced hot-weather, and desert BDU, and the BDU field jacket, as described above. The SSI–FWTS is not authorized for wear on organizational uniforms, except as prescribed in this paragraph.

(3) Other services. The Department of the Navy, the United States Marine Corps, and the Air Force do not authorize wear of SSI. Therefore, personnel who served in one of the designated areas during one of the specified periods, but who were not members of the U.S. Army, are not authorized to wear the SSI–FWTS on their right shoulder. The only exception to this policy is for U.S. Army members who served with the United States Marines Corps during World War II from 15 March 1943 through 2 September 1946.

*d.* Soldiers who are authorized to wear more than one SSI–FWTS have the option of choosing which SSI–FWTS they will wear. Soldiers may elect not to wear SSI–FWTS. (See appendix F for further guidance on the wear of the SSI–FWTS.)

## 28–18. Wear of full-color U.S. flag cloth replica
*a.* General. All soldiers throughout the Force, regardless of deployment status, will wear the full-color U.S. flag cloth replica on utility and organizational uniforms.

*b.* Description. The colors of the U.S. flag cloth replica are red, white, and blue. The size is approximately 2 inches by 3 inches.

*c.* How worn.

(1) When approved for wear, the full-color U.S. flag cloth replica is sewn ½ inch below the right shoulder seam of the temperate, hot-weather, enhanced hot-weather, and desert BDU; the BDU field jacket; and the cold-weather uniform (see fig 28–135). If the SSI–FWTS is worn on the right shoulder of the utility uniform, the full-color U.S. flag cloth replica is placed ⅛ inch below the right shoulder sleeve insignia (see fig 28–136). The SSI–FWTS is not authorized for wear on organizational uniforms, unless indicated above.

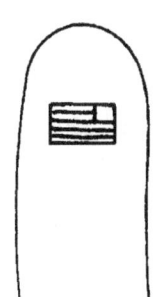

**Figure 28–135. Wear of full-color flag cloth replica, right sleeve**

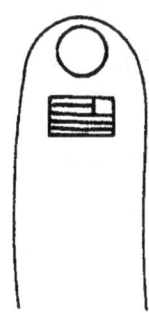

**Figure 28–136. Wear of shoulder sleeve insignia-former wartime service, with flag replica, right sleeve**

(2) The full-color U.S. flag cloth replica is worn so that the star field faces forward, or to the flag's own right. When worn in this manner, the flag is facing to the observer's right, and gives the effect of the flag flying in the breeze as the wearer moves forward. The appropriate replica for the right shoulder sleeve is identified as the reverse side flag.

## 28–19. Branch colors

*a.* Adjutant General Corps: dark blue and scarlet (cable numbers 65012 and 65006).

*b.* Air Defense Artillery: scarlet (cable number 65006).

*c.* Armor: yellow (cable number 65002).

*d.* Army Medical Specialist Corps: maroon and white (cable numbers 65017 and 65005).

*e.* Army Nurse Corps: maroon and white (cable numbers 65017 and 65005).

*f.* Aviation: ultramarine blue and golden orange (cable numbers 65010 and 65003).

*g.* Branch Immaterial: teal blue and white (cable numbers 65024 and 65005).

*h.* Cavalry: yellow (cable number 65002).

*i.* Chaplains: black (cable number 65018).

*j.* Chemical Corps: cobalt blue and golden yellow (cable numbers 65011 and 65001).

*k.* Civil Affairs, USAR: purple and white (cable numbers 65009 and 65005).

*l.* Corps of Engineers: scarlet and white (cable numbers 65006 and 65005).

*m.* Dental Corps: maroon and white (cable numbers 65017 and 65005).

*n.* Field Artillery: scarlet (cable number 65006).

*o.* Finance Corps: silver gray and golden yellow (cable numbers 65008 and 65001).

*p.* General staff: no color assigned.

*q.* Infantry: light blue (cable number 65014).

*r.* Inspector General: dark blue and light blue (cable numbers 65012 and 65014).

*s.* Judge Advocate General's Corps: dark blue and white (cable numbers 65012 and 65005).

*t.* Medical Corps: maroon and white (cable numbers 65017 and 65005).

*u.* Medical Service Corps: maroon and white (cable numbers 65017 and 65005).

*v.* Military Intelligence: oriental blue and silver gray (cable numbers 65027 and 65008).

*w.* Military Police Corps: green and yellow (cable numbers 65007 and 65002).

*x.* National Guard Bureau: dark blue (cable number 65012).

*y.* Ordnance Corps: crimson and yellow (cable numbers 65013 and 65002).

*z.* Quartermaster Corps: buff (cable number 65015).

*aa.* Signal Corps: orange and white (cable numbers 65004 and 65005).

*ab.* Special Forces: jungle Green (cable number 65025).

*ac.* Staff specialist, USAR: green (cable number 65007).

*ad.* The Sergeant Major of the Army. no color assigned.

*ae.* Transportation Corps: brick red and golden yellow (cable numbers 65020 and 65001).

*af.* Veterinary Corps: maroon and white (cable numbers 65017 and 65005).

*ag.* Warrant officers: brown (cable number 65016).

## 28–20. Branch scarves

*a.* General. Personnel may wear branch scarves with service and utility uniforms, only when issued and prescribed by the local commander for ceremonial occasions.

*b.* Description. These scarves are a bib-type design in the following colors, for wear by personnel as indicated.

(1) Black: chaplain.

(2) Brick red: transportation.

(3) Buff: supply, quartermaster, supply and service, supply and transportation, and support.

(4) Cobalt blue: chemical.

(5) Crimson: ordnance and maintenance.

(6) Dark blue: National Guard Bureau, Judge Advocate General, Inspector General and Adjutant General.

(7) Green: Military Police and staff specialist.

(8) Infantry Blue: Infantry.

(9) Jungle green: Special Forces.

(10) Maroon: Army medical specialist, Nurse, Dental, Medical, Medical Service, and Veterinary Corps.

(11) Orange: signal.

(12) Oriental blue: intelligence.

(13) Purple: civil affairs.

(14) Scarlet: artillery, engineers and permanent professors, registrar and civilian instructors of the U.S. Military Academy.

(15) Silver gray: finance.

(16) Teal blue: branch immaterial.

(17) Ultramarine blue: aviation.

(18) Yellow: armor and cavalry.

(19) Camouflage: as determined by local commander.

*c.* Branch scarves are provided without cost to all personnel, when prescribed for wear.

## 28–21. Leaders identification insignia

*a.* Leaders in all units (Active Army, Army National Guard, and Army Reserves), regardless of unit category (MTOE or TDA), will wear the leaders identification (LI) insignia.

*b.* The following specific leaders are authorized to wear the leaders identification insignia.

(1) Commanders.

(2) Deputy commanders.

(3) Platoon leaders.

(4) Command sergeants major.

(5) First sergeants.

(6) Platoon sergeants.

(7) Section leaders.

(8) Squad leaders and tank commanders.

(9) Team leaders.

(10) Assistant SF detachment commanders.

(11) SF operational detachment "B" sergeants major.

(12) SF operational detachment "A" senior sergeants.

*c.* The LI insignia is a green cloth loop, 1⅝ inches wide, worn in the middle of both shoulder loops on the Army green coat, the cold-weather coat (field jacket) and on the center tab of the extended cold-weather clothing system (ECWCS) (Gortex) parka. When the LI is worn on the parka, personnel wear their grade insignia centered on the LI. Personnel may wear pin-on grade insignia, or they may sew onto the LI the same cloth grade insignia that is worn on the collars of the utility uniform (see fig 28–137).

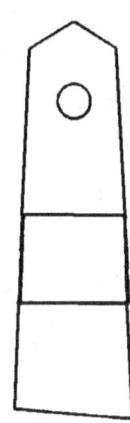

**Figure 28–137. Wear of combat leaders identification on shoulder loops**

*d.* Personnel will not wear the LI when reassigned from a command position or from an organization designated above, or when taking an official photo.

## 28–22. Distinctive unit insignia

*a.* Authorization. Distinctive unit insignia (DUI) of a design approved by The Institute of Heraldry, U.S. Army, are authorized and prescribed for wear on the service uniforms of personnel in the following echelons.

(1) MACOM: one design for each MACOM.

(2) Field armies: one design for each field Army.

(3) Regional readiness commands.

(4) Corps: one design for each corps.

(5) Division: one design for each division.

(6) Separate brigades: one design for each separate TOE brigade.

(7) Numbered group: one design for each TOE numbered group.

(8) Color-bearing regiments; training support battalions aligned to color-bearing regiments; and separate battalions, fixed type: one design for each regiment and separate TOE battalion.

(9) Battalions, flexible: one design for each TOE battalion.

(10) Hospitals: one design for each TOE hospital.

(11) U.S. Army service schools established by the Department of the Army: one design for each service school.

(12) U.S. Army Training and Doctrine Command training centers: one design for each training center.

(13) U.S. Army medical centers: one design for each center.

(14) U.S. Army medical department activities: one design for each activity.

(15) U.S. Army hospital centers: one design for each center.

(16) U.S. Army dental activities: one design for each activity.

(17) Army National Guard TASS: one design for all TASS activities identified in paragraph 28–16*d*(10)*(c)*, above.

(18) U.S. Army Reserve schools: one design for all USAR schools.

(19) Field operating agencies: one design for each activity based on the following criteria.

*(a)* An identifiable command structure.

*(b)* A valid justification in terms of unit mission, enhancement of unit morale, and degree of unit permanency.

*(c)* At least 250 military personnel assigned to the activity.

(20) Other organizations: one design for each organization, except U.S. Army garrison (active and reserve), meeting the following criteria.

*(a)* An identifiable command structure.

*(b)* A valid justification in terms of unit mission, enhancement of unit morale, and degree of unit permanency.

*(c)* At least 500 military personnel assigned to the organization.

(21) Other.

*(a)* Organizations not in the categories listed above, which have a DUI by virtue of previous HQDA authority, are permitted to retain that DUI if it was manufactured and worn by members of the subject organization. In each case, such insignia is authorized for wear only after The Institute of Heraldry, U.S. Army, has determined the propriety, and granted approval of the insignia.

*(b)* Units not authorized a DUI in their own right will wear the DUI of the command to which assigned. Those units not authorized a DUI in their own right, and not assigned to a higher echelon that is authorized a DUI, may, with the approval of the Army commander concerned, wear the DUI of the Army area in which located. Personnel participating in the AGR and ROTC simultaneous membership programs will wear the DUI of the commands, units, and agencies to which attached.

*(c)* Personnel assigned to a joint command, DOD, or Federal agency will wear the DUI designated for joint or DOD agencies.

*b.* Approval of design. Units meeting the criteria established above will submit requests for authorization of DUI through channels, with a copy of permanent orders activating the unit to: Director, The Institute of Heraldry, U.S. Army, 9325 Gunston Road, Room S112, Fort Belvoir, VA 22060–5579. Requests will include three proposed mottoes, if the organization requests a motto with the design. Once approved, no changes are made in a design of the insignia.

*c.* Provisional units. The authorization of a DUI will not be granted for provisional units.

*d.* By whom worn.

(1) When a DUI is authorized, all personnel assigned to the organization wear the insignia, except general officers and the Sergeant Major of the Army. General officers wear their regimental distinctive insignia (RDI) on the black pullover sweater. The Sergeant Major of the Army wears the SMA insignia in lieu of the DUI. Reserve component units with WARTRACE alignments may wear the DUI of the Active unit to which they are aligned, in lieu of their peacetime DUI, provided major RSC or state TAG, and MACOM commanders agree on such wear.

(2) A complete set of the distinctive unit insignia consists of three pieces. The procurement of distinctive insignia not approved by The Institute of Heraldry, U.S. Army, is prohibited. Units may purchase approved DUIs through the use of appropriated or nonappropriated funds.

*e.* Where worn. The design of the DUI is metal, or metal and enamel, only. Enlisted personnel wear the insignia on the Army green uniform coat, the black pullover sweater, and the beret.

*f.* How worn.

(1) Enlisted personnel wear the DUI on the green service uniform coat, centered on the shoulder loops an equal distance from the outside shoulder seam to the outside edge of the button, with the base of the insignia toward the outside shoulder seam. Enlisted personnel are not authorized to wear the DUI on the enlisted green dress uniform (worn with white shirt and necktie/neck tab). Officers wear the DUI centered on the shoulder loops, an equal distance from the inside edge of their grade insignia to the outside edge of the button, with the base of the insignia toward the outside shoulder seam (see fig 28–138).

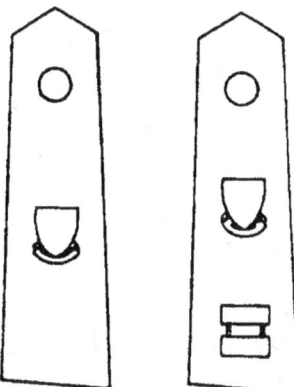

Figure 28–138. Wear of distinctive unit insignia on shoulder loops

(2) On the beret, enlisted personnel wear the DUI centered on the organizational flash. Soldiers assigned to units not authorized a DUI wear the RDI on the beret in the same manner as the DUI.

(3) Soldiers (except chaplains, general officers, and the SMA) wear the DUI centered above the nameplate on the black pullover sweater, with the top edge of the insignia ¼ inch below the top edge of the patch on the sweater. Soldiers assigned to units not authorized the DUI wear the RDI on the black pullover sweater in the same manner as the DUI (see fig 28–139). Chaplains wear their branch insignia, general officers wear the RDI, and the SMA wears the SMA insignia in the same manner. All soldiers may adjust the placement of the DUI or RDI, up or down on the patch, to allow for large size DUI or RDI, or to adjust to body configuration.

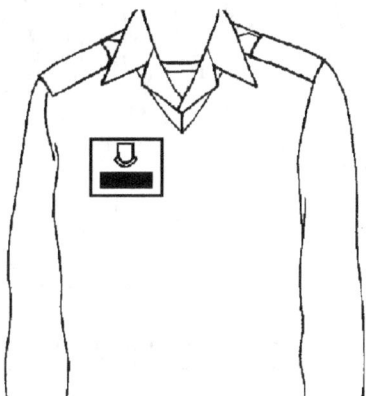

Figure 28–139. Wear of distinctive unit insignia/regimental distinctive insignia, on black pullover sweater

## 28–23. Regimental distinctive insignia

*a.* Authorization. Regimental distinctive insignia (RDI) of a design approved by the Institute of Heraldry, U.S. Army, are authorized and prescribed for wear by all soldiers affiliated with a regiment or whole-corps regiment, as described in AR 600–82 and NGR 600–82.

*b.* How worn.

(1) Males.

*(a)* On the Army green, white, and blue uniforms, and the AG 415 shirt, males wear the RDI centered ⅛ inch above the top of the pocket flap, or ¼ inch above any unit awards or foreign badges that are worn. When the coat lapel obscures the insignia, soldiers may wear the RDI aligned to the right edge of unit awards or the nameplate. Wear of the RDI on the AG 415 shirt is optional (see fig 28–140).

**Figure 28–140. Wear of regimental distinctive insignia on Army green, blue, and white uniforms, male**

*(b)* On the white and blue mess and evening mess uniforms, male personnel wear the RDI on the right lapel. On the blue mess uniform, the RDI is worn centered on the satin facing, ½ inch below the notch in the lapel. On the white mess uniform, the RDI is worn ½ inch below the notch, centered on the lapel. The RDI is worn so that the vertical axis of the insignia is perpendicular to the ground (see fig 28–141).

**Figure 28–141. Wear of regimental distinctive insignia on Army blue and white mess uniforms, male**

(2) Females.

*(a)* On the Army green, blue, and white uniforms, the Army maternity tunic, and the AG 415 shirt, females wear the RDI centered ½ inch above the nameplate, or ¼ inch above any unit awards or foreign badges that are worn. When the coat lapel obscures the RDI, soldiers may wear the RDI aligned to the right edge of unit awards or the nameplate. Wear of the RDI on the AG 415 shirt is optional (see fig 28–144).

*(b)* On the blue mess and evening mess, and the new version white mess and evening mess uniforms, females wear the RDI centered on the right lapel, with the top of the RDI aligned with the top row of miniature medals. On the black mess and evening mess, and the old version white mess and evening mess uniforms, females wear the RDI centered on the right side of the jacket (not on the lapels). The RDI is centered between the lapel and shoulder seam, with the top of the RDI aligned with the top row of miniature medals. The RDI is worn so that the vertical axis is perpendicular to the ground (see fig 25–2).

(3) The RDI and DUI will be the same for soldiers who are assigned to, and affiliated with the same unit. Soldiers who are assigned to a unit or agency not authorized a DUI will wear the RDI on the beret and the black pullover sweater in lieu of a DUI (see fig 28–139).

## 28–24. Insignia, distinguishing, U.S. Army nametape and nameplate

*a.* Insignia, distinguishing, U.S. Army.

(1) Description.

*(a)* For woodland camouflage or olive-green uniforms, the insignia is a woven tape of olive-green cloth, 1 inch wide, with the inscription "U.S. ARMY" in black block letters, ¾ inch high. For desert camouflage uniforms, the insignia is a woven tape of khaki, 1 inch wide, with the inscription "U.S. ARMY" in spice-brown block letters, ¾ inch high.

*(b)* As an option, soldiers may purchase and wear 1-inch wide tape with embroidered ¾-inch block letters. The length of the U.S. Army distinguishing insignia tape is 4½ inches, or it extends to the edge of the pocket flap when sewn on the uniform (see fig 28–142).

**Figure 28–142. Insignia, distinguishing, U.S. Army tape**

(2) How worn. The U.S. Army distinguishing insignia tape is worn immediately above, and parallel to the top edge of the left breast pocket of the uniform shirt, only. The insignia is worn on the temperate, hot-weather, enhanced hot-weather, maternity, aviation, and desert BDU shirts; BDU field jackets; and on organizational clothing when required and prescribed by the commander issuing the organizational clothing. Personnel will not wear the U.S. Army insignia tape on the hospital duty and food service uniforms. Personnel are not authorized to have the words U.S. Army embroidered directly on the uniform (see fig 28–143).

**Figure 28–143. Wear of nametape and U.S. Army distinguishing tape**

*b.* Insignia, nametape.

(1) Description.

*(a)* For woodland camouflage or olive-green uniforms (except for the ECWCS parka), the nametape is a strip of olive-green cloth, 1 inch wide, with the individual's last name in black block letters, ¾ inch in height. Last names consisting of 11 letters or more are constructed using Franklin gothic extra-condensed print (48 point), ½ inch high. The nametape insignia is 4½ inches in length, or extends to the edge of the pocket flap when sewn on the uniform.

*(b)* For desert camouflage uniforms, the nametape is a strip of khaki tape with spice-brown lettering, of the same description as in paragraph *b*(1)(a), above.

*(c)* For the extended cold-weather clothing system (ECWCS) (Gortex) parka, the nametape is a strip of olive-green cloth, 3½ inches long and ½ inch wide, with ¼-inch black block lettering. The nametape can accommodate up to 14 characters. No other size nametape is authorized for wear on the Gortex parka.

*(d)* See para 28–3*g*(1) for wear of nametapes on helmet bands.

(2) How worn.

*(a)* All personnel will wear the nametape above the top right breast pocket on the same uniforms and in the same manner as described for the "U.S. ARMY" tape in paragraph *a*(1)(a), above. When the nametape is worn with the U.S. Army tape, both must be the same size, 4½ inches in length, or they must extend to the edge of the pocket flaps. Personnel are not authorized to have the last name embroidered directly onto the uniform. Personnel may wear embroidered nametapes with woven U.S. Army insignia (see fig 28–143).

*(b)* All personnel will wear the nametape on the ECWCS (Gortex) parka, on the left-sleeve pocket flap, ¼ inch above the bottom of the flap, and centered left to right on the flap. Personnel are not authorized to wear the nametape in any other location on the parka than the pocket flap, and they are not authorized to embroider the name directly on the pocket flap.

(3) How to obtain. Initial and replacement nametapes are provided at no cost to enlisted members and are procured from appropriated funds. If facilities are not available at installations for inscribing and attaching nametapes, contracting for such services with local vendors is authorized.

*c.* Nameplate.

(1) Description.

*(a)* The nameplate is a black, laminated plastic plate, 1 inch by 3 inches, 1/16 inch thick, with a white border not to exceed 1/32 inch in width. Lettering is block type, indented white lettering, ⅜ inch in height, and centered on the plate. Only last names are used on the nameplates. Gloss or non-gloss finish is authorized on the nameplate.

*(b)* Modifications to the nameplate to add other insignia or information are prohibited unless authorized by HQDA. Personnel will not wear nameplates with authorized additions or translations outside of the area for which they are authorized.

(2) How worn.

*(a)* Male personnel. On the AG shade 415 shirts, and on the coats of the Army green, white, and blue uniforms, the nameplate is worn centered left to right on the flap of the right breast pocket, and centered between the top of the button and the top of the pocket. (See illustrations in individual uniform chapters.) On the black pullover sweater, the nameplate is worn centered on the black patch of the sweater, except when wearing the DUI or RDI. When wearing a DUI or RDI, the nameplate is placed ¼ inch above the bottom of the black patch, with the top of the DUI or RDI placed ¼ inch below the top edge of the patch, and centered left to right. Personnel may adjust the placement of the nameplate and DUI or RDI, up or down on the patch, to allow for large size DUI or RDI, or to adjust to body configuration (see fig 28–139).

*(b)* Female personnel. On the Army green uniform, and the new style Army blue and white uniforms, the nameplate is worn 1 to 2 inches above the top button of the coat and centered horizontally on the wearer's right side (see fig 28–144). On the AG 415 shirts, maternity tunic, hospital duty, and food service uniforms, the nameplate is worn in a comparable position. On the old-style Army blue and white uniforms the nameplate is worn centered horizontally on the wearer's right side, slightly above the top edge of the top button. (See illustrations in individual uniform chapters.) On the black pullover sweater, the nameplate is worn centered on the black patch of the sweater, except when the DUI or RDI is worn. When wearing a DUI or RDI, the nameplate is placed ¼ inch above the bottom of the black patch, with the top of the DUI or RDI placed ¼ inch below the top edge of the patch, and centered left to right. Personnel may adjust the placement of the nameplate and DUI or RDI, up or down on the patch, to allow for large size DUI or RDI, or to adjust to body configuration (see fig 28–139).

Figure 28–144. Wear of nameplate on Army green and new version blue and white uniforms, female

## 28–25. Aiguillette, service

*a.* Description. The service aiguillette is a one-piece braided gold, gold-colored nylon, or synthetic metallic gold-colored cord, 3/16 inch in diameter, and 30½ inches in length, with each end equipped with a hook, and one end equipped with an eye. The front part of the aiguillette is 8½ inches in length and consists of 1½ inches of cord equipped with a hook, a knot 1¾ inches in length, a cord 2 inches in length, and a 3-inch ferrule.

*b.* How worn. The military aide to the President, White House social aides while on duty with the First Family, and officers designated as aides to foreign heads of state wear the service aiguillette on the right side of the uniform. All other aides wear aiguillettes on the left side. The cord is placed under the arm with the hook engaging the eyes on each side of the appropriate shoulder loop. The end equipped with the eye is worn to the front. The hook of the front part of the aiguillette is engaged in the eye of the cord (see fig 28–145).

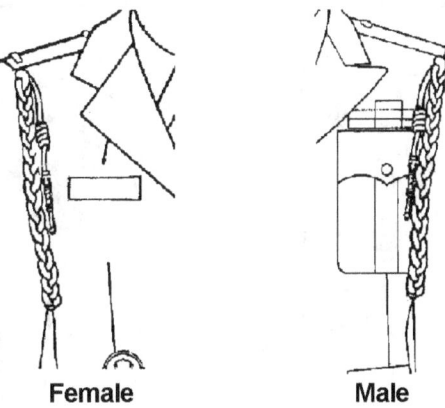

Female          Male

Figure 28–145. Wear of service aiguillettes

*c.* By whom worn. Army attachés, assistant Army attachés, and aides wear the service aiguillette on the Army green, blue, and white uniforms when they are worn for informal occasions. Males will wear the four-in-hand necktie with the uniform when wearing the service aiguillette. When personnel wear the black all-weather coat, they may wear the service aiguillette on the outside of the garment. The aiguillette is worn only when personnel are performing duties as aides.

### 28–26. Aiguillette, dress

*a.* Description.

(1) The front of the dress aiguillette is the same as the service aiguillette, except the front part is replaced by a piece that is 25 inches in length, with 15 inches of braiding, with 2 inches from the braiding to the button loop and knot. The knot is 1¾ inches in length, the cord is 3¼ inches, and the ferrule is 3 inches. The braided end is equipped with a hook.

(2) The back of the dress aiguillette consists of a braided gold cord, or gold-colored nylon cord, 3/16 inch in diameter and 30½ inches in length, with an additional part 34 inches in length that consists of 24 inches of braiding, with 2 inches from the braiding to the button loop and knot. The knot is 1¾ inches in length, the cord is 3¼ inches, and the ferrule is 3 inches and is fastened to a triangular piece of brass with a hook on the inside. This hook is attached to a small strip of brass which slips under the shoulder loop, shoulder strap, or shoulder knot. The brass strip for the shoulder strap is curved to conform to the contour of the shoulder, and is ⅝ inch in width and 3⅞ inches in length, with a rectangular opening at each end, ⅜ inches in length. The brass strip for shoulder knots is ⅝ inch in width and 3⅜ inches in length, with an extra piece fastened to form a standing loop 1 inch in length, that permits the flexible backing of the shoulder knot to pass through. The brass strip for the shoulder loop of the Army white mess uniform coat is the same as that used for the shoulder knot, without the standing loop.

*b.* How worn. The military aide to the President, White House social aides while on duty with the First Family, and officers designated as aides to foreign heads of state wear the aiguillette on the right side of the uniform. All other authorized personnel wear aiguillettes on the left side. Aiguillettes are secured to the coat before the opening of the brass strip, and the front part is hooked into the eye of the service aiguillette. The 34-inch part is passed under the arm, and the button loop of the 25-inch part is inserted through the button loop of the 34-inch part, past the button loop of the 25-inch part notch in the lapel, and attached to the button under the collar. The button under the collar is attached to the body of the coat so that the knot of the 25-inch part will easily clear the notch in the lapel. The loops of both cords cross on the outside of the arm with front loop on top. Either gold cord or gold-colored nylon cord may be worn, depending upon the importance of the occasion and the individual's preference (see fig 28–146).

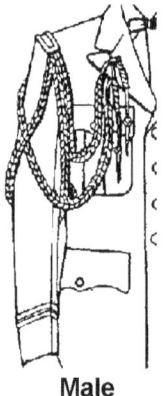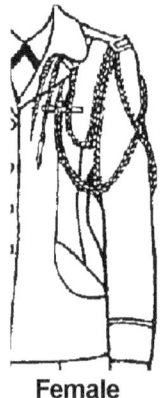

Male        Female

Figure 28–146. Wear of dress aiguillettes

*c.* By whom worn. The dress aiguillette is worn only when personnel are performing duties as aides. Army attachés, assistant Army attachés, and aides wear the dress aiguillette with the Army blue, white, and black mess and evening mess uniforms, when prescribed. Personnel may wear the dress aiguillette with the Army blue or white uniform only at formal occasions (when the bow tie is worn).

*d.* How to obtain. Aiguillettes are procured locally as expendable property by the organization to which the individual is assigned for supply purposes. A gold cord, gold-colored nylon cord, or synthetic metallic gold-colored cord are authorized for purchase.

## 28–27. Service stripes

*a.* Large.

(1) A goldenlite, rayon-embroidered diagonal stripe, 3/16 inch wide and 1–5/16 inches long, on an Army green background that forms a 3/32–inch border around the stripe. All soldiers are authorized to wear the large service stripes on the green background on the Army green uniform. Soldiers must wear the large service stripes with large rank insignia.

(2) A gold-colored rayon or a goldenlite rayon or nylon braid, ½ inch wide, and of variable length. The large service stripe braid is authorized for wear by all enlisted soldiers on the Army blue and white dress, mess, and evening mess uniforms. Soldiers must wear the large service stripes with large rank insignia.

*b.* Small.

(1) A goldenlite rayon-embroidered diagonal stripe, 5/32 inch wide and 1¼ inches long on an Army green background, which forms a 5/64 inch border around the stripe. All enlisted soldiers are authorized to wear the small service stripes on the green background on the Army green uniform. Soldiers must wear the small service stripes with small rank insignia.

(2) A gold-colored rayon or goldenlite rayon or nylon braid, ¼ inch wide, and of variable length. The small service stripe braid is authorized for wear by all enlisted soldiers on the Army blue and white dress, mess, and evening mess uniforms. Soldiers must wear the small service stripes with small rank insignia.

*c.* How worn.

(1) The service stripes are worn centered on the outside bottom half of the left sleeve on the Army green uniform coat. The service stripe is placed at an angle of 45 degrees with the lower end toward the inside seam of the sleeve, and it is placed 4 inches from the bottom of the sleeve. For each additional period of 3 years honorable service, another service stripe is added above and parallel to the first stripe, with a 1/16-inch space between stripes (see fig 28–147.)

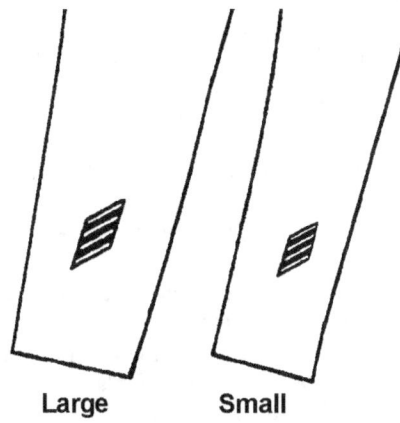

**Large**　　**Small**

Figure 28–147. Wear of service stripes, enlisted

(2) Service stripes covered in paragraphs *a*(2) and *b*(2), above, are worn on the Army blue and white dress, mess, and evening mess uniforms. The service stripe is worn centered from seam-to-seam on the outside bottom half of both sleeves. The first stripe is sewn on an angle of 30 degrees, with the lower end inserted in the front inside seam, ¼ inch above the cuff braid. The upper end of the stripe is inserted in the back seam of the sleeve on the Army blue dress, mess, and evening mess uniforms, and on the Army white mess and evening mess uniforms; and 3 inches above the bottom of the sleeve on the Army white dress uniform. Each additional stripe is spaced ⅛ inch apart from the last, and above the first stripe (see fig 28–148).

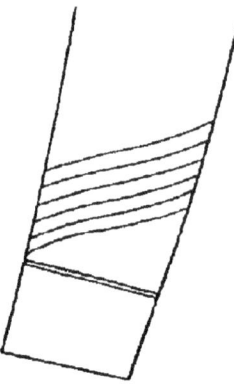

**Figure 28–148. Wear of service stripes on Army blue and white uniforms, enlisted**

*d.* By whom worn. Enlisted personnel wear the service stripes as members of the Active Army, Army National Guard, and U.S. Army Reserve, when they have served honorably, as indicated below.

(1) In Active Federal service as a commissioned officer, warrant officer, or enlisted member of the Army, Navy, Air Force, Marine Corps, or Coast Guard.

(2) In Active Reserve service creditable for retirement for non-regular service, in accordance with chapter 1223, title 10, United States Code, as a commissioned officer, warrant officer, or enlisted member of any reserve component of the Armed Forces, including the Women's Army Auxiliary Corps.

*e.* One stripe is authorized for each 3 years of honorable active Federal service; active Reserve service creditable for retired pay for non-regular service; or a combination. There is no limit to the number of stripes worn; however, service stripes will not cover the chevrons. Service need not have been continuous, and the 10th stripe is authorized after 29½ years. Individuals authorized more than 10 service stripes may elect whether or not to wear them.

### 28–28. Overseas service bars

*a.* Large. A goldenlite rayon-embroidered bar, 3/16 inches wide 1–5/16 inches long, on a green background that forms a 3/32-inch border around the bar. All personnel are authorized to wear the large overseas service bar. Enlisted soldiers must wear large overseas service bars with large rank and service stripe insignia.

*b.* Small. A goldenlite rayon-embroidered bar, 5/32 inch wide and 13/32 inch long, on a green background that forms a 5/64-inch border around the bar. All personnel are authorized to wear the small overseas service bar. Enlisted soldiers must wear small overseas service bars with small rank and service stripe insignia.

*c.* How worn. The overseas service bar is worn centered on the outside bottom half of the right sleeve of the Army green uniform coat. The lower edge of the overseas service bar is placed ¼ inch above the sleeve braid of the coat for officer personnel, and 4 inches above and parallel to the bottom of the sleeve for enlisted personnel. Each additional bar is spaced 1/16 inch above, and parallel to the first bar (see fig 28–149).

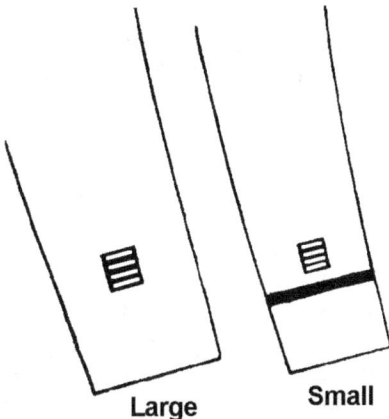

**Figure 28–149. Wear of overseas service bars, all ranks**

*d.* By whom worn. Soldiers are authorized wear of the overseas service bar as indicated below.

(1) One overseas service bar is authorized for each 6–month period of active Federal service as a member of a U.S. Service outside CONUS, from 7 December 1941 until 2 September 1946, both dates inclusive. In computing overseas service, Alaska is considered outside CONUS. An overseas service bar is not authorized for a fraction of a 6–month period.

(2) One overseas service bar is authorized for each 6–month period of active Federal service as a member of a U.S. Service in Korea, from 27 June 1950 until 27 July 1954, both dates inclusive. Credit toward an overseas service bar is authorized for each month of active Federal service as a member of the U.S. Army serving in the designated hostile fire area in Korea from 1 April 1968 until 31 August 1973. The months of arrival to, and departure from the hostile fire pay area are counted as whole months. When credit is given for a month for hostile fire pay, credit for a corresponding month is given toward an overseas service bar.

(3) One overseas service bar is authorized for each 6–month period active Federal service as a member of a U.S. Service in Vietnam, from 1 July 1958 to 28 March 1973. The months of arrival to, and departure from Vietnam are counted as whole months for credit toward the overseas service bar. Periods of TDY service in Vietnam where credit is given for hostile fire pay for 1 month, also may be given credit for a corresponding month towards award of an overseas service bar.

(4) One overseas service bar is authorized for each 6–month period of Federal service as a member of a U.S. Service in the Dominican Republic, from 29 April 1965 to 21 September 1966, both dates inclusive.

(5) One overseas service bar is authorized for each 6–month period of Federal service as a member of a U.S. Service in Laos, from 1 January 1966 to 28 March 1973.

(6) One overseas service bar is authorized for each 6–month period of Federal service as a member of a U.S. Service in Cambodia from 1 January 1971 until 28 March 1973. Personnel must qualify for hostile fire pay to receive credit for an overseas service bar. The months of arrival to, and departure from the hostile fire pay area are counted as whole months.

(7) One overseas service bar is authorized for each 6–month period of Federal service as a member of a U.S. Service in Lebanon, from 6 August 1983 to 24 April 1984, for the two units listed in paragraph 28–17*b*(6). The months of arrival to, and departure from the hostile fire pay area are counted as whole months.

(8) One overseas service bar is authorized for each 6–month period of Federal service as a member of a U.S. Service in the Persian Gulf from 27 July 1987 to 1 August 1990, for Operation Earnest Will. The months of arrival to, and departure from Operation Earnest Will are counted as whole months.

(9) One overseas service bar is authorized for each 6–month period of Federal service as a member of a U.S. Service in the Persian Gulf from 17 January 1991 to 31 August 1993, for Operation Desert Storm. The months of arrival to, and departure from Operation Desert Storm are counted as whole months.

(10) One overseas service bar is authorized for each 6–month period of Federal service as a member of a U.S. Service who participated in El Salvador, from 1 January 1981 to 1 February 1992. The months of arrival to, and departure from El Salvador are counted as whole months.

(11) One overseas service bar is authorized for each 6-month period of Federal service as a member of a U.S.

Service in Somalia, from 5 December 1992 to 31 March 1995. The months of arrival to, and departure from Somalia are counted as whole months.

(12) One overseas service bar is authorized for each 6-month period of Federal service as a member of a U.S. Service participating in Operation Enduring Freedom, the CENTCOM area of operations, or under the control of the Combatant Commander, CENTCOM, from 19 September 2001 to a date to be determined. The months of arrival to, and departure from the CENTCOM area of operations are counted as whole months.

(13) One overseas service bar is authorized for each 6–month period of Federal service as a member of a U.S. Service participating in Operation Iraqi Freedom, the CENTCOM area of operations, or under the control of the Combatant Commander, CENTCOM, from 19 March 2003 to a date to be determined. The months of arrival to, and departure from the CENTCOM area of operations are counted as whole months.

(14) Service as a member of a U.S. Armed Service for periods of less than 6 months duration, which otherwise meets the requirements for the award of overseas service bars, may be combined by adding the number of months to determine creditable service toward the total number of overseas service bars authorized for the following: World War II, Korea, Vietnam, The Dominican Republic, Laos, Cambodia, Lebanon, Operation Earnest Will, Grenada, Operation Just Cause, Operation Desert Storm, El Salvador, Somalia, Operation Enduring Freedom, and Operation Iraqi Freedom.

*e.* Computation of World War II service.

(1) Service is computed between the dates of departure from, and arrival to a port in the United States or the boundary of CONUS. The day of departure and the day of return are included. The expression "each 6-month period of Federal service" is interpreted to authorize the wear of an overseas service bar for overseas service of various lengths, performed either continuously or at intervals, when the total service equaled or exceeded 6 months. Thus, an individual who served 4 months and 10 days outside CONUS and returned there, and subsequently departed from the United States to the same or another theater or country, and served an additional 1 month and 20 days, is entitled to one bar. All active duty or service outside CONUS (permanent, temporary, detached, and so forth) is included in computing length of service, provided that the official duty of the individual required his or her presence outside CONUS.

(2) Military personnel who served on transport vessels and on aircraft became eligible to wear the bar when their total service outside CONUS equaled or exceeded 6 months.

(3) Service on the Great Lakes and in any harbor, bay, or other enclosed arm of the sea along the coast, and that part of the sea which is within 3 miles of the continental limits of the United States, is not included in computing length of service required.

(4) Periods during which military personnel were absent without leave or were in a desertion status, are not included in computing length of service required.

(5) Periods during which military personnel were in the United States on temporary duty, detached service, or leave (even though the individual was assigned overseas) are not included in computing length of service required.

(6) Periods during which military personnel were in confinement, which resulted in time lost as described in section 6 of the Uniform Code of Military Justice (chapter 47, title 10, United States Code), are not included in computing length of service required.

## 28–29. Brassards

*a.* Brassards are worn as identification to designate personnel who are required to perform a special task or to deal with the public. Brassards are made of cloth; they are 17 to 20 inches long and 4 inches wide and of colors specified. When more than one color is specified for the brassard, the colors are of equal width and run lengthwise on the brassard. Brassards are worn on the left sleeve of the outer garment, with the bottom edge of the brassard approximately 2 inches above the elbow (see fig 28–150).

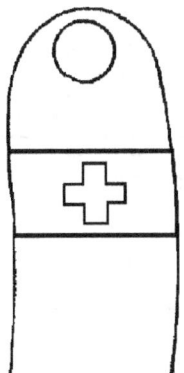

**Figure 28–150. Wear of brassards**

*b.* Descriptions of current authorized brassards.

(1) Acting noncommissioned officer brassard. The brassard consists of gold-colored chevrons on a dark blue background. Trainees or candidates acting as noncommissioned officers in schools or training centers wear this brassard. (See figs 28–151 and 28–152 for the sergeant and corporal brassards.)

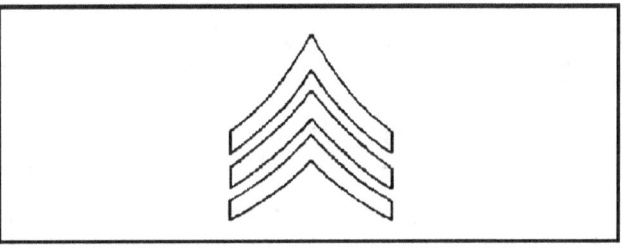

**Figure 28–151. Brassard, sergeant**

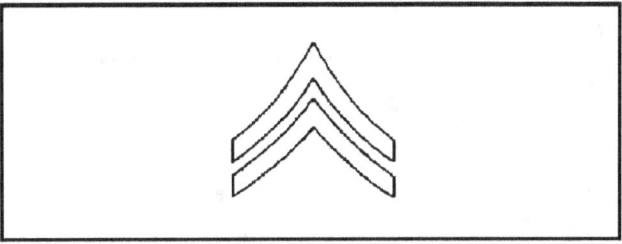

**Figure 28–152. Brassard, corporal**

(2) Acting officer brassard. The brassard consists of white stripes on an olive-drab background, centered, and parallel with the long side of the brassard. Trainees or candidates acting as commissioned officers in schools or training centers wear this brassard.

*(a)* Captain: three white stripes (see fig 28–153).

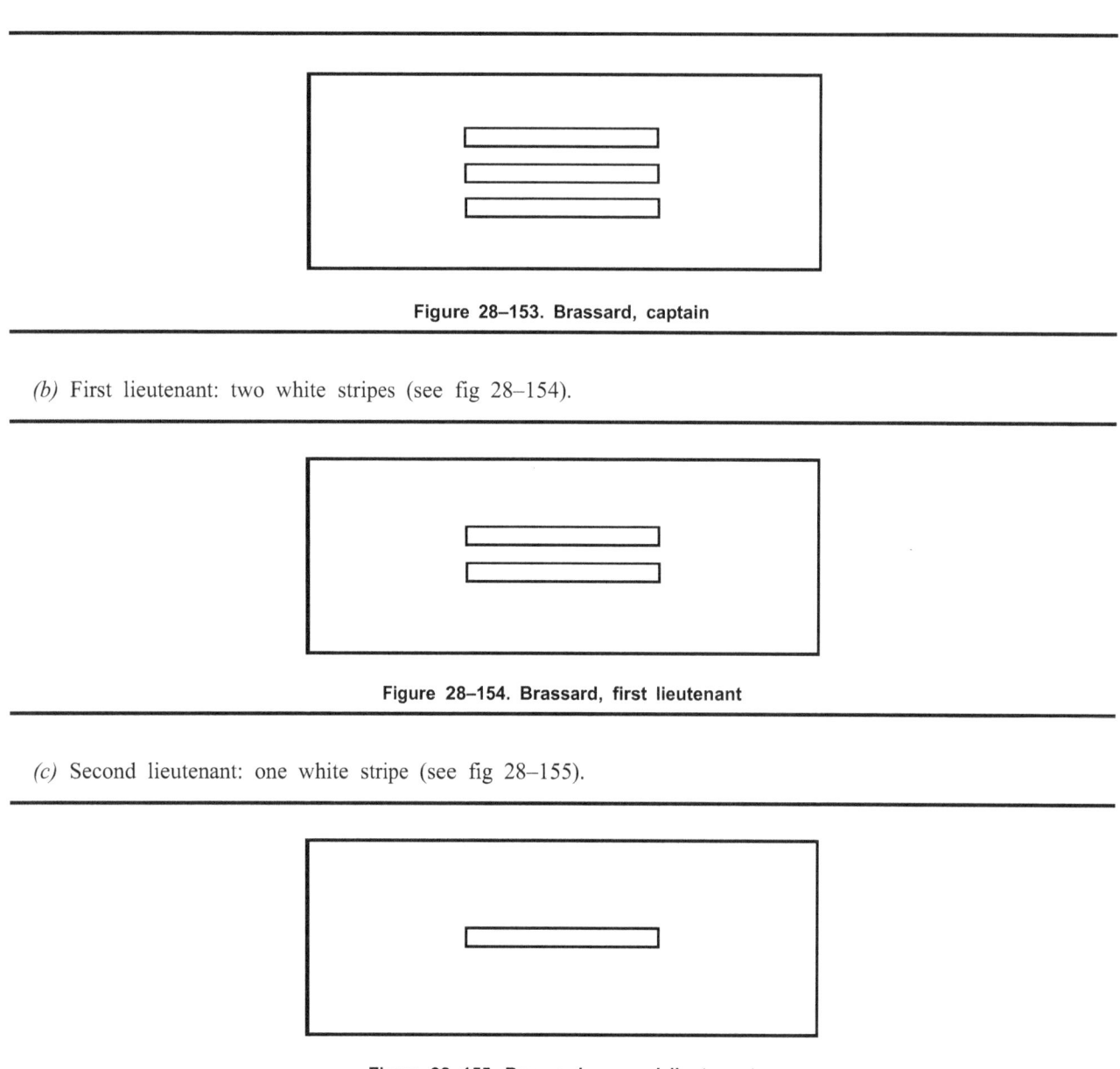

Figure 28–153. Brassard, captain

*(b)* First lieutenant: two white stripes (see fig 28–154).

Figure 28–154. Brassard, first lieutenant

*(c)* Second lieutenant: one white stripe (see fig 28–155).

Figure 28–155. Brassard, second lieutenant

(3) Armed Forces Police brassard. The brassard consists of the words "Armed Forces Police" on three lines in yellow block letters on a black cloth background, 20 inches long and 4 inches wide, with a cloth extension 5–11/16 inches high, centered above the words, for display of shoulder sleeve insignia. Personnel wear the shoulder sleeve insignia ½ inch below the top of the brassard. Members of armed forces police detachments wear the brassard while on duty (see fig 28–156).

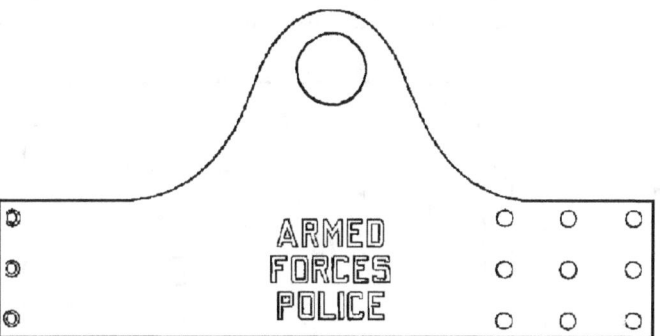

Figure 28–156. Brassard, Armed Forces Police

(4) Army community service brassard. The brassard consists of the Army community service emblem in appropriate colors centered over the words "ARMY COMMUNITY SERVICE," aligned vertically on a blue background. Military personnel, civilian employees, and volunteer personnel engaged in Army community service activities wear the brassard when ready identification is required (see fig 28–157).

Figure 28–157. Brassard, Army Community Service

(5) Explosive ordnance disposal brassard. The brassard consists of a black projectile shape pointed downward, bearing a red conventional drop bomb fringed in yellow, on a dark-blue background. Explosive ordnance disposal personnel wear the brassard while performing disposal activities (see fig 28–158).

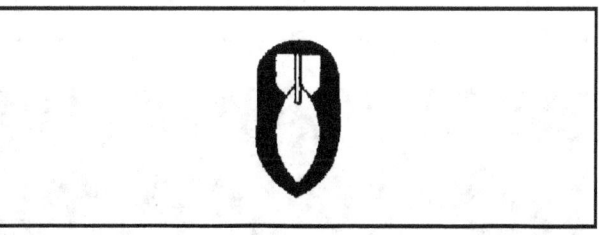

Figure 28–158. Brassard, explosive ordnance disposal

(6) Gas brassard. The brassard consists of the word "GAS" in golden orange letters, on a cobalt-blue background. Personnel assigned gas duties in a theater of operations wear the brassard (see fig 28–159).

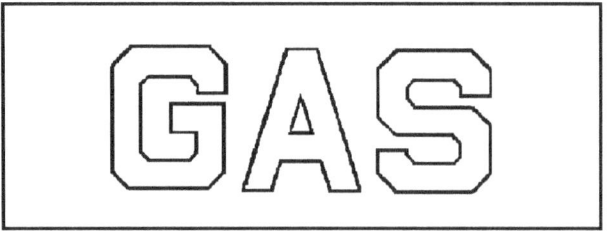

Figure 28–159. Brassard, gas

(7) Geneva Convention brassard. The brassard consists of a red Geneva cross on a white background. Medical personnel wear the brassard, subject to the direction of competent military authority. When the brassard is worn, personnel are exclusively engaged in the search for, collection, transport, or treatment of the wounded or sick; or in the prevention of disease. The brassard also is worn by staff exclusively engaged in the administration of medical units and establishments, and it is worn by chaplains attached to the armed forces. Veterinary units are not considered medical units and do not wear the Geneva Convention brassards; they wear the Veterinary Corps brassard (see fig 28–160).

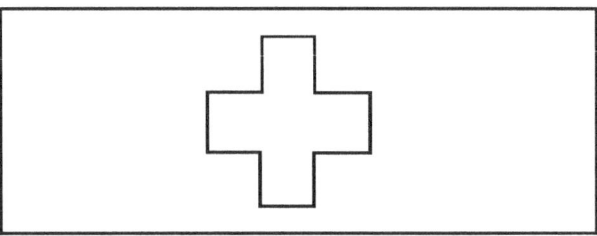

Figure 28–160. Brassard, Geneva Convention

(8) Mourning brassard. The brassard consists of plain black, or black crepe material. Personnel wear the brassard on the Army uniform, at the discretion of the wearer, only when actually present at a funeral, or en route to or from the funeral. Funeral escorts wear the brassard when prescribed by the Secretary of the Army (see fig 28–161).

Figure 28–161. Brassard, mourning

(9) Military Police brassard.

*(a)* Non-subdued. The brassard consists of the letters "MP" in white block letters, 2½ inches high, on a dark-blue or black background, 20 inches long and 4⅛ inches wide, with an extension 5–11/16 inches high, centered above the letters for display of shoulder sleeve insignia. The blue or black brassard is worn with the Army green uniform coat, or when the AG 415 shirt, black pullover or unisex cardigan sweaters, and the black windbreaker or black all-weather coat are worn as outer garments. Military Police personnel wear these brassards when authorized by the local commander.

*(b)* Subdued. The subdued MP brassard is worn with utility uniforms when performing tactical duties in the field. The subdued version has black lettering on an olive-green background or spicebrown embroidery on khaki background for the desert camouflage uniform, and it has a Velcro closure. The local commander may authorize wear of the non-subdued MP brassard when personnel are performing garrison law enforcement duties. Personnel will not wear the MP brassard and badge at the same time. Military Police personnel wear these brassards when authorized by the local commander (see fig 28–162).

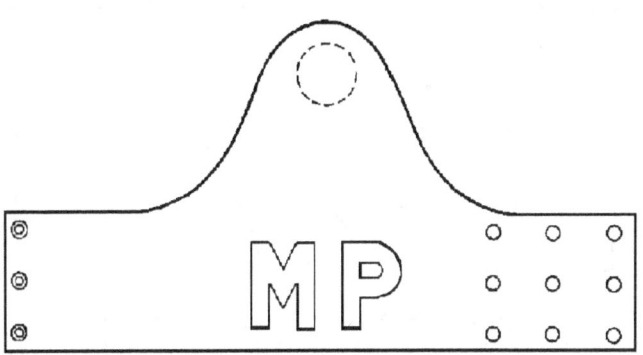

**Figure 28–162. Brassard, Military Police**

(10) Movement control brassard. The brassard consists of the words "MOVEMENT CONTROL" in golden yellow block letters on a brick-red background. Military movement control personnel wear the brassard. Other designated personnel may wear the brassard in the field, when prescribed (see fig 28–163).

**Figure 28–163. Brassard, movement control**

(11) Officer of the day brassard. The brassard consists of the letters "OD" in yellow block letters on a dark blue background. The officer of the day wears the brassard, as designated by the appropriate commander (see fig 28–164).

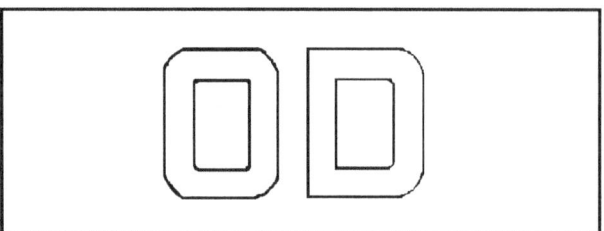

**Figure 28–164. Brassard, officer of the day**

(12) Officer of the guard brassard. The brassard consists of the letters "OG" in yellow block letters on a dark blue background. The officer of the guard wears the brassard, as designated by the appropriate commander (see fig 28–165).

**Figure 28–165. Brassard, officer of the guard**

(13) Photographer brassard. The brassard consists of the words "US ARMY PHOTOGRAPHER" on two lines, in golden-orange block letters on an ultramarine-blue background. U.S. Army photographers wear the brassard when actually performing photographic duties (see fig 28–166).

**Figure 28–166. Brassard, photographer**

(14) Port brassard. The brassard consists of the letters "TC" in golden-yellow block letters on a brick-red background. Transportation Corps military personnel wear the brassard when prescribed by the port or Army terminal commander (see fig 28–167).

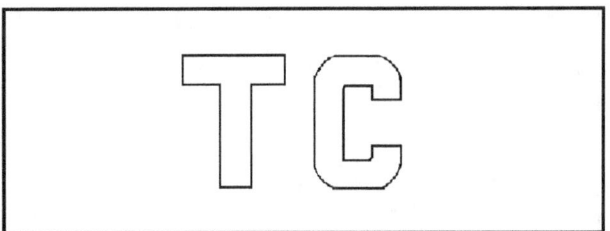

**Figure 28–167. Brassard, port**

(15) Trainees in leadership courses brassard. The brassard consists of a golden-yellow and dark-blue "compass rose" on a dark-blue background. All students attending leadership courses wear the brassard (see fig 28–168).

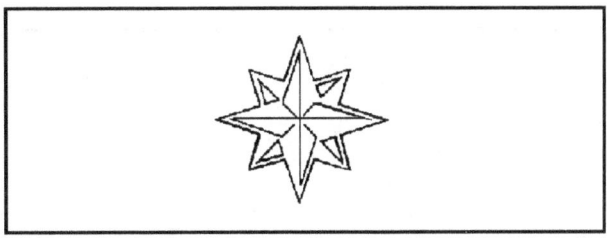

**Figure 28–168. Brassard, trainee in leadership position**

(16) Unit Police brassard. The brassard consists of the letters "UP" in yellow block letters on a dark-blue background. Army personnel, other than members of the Military Police Corps, wear the brassard while performing duties as unit traffic guides, courtesy patrols, security guards, or other police-type functions, when prescribed by the appropriate commander (see fig 28–169).

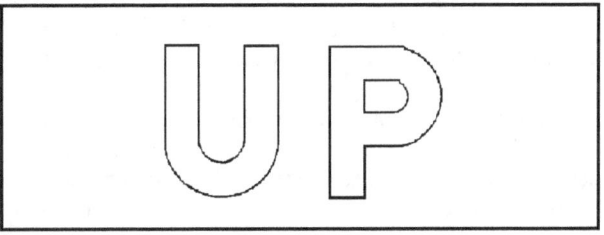

**Figure 28–169. Brassard, unit police**

(17) Veterinary Corps brassard. The brassard consists of a green cross on a white background. Members of the Veterinary Service wear the brassard, when prescribed (see fig 28–170).

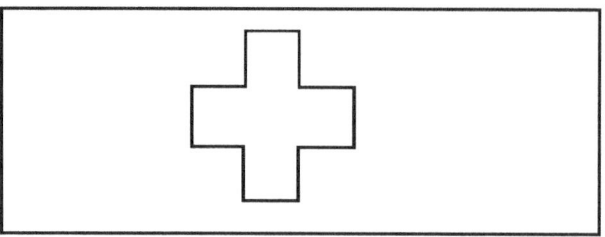

Figure 28–170. Brassard, Veterinary Corps

(18) CID brassard.

*(a)* Non-subdued. The brassard consists of white lettering (CID) on a blue background. Special agents of the USACIDC and accredited supervisors wear the brassard, as determined by the appropriate USACIDC commander (see fig 28–171).

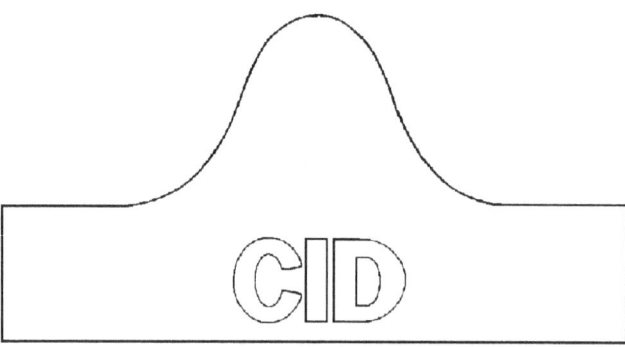

Figure 28–171. Brassard, CID

*(b)* Subdued and desert brassards. The brassard is available in subdued and desert versions. The subdued brassard has black lettering on an olive-green background. The desert brassard has spice-brown lettering on a khaki background. Special agents of the USACIDC and accredited supervisors wear the subdued and desert brassards, as determined by the appropriate USACIDC commander.

(19) Personnel assistance point brassard. The brassard consists of the words "MILITARY ASSISTANCE" on two lines, in white lettering on a black background, 20 inches long and 4¼ inches wide, with an extension 5¾ inches high centered above the letters for display of shoulder sleeve insignia. Qualified personnel working at personnel assistance points wear the brassard, at the direction of the Total Army Personnel Command commander (see fig 28–172).

Figure 28–172. Brassard, military assistance

## 28–30. Distinctive items authorized for infantry personnel

*a.* Cord, shoulder.

(1) Description. The shoulder cord is infantry blue, and it is formed by a series of interlocking square knots around a center cord.

(2) Approval authority. The commanding general of the U.S. Army Infantry Center authorizes the award of the shoulder cord to infantrymen who have successfully completed the appropriate training. For Army National Guard soldiers, commanders of divisions, separate brigades, infantry regiments, the infantry scout group, and state adjutants general for separate infantry battalions and companies are authorized to award the shoulder cord to Army National Guard soldiers who have successfully completed the appropriate training.

(3) How worn. The shoulder cord is worn on the right shoulder of the Army green, blue, and white uniform coats, and the AG 415 shirts. The cord is passed under the arm and over the right shoulder under the shoulder loop, and secured to the button on the shoulder loop. In order to attach the cord, officer personnel will attach a 20-ligne button to the right shoulder seam, ½ inch outside the collar edge (see fig 28–173).

**Figure 28–173. Distinctive items authorized for infantry personnel**

(4) By whom worn.

*(a)* Officers and enlisted personnel of the infantry, holding an infantry PMOS or specialty, who have been awarded the Combat Infantryman badge, the Expert Infantry badge, or who have successfully completed the basic unit phase of an Army training program or equivalent.

*(b)* Enlisted personnel who have completed one station unit training (OSUT) resulting in the award of an infantry PMOS.

*(c)* Infantry officers who have graduated from the resident infantry officer basic or advanced course.

*(d)* Infantry officers who have graduated from the Infantry Officer Candidate Course (during mobilization).

*(e)* Infantry officers and enlisted personnel in the Reserve components who hold an infantry PMOS or specialty.

(5) When worn. Infantry personnel (as described above) may wear the infantry cord as follows.

*(a)* During the period of assignment to an infantry regiment, brigade, separate infantry battalion, infantry company (including the headquarters and headquarters company of an infantry division), infantry platoon, or infantry TDA unit. In addition, infantrymen assigned to infantry sections or squads within units other than infantry units may wear the cord when authorized by battalion or higher-level commanders.

*(b)* During the period assigned for duty as an Army recruiter or advisor, ROTC instructor, or member of the staff and faculty of the U.S. Military Academy, as long as personnel retain their infantry PMOS.

*(c)* During the period of assignment at brigade- or lower-level BT or advance individual training units, or in OSUT infantry units, as long as personnel retain their infantry PMOS.

*(d)* Infantry OSUT and IOBC graduates may wear the cord en route to their initial follow-on infantry assignment.

*(e)* Soldiers en route from an assignment where wear of the shoulder cord was authorized are permitted to wear the shoulder cord if they are pending reassignment to another organization authorized wear of the cord, or when assigned to a separation point for discharge purposes.

*b.* Insignia disk; branch and U.S. insignia.

(1) Description. A plastic disk in infantry blue, 1–1/14 inches in diameter.

(2) Approval authority. The same as in paragraph *a*(2), above. The insignia is issued without cost to enlisted personnel.

(3) How worn. The blue infantry disk is worn secured beneath the branch and U.S. insignia disks, with a ⅛-inch border around the insignia. infantry personnel wear the insignia on the Army green, blue, and white uniforms (see fig 28–173).

(4) By whom worn.

*(a)* Enlisted infantry personnel, who hold an infantry PMOS; who were awarded the Combat Infantryman badge or the Expert Infantry badge, or who have successfully completed the basic unit phase of an Army training program, or the equivalent.

*(b)* Enlisted personnel who completed one station unit training (OSUT) and were awarded an infantry PMOS.

*(c)* Enlisted personnel of the Reserve components holding an infantry PMOS.

(5) When worn. The same as in paragraph *a*(5), above.

*c.* Insignia disk, service cap.

(1) Description. A plastic disk in infantry blue, 1¾ inches in diameter.

(2) Approval authority. The same as in paragraph *a*(2), above. The insignia is issued without cost to enlisted personnel.

(3) How worn. The blue infantry disk is worn secured beneath the insignia on the blue and green service caps and the male drill sergeant hat (see fig 28–173).

(4) By whom worn. The same as in paragraph *b*(4), above.

(5) When worn. The same as in *b*(5), above.

## 28–31. Distinctive items authorized for other than infantry personnel

*a.* Organizational flash.

(1) Description. A shield-shaped embroidered patch, with a semicircular bottom, approximately 2¼ inches long and 1⅞ inches wide.

(2) Approval authority. The Institute of Heraldry, U.S. Army, approves the color selection or color combination of the flash for each organization. The flash is provided without cost to enlisted personnel.

(3) How worn. The flash is sewn centered on the stiffener of the beret (see figs 28–11 and 28–12).

(4) By whom worn. Personnel authorized to wear the maroon, tan, or green berets wear their distinctive organizational flash. All other soldiers wear the Army flash on the black beret, unless authorization for another flash was granted before the implementation of the black beret as the standard Army headgear (see para 3–5*a*(3)*(c)*).

*b.* Airborne background trimming.

(1) Description. An oval-shaped embroidered device in distinctive colors, 1⅜ inches in height and 2¼ inches in width.

(2) Approval authority. Subject to the approval of The Institute of Heraldry, U.S. Army, a background trimming is authorized for organizations designated (by structure, equipment, and mission) "Airborne" or "Air Assault" by HQDA. Qualified personnel are authorized to wear the background trimming with the Parachutist or Air Assault badges. Personnel wear only one background trimming at a time. Appropriated funds are used to provide enlisted personnel with the background trimming without cost. If appropriated funds are not available, units may purchase background trimming with non-appropriated funds.

(3) How worn.

*(a)* Personnel wear the background trimming beneath any of the authorized parachutist or air assault badges on the Army green coat and AG 415 shirt. The basic portion of the badge is centered on the background trimming; however, the wreath and star on the Master and Senior Parachutist badges project slightly above the background trimming. On the AG 415 shirt when ribbons are worn, all personnel wear the trimming so the bottom edge of the trimming is ¼ inch above the ribbons. When ribbons are not worn, males wear the trimming ¼ inch above the pocket seam, and females wear the trimming in a comparable position.

*(b)* On the green uniform coat, males wear the background trimming and applicable badge on the pocket flap so the space between the seam of the pocket flap and the top of the background trimming, wreath, or star is ⅛ inch (see fig 28–174). Females wear the trimming and applicable badge on the green coat and the maternity uniform tunic so the bottom edge of the background trimming is ¼ inch above the ribbons (see fig 28–175). When worn below the ribbons, the top of the background trimming is ¼ inch below the bottom ribbon row.

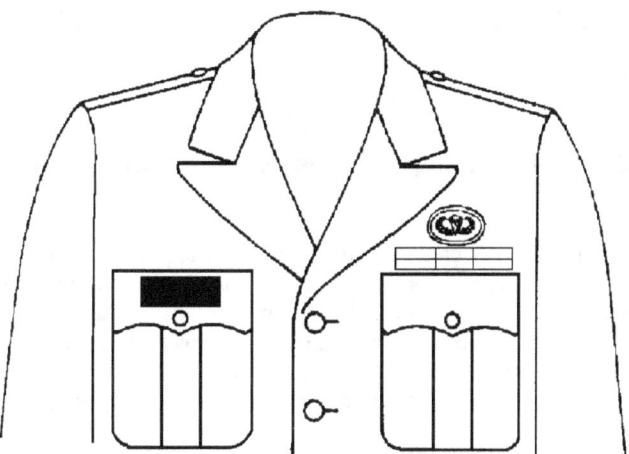

Figure 28–174. Wear of airborne background trimming

Figure 28–175. Wear of airborne background trimming, maternity tunic

(4) By whom worn. All personnel of an organization authorized a background trimming, and who were awarded one of the parachutist or air assault badges.

c. Cord, shoulder, marksmanship.

(1) Description. A blue cord, 3/16 inch in diameter, bearing a band composed of serrated markings at 9/16-inch intervals. Each marking consists of 1/16-inch white, 1/16-inch red, and 1/16-inch white markings. The overall length of the shoulder cord will not exceed 52 inches (includes double cord).

(2) By whom worn. All personnel assigned to the U.S. Army marksmanship unit, subordinate marksmanship training units, and the ARNG marksmanship training unit. The shoulder cord is issued at no cost to the individual.

(3) How worn. The shoulder cord is worn on the right shoulder of the Army green uniform coats and the AG 415 shirt, when it is worn as an outer garment. The cord is passed under the arm and over the right shoulder under the shoulder loops, and secured to the button on the shoulder loop.

(4) When worn. Personnel wear the marksmanship cord during the period of assignment to the U.S. Army marksmanship unit, one of the marksmanship training units, or the ARNG marksmanship training unit. Personnel who

are transferred from these units are not authorized to wear the shoulder cord. Personnel in an attached or TDY status with these units, or the State small arms readiness training teams, are not authorized to wear the shoulder cord.

## Chapter 29
## Wear of Decorations, Service Medals, Badges, Unit Awards, and Appurtenances

### 29–1. General
This chapter covers the decorations, medals, badges, unit awards and appurtenances, both U.S. and foreign, authorized for wear on Army uniforms. The term "awards" is an all-inclusive term covering any decoration, medal, badge, ribbon, or appurtenance bestowed on an individual or unit. The term "awards" is used throughout this chapter. The term "ribbon" is an all-inclusive term covering that portion of the suspension ribbon of a service medal or decoration that is worn instead of the service medal or decoration. The ribbon is made in the form of a ribbon bar, 1⅜ inches long by ⅜ inches wide. The term "ribbon" is used throughout this chapter, and it includes service and training ribbons.

### 29–2. Authorization
*a.* Commanders may require the wear of awards on the following occasions.
(1) Parades, reviews, inspections, and funerals.
(2) Ceremonial and social occasions.
*b.* Awards are worn at the option of the wearer when not prohibited during normal duty hours. Personnel also may wear awards on appropriate uniforms when off duty (see para 29–4, below). Personnel are encouraged to wear authorized awards on the service, dress, and mess uniforms.
*c.* Soldiers may wear awards on the class B uniform during duty hours and when off duty, at their option.

### 29–4. When wear of awards is prohibited
The wear of awards is prohibited in the following circumstances.
*a.* On any uniform other than those authorized in this regulation. (See section 704, title 18, United States Code (18 USC 704) for the penalty for unauthorized wear of the uniform.)
*b.* When serving a sentence of confinement.
*c.* When wearing civilian clothing, except for civilian awards, lapel buttons, or rosettes intended for wear with civilian clothing. Soldiers may wear miniature medals on formal civilian attire at formal social functions, when the wear of the Army uniform is inappropriate or not authorized.

### 29–5. Order of precedence by category of medal
The following list indicates the order of precedence by category when medals from two or more categories are worn at the same time.
*a.* U.S. military decorations.
*b.* U.S. unit awards.
*c.* U.S. non-military decorations.
*d.* U.S. service (campaign) medals, and service and training ribbons.
*e.* U.S. Merchant Marine awards.
*f.* U.S. non-military unit awards.
*g.* Foreign military decorations.
*h.* Foreign unit awards.
*i.* Non-U.S. service awards.
*j.* State awards for ARNG soldiers.

### 29–6. Order of precedence within categories of medals
The following lists indicate the order of precedence within each category, when two or more medals from each category are worn at the same time.
*a.* U.S. military decorations. A decoration is an award given to an individual as a distinctively designed mark of honor denoting heroism, or meritorious or outstanding service or achievement. U.S. military decorations authorized for wear on Army uniforms are listed below in order of precedence.
(1) Medal of Honor (Army, Navy, Air Force).
(2) Distinguished Service Cross.
(3) Navy Cross.
(4) Air Force Cross.
(5) Defense Distinguished Service Medal.

(6) Distinguished Service Medal (Army, Navy, Air Force, Coast Guard).

(7) Silver Star.

(8) Defense Superior Service Medal.

(9) Legion of Merit.

(10) Distinguished Flying Cross.

(11) Soldier's Medal.

(12) Navy and Marine Corps Medal.

(13) Airman's Medal.

(14) Coast Guard Medal.

(15) Bronze Star Medal.

(16) Purple Heart.

(17) Defense Meritorious Service Medal.

(18) Meritorious Service Medal.

(19) Air Medal.

(20) Aerial Achievement Medal

(21) Joint Service Commendation Medal.

(22) Army Commendation Medal.

(23) Navy Commendation Medal.

(24) Air Force Commendation Medal.

(25) Coast Guard Commendation Medal.

(26) Joint Service Achievement Medal.

(27) Army Achievement Medal.

(28) Navy Achievement Medal.

(29) Air Force Achievement Medal.

(30) Coast Guard Achievement Medal.

(31) Combat Action Ribbon.

*b.* U.S. unit awards. A unit award is given to an operating unit and is worn by members of that unit who participated in the cited action. Personnel who did not participate in the cited action, but who are assigned in the cited unit, are authorized temporary wear of some unit awards. U. S. unit awards authorized for wear on Army uniforms are listed below in their order of precedence.

(1) Presidential Unit Citation (Army, Air Force).

(2) Presidential Unit Citation (Navy).

(3) Joint Meritorious Unit Award.

(4) Valorous Unit Award.

(5) Meritorious Unit Commendation (Army).

(6) Navy Unit Commendation.

(7) Air Force Outstanding Unit Award.

(8) Coast Guard Unit Commendation.

(9) Army Superior Unit Award.

(10) Meritorious Unit Commendation (Navy).

(11) Navy "E" Ribbon.

(12) Air Force Organizational Excellence Award.

(13) Coast Guard Meritorious Unit Commendation.

*c.* U.S. non-military decorations. U.S. non-military decorations authorized for wear on Army uniforms are listed below in their order of precedence. Personnel will wear other U.S. non-military (Federal agency) decorations based upon date of receipt. If more than one decoration is awarded by the same agency, the decorations are worn in the order of precedence, as established by the awarding agency. Personnel will not wear U.S. non-military decorations that duplicate recognition for service or an act for which a military decoration has already been awarded. Awards given by a jurisdiction inferior to the Federal Government are not authorized for wear on the Army uniform, except as specified in paragraph *j*, below.

(1) Presidential Medal of Freedom.

(2) Presidential Citizen's Medal.

(3) President's Award for Distinguished Federal Civilian Service Award.

(4) Department of Defense Distinguished Civilian Service Award.

(5) Secretary of Defense Medal for the Defense of Freedom.

(6) Secretary of Defense Meritorious Civilian Service Award.

(7) Office of the Secretary of Defense Exceptional Civilian Service Award.

(8) Surgeon General's Exemplary Service Medal.

(9) NASA Space Flight Medal.

(10) Public Health Service Commendation Medal.

(11) Public Health Service Achievement Medal.

(12) Department of State Superior Honor Award.

(13) Decoration for Exceptional Civilian Service.

(14) Meritorious Civilian Service Award.

(15) Superior Civilian Service Award.

(16) Commander's Award for Civilian Service.

(17) Achievement Medal for Civilian Service.

*d.* U.S. service (campaign) medals, and service and training ribbons. U.S. service (campaign) medals, and service and training ribbons authorized for wear on the uniform are listed below, in their order of precedence. Personnel may wear service medals and service and training ribbons awarded by other U.S. Services on the Army uniform, except for the Air Force Longevity Service Award ribbon and Air Force, Navy, and Coast Guard marksmanship medals and ribbons. Personnel will wear service and training medals and ribbons awarded by other U.S. Services after U.S. Army service and training ribbons, and before foreign awards.

(1) Prisoner of War Medal.

(2) Good Conduct Medal. Good Conduct Medals from the other Services follow the Army Good Conduct Medal in order of precedence. The Army reserve components' Achievement Medal and equivalents awarded by other Service reserve components follow the Army Good Conduct Medal and Good Conduct Medals from the other U.S. Services, in order of precedence.

(3) American Defense Service Medal.

(4) Women's Army Corps Service Medal.

(5) American Campaign Medal.

(6) Asiatic-Pacific Campaign Medal.

(7) European-African-Middle Eastern Campaign Medal.

(8) World War II Victory Medal.

(9) Army of Occupation Medal.

(10) Medal for Humane Action.

(11) National Defense Service Medal.

(12) Korean Service Medal.

(13) Antarctica Service Medal.

(14) Armed Forces Expeditionary Medal.

(15) Vietnam Service Medal.

(16) Southwest Asia Service Medal.

(17) Global War on Terrorism—Expeditionary Medal.

(18) Global War on Terrorism—Service Medal.

(19) Kosovo Campaign Medal.

(20) Korean Defense Service Medal.

(21) Armed Forces Service Medal.

(22) Humanitarian Service Medal.

(23) Military Outstanding Volunteer Service Medal.

(24) Armed Forces Reserve Medal.

(25) NCO Professional Development Ribbon.

(26) Army Service Ribbon.

(27) Overseas Service Ribbon.

(28) Army Reserve Components Overseas Training Ribbon.

(29) Coast Guard Special Operations Service Ribbon.

(30) Air Force Combat Readiness Medal.

(31) Navy Sea Service Deployment Ribbon.

*e.* U.S. Merchant Marine awards. Listed below in their order of precedence are the U.S. Merchant Marine awards authorized for wear on the Army uniform.

(1) Distinguished Service Medal.

(2) Meritorious Service Medal.

(3) Gallant Ship Citation.

(4) Mariner's Medal.

(5) Combat Medal.

(6) Defense Medal.

(7) Atlantic War Zone Medal.

(8) Pacific War Zone Medal.

(9) Mediterranean-Middle East War Zone Medal.

(10) Victory Medal.

(11) Korean Service Medal.

(12) Vietnam Service Medal.

(13) Expeditionary Medal.

(14) Philippine Defense Ribbon.

(15) Philippine Liberation Ribbon.

*f.* U.S. non-military unit awards. The Public Health Service Unit Award and the National Intelligence Meritorious Unit Citation are authorized for wear on the Army uniform.

*g.* Foreign military decorations. Personnel who are specifically authorized by law to accept decorations from foreign governments may wear them in the order of their receipt after all U.S. decorations, the Good Conduct Medal, campaign and service medals, and service and training ribbons. (See chap 9, AR 600–8–22, for application procedures to request authorization to accept and wear foreign decorations.) Personnel may not wear any foreign decorations on the uniform unless at least one U.S. decoration or service medal is worn at the same time. Personnel will not wear foreign awards that do not conform to the standard U.S. size ribbon bar or medal.

*h.* Foreign unit awards. The following foreign unit awards, listed in their order of precedence, are authorized for wear on the Army uniform, when at least one U.S. decoration, service medal, or ribbon is worn at the same time.

(1) Philippine Republic Presidential Unit Citation.

(2) Republic of Korea Presidential Unit Citation.

(3) Vietnam Presidential Unit Citation.

(4) Republic of Vietnam Gallantry Cross Unit Citation.

(5) Republic of Vietnam Civil Actions Unit Citation.

(6) Fourrageres (no order of precedence).

*(a)* French Fourragere.

*(b)* Belgian Fourragere.

*(c)* Netherlands Orange Lanyard.

*i.* Non-U.S. service awards. The following non-U.S. service awards, listed in their order of precedence, are authorized for wear on the Army uniform when at least one U.S. decoration, service medal, or ribbon is worn at the same time. An individual may not wear any other foreign service medal, unless the wearer was awarded such medal while a bona fide member of the armed forces of a friendly foreign nation and has received HQDA approval to wear the medal or ribbon. (See chap 9, AR 600–8–22, for application procedures to request authorization to accept and wear foreign service medals or ribbons.)

(1) Philippine Defense Ribbon.

(2) Philippine Liberation Ribbon.

(3) Philippine Independence Ribbon.

(4) United Nations Service Medal.

(5) Inter-American Defense Board Medal.

(6) United Nations Medal.

(7) NATO Medal.

(8) Multinational Force and Observers Medal.

(9) Republic of Vietnam Campaign Medal.

(10) Kuwait Liberation Medal (Saudi Arabia).

(11) Kuwait Liberation Medal (Government of Kuwait).

(12) Republic of Korea War Service Medal.

*j.* State awards for ARNG soldiers. Army National Guard personnel are authorized to wear State awards under applicable State laws or regulations when assigned to the ARNG under the command and control of the Governor or Adjutant General, under the provisions of title 32, United States Code. The term "State" includes the 50 states, U.S. territories (which include Guam and the U.S. Virgin Islands), Puerto Rico, and the District of Columbia. The following personnel statuses are included in this authorization: AGR; active duty for training (ADT), active duty for special work (ADSW); full-time National Guard duty (FTNGD) for special work or training, annual training; and inactive duty training (drill status), including periods when personnel may be attached to the active component or reserve of any service, whether paid or unpaid. Personnel will wear such awards in the State order of precedence, after Federal and foreign awards. Soldiers on active Federal Service, under the provisions of title 10, United States Code, are authorized to accept but not wear State or Territory awards.

## 29–7. Wear of service ribbons and lapel buttons

*a.* Ribbons.

(1) Where worn. Personnel may wear ribbons representing decorations, service medals, service ribbons, and training ribbons on the following uniforms.

*(a)* Male personnel. On the coats of the Army green, blue, and white uniforms, and on the AG shade 415 shirt.

*(b)* Female personnel. On the coats of the Army green, blue, and white uniforms, the maternity tunic, and the AG shade 415 shirt.

(2) How worn.

*(a)* General. Ribbons are worn in order of precedence from the wearer's right to left, in one or more rows, with either no space between rows or ⅛-inch space between rows. No more than four ribbons are worn in any one row. Soldiers will not start a second row unless they are authorized to wear four or more ribbons. The determination of whether three or four ribbons are worn in each row is based upon the size of the coat and the position of the lapel. The first and second rows will contain the same number of ribbons (three or four) before starting a third row. The third and succeeding rows will contain the same number of ribbons as the first two rows, but may contain less. The top row is centered on the row beneath, or may be aligned to the wearer's left, whichever presents the best appearance (see fig 29–1).

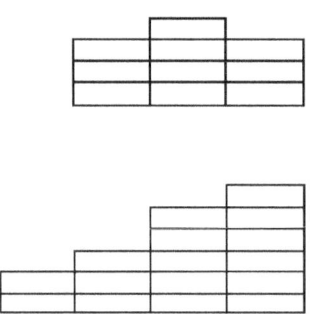

**Figure 29–1. Wear of ribbons centered and aligned to the left**

*(b)* Personnel are authorized to have their ribbons commercially mounted on a cloth background, on an optional basis. Soldiers who choose this option must ensure the color of the cloth background is black, or that it matches the color of the uniform fabric. The border trim should not exceed ⅛ inch. Soldiers will not wear a black background on the AG shade 415 and 469 shirts. Plastic or plastic-coated, commercially mounted ribbons are not authorized.

*(c)* Male personnel. On the coats of the Army green, blue, and white uniforms, and on the AG shade 415 shirt, males wear the ribbons centered ⅛ inch above the left breast pocket. Ribbon mounts will remain centered above the pocket even if the top ribbon row is offset (see fig 29–2).

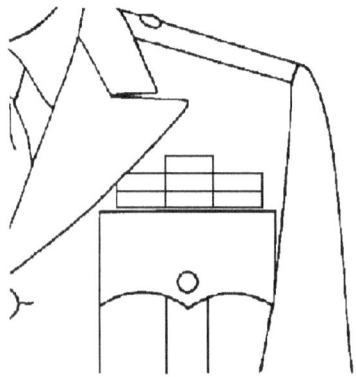

**Figure 29–2. Wear of ribbons, Army green, blue, and white uniforms, male**

*(d)* Female personnel. On the coats of the Army green, blue, and white uniforms, the maternity tunic, and the AG shade 415 shirt, females wear the ribbons centered on the left side, with the bottom row positioned parallel to the bottom edge of the nameplate. Females may adjust the placement of the ribbons to conform to individual body-shape differences (see fig 29–3).

**Figure 29–3. Wear of ribbons, Army green, blue, and white uniforms, female (new version coats)**

*b.* Lapel buttons. Lapel buttons are miniature enameled replicas of an award that are worn only on civilian clothing. Males wear the buttons on the left lapel of civilian clothing; females wear the buttons in a similar location on their civilian attire.

## 29–8. Wear of full-size U.S. and foreign decorations and service medals

*a.* Where worn. All personnel may wear full-size decorations and service medals on the Army blue and white uniforms. When the Army green dress uniform is worn to social functions, enlisted personnel may wear full-size decorations and service medals on the coat of the green dress uniform.

*b.* How worn. Personnel wear all full-size decorations, except the Medal of Honor (see para *c*, below) in the order of precedence from the wearer's right to left, in one or more rows, with ⅛-inch space between rows. Second and subsequent rows will not contain more medals than the row below. Personnel will not wear service and training ribbons when full-size decorations and service medals are worn. Personnel may wear U.S. and foreign unit award emblems as prescribed, when wearing full-size medals. Full-size medals are worn as follows:

(1) Males wear full-size medals immediately above the left breast pocket, in as many rows as necessary. The number of medals worn in each row depends upon the size of the coat. Full-size decorations or medals will not overlap within a row. When full-size medals are worn, up to three full-size or miniature combat and special skill badges from groups 1 to 5 are authorized for wear above the medals, in order of group precedence (see para 29–17*a*). Males may not wear the Driver and Mechanic badges with full-size medals, and they may not wear special skill and marksmanship badges on the pocket flap below the medals (see fig 29–4).

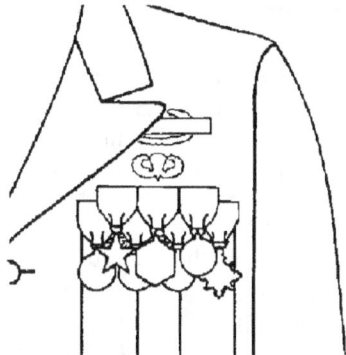

**Figure 29–4. Wear of full-size and miniature medals, Army blue and white uniforms, male**

(2) Females wear full-size medals centered on the left side of the coat. The bottom row of the medal pendants are positioned parallel to the bottom of the nameplate. Females may adjust the placement of the medals and nameplate to conform to individual body shape differences. The number of medals worn in each row depends upon the size of the coat. When full-size medals are worn, up to three full-size or miniature combat and special skill badges from groups 1 to 5 are authorized for wear above the medals, in order of group precedence (see para 29–17a). Females may not wear the Driver and Mechanic badges with full-size medals, and they may not wear special skill and marksmanship badges below the medals (see fig 29–5).

**Figure 29–5. Wear of full-size and miniature medals, Army blue and white uniforms, female (new version coats)**

c. Medal of Honor. The Medal of Honor is worn with the neckband ribbon around the neck, outside the shirt collar and inside the coat collar, with the medal hanging over the necktie. Authorized foreign neck decorations are worn beneath the Medal of Honor (see fig 29–6).

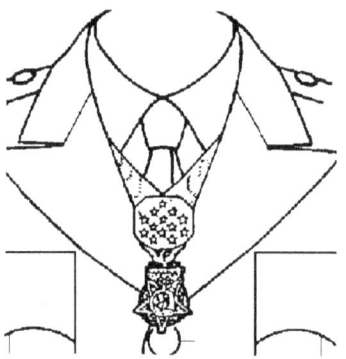

**Figure 29–6. Wear of Medal of Honor**

## 29–9. Wear of miniature decorations and service medals

a. Miniature medals are replicas of regular size medals, made to a scale of one-half the size of the original. Except for the Medal of Honor, for which there is no miniature, only miniature decorations and service medals are authorized for wear on the mess and evening mess uniforms. Personnel will not wear full-size medals, service and training ribbons, or U.S. and foreign unit award emblems with miniature medals. Only the dress miniature-size combat and special skill badges are worn with miniature medals.

b. Miniature decorations and service medals are authorized for wear on the following uniforms.

(1) Male personnel. On the Army white and blue uniforms, the white and blue mess and evening mess uniforms; and on the left lapel of formal civilian attire, when wear of Army uniforms is inappropriate or not authorized. Miniature badges are authorized for wear on the AG shade 415 shirt. (See para 29–17b for wear of combat and special

skill badges with miniature medals; see paragraphs 29–17c and 29–18d for wear of combat and special skill badges on the AG shade 415 shirt.)

(2) Female personnel. On the Army white and blue uniforms; the white, all-white, black, or blue mess uniforms; the Army white, blue, or black evening mess uniforms; and on the left side of formal civilian attire when wear of Army uniforms is inappropriate or not authorized. Miniature badges are authorized for wear on the AG shade 415 shirt. (See para 29–17b for wear of combat and special skill badges with miniature medals; see paragraphs 29–17c and 29–18d for wear of combat and special skill badges on the AG shade 415 shirt.)

c. The maximum length of holding bars for miniature medals is 2¾ inches. Miniature decorations and service medals are worn in the order of precedence from the wearer's right to left, with the medal of highest precedence worn on the top row, if more than one row is required. Miniature medals are worn side by side when four or less are worn in the same row, and they may be overlapped. If the medals are overlapped, the overlap will not exceed 50 percent and will be equal for all medals. When more than one row of miniature medals are worn, the second and subsequent rows are positioned so that the medal pendants on the row below are visible. The top row of miniature medals is centered over the row immediately below. Miniature medals are worn as follows:

(1) Male personnel. Miniature medals are worn centered on the left lapel, approximately ½ inch below the notch of the mess and evening mess uniforms, and will not extend beyond the edge of the lapel. Personnel may adjust placement of the medals to accommodate the wear of dress miniature badges (see fig 29–7). Personnel will wear miniature medals on the Army blue and white uniforms only when these uniforms are worn as formal dress uniforms (with bow tie). When worn on the blue and white uniforms, the miniature medals are worn above the left breast pocket in the same position as full-size medals (see fig 29–4). (See para 29–17c for wear of dress miniature badges with miniature medals on the blue and white uniforms.)

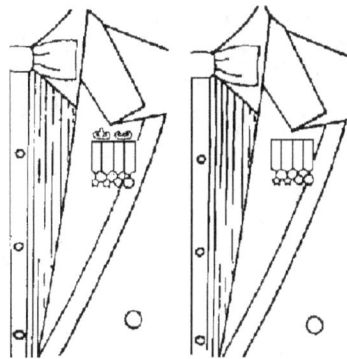

Figure 29–7. Wear of miniature medals on mess uniforms, male

(2) Female personnel. Miniature medals are worn centered on the left lapel of the Army blue mess and the new versions of the Army white mess uniforms. On the black mess uniform, the old version of the white mess jackets, and on the Army white and blue uniform coats, females wear the medals centered on the left side of the jacket (not on the lapels). The medals are placed so the bottom line is positioned parallel to the top edge of the top button of the Army white and blue uniform coats, and in a similar position on the new version of the white mess uniforms, and the blue mess and evening mess uniforms (see fig 29–8). Females may adjust placement of the medals to conform to differences in individual body shape. Personnel may wear miniature medals on the Army blue and white uniform coats only when these uniforms are worn as formal dress uniforms. (See para 29–17c for wear of dress miniature badges with miniature medals on the Army blue and white dress uniforms.)

**Figure 29–8. Wear of miniature medals on mess uniforms, female**

## 29–10. Wear of multiple neck ribbons, broad sashes, and stars

*a.* An individual awarded more than one decoration that includes a broad ribbon, sash, or star, will wear only one broad ribbon or sash, and no more than four stars at one time. The Presidential Medal of Freedom broad ribbon with badge and star has precedence over all other broad ribbons, sashes, or stars. Stars are worn above the waistline on the side, as described by the awarding country (see figs 29–11 and 29–12). Stars are worn as follows:

(1) Two stars. Along side or above the first star.

(2) Three stars. In a triangle, with the point of the triangle up.

(3) Four stars. The fourth star is centered beneath the triangle of three stars.

*b.* An individual may not wear more than two decorations with neck ribbons at one time. The decoration with the highest precedence is worn suspended above the other. The Medal of Honor takes precedence over all other decorations with neck ribbons (see figs 29–6, 29–9, and 29–10).

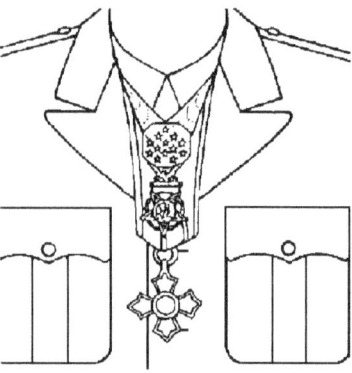

**Figure 29–9. Wear of multiple neck ribbons, male**

Figure 29–10. Wear of multiple neck ribbons, female

Figure 29–11. Wear of sash and stars, male

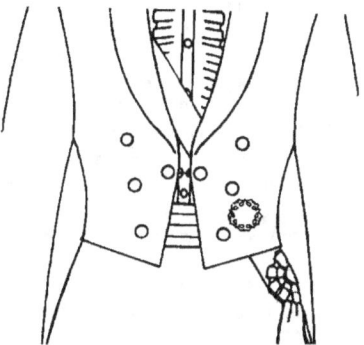

Figure 29–12. Wear of sash and stars, female

## 29–11. Wear of U.S. and foreign unit awards

*a.* Description. Unit award emblems awarded with frames are worn with the laurel leaves of the frame pointing upward. Unit awards are worn on the right side of the uniform, regardless of which service awarded them. Only one emblem representing the same unit award is worn at one time. Personnel may wear unit awards when wearing full-size medals or service ribbons, but they may not wear them with miniature medals. Unit awards received from other U.S. Services that have a frame are worn with the Army (large-size) unit award citation frame. Unit awards of the other U.S. Services that do not have frames are worn on the right side, without frames. (See table 29–1 for authority to wear U.S.

unit awards on a temporary or permanent basis.) The criteria for permanent and temporary wear of foreign unit awards are contained in AR 600–8–22.

**Table 29–1**
**Authority for wear—U.S. unit award emblems**

| Emblem in order of precedence | Authority for wear | | Subsequent award | |
|---|---|---|---|---|
| | Permanent[1] | Temporary[2] | Oak leaf cluster | Star |
| Presidential Unit Citation (Army and Air Force)[3] | X[4] | X | X[5] | |
| Presidential Unit Citation (Navy) | X | | | X |
| Joint Meritorious Unit Award | X | | X | |
| Valorous Unit Award | X | X | X | |
| Meritorious Unit Commendation (Army) | X | X | X | |
| Navy Unit Commendation | X[4] | | | X |
| Meritorious Unit Commendation (Navy) | X[4] | | | X |
| Air Force Outstanding Unit Award[6] | X[4] | | X | |
| Air Force Organization Excellence Award[6] | X[4] | | X | |
| Army Superior Unit Award | X | X | X | |
| Navy "E" Ribbon | X | | | |
| Coast Guard Unit Commendation | X[7] | | X | |
| Coast Guard Meritorious Unit Commendation | X[7] | | X | |

Notes:

[1] A soldier may wear the unit award permanently if the individual was assigned to, and present for duty with the unit any time during the period cited; or who was attached by competent orders to, and present for duty with the unit during the entire period, or for at least 30 consecutive days of the period cited. When a soldier is permanently awarded a unit award and is subsequently assigned to a unit that has received the same unit award, the soldier will wear the permanent award in lieu of the temporary unit award.

[2] A soldier may wear the unit award temporarily if the individual was not present with the unit during the period cited but was subsequently assigned to the unit. Soldiers may wear the unit award only while assigned to the cited unit. For elements of regiments organized under the New Manning System or Combat Arms Regimental System, only personnel of the earning unit wear the emblem temporarily.

[3] Personnel may not wear the Air Force Presidential Unit Citation on a temporary basis.

[4] The 30-day requirement for attached personnel does not apply to Navy and Air Force awards.

[5] Army and Air Force awards are equal in precedence, and the emblems are identical. An individual authorized to wear both an Army and Air Force emblem would wear a single emblem with an oak leaf cluster.

[6] When awarded for combat or direct combat support, a bronze "V" device is worn on the emblem.

[7] Authorized for wear by an individual who was assigned to, or who was attached to and present for duty with the unit during at least 1 day of the period cited, for awards issued prior to 28 August 1979. For awards issued on or after 28 August 1979, the individual must have been assigned or attached by competent orders to the unit, and have been present for duty during the entire period, or for at least 50 percent of the period cited.

*b.* Where worn. Personnel may wear U.S. and foreign unit award emblems on the following uniforms.

(1) Male personnel. On the coats of the Army green, blue, and white uniforms, and the AG shade 415 shirt.

(2) Female personnel. On the coats of the Army green, blue, and white uniforms, the Army green maternity tunic, and the AG shade 415 shirt.

(3) Fourrageres and lanyards. Fourrageres and lanyards are authorized for wear on the coats of the uniforms listed in paragraphs (1) and (2), above.

*c.* How worn. All permanent and temporary unit award emblems, with and without frames, are worn in the order of precedence from the wearer's right to left. Award emblems are worn in rows containing no more than three emblems per row, with no space between emblems, and with up to ⅛ inch space between rows, depending upon the size of emblems with frames. The emblems are worn as follows:

(1) Male personnel. Emblems with or without frames are worn centered with the bottom edge of the emblem 1/8 above the right breast pocket flag (see fig 29-13).

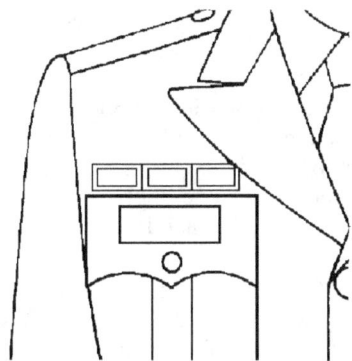

**Figure 29–13. Wear of unit awards, male**

(2) Female personnel. Emblems with or without frames are worn centered on the right side of the uniform, with the bottom edge ½ inch above the top edge of the nameplate (see fig 29–14).

**Figure 29–14. Wear of unit awards, female**

(3) Fourrageres and lanyards. Permanent and temporary fourrageres and lanyards, when authorized for wear according to AR 600–8–22, are worn on the left shoulder, with the cord passing under the sleeve and attached to the shoulder loop on the coat of the green and white uniforms, and on the enlisted blue uniforms. Officer personnel authorized to wear a fourragere or lanyard on the blue coat must attach a 20-ligne button to the left shoulder seam, ½ inch outside the collar edge, to attach these awards. Only one fourragere, lanyard, aiguillette, or cord is authorized for wear on each shoulder.

*d.* Foreign unit awards. If a foreign unit award is worn, personnel must wear at least one other U.S. decoration, service medal, or unit award. Foreign unit awards are worn after U.S. unit awards, by date of receipt. (See AR 600–8–22 for criteria for acceptance of foreign unit awards.) Foreign unit awards are worn as follows:

(1) French fourragere: when authorized for permanent or temporary wear.

(2) Belgian fourragere: only when authorized for permanent wear.

(3) Netherlands orange lanyard: only when authorized for permanent wear.

(4) The Philippine Republic Presidential Unit Citation is authorized for permanent wear, only. The blue portion of the badge is worn to the wearer's right. No oak leaf cluster or other appurtenance is authorized for wear with this award.

(5) The Republic of Korea Presidential Unit Citation is authorized for temporary or permanent wear, when authorized. The red portion of the central figure is worn uppermost. No oak leaf cluster or other appurtenance is authorized for wear with this award.

(6) The Vietnam Presidential Unit Citation is authorized for permanent wear only.

(7) The Republic of Vietnam Gallantry Cross Unit Citation is authorized for permanent wear only.

(8) The Republic of Vietnam Civil Actions Unit Citation is authorized for permanent wear only.

(9) Individuals may not wear more than one Gallantry Cross Unit Citation and one Civil Actions Unit Citation; this precludes wear of the Vietnamese fourrageres, which represent additional unit awards.

## 29–12. Wear of appurtenances

Appurtenances are devices affixed to service or suspension ribbons, or worn in lieu of medals or ribbons. They are worn to denote an additional award, participation in a specific event, or some other distinguishing characteristic of an award. The following appurtenances are authorized for wear on decorations, medals, ribbons and other awards, when authorized by appropriate authority. When more than one appurtenance is worn, soldiers will ensure all devices are centered on the ribbon. (See AR 600–8–22 for additional information.)

*a.* Oak leaf clusters.

(1) A bronze twig of four oak leaves with three acorns on each stem is worn to denote award of second and succeeding awards of decorations (other than the Air Medal), the Army Reserve Components Achievement Medal, and unit awards. A silver oak leaf cluster is worn in lieu of five bronze oak leaf clusters. It is worn to the wearer's right of a bronze oak leaf cluster and to the left of the "V" device. Oak leaf clusters, 5/16 inch in length, are worn on service ribbons, the suspension ribbon of miniature medals, and unit awards. Oak leaf clusters, 13/32 inch in length, are worn on the suspension ribbon of full-size medals. Oak leaf clusters 5/16 inch in length, joined together in series of two, three, and four clusters, are authorized for optional purchase and wear on service ribbons and unit award emblems. Personnel wear oak leaf clusters centered on the service ribbon and suspension ribbon, with the stems of the leaves pointing to the wearer's right. If four oak leaf clusters are worn on the suspension ribbon on either full-size or miniature medals, the fourth one is placed above the middle one in the row of three. No more than four oak leaf clusters can be worn side-by-side on service ribbons.

(2) If the number of authorized oak leaf clusters exceeds four and will not fit on a single ribbon, a second ribbon is authorized for wear. When the second ribbon is worn, it is placed after the first ribbon; the second ribbon counts as one award. Personnel may wear no more than four oak leaf clusters on each ribbon. If the receipt of future awards reduces the number of oak leaf clusters sufficiently (that is, a silver oak leaf for five awards), personnel will remove the second ribbon and place the appropriate number of devices on a single ribbon.

*b.* "V" device. The "V" device is a bronze block letter, "V," ¼ inch high. It is worn to denote participation in acts of heroism involving conflict with an armed enemy. The "V" device is worn centered on the suspension ribbon and service ribbon on the Air Medal, Bronze Star Medal, Army Commendation Medal, and the Joint Service Commendation Medal. Not more than one "V" device is worn on a ribbon. When worn with an oak leaf cluster or numerals, the "V" device is worn on the wearer's right.

*c.* Numerals. Arabic numerals, 3/16 inch in height, are issued in lieu of a medal or ribbon for second and succeeding awards of the Air Medal, Army Reserve Components Overseas Training Ribbon, the Overseas Service Ribbon, the Multinational Force and Observers Medal, and with succeeding awards of the "M" device with the Armed Forces Reserve Medal. The ribbon denotes the first award, and numerals starting with the numeral 2 denote second and subsequent awards. The numeral worn on the NCO Professional Development Ribbon denotes the highest level of NCO development, as follows:(ribbon=the primary course; 2=basic course; 3=advanced course; 4=U.S. Army sergeants major academy course completion, or equivalent level training approved by HQDA.) The numerals are worn centered on the suspension ribbon of the medal or the ribbon. (See para *i*, below, for placement of a numeral with the "M" device.)

*d.* Clasps.

(1) The Good Conduct Medal clasp is worn on the service ribbon and suspension ribbon of the Good Conduct Medal to denote second and subsequent awards. The clasp is worn centered on the Good Conduct Medal suspension ribbon and service ribbon. The clasp of the full-size medal and service ribbon is a bar, ⅛ inch by 1⅜ inches, made of bronze, silver, or gold, with loops to indicate each period of service. The clasp for the miniature medal is 1/16 inch by ⅝ inch. (See table 29–2 for a description of the clasps authorized for second and subsequent awards. See chap 4, AR 600–8–22, for criteria for award of the Good Conduct Medal.)

(2) The Antarctic wintered-over clasp is a clasp, with the words "Wintered Over," that is worn centered on the suspension ribbon of the Antarctica service medal. A disk with an outline of the Antarctic Continent is worn on the service ribbon. The clasp and disc are bronze for the first winter, gold for the second winter, and silver for three or more winters.

(3) All other clasps are worn only on the suspension ribbon of the award and denote battle campaigns and service campaigns; they are not worn on the service ribbon.

**Table 29–2**
**Clasps authorized for second and subsequent awards of the Good Conduct Medal.**

| Award | Clasp |
|-------|-------|
| 2d | Bronze, 2 loops |
| 3d | Bronze, 3 loops |
| 4th | Bronze, 4 loops |
| 5th | Bronze, 5 loops |
| 6th | Silver, 1 loop |
| 7th | Silver, 2 loops |
| 8th | Silver, 3 loops |
| 9th | Silver, 4 loops |
| 10th | Silver, 5 loops |
| 11th | Gold, 1 loop |
| 12th | Gold, 2 loops |
| 13th | Gold, 3 loops |
| 14th | Gold, 4 loops |
| 15th | Gold, 5 loops |

*e.* Service stars. The service star is a bronze or silver five-pointed star, 3/16 inch in diameter. A silver service star is worn in lieu of five bronze service stars. It is worn to the wearer's right of a bronze service star and to the left of an arrowhead. (See AR 600–8–22 for the criteria for wear.) Service stars are worn to denote an additional award or service in a named campaign and are centered on the ribbon and suspension ribbon with one point upward. Additional service stars are worn side by side, each with one point upward. Three-sixteenths-inch service stars, joined together in a series of two, three, and four stars, are authorized for optional purchase and wear on ribbons. The bronze service star is affixed to the parachutist badge and the military free fall parachutist badge to denote participation in a combat parachute jump.

*f.* Arrowhead. The arrowhead is a bronze replica of an Indian arrowhead, ¼ inch high. It denotes participation in a combat parachute jump, combat glider landing, or an amphibious assault landing while assigned or attached as a member of an organized force carrying out an assigned tactical mission. It is worn on the suspension ribbon and service ribbon of the Asiatic-Pacific Campaign, European-African-Middle Eastern Campaign, and World War II Campaign medals; the Korean Service and Vietnam Service medals; and the Armed Forces Expeditionary Medal. The arrowhead is worn with the point facing upward, and is worn to the wearer's right of all service stars. Only one arrowhead is worn on any ribbon.

*g.* Berlin Airlift device. The Berlin Airlift device is a miniature replica of a C-54 aircraft and is worn on the suspension and service ribbons of the Army of Occupation Medal, with the nose pointed upward at a 30-degree angle, to the wearer's right. When the device is worn on the suspension ribbon of the medal, it is centered above the "Germany" clasp.

*h.* Ten-Year device. The Ten-Year device is an hourglass that is worn centered on the suspension ribbon or service ribbon of the Armed Forces Reserve Medal to denote each succeeding 10–year period in addition to, and under the same conditions as prescribed for the award of the Armed Forces Reserve Medal. If two or more devices are authorized, they are placed side-by-side. A bronze device denotes the completion of the first 10–year period (10 years); a silver device denotes completion of the second period (20 years); a gold device denotes completion of the third period (30 years), and a gold device followed by a bronze device denotes completion of the fourth period (40 years). The Ten-Year device, 11/32 inch in height, is worn on the suspension ribbon of full-size medals and on the service ribbon; the Ten-Year device, 3/16 inch in height, is worn on the suspension ribbon of miniature medals.

*i.* "M" device. The "M" device is a bronze letter "M" that is worn on the suspension ribbon or service ribbon of the Armed Forces Reserve Medal to denote service during a mobilization or contingency designated by the Secretary of Defense. If personnel served during more than one mobilization or contingency, a numeral is worn to the wearer's left of the "M" device, to indicate the number of times mobilized. If worn alone, the "M" device is worn centered on the ribbon. When worn with the Ten-Year device, the "M" device is centered on the ribbon, and the Ten-Year device is worn to the wearer's right. If a numeral is worn, it is placed on the ribbon to the wearer's left, with the "M" device in the center and the Ten-Year device to the wearer's right.

## 29–13. Badges authorized for wear on Army uniforms

A badge is awarded to an individual for identification purposes, or for attaining a special skill or proficiency. The criteria for the award of Army badges are contained in AR 600–8–22, and in NGR 601–1 for Army National Guard Recruiting and Retention identification badges. Most combat and special skill badges are available in full, miniature, and dress miniature sizes. The following badges are authorized for wear on the Army uniform.

*a.* Military badges awarded by the Department of Army, U.S. Air Force, Navy, Coast Guard, and the Director of Civilian Marksmanship. (See para *g*, below, for additional information.)

*b.* Badges awarded by the Regular Army and Navy Union, and by the Army and Navy Union of the United States.

*c.* Marksmanship badges pertaining to national matches and approved by HQDA. Marksmanship badges from other U.S. Services are not authorized for wear on the Army uniform.

*d.* Badges of civic and quasi-military societies of the United States, and international organizations of a military nature. These include badges of organizations originally composed of members who served in a U.S. force during the Revolutionary War; the War of 1812; the Mexican War; the Civil War; the Spanish-American War; the Philippine Insurrection; and the Chinese Relief Expedition of 1900. The badges are worn only while the wearer is actually attending meetings or functions of such organizations, or on occasions of ceremony. Personnel will not wear these badges to and from such meetings or events.

*e.* Badges awarded by friendly foreign nations in recognition of military activities, and as authorized by AR 600–8–22.

*f.* Tabs indicating marksmanship or special skill. The Sapper, Ranger, Special Forces and President's Hundred tabs are the only tabs authorized for permanent wear. Tabs such as Airborne, Honor Guard, Mountain, and Pershing are authorized for temporary wear only. These tabs are considered an integral part of the shoulder sleeve insignia and soldiers are not authorized to wear them when they are reassigned from the organization that prescribed wear of the shoulder sleeve insignia with tab.

*g.* In accordance with AR 600–8–22, personnel must obtain authority from HQDA before wearing badges on the uniform that were awarded by other U.S. Services, or by the Director of Civilian Marksmanship. The following rules apply when wearing badges from other U.S. Services.

(1) Military combat or special skill badges awarded by other U.S. Services that are similar to U.S. Army combat or special skill badges are worn on the Army uniform in the same manner as U.S. Army combat or special skill badges, only if no Army badges are authorized for wear in the same group. For example, a soldier who had no group 3 badges could wear aviation badges awarded by the U.S. Air Force (USAF) as group 3 badges (as Army Aviation and Aviator badges are worn). However, if the individual was authorized to wear an Army badge in group 3, the soldier would not be authorized to wear the group 3 badge from the USAF.

(2) Skill badges awarded by other U.S. Services that are not similar to Army skill badges are worn as group 4 badges.

(3) Badges from other U.S. Services that indicate career fields are not authorized for wear, such as USAF medical insignia, or badges used to identify the duty, function, or classification of the wearer. Some examples are USAF fire protection, air training command instructor, security police, or the Naval aviation warfare specialist.

(4) Personnel will not wear badges awarded by other U.S. Services which, because of size or configuration, cannot be worn as group 4 badges. Subdued embroidered or metal skill badges authorized for wear by another U.S. Service, and that are authorized for wear on the Army uniform, may be worn on utility uniforms in the same manner as prescribed for Army badges.

## 29–14. Badges not authorized for wear on Army uniforms

*a.* Badges awarded by States and other jurisdictions inferior to the U.S. Government, except as provided in paragraph 29–6*j* for ARNG soldiers in their state status.

*b.* Badges awarded by jurisdictions inferior to foreign national governments.

*c.* Badges awarded by foreign civilian organizations.

*d.* Foreign military badges, except as previously authorized.

*e.* Marksmanship badges awarded by other U.S. Services.

*f.* Locally authorized badges.

## 29–15. Categories of badges authorized for wear on Army uniforms

The following categories of badges are worn on the Army uniform.

*a.* Marksmanship badges and tab.

*b.* Combat and special skill badges and tabs.

*c.* Identification badges.

*d.* Foreign badges.

## 29–16. Marksmanship badges and tab

*a.* Listed below in their order of precedence are the marksmanship badges authorized for wear on the Army uniform.

(1) Distinguished International Shooter badge (see fig 29–15).

**Figure 29–15. U.S. Distinguished International Shooter badge**

(2) Distinguished Rifleman badge (see fig 29–16).

**Figure 29–16. Distinguished Rifleman badge**

(3) Distinguished Pistol Shot badge (see fig 29–17).

**Figure 29–17. Distinguished Pistol Shot badge**

(4) National Trophy Match badge.
(5) Interservice Competition badge.
(6) U.S. Army Excellence in Competition Rifleman badge (see fig 29–18).

**Figure 29–18. U.S. Army Excellence in Competition Rifleman badge**

(7) U.S. Army Excellence in Competition Pistol Shot badge (see fig 29–19).

**Figure 29–19. U.S. Army Excellence in Competition Pistol Shot badge**

(8) Marksmanship Qualification badges (Expert, Sharpshooter and Marksman) (see fig 29–20).

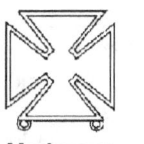
**Marksman**

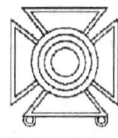
**Sharpshooter**

**Expert**

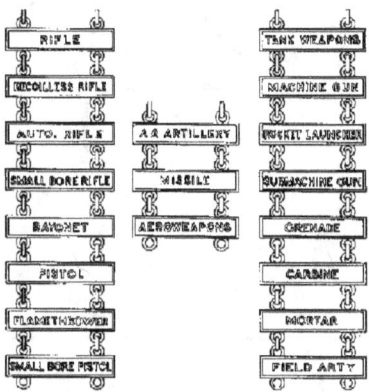

**Marksman Qualification Clasps**

**Figure 29–20. Marksmanship qualification badges**

*b.* No more than three marksmanship badges (does not include marksmanship tab; see para *c*, below) are authorized for wear. Personnel will not attach more than three clasps to marksmanship badges. The total number of marksmanship and special skill badges worn on the pocket flap or below the ribbons will not exceed three.

(1) Where worn. Marksmanship badges are authorized for wear on the following uniforms.

*(a)* Male personnel. On the coat of the Army green, white, and blue uniforms, and the AG shade 415 shirt.

*(b)* Female personnel. On the coats of the Army green, white, and blue uniforms, maternity tunic, and the AG shade 415 shirt.

(2) How worn. Marksmanship badges are worn in order of precedence from the wearer's right, and to the left of any special skill badges that are worn. Normally, all soldiers wear at least one marksmanship badge, unless they fail to qualify or are exempt from qualification by Army regulations.

*(a)* Male personnel. Marksmanship badges are worn on the upper portion of the left breast pocket flap, or on the lower portion of the pocket flap, if special skill badges are worn. (See para 29-17 for a description and the wear policy for special skill badges.) Marksmanship badges and special skill badges are authorized for wear on the pocket flap of the Army green, blue, and white uniforms, as prescribed below, with the exception of the Sapper, Ranger, and Special Forces tab metal replicas. When the Sapper, Ranger, or Special Forces metal tab replicas are worn on the pocket flap of the blue or white dress uniforms, the replicas are worn approximately 1/8 inch below the top of the pocket. (See para 29-17*e* for a description of, and the wear policy for metal tab replicas.) When airborne background trimming is worn beneath the Parachutist or Air Assault badge, personnel will center the badge on the trimming and place it so that the space between the pocket flap seam and the top of the background trimming is 1/8 inch.

*(b)* Female personnel. On the service or dress uniform coats and on the maternity tunic, marksmanship badges are worn on the left side, ¼ inch below the bottom ribbon row, or in a similar location if ribbons are not worn. Personnel may adjust the placement of badges to conform to individual body-shape differences. Marksmanship badges and special skill badges authorized for wear below ribbons are worn as prescribed below. (See para 29–17 for a description and the

wear policy for special skill badges.) When airborne background trimming is worn beneath the Parachutist or Air Assault badge, personnel will center the badge on the trimming and place it so that the space between the bottom of the ribbon bar and the top of the background trimming is ¼ inch.

(3) Following are descriptions of the placement of badges when more than one marksmanship badge is worn, or when special skill badges are worn with marksmanship badges.

*(a)* One marksmanship or one special skill badge. Males wear the badge centered on the pocket flap, from left to right, with the upper portion of the badge approximately ⅛ inch below the top of the pocket (see fig 29–21). Females wear the badge on the left side, centered below the ribbons, with the upper portion of the badge ¼ inch below the ribbon bar (see fig 29–22).

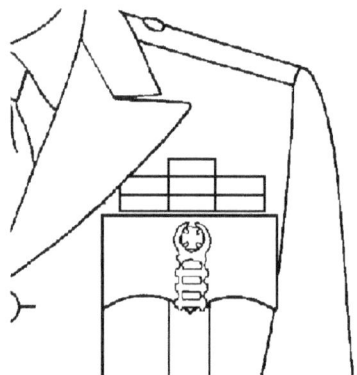

Figure 29–21. Wear of one marksmanship or special skill badge on pocket flap, male

Figure 29–22. Wear of one special skill or one marksmanship badge, female

*(b)* Two special skill or two marksmanship badges, or one special skill and one marksmanship badge. Males wear these badges equally spaced on the pocket flap, from left to right, with the upper portion of the badges approximately ⅛ inch below the top of the pocket, and with at least 1 inch between badges (see figs 29–23 and 29–25). Females wear these badges with the upper portion ¼ inch below the ribbon bar, and with at least 1 inch between badges (see figs 29–24 and 29–26). Special skill badges are worn to the wearer's right of the marksmanship badges.

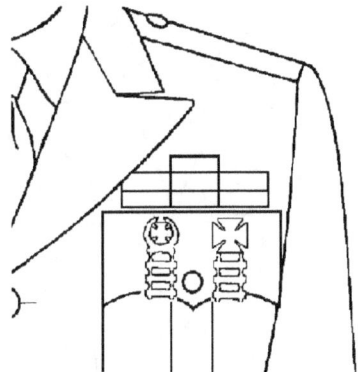

**Figure 29–23. Wear of two marksmanship or two special skill badges on pocket flap, male**

**Figure 29–24. Wear of two marksmanship or two special skill badges below ribbons, female**

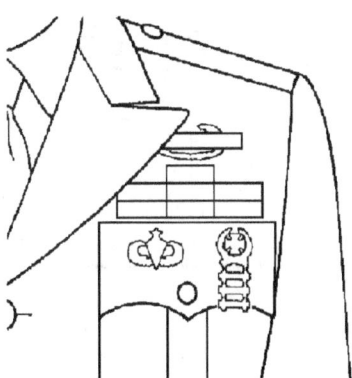

**Figure 29–25. Wear of one marksmanship and one special skill badge on pocket flap, male**

**Figure 29–26. Wear of one marksmanship and one special skill badge below ribbons, female**

*(c)* One special skill and two marksmanship badges. Males wear these badges equally spaced on the pocket flap, from left to right, with the upper portion of the badges approximately ⅛ inch below the top of the pocket. Males will wear marksmanship badges that have attaching devices at the top of the badge, such as the Excellence in Competition Rifleman badge, in this manner (see fig 29–27). When no badges are worn that have devices attached at the top, males have the option of wearing the special skill badge centered on the pocket flap, from left to right, with the upper portion of the badge approximately ⅛ inch below the top of the pocket. Each marksmanship badge is centered between the button and the left or right side of the pocket. The bottom of the badges (not the clasp holder or clasps) is adjacent to the bottom of the pocket flap (see fig 29–28). Females wear these badges with the upper portion of the badges ¼ inch below the ribbon bar and spaced an equal distance apart (see fig 29–30).

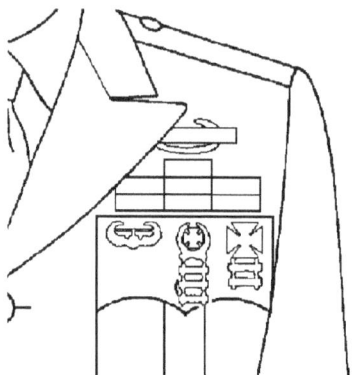

**Figure 29–27. Wear of one special skill and two marksmanship badges on pocket flap, male**

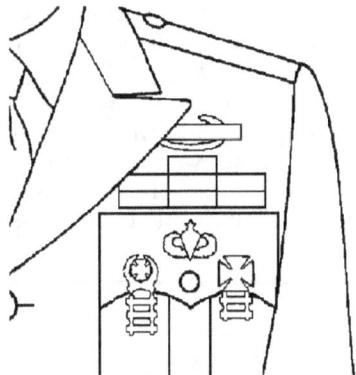

Figure 29–28. Wear of one special skill and two marksmanship badges on pocket flap, male

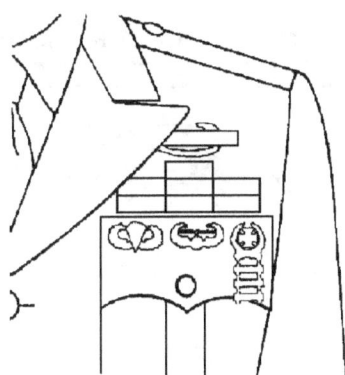

Figure 29–29. Wear of two special skill and one marksmanship badge on pocket flap, male

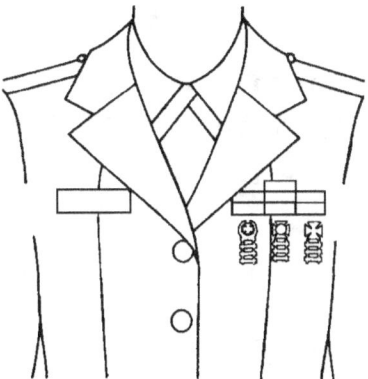

Figure 29–30. Wear of two special skill and one marksmanship; or one special skill and two marksmanship badges, female

(d) Two special skill and one marksmanship badge, or one special skill and two marksmanship badges, or three marksmanship badges. Males wear these badges equally spaced on the pocket flap, approximately ⅛ inch below the top of the pocket (see fig 29–29). Females wear these badges with the upper portion of the badges ¼ inch below the ribbon bar and spaced an equal distance apart (see fig 29–30).

*c.* President's Hundred tab (rifle or pistol). The President's Hundred tab is a full-color tab of yellow cloth, 4¼ inches long and ⅝ inch high, with the words "President's Hundred" centered in ¼-inch-high green letters (see fig 29–31). The President's Hundred tab is worn ½ inch below the shoulder seam on the left sleeve of the male and female Army green uniform coats (see fig 29–32). The President's Hundred tab is available in a subdued version for wear on the BDUs. The President's Hundred bronze metallic brassard is not authorized for wear on the Army uniform.

Figure 29–31. President's Hundred tab

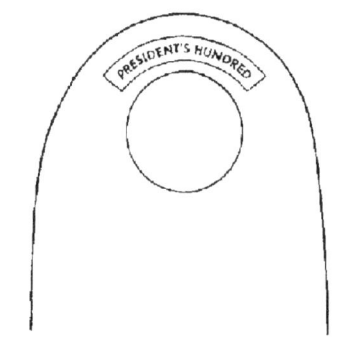

Figure 29–32. Wear of President's Hundred tab

## 29–17. Combat and special skill badges and tabs

*a.* Listed below in order of group precedence are combat and special skill badges authorized for wear on the Army uniform.

(1) Group 1. Combat Infantryman badges (three awards)(see fig 29–33); Expert Infantryman badge (see fig 29–34).

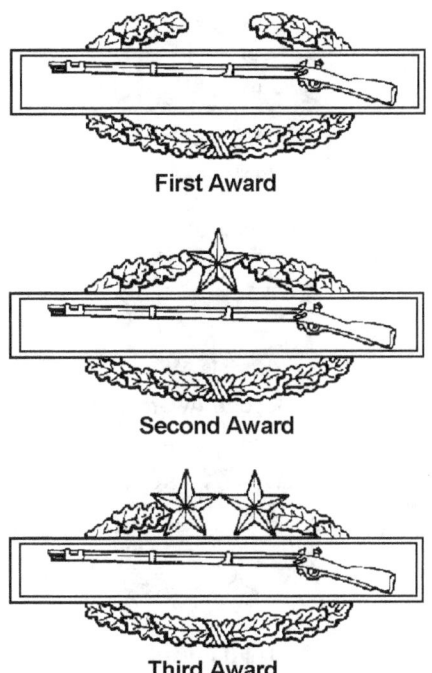

**First Award**

**Second Award**

**Third Award**

**Figure 29–33. Combat Infantryman badges**

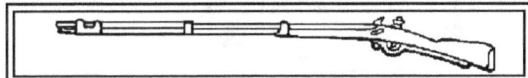

**Figure 29–34. Expert Infantryman badge**

(2) Group 2. Combat Medical badges: (three awards) (see fig 29–35); Expert Field Medical badge (see fig 29–36).

First Award

Second Award

Third Award

**Figure 29–35. Combat medical badges**

**Figure 29–36. Expert Field Medical badge**

(3) Group 3. Army Astronaut device (worn attached to any aviation badge) (see fig 29–37); Army Aviator badges (three degrees) (see fig 29–38); Flight Surgeon badges (three degrees) (see fig 29–39); Aviation badges (three degrees) (see fig 29–40); Explosive Ordnance Disposal badges (three degrees) (see fig 29–41).

Device

Device Worn on any Aviator Badge

**Figure 29–37. Army Astronaut device**

**Army Aviator**

**Senior Army Aviator**

**Master Army Aviator**

Figure 29–38. Army Aviator badges

**Flight Surgeon**

**Senior Flight Surgeon**

**Master Flight Surgeon**

Figure 29–39. Flight Surgeon badges

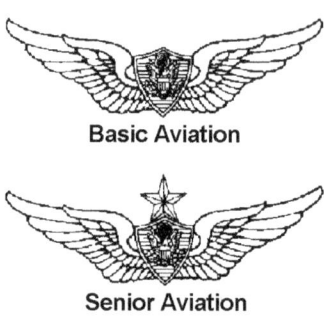

**Basic Aviation**

**Senior Aviation**

**Master Aviation**

Figure 29–40. Aviation badges

**Explosive Ordnance Disposal**

**Senior Explosive Ordnance Disposal**

**Master Explosive Ordnance Disposal**

Figure 29–41. Explosive Ordinance Disposal badges

(4) Group 4. Glider badge (see fig 29-42); Parachutist badges (three degrees) (see fig 29-43); Parachutist badges with combat jump device (four degrees are shown at figure 29-44); Pathfinder badge (see fig 29-45); Military Freefall Parachutist badges (two degrees) (see fig 29-46); Military Freefall Parachutist badges with combat jump device; Air Assault badge (see fig 29-47); Sapper, Ranger, and Special Forces tab metal replicas (see fig 29-61).

**Figure 29–42. Glider badge**

**Parachutist**

**Senior Parachutist**

**Master Parachutist**

**Figure 29–43. Parachutist badges**

One jump

Two jumps

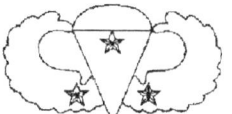

Three jumps

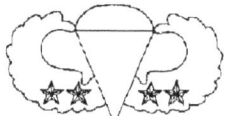

Four jumps

Figure 29–44. Parachutist badges with Combat Jump device

**Figure 29–45. Pathfinder badge**

**Basic**

**Jumpmaster**

**Figure 29–46. Military Freefall Parachutist badge**

**Figure 29–47. Air Assault badge**

**Figure 29–59. Ranger tab**

**Figure 29–63. Special Forces tab**

(5) Group 5. Diver badges (five badges) (see fig 29–48); Driver and Mechanic badge (see fig 29–49); Parachute Rigger badge (see fig 29–50).

**Salvage diver**

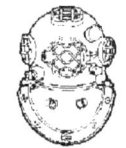

**Second class diver**

**First class diver**

**Master diver**

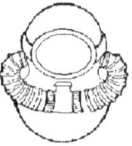

**Scuba diver**

**Figure 29–48. Diver badges**

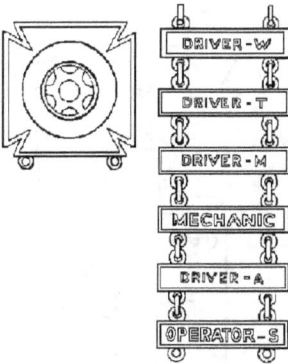

**Figure 29–49. Driver and Mechanic badges and clasps**

**Figure 29–50. Parachute Rigger badge**

(6) Physical Fitness badge. The Physical Fitness badge is authorized for wear on the Physical fitness uniform and the improved physical fitness uniform, only (see fig 29–51).

**Figure 29–51. Physical Fitness badge**

*b.* Wear of combat and special skill badges.

(1) Wear of commercial, mirror-like finish combat and special skill badges is authorized. However, soldiers may not mix these badges with combat and special skill badges that do not have the mirror-like finish.

(2) A total of five combat and special skill badges are authorized for wear at one time; this total does not include special skill tabs (see figs 29–52 and 29–53). Personnel may wear only one badge each from groups 1, 2, and 3, as listed in paragraph *a*, above. Personnel also may wear three badges from group 4, and two badges from group 5, but the total number of badges cannot exceed five. Combat badges have precedence over special skill badges within the same group. For example, if an individual is authorized to wear the Combat Infantry badge and the Expert Infantry badge, the Combat Infantry badge is worn. There is no precedence for special skill badges within the same group. For example, personnel who are authorized to wear the Parachutist and Air Assault badges may determine the order of wear. The above policies apply to the wear of both non-subdued and subdued badges.

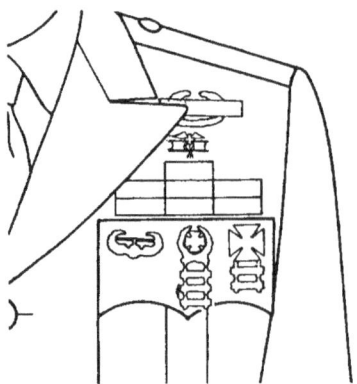

Figure 29–52. Wear of five badges, male

Figure 29–53. Wear of five badges, female

(3) Only three badges, to include marksmanship badges, can be worn on the pocket flap at one time. Personnel will wear the Driver and Mechanic badges only on the left pocket flap of service and dress uniforms, or in a similar location on uniforms without pockets. Personnel may attach no more than three clasps to the Driver and Mechanic badges. The Driver and Mechanic badges are not authorized for wear on utility uniforms.

(4) The Physical Fitness badge is authorized only as a cloth badge and is worn on the physical fitness uniform and on the improved physical fitness uniform, only. The badge is worn centered on the left front side above the breast on the PFU or IPFU T-shirt, and on the PFU sweatshirt. On the IPFU running jacket, the insignia is sewn centered ½ inch above the word "Army."

c. Wear of non-subdued full-size and miniature combat and special skill badges, with or without ribbons, on male and female service and dress uniforms.

(1) On the service and dress uniforms, personnel may wear up to three combat and special skill badges from groups 1 through 3, above the ribbons or pocket flap, or in a similar location for uniforms without pockets. When no badges from groups 1 through 3 are worn, personnel may wear a total of three combat and special skill badges from groups 4 and 5 above the ribbons or pocket flap, or in a similar location on uniforms without pockets. When three badges are worn above the ribbons or pocket flap, three badges, to include marksmanship badges, can be worn side-by-side on the pocket flap, or below the ribbons on uniforms without pockets, in order of group precedence from the wearer's right to left. (Para 29–8b describes wear of combat and special skill badges with full-size medals; para 29–16b describes wear of badges on the pocket flap, or below the ribbons.)

(2) How worn. Combat and special skill badges are worn on the coats of the Army green, blue, and white uniforms; the AG shade 415 shirt, and on the Army maternity tunic (females only). Personnel wear the badges ¼ inch above the ribbons or the top of the pocket, one above the other, with ½ inch between badges, or they are worn on the pocket flap, as described in paragraph 29–16b, or in a similar location for uniforms without pockets. In those instances where the

coat lapel obscures the ribbons or medals, personnel may wear the badges (or airborne background trimming, if worn beneath the badge) aligned with the left edge of the ribbons or medals (see figs 29–54 through 29–57).

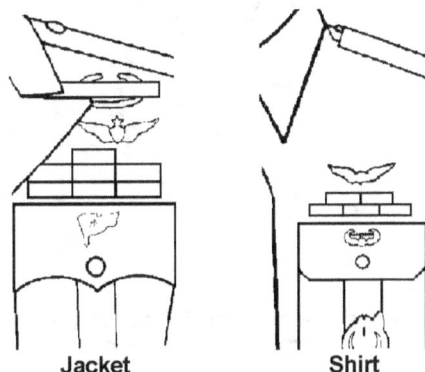

Figure 29–54. Wear of combat and special skill badges above and below ribbons, Army green, white, or blue coats and AG 415 shirt, male

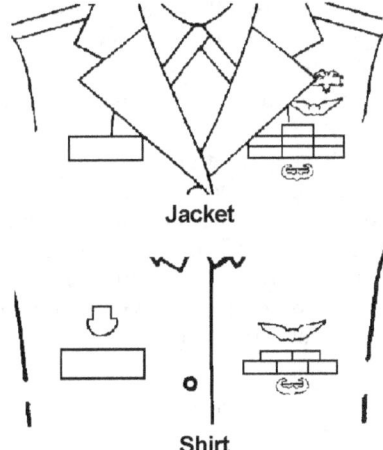

Figure 29–55. Wear of combat and special skill badges above and below ribbons, Army green, white, or blue coats and AG 415 shirt, female (new version coats)

Figure 29–56. Wear of special skill badges above ribbons, male

**Figure 29–57. Wear of special skill badges above ribbons, female**

(3) Dress miniature badges.

*(a)* The dress miniature combat and special skill badges are worn on the blue and white dress uniforms only when miniature medals are worn. (Dress miniature badges and miniature medals are worn on the Army blue and white dress uniforms only when these uniforms are worn as formal dress uniforms (with bow tie).) When miniature medals are worn on these uniforms, personnel may wear up to three dress miniature combat and special skill badges from groups 1 through 5 (see para 29–17*a*, above), one above the other, above the miniature medals in order of group precedence. When miniature medals are worn, personnel will not wear dress miniature combat and special skill and marksmanship badges on the pocket flap, or below the medals on uniforms without pockets.

*(b)* Dress miniature combat and special skill badges are worn on all mess and evening mess uniforms. Personnel may wear up to five combat and special skill badges from groups 1 through 5. If no badge from groups 1 through 3 is worn, personnel may wear five badges from groups 4 and 5. When two badges are worn, they are placed side-by-side immediately above the miniature medals. When three badges are worn, two are placed side-by-side immediately above the medals, and the third is centered 1/4 inch above the other two badges. When four badges are worn, the third and fourth badges are centered side-by-side 1/4 inch above the other two badges. When five badges are worn, the fifth will be worn centered 1/4 inch above the third and fourth badges. Badges are worn in order of group precedence; on the male mess uniform, badges will not extend beyond the lapel. (Para 29–9 describes wear of miniature medals on the mess uniforms (see figs 29–7 and 29–8).)

*(c)* Personnel may wear dress miniature combat and special skill badges on the AG shade 415 shirt. However, they may not mix dress miniature combat and special skill badges with full-size and miniature combat and special skill badges on the shirt.

*d.* Subdued pin-on and embroidered sew-on combat and special skill badges. Personnel may wear no more than five subdued combat and special skill badges on the temperate, hot weather, enhanced hot weather, maternity, aviation, and desert BDU shirts. Badges are worn one above the other, centered above the U.S. Army tape, in order of group precedence. When five badges are worn, three are centered ¼ inch above the U.S. Army tape in a vertical line with ½ inch between badges, and two are worn on the pocket flap, ⅛ inch below the top of the pocket, with at least 1 inch between badges. When four badges are worn, three are centered ¼ inch above the U.S. Army tape in a vertical line with ½ inch between badges, and one is worn on the pocket flap, ⅛ inch below the top of the pocket, with at least 1 inch between badges. When three badges are worn, two badges are centered ¼ inch above the U.S. Army tape in a vertical line with ½ inch between badges, and one is worn centered on the pocket flap, ⅛ inch below the top of the pocket. When two badges are worn, both are centered ¼ inch above the U.S. Army tape in a vertical line with ½ inch between badges. If only one badge is worn, it is centered ¼ inch above the U.S. Army tape (see fig 29–58).

**Figure 29–58. Wear of subdued combat and special skill badges**

*e.* Wear of special skill tabs.

(1) Ranger tab.

*(a)* The full-color tab is 2⅜ inches long, 11/16 inch wide, with a ⅛-inch yellow border and the word "RANGER" inscribed in yellow letters 5/16 inch high. The subdued tab is identical, except the background is olive-drab and the word "RANGER" is in black letters (see fig 29–59).

*(b)* How worn. The full-color tab is worn ½ inch below the shoulder seam on the left sleeve of the Army green coat. The subdued tab is worn ½ inch below the shoulder seam on the left sleeve of utility uniforms, field jackets, and the desert BDU.

*(c)* By whom worn. All personnel who are authorized, in accordance with the criteria provided in AR 600–8–22.

*(d)* Ranger tab metal replica. The Ranger tab metal replica is available in two sizes, full and dress miniature. Soldiers authorized to wear the Ranger tab may wear the Ranger tab metal replica as prescribed below. The full-size version is approximately 1–5/32 inches wide and is worn only on the blue and white dress uniforms, and the AG shade 415 shirt. The dress miniature version is 13/16 inch wide and is worn on the blue and white mess and evening mess uniforms. When miniature medals are worn on the blue and white dress uniforms, personnel may wear the dress miniature Ranger tab metal replica (see figs 29–60 and 29–61).

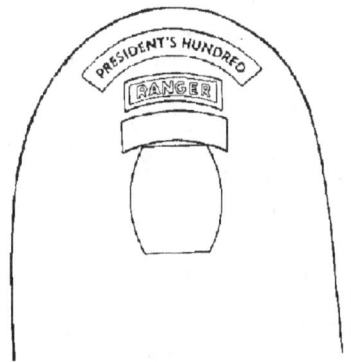

**Figure 29–60. Wear of multiple special skill tabs**

**Figure 29–61. Wear of metal tab replicas on Army blue or white uniforms, male**

(2) Special Forces tab.

*(a)* Description. The Special Forces tab is a teal blue arc, 3¼ inches wide and 11/16 inch high, with the designation "SPECIAL FORCES" in yellow letters, 5/16 inch high. The subdued tab is identical in shape to the full-color tab, but the background color is olive-drab and the words "SPECIAL FORCES" are in black letters (see fig 29–63).

*(b)* How worn. The Special Forces tab is worn the same as the Ranger tab (see para (1)(b) above).

*(c)* By whom worn. All personnel who are authorized, in accordance with the criteria provided in AR 600–8–22.

*(d)* Special Forces tab metal replica. The Special Forces tab metal replica is available in two sizes. Soldiers authorized to wear the Special Forces tab may wear the Special Forces tab metal replica, as prescribed below. The full-size version is approximately 1–9/16 inches wide and is worn on the blue and white dress uniforms (see figs 29–61 and 29–62). The dress miniature version is 1 inch wide and is worn on the blue and white mess and evening mess uniforms (see fig 29–62). When miniature medals are worn on the blue and white dress uniforms, personnel may wear the dress miniature Special Forces tab metal replica.

(3) Sapper tab.

*(a)* Description. The Sapper tab is a red arc 2 3/8 inches long, 11/16 inch wide, with a 1/8-inch red border and the word "SAPPER" inscribed in white letters 5/16 inch high. The subdued tab is identical in shape to the full-color tab, except the background is olive drab and the word "SAPPER" is in black letters for the BDU, and khaki with the word "SAPPER" in spice brown letters for the Desert BDU.

*(b)* How worn. The Sapper tab is worn the same as the Ranger tab (see para (1)*(b)*, above).

*(c)* By whom worn. All personnel who are authorized in accordance with the criteria provided in AR 600–8–22.

*(d)* Sapper tab metal replica. The Sapper tab metal replica is available in two sizes. Soldiers authorized to wear the Sapper tab may wear the Sapper tab metal replica as prescribed below. The full-size version is approximately 1-5/32 inches wide and is worn only on the blue and white dress uniforms. The dress miniature version is 13/16 inch wide and is worn on the blue and white mess and evening mess uniforms. When miniature medals are worn on the blue and white dress uniforms, personnel may wear the dress miniature Sapper tab metal replica.

(4) For purposes of classification and wear policy, the Sapper, Ranger, and Special Forces tab metal replicas are classified as group 4 special skill badges.

(5) As an option, soldiers may wear the full-size and dress miniature Sapper, Ranger, and Special Forces tab metal replicas on the AG shade 415 shirt. If soldiers wear the dress miniature versions of the tabs, they cannot mix them with other sizes of combat and special skill badges on the shirts. When personnel wear metal tab replicas on the pocket flap of the blue or white dress uniforms, or the AG shade 415 shirt, the tab is placed approximately 1/8 inch below the top of the pocket. If no badges are worn from groups 1 to 3, personnel may wear the metal tab replica above the ribbons.

*f.* Wear of three special skill tabs. Soldiers may wear the full-color Sapper, Ranger, and Special Forces tabs together on Army uniforms.

(1) On the Army green service uniform, the Special Forces tab is centered on the left shoulder sleeve, 1/2 inch from the shoulder seam, the Ranger tab is centered 1/8 inch below the Special Forces tab, and the Sapper tab is centered 1/8 inch below the Ranger tab. The current unit shoulder sleeve insignia is centered 1/4 inch below the Sapper tab. On the utility uniforms and the cold weather jackets, personnel wear the subdued tabs in the same positions as on the Army green service uniform (see fig 29-60).

(2) On the Army blue and white uniforms, and on the AG shade 415 shirt, personnel wear the full-size metal tab

replicas on the pocket flap, 1/8 inch from the top of the pocket, with approximately 1/2 inch between the tabs. If no badges are worn from groups 1 to 3, personnel may wear the metal tab replicas above the ribbons (see fig 29-61).

(3) See paragraph 29–17c(3)(b)for a description of how to wear the dress miniature metal Sapper, Special Forces, and Ranger tab replicas together on the Army blue and white mess and evening mess uniforms (see fig 29–62).

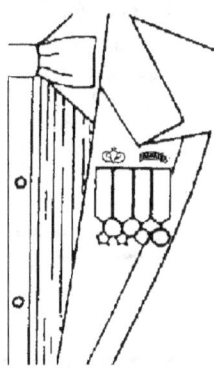

**Figure 29–62. Wear of metal tab replicas on Army mess uniforms, male**

## 29–18. Identification badges

*a.* The following is the order of precedence of U.S. military identification (ID) badges authorized for wear on the Army uniform:

(1) Presidential Service identification badge (see fig 29–64).

**Figure 29–64. Presidential Service identification badge**

(2) Vice-Presidential Service identification badge (see fig 29–65).

**Figure 29–65. Vice-presidential Service identification badge**

(3) Secretary of Defense identification badge (see fig 29–66).

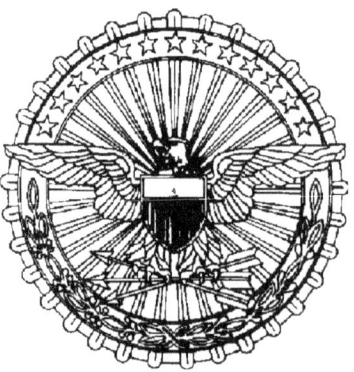

**Figure 29–66. Secretary of Defense identification badge**

(4) Joint Chiefs of Staff identification badge (see fig 29–67).

**Figure 29–67. Joint Chiefs of Staff identification badge**

(5) Army Staff identification badge (see fig 29–68).

**Figure 29–68. Army Staff identification badge**

(6) Guard, Tomb of the Unknown Soldier identification badge (see fig 29–69).

**Figure 29–69. Guard, Tomb of the Unknown Soldier identification badge**

(7) Drill Sergeant identification badge (see fig 29–70).

**Figure 29–70. Drill Sergeant identification badge**

(8) U.S. Army Recruiter identification badge (Active Army/Army Reserve) (see fig 29–71).

**Figure 29–71. U.S. Army Recruiter identification badge, Active Army and Army Reserve**

(9) Army Career Counselor identification badge (see fig 29–72).

**Figure 29–72. Army Career Counselor identification badge**

(10) Recruiting and Retention identification badge, Master (ARNG) (see fig 29–73).

**Figure 29–73. Army National Guard Recruiting and Retention identification badge, Master**

*b.* Temporary badges. The following badges are authorized for temporary wear. Personnel will not wear these badges for official photographs or for promotion/selection boards. Upon termination of assignment to the command that directs the wear of these badges, soldiers will discontinue wearing these badges on the uniform.

(1) Unified Combatant Command identification badge. The order of precedence for this badge is after the Joint Chiefs of Staff identification badge.

(2) National Defense University identification badge. The order of precedence for this badge is after the Unified Combatant Command identification badge.

(3) The following badges do not have an order of precedence in relation to other identification badges in this chapter.

*(a)* Recruiting and Retention identification badge, Basic and Senior (ARNG) (see fig 29–74).

**Figure 29–74. Army National Guard Recruiting and Retention identification badge, Basic and Senior**

*(b)* Military Police identification badge (see fig 29–75).

**Figure 29–75. Military Police identification badge**

*c.* U.S. non-military identification badges. The Secretary of Health and Human Services identification badge is authorized for wear on the uniform (see fig 29–76).

Figure 29–76. Secretary of Health and Human Services identification badge

*d.* Wear of identification badges. Personnel may wear no more than two identification badges on one pocket or side of the coat of the uniforms prescribed below. When two identification badges are worn on the same side or pocket, the precedence of the badges is from the wearer's right (highest) to left (lowest), as listed in *a*, above. When more than two badges are awarded that are worn on the same side, the individual may determine which two badges are worn on the uniform (see fig 29–77). Identification badges are worn as follows.

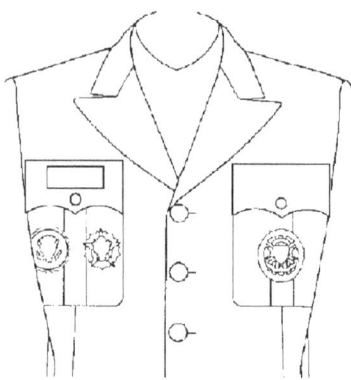

Figure 29–77. Wear of identification badges on Army green, blue, and white uniforms, male

(1) Male personnel.

*(a)* On service and dress uniforms, and the AG 415 shirt, ID badges are worn centered on the pocket of the coat or shirt. The badge is centered between the bottom of the pocket flap and the bottom of the pocket, and centered from left to right. When two badges are worn on the same side, they are spaced equally from left to right on the pocket. Personnel may wear miniature badges on the AG 415 shirt.

*(b)* Subdued badges are worn on the temperate, hot weather, enhanced hot weather, maternity, aviation, and desert BDU shirts, and on the field jacket, with the badge centered on the appropriate breast pocket between the bottom of the pocket flap and the bottom of the pocket, or in a similar location on uniforms without pockets. When two badges are worn on the same side, they are spaced equally from left to right on the pocket.

*(c)* On the mess and evening mess uniforms, ID badges are worn centered between the upper two buttons of the jacket, with one inch between badges when two are worn on the same side (see fig 29–78). Personnel are authorized to wear full-size identification badges on the mess and evening mess uniforms when the badges are not available in miniature size.

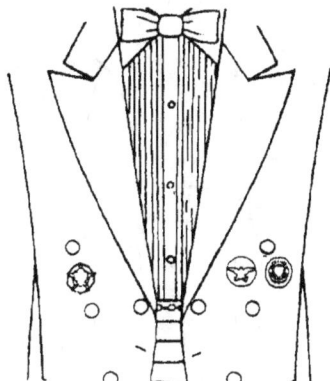

Figure 29–78. Wear of identification badges on white and blue mess uniforms, male

(2) Female personnel.

*(a)* On service and dress uniforms, the identification badge is worn parallel to the waistline on the coat of the Army green uniform, with one inch between badges when two are worn on the same side. Badges are worn in a comparable position on the Army blue and white uniform coats, the maternity tunic, and the AG shade 415 shirt (see fig 29–79). If no other awards, decorations, or insignia (other than the nameplate and rank) are worn on the AG shade 415 shirt, females may place the ID badge parallel to the nameplate, or approximately 1 inch above the nameplate, depending upon which side the badge is worn (see fig 29–80). Females may adjust placement of badges to conform to individual body-shape differences. Personnel may wear miniature badges on the AG 415 shirt.

Figure 29–79. Wear of identification badges on Army green, blue, and white uniforms, female

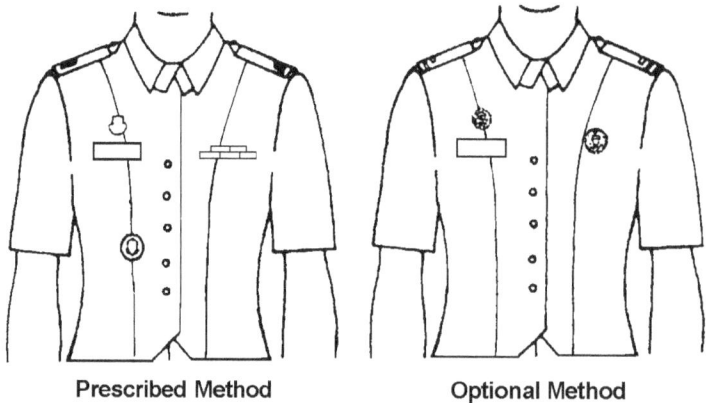

Prescribed Method          Optional Method

**Figure 29–80. Wear of identification badges on AG 415 shirt, female**

*(b)* Subdued badges are worn on the utility uniforms, the field jacket, and the desert BDU with the badge centered on the appropriate breast pocket between the bottom of the pocket flap and the bottom of the pocket, or in a similar location on uniforms without pockets. When two badges are worn on the same side, they are spaced equally from left to right on the pocket.

*(c)* On the mess and evening mess uniforms, ID badges are worn centered between the lower two buttons of the jacket, with one inch between badges when two are worn on the same side (see fig 29–81). Personnel are authorized to wear full-size identification badges on the mess and evening mess uniforms when the badges are not available in miniature size.

**Figure 29–81. Wear of identification badges on white and blue mess uniforms, female**

*e.* Position of wear of identification badges. Badges are worn as prescribed in paragraph *c*, above.

(1) The Presidential Service identification badge is worn on the right side.

(2) Vice-Presidential Service identification badge is worn on the right side.

(3) The Secretary of Defense identification badge is worn on the left side.

(4) The Joint Chiefs of Staff identification badge is worn on the left side.

(5) The Army Staff identification badge is worn on the right side.

(6) The Guard, Tomb of the Unknown Soldier identification badge is worn on the right side. This badge is authorized as a non-subdued metal badge, and as a subdued embroidered cloth badge.

(7) The Drill Sergeant identification badge is worn on the right side.

*(a)* This badge is authorized as a non-subdued metal badge, and as a subdued embroidered cloth badge. The subdued badge has black details and letters embroidered on olive green cloth. The subdued badge is worn on utility uniforms and field jackets, with the badge centered on the right breast pocket between the bottom of the pocket flap and the

bottom of the pocket, as measured from the insignia, not the cloth backing. Personnel will wear the subdued badge with the background material intact.

*(b)* When personnel wear both the subdued Drill Sergeant and Career Counselor badges on utility uniforms, the Drill Sergeant badge is worn to the right of the Career Counselor badge. Officers who were awarded the Drill Sergeant badge as a permanent award while in an enlisted status are authorized to wear the badge.

(8) The U.S. Army Recruiter identification badge, Active Army/Army Reserve, is worn on the left side.

*(a)* This badge is authorized for wear by military personnel assigned or attached to the U.S. Army Recruiting Command (USAREC) as designated by the CG, USAREC. (See AR 600–8–22 for eligibility criteria.) Personnel may wear only one recruiter badge at a time.

*(b)* This badge is authorized as a non-subdued metal badge and as a subdued embroidered cloth badge. The subdued badge is embroidered on olive-green cloth (silver badge) or black cloth (gold badge). The subdued badge is worn on utility uniforms and field jackets, with the badge centered on the left breast pocket between the bottom of the pocket flap and the bottom of the pocket, as measured from the insignia, not the cloth backing. Personnel will wear the subdued badge with the background material intact.

*(c)* Officers who were awarded the U.S. Army Recruiter badge as a permanent award while in an enlisted status are authorized to wear the badge.

(9) The Career Counselor identification badge is worn on the right side. Only enlisted personnel in CMF 79 are authorized wear of this badge. (See AR 600–8–22 for eligibility criteria.)

*(a)* The badge is authorized as a non-subdued metal badge in a small and large version, and as a subdued embroidered cloth badge. The subdued badge is embroidered on green cloth and is worn on the utility uniforms and field jackets with the badge centered on the right breast pocket, between the bottom of the pocket flap and the bottom of the pocket, as measured from the insignia, not the cloth backing. Personnel will wear the subdued badge with the background material intact.

*(b)* When both the Career Counselor identification and Drill Sergeant badges are worn, the Drill Sergeant badge is worn to the right of the Career Counselor badge. Personnel wear the non-subdued Career Counselor badge on the black pullover sweater instead of the DUI or RDI.

(10) The Recruiting and Retention identification badges, ARNG, are worn on the left side.

*(a)* Basic and Senior badges. (See NGR 601–1 for eligibility criteria.) These badges are authorized as non-subdued metal badges and as subdued embroidered cloth badges. The non-subdued basic badge is silver and the senior badge is gold. The subdued basic badge is a black minuteman on green cloth, and the subdued senior badge is a green minuteman on black cloth. The basic and senior badges are authorized for temporary wear only while assigned to a recruiting position, or to occasional recruiting duties. Officers may wear this as a temporary badge if assigned to recruiting duties.

*(b)* Master badge. The non-subdued master badge is a gold badge surrounded by a wreath. The subdued badge is a black minuteman on green cloth, surrounded by a black wreath. This badge is authorized for permanent wear. After ARNG master-level recruiters leave recruiting duty, they may wear the master badge on the class A uniform; they may wear the badge on the AG shade 415 shirt only when all other awards and decorations are worn. Officers who were awarded the Recruiting and Retention badge, Master, as a permanent award while in an enlisted recruiter status, or as an AMEDD recruiter, are authorized to wear the badge.

*(c)* Personnel wear the subdued badges on utility uniforms and field jackets, with the badge centered on the left breast pocket between the bottom of the pocket flap and the bottom of the pocket, as measured from the insignia, not the cloth backing. Personnel will wear the subdued badge with the background material intact. Only one recruiter badge is authorized for wear at a time. Soldiers currently on recruiting duty will wear the recruiter badge of their component.

(11) The Unified Combatant Commander identification badge is worn on the left side. The design of the badge is unique to the respective command. The badge is authorized for wear by personnel assigned to the Combatant Commander's staff, and by personnel assigned to subordinate unified commands and direct reporting units to the unified command, at the direction of the Unified Combatant Commander. The badge is worn on the class A and B uniforms, and on the Army dress, mess, and evening mess uniforms.

(12) The National Defense University (NDU) identification badge is worn on the right side. Personnel assigned to the faculty or staff of NDU; the National War College, Industrial College of the Armed Forces; or the Armed Forces Staff College are authorized to wear the badge during their assignment.

(13) The Military Police badge is worn on the left side. The Military Police badge is the symbol of law enforcement authority vested in Military Police and is worn only in the performance of law enforcement duties.

*(a)* The Military Police badge is worn on the Army green uniform coat when MPs wear the coat as an outer garment. Males wear the badge centered below the pocket flap on the left breast pocket (see fig 29–82). Females wear the badge centered or aligned to the left above the service ribbons (see fig 29–83). The badge is attached to the outer garment by using a pin clasp or a leather fob.

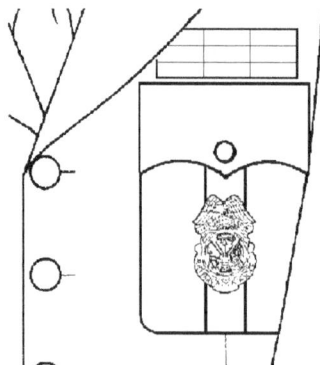

**Figure 29–82. Wear of Military Police identification badge, male**

**Figure 29–83. Wear of Military Police identification badge, female**

*(b)* Brassards are worn when MPs wear utility uniforms, the AG shade 415 shirt, the black pullover sweater, black windbreaker, or black overcoat as outer garments. (See paragraph 28–29*b*(9) for brassard wear policy.)

(14) DOD/Joint Agency identification badges. DOD/Joint Agency badges are worn by personnel during their assignment to specific DOD and Joint Agencies. Badges may be worn on either pocket/side of the uniform, as long as they do not interfere with the positioning of other badges listed in this chapter. Manner of wear is determined by the agency.

(15) The Secretary of Health and Human Services badge is worn on the right side. Officers wear this badge temporarily upon initial assignment within the Office of the Secretary of Health and Human Services (OSHHS). After one year of duty in OSHHS, officers may wear the badge permanently.

*Note.* Subdued badges, worn on desert BDUs, are available in spicebrown/brown/khaki.

### 29–19. Wear of foreign badges

*a.* Personnel may not wear more than one foreign badge at a time. Only those badges awarded in recognition of military activities by the military department of the host country are authorized for acceptance and permanent wear on the Army uniform. The only Vietnamese badges authorized for wear are the parachute, ranger, and explosive ordnance disposal badges. Soldiers must obtain approval from HQDA, in accordance with the procedures provided in AR 600–8–22, to accept, retain, and wear a foreign badge.

*b.* Males wear a foreign badge ⅛ inch above the right pocket flap, or ½ inch above any unit awards that are worn (see fig 29–84). Females wear the badge ½ inch above the nameplate, or ½ inch above any unit awards that are worn (see fig 29–85). Personnel may not wear a foreign badge unless at least one U.S. medal or service ribbon is worn at the same time. Foreign badges are not authorized for wear on mess or utility uniforms. Personnel may not wear foreign badges that are awarded only as cloth badges. Personnel may not wear foreign badges that cannot be worn properly because of size or configuration.

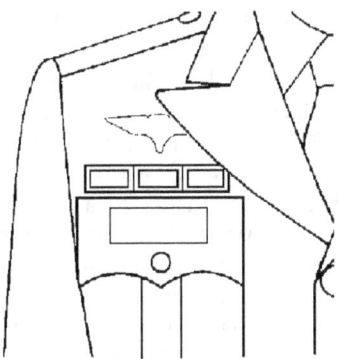

Figure 29–84. Wear of foreign award, male

Figure 29–85. Wear of foreign award, female

*c.* The German Marksmanship Award (Schuetzenschnur) is authorized for wear only by enlisted personnel. Officers may accept, but may not wear the Schuetzenschnur. If authorized, personnel wear the award on the right side of the uniform coat, with the upper portion attached under the center of the shoulder loop, and the bottom portion attached under the lapel to a button mounted specifically for wear of this award.

# Chapter 30
# Wear of the Army Uniform by Reserve, Retired, Separated, and Civilian Personnel

## 30–1. Occasions of ceremony
*a.* As used in this regulation, the phrase "occasions of ceremony" means occasions essentially of a military character, at which the uniform is more appropriate than civilian clothing. These functions include, but are not limited to: military balls, military parades, weddings, and military funerals; memorial services, meetings and conferences; or functions of associations formed for military purposes, of which the membership is composed largely or entirely of current or honorably discharged veterans of the Armed Forces or reserve components. Authority to wear the uniform includes wear while traveling to and from the ceremony or function, provided the travel in uniform can be completed on the day of the ceremony or function.

*b.* All persons wearing the Army uniform will wear awards, decorations, and insignia in the same manner as prescribed in this regulation for active duty soldiers. For civilian attire, individuals may wear only those awards, decorations, or insignia authorized by this regulation for wear on civilian clothing, in the same manner and approximate location as the equivalent military uniform.

## 30–2. Wear of the uniform by members of the Army National Guard and U.S. Army Reserve
*a.* All members of the ARNG and USAR on any form of paid or unpaid inactive duty, active duty, annual training,

or full-time National Guard, or AGR duty will wear the uniform and insignia prescribed for personnel in the Active Army. Army National Guard and USAR personnel are authorized to wear the Army uniform on the following occasions.

*b.* When ARNG AND USAR personnel are within the limits of the United States or its possessions. Army National Guard and USAR personnel not on active duty may wear the Army uniform only as follows.

(1) When participating in reserve training assemblies (inactive duty training), exercises, conferences, or ceremonies in an official capacity as members of the ARNG or the USAR under competent orders.

(2) When engaged in military instruction or in attendance as a student under appropriate orders at any school or course of instruction under the auspices of the armed forces or the reserve components.

(3) When instructors at an educational institution conducting courses of instruction approved by the armed forces, or when responsible for military discipline at like institutions.

(4) When attending social functions or informal gatherings of a military character. All current and former soldiers will conform to the wear and appearance standards in this regulation while wearing the uniform under the provisions of this chapter.

(5) When enrolled as undergraduates in educational institutions in which there is an active ROTC unit or an established USAR unit. Individuals may wear the uniforms and insignia of their grade only upon such occasions expressly desired or authorized by the professor of military science, or other proper official of the school. Members of the USAR attending institutions at which military training is considered as required curricular activity are authorized, and may be required to wear, the uniform prescribed by the institution, including the insignia of any grade or rating held in the student unit.

(6) Army National Guard military technicians who are required to wear the uniform as a condition of their employment will wear the uniform for their federally recognized grades, as prescribed by the Adjutant General of their state, commonwealth, territory, or district.

(7) U. S. Army Reserve technicians who are also members of the U.S. Army Reserve may wear the Army uniform at their option while performing in their civil service status.

*c.* When outside the limits of the United States or its possessions. Army National Guard and USAR personnel not on active duty and outside the limits of the United States or its possessions will not wear the Army uniform, unless granted authority by HQDA. However, on occasions of military ceremony or other military functions in a foreign country, ARNG and USAR personnel may be granted authority to wear the Army uniform after they have their status accredited by the nearest Army attaché. In a foreign country that does not have an Army attaché, however, ARNG and USAR personnel must obtain authority to wear the Army uniform for a specific occasion from the military authorities of the country concerned.

*d.* Army National Guard personnel also may wear the Army uniform in the performance of State service, when authorized to do so by their State Adjutant General.

*e.* United States Army Reserve personnel.

(1) Warrant officers and enlisted personnel serving on active duty who also hold commissions in the USAR may wear the uniform indicative of their grade in the USAR only as follows.

*(a)* When undergoing authorized voluntary training designed for Reserve officers which they are authorized to take, and while traveling to and from that training.

*(b)* When attending meetings or functions of associations formed for military purposes, of which membership is composed largely or entirely of officers of the United States Army, or of former members of the Army.

(2) Warrant officers and enlisted personnel serving on active duty who also hold commissions in the USAR may not wear the uniform indicative of their grade in the USAR as follows.

*(a)* When in an office of the Department of Defense.

*(b)* When they will be in association with troops of the active Army or of the ARNG when called into Federal service, except when the individual is on active duty as a Reserve officer, or as otherwise authorized in paragraph (1), above.

## 30–3. Wear of the uniform by retired personnel

*a.* Personnel who will be advanced to a higher grade upon retirement have the option of wearing the insignia of that grade thereafter.

*b.* Retired personnel on active duty will wear their uniform and insignia in the same manner as prescribed for personnel in the Active Army of corresponding grade and branch.

*c.* Retired personnel not on active duty may wear either the uniform reflecting their grade and branch on the date of their retirement, or the uniform for personnel in the Active Army of corresponding grade and branch, when appropriate, but may not intermix the two uniforms. Personnel will wear the grade as shown on the retired grade of rank line on the retirement order.

*d.* Retired personnel not on active duty are not authorized to wear shoulder sleeve insignia, except as follows:

(1) Personnel performing instructor duties at an educational institution conducting courses of instruction approved

by the Armed Forces will wear the shoulder sleeve insignia of the command that is responsible for the course of instruction. Senior and junior ROTC instructors will wear the Cadet Command shoulder sleeve insignia on their left shoulder (see AR 145–1 and 145–2 for wear of the uniform by senior and junior ROTC instructors, respectively).

(2) Retired personnel are authorized to wear the shoulder sleeve insignia for U.S. Army Retirees on the left shoulder. The insignia consists of a white cloth disc with a blue border, and an inner white disc with a red border, which bears a blue and white adaptation of the coat of arms of the United States. The outer disk that surrounds the coat of arms contains the inscription "UNITED STATES ARMY" in red letters at the top, and the word "RETIRED" in blue letters at the bottom (see fig 30–1).

**Figure 30–1. Shoulder sleeve insignia, retirees**

(3) Retired personnel may wear the shoulder sleeve insignia for former wartime service (SSI–FWTS) on the right shoulder if they were authorized wear of the SSI–FWTS while on active duty.

*e.* Retired personnel not on active duty are not authorized to wear the Army uniform when they are instructors or responsible for military discipline at an educational institution, unless the educational institution is conducting courses of instruction approved by the Armed Forces.

*f.* In addition to the occasions for wear listed above, retired personnel are authorized to wear the uniform only on the following occasions. Uniforms for these occasions are restricted to service and dress uniforms; the BDU and physical fitness uniforms will not be worn.

(1) While attending military funerals, memorial services, weddings, inaugurals, and other occasions of ceremony.

(2) Attending parades on national or state holidays, or other patriotic parades or ceremonies in which any active or reserve United States military unit is taking part. Wear of the Army uniform at any other time, or for any other purpose than stated above is prohibited.

*g.* Retirees are authorized to wear the physical fitness uniform (PFU) or the improved physical fitness uniform (IPFU) under the following provisions:

(1) May wear the PFU or the IPFU with civilian attire off the installation.

(2) When wearing the PFU or the IPFU as a complete uniform, retirees will—

*(a)* Wear only authorized accessories corresponding to those worn by personnel of the Active Army.

*(b)* Keep the sleeves down on the sweatshirt or jacket, the legs down on the pants, and the t-shirt tucked inside the trunks.

*(c)* Not roll or push up the sleeves of the IPFU sweatshirt or the PFU/IPFU jacket.

*(d)* Wear the sleeves of the IPFU sweatshirt cuffed or uncuffed; may not cuff the IPFU jacket sleeves.

*(e)* Wear the black knit cap pulled down snugly on the head, with the bottom edge of the cap folded up; will not roll the edge of the cap. A similar, commercially designed black knit cap is authorized for wear.

*h.* Pregnant retirees are authorized to wear the t-shirt/sweatshirt outside the trunks/sweatpants.

## 30–4. Wear of the uniform by former members of the Army

*a.* Unless qualified under another provision of this regulation, or under the provisions of section 772, title 10, United

States Code (10 USC 772), former members of the Army may wear the uniform if they served honorably during a declared or undeclared war, and if their most recent service was terminated under honorable conditions. Personnel who qualify under these conditions will wear the Army uniform in the highest grade they held during such war service, in accordance with 10 USC 772.

b. The uniform is authorized for wear only for the following ceremonial occasions, and when traveling to and from the ceremony or function. Uniforms for these occasions are restricted to service and dress uniforms; the BDU and physical fitness uniforms will not be worn.

(1) When attending military funerals, memorial services, weddings, inaugurals, and other occasions of ceremony.

(2) When attending parades on national or state holidays, or other patriotic parades or ceremonies in which any active or reserve United States military unit is taking part. Wear of the Army uniform at any other time, or for any other purpose than stated above, is prohibited.

### 30–5. Wear of the uniform by Medal of Honor recipients.

Personnel awarded the Medal of Honor may wear the Army uniform at their pleasure, except under the circumstances in paragraph 1–10*j*.

### 30–6. Wear of medals on civilian clothes

Retired personnel and former members of the Army (as described above) may wear all categories of medals described in this regulation on appropriate civilian clothing. This includes clothes designed for veteran and patriotic organizations on Veteran's Day, Memorial Day, and Armed Forces Day, as well as at formal occasions of ceremony and social functions of a military nature. Personnel may wear either full-size or miniature medals. Personnel who wear medals on civilian clothes should place the medals on the clothing in approximately the same location and in the same manner as for the Army uniform, so they look similar to medals worn on the Army uniform.

### 30–7. When wear of the uniform is prohibited

The wear of the Army uniform by ARNG, USAR, retired, separated, and civilian personnel is prohibited under the circumstances listed in paragraph 1–10*j*.

### 30–8. Wear of a uniform similar to the Army uniform

a. A person for whom one of the following uniforms is prescribed may wear the uniform, provided it includes distinctive insignia prescribed by the Secretary of the Army to distinguish it from the U.S. Army uniform.

(1) Instructors or members of an organized cadet corps at a state university, college, or public high school that has a regular course of military instruction will wear the uniform prescribed by the academic organization.

(2) Instructors or members of an organized cadet corps at an educational institution that has a regular course of military instruction in military science with an Army instructor, will wear the uniform prescribed by the academic organization.

(3) When authorized by regulations prescribed by the Secretary of the Army, members of a military society composed of persons discharged honorably or under honorable conditions from the U.S. Army may wear the uniform prescribed by the military society.

b. According to section 773(b), title 10, United States Code (10 USC 773(b)), none of the uniforms prescribed in paragraph *a*, above, may include insignia or grade the same as or similar to those prescribed for officers of the Army, Navy, Air Force, or Marine Corps.

c. State defense forces (SDF) may adopt the Army service and BDU uniforms, provided all service uniform buttons, cap devices, and other insignia differ significantly from that prescribed for wear by members of the U.S. Army. State insignia will not include "United States," "U.S.," "U.S. Army," or the Great Seal of the United States. Personnel of the SDF may wear a State-designed SDF distinguishing badge or insignia centered on the left pocket flap. The red nametape or nameplate will include the full title of the SDF (for example, "Texas State Guard"). The utility uniforms will contain a State SDF tape in lieu of "U.S. Army" over the left breast pocket. States wishing to adopt the Army service and utility uniforms will register with the Chief, National Guard Bureau.

### 30–9. Wear of distinctive unit insignia on civilian clothing

Former members of an Army unit may wear the distinctive unit insignia on the breast pocket or lapel.

### 30–10. Wear of uniforms by U.S. civilians

a. Authorized U.S. civilian personnel attached to, or authorized to accompany forces of the United States, including DA civilians, are authorized to wear utility uniforms only when required in the performance of their duties, and when authorized by the MACOM commander. The procedures for purchasing uniforms, footwear, and insignia are contained in AR 700–84, chapter 3. Only the insignia described below is authorized for wear on these uniforms.

b. Insignia for civilians.

(1) Description. The woodland subdued insignia is a black equilateral triangle, 1¼ inches long per side, with the

letters "U.S." in olive-drab color, ¼ inch wide and ½ inch high. The triangle is printed on an olive-green colored cloth background, 3 inches long and 2–½ inches wide. If applicable, the insignia also indicates the designated assignment in black letters, ¼ inch high. The desert subdued insignia is the same size, with khaki or tan letters on a black cloth triangle. The triangle is printed on a khaki or tan cloth background.

(2) The authorized designations are as follows.

*(a)* Scientific consultant.

*(b)* Operations analyst.

*(c)* War correspondent.

*(d)* Technical observer.

*(e)* Ordnance technician.

*(f)* Chauffeur.

*(g)* Messenger.

*(h)* Logistics specialist.

*(i)* Safety.

*(j)* Ammunition surveillance.

(3) Insignia for civilians performing duties not listed above, or when specific designations are not required, will conform to previously described insignia, except the insignia will not denote duty assignment (see fig 30–2).

**Figure 30–2. Insignia for civilians**

(4) How worn. Personnel will wear the insignia centered directly above the left pocket, or on the left sleeve on the utility uniform, and in a similar location on outer garments. Personnel will center the insignia on the front of the BDU cap.

(5) Nametape or nameplate. Personnel will wear a standard size nametape or nameplate in the same manner as for U.S. Army personnel (see figs 28–139 through 28–144).

# Appendix A
## References

### Section I
### Required Publications

**AR 600–8–22**
Military Awards (Cited in paras 1–5, 14–5, 29–6, 29–11, 29–12, 29–13, 29–17, 29–18, and 29–19, .)

**AR 600–9**
The Army Weight Control Program (Cited in para 1–7.)

**AR 600–20**
Army Command Policy (Cited in paras 1–7, 1–8, 3–6, and 5–5.)

**AR 614–100**
Officers Assignment Policies, Details, and Transfers (Cited in para 28–9.)

**AR 700–84**
Issue and Sale of Personal Clothing (Cited in paras 1–4, 1–9, 1–10, 2–6, 2–7, 3–6, 15–11, 16–12, 17–1, 17–3, and 30–10.)

**CTA 50–900 (added Web site)**
Clothing and Individual Equipment (Cited in paras 2–6, 2–7, 3–2, 4–2, 5–2, 6–1, 6–2, 6–5, 7–2, 7–5, 7–6, 7–7, 8–2, 9–2, 10–1, 10–2, 10–5, 11–1, 11–2, 11–5, 12–1, 12–2, 12–5, 13–1, 13–2, 17–1, , 17–3, 18–1, 19–1, 20–1, 20–11, 21–1, 21–12, 22–1, 23–1, 27–3, 28–1, app B, table C–1, and terms.) (Available at https://WEBTAADS.BELVOIR.ARMY.MIL/USAFMSA.)

### Section II
### Related Publications
A related publication is a source of additional information. The user does not have to read a related publication to understand this regulation.

**AR 10–5 (obsolete)**
Headquarters, Department of the Army

**AR 11–30 (obsolete)**
WARTRACE Program

**AR 70–1**
Army Acquisition Policy

**AR 95–1**
Flight Regulations

**AR 140–10**
Assignments, Attachments, Details, and Transfers

**AR 145–1**
Senior Reserve Officers' Training Corps Program: Organization, Administration, and Training

**AR 145–2**
Organization, Administration, Operation, and Support

**AR 165–1 (updated title)**
Army Chaplain Corps Activities

**AR 190–30**
Military Police Investigations

**AR 310–25 (obsolete)**
Dictionary of United States Army Term

**AR 385–10**
The Army Safety Program

**AR 600–8–10**
Leave and Passes

**AR 600–8–14**
Identification Cards for Members of the Uniformed Services, Their Family Members, and Other Eligible Personnel

**AR 600–8–24**
Officer Transfers and Discharges

**AR 600–82**
The U.S. Army Regimental System

**AR 635–200**
Active Duty Enlisted Administrative Separations

**AR 672–8**
Manufacture, Sale, Wear, and Quality Control of Heraldic Items

**AR 672–20**
Incentive Awards

**AR 702–7–1 (updated title)**
Reporting of Product Quality Deficiencies within the U.S. Army

**CTA 8–100 (added Web site)**
Army Medical Department Expendable/Durable Items (Available at https://WEBTAADS.BELVOIR.ARMY.MIL/ USAFMSA.)

**CTA 50–909 (added Web site)**
Field and Garrison Furnishings and Equipment (Available at https://WEBTAADS.BELVOIR.ARMY.MIL/USAFMSA.)

**CTA 50–970 (added Web site)**
Expendable Durable Items (Except: Medical, Class V, Repair Parts, and Heraldic Items) (Available at https:// WEBTAADS.BELVOIR.ARMY.MIL/USAFMSA.)

**DA Pam 672–3**
Unit Citation and Campaign Participation Credit Register

**DA Pam 710–2–1**
Using Unit Supply System (Manual Procedures)

**DA Pam 750–8 (superseded by AR 750–8)**
The Army Maintenance Management System (TAMMS) Users Manual

**NGR 600–82**
U.S. Army Regimental System—Army National Guard (Available at www.ngbpdc.ngb.army.mil/.)

**NGR 600–102**
Commissioned and Warrant Officers Assigned to Selective Service Sections State Area Commands (Available at www. ngbpdc.ngb.army.mil/.)

**NGR 601–1**
Army National Guard Strength Maintenance Program (Available at www.ngbpdc.ngb.army.mil/.)

**TB Med 287**
Pseudofolliculitis of the Beard and Acne Keloidalis Nuchae

**TM 10–227**
Fitting of Army Uniforms and Footwear

**TM 10–8400–201–23**
Unit and Direct Support Maintenance Manual for General Repair Procedures for Clothing

**DOD 4500.54–G**
DOD Foreign Clearance Guide (Available at www.fcg.pentagon.mil/.)

**10 USC 2533a (added)**
Requirement to buy certain articles from American sources; exceptions (Available at http://uscode.house.gov/.)

## Section III
## Prescribed Forms
This section contains no entries.

## Section IV
## Referenced Forms
Unless otherwise indicated, DA forms are available on the Army Publishing Directorate (APD) Web site (http://www.apd.army.mil/); DD Forms are available on the Office of the Secretary of Defense (OSD) Web site (http://www.dtic.mil/whs/directives/infomgt/forms/index.htm); and Standard Forms (SF) are available on the U.S. General Services Administration (GSA) Web site (http://www.gsa.gov/).

**DA Form 2028 (added)**
Recommended Changes to Publications and Blank Forms

**DD Form 1610**
Request and Authorization for TDY Travel of DOD Personnel

**SF Form 368**
Product Quality Deficiency Report

# Appendix B
# Prescribed Dress

Table B–1 summarizes the attire that makes up various kinds of prescribed dress.

**Table B–1**
**Table of prescribed dress**

| Prescribed | Attire |
|---|---|
| Duty uniform | Duty uniform as locally prescribed. |
| Informal uniform | Army blue or white with four-in-hand tie or neck tab.[1] Enlisted personnel may wear the class A Army green uniforms (with skirt for females) with white shirt and black bow tie (after retreat), four-in-hand necktie (before retreat), or neck tab as a substitute. |
| Civilian equivalent | Civilian business suit. |
| Black tie uniform | Army blue or white uniform with black bow tie; blue, white, or black mess uniforms.[1] Enlisted personnel may wear the Army green uniform (with skirt for females) with white shirt and black bow tie or neck tab. |
| Civilian equivalent | Civilian dinner jacket (tuxedo). |
| White tie uniform | Army blue or black evening mess uniforms. |
| Civilian equivalent | Evening full dress (tail coat). |

Notes:

[1] Unless otherwise indicated by the host, the uniform equivalent of specified civilian attire may be worn. Invitations may prescribe dress as indicated above; for example, "Army blue or Army blue mess." The Army white and white mess uniforms are normally worn from April to October, except in clothing zones 1 and 2, in accordance with CTA 50–900.

# Appendix C
## Officer Uniform Requirements

### C–1. General
Officers are responsible for procuring and maintaining uniforms appropriate to their assigned duties. Officers will procure and maintain sufficient quantities of personal items necessary to ensure acceptable standards of personal hygiene and appearance. It is mandatory that all officers dress in accordance with their position as an officer of the United States Army, and in accordance with the traditions and customs of the service.

### C–2. List of major components
The major items of uniform clothing that are normally prescribed by commanders, with the minimum quantities that all officers should have in their possession, are shown in table C–1 (see note 1).

**Table C–1**
**List of major components**

| Item[1] | Male Minimum No. | Female Minimum No. |
|---|---|---|
| Coat, black, all weather | 1 | 1 |
| Uniform, Army green | 1 | 1[2] |
| Uniform, Army blue[3, 6] | 1 | 1 |
| Uniform, Army green maternity[4] | NA | 2 |
| Uniform, battle dress[5] | 4 | 4 |
| Coat, cold weather, woodland pattern, camouflage (field jacket) | 1 | 1 |
| Uniform, improved physical fitness | | |
|   SS T-shirt | 2 | 2 |
|   LS T-shirt | 1 | 1 |
|   Trunks | 2 | 2 |
|   Jacket | 1 | 1 |
|   Pants | 1 | 1 |

Notes:
[1] Commanders may prescribe items not on this list for the performance of duties.
[2] Three-piece ensemble (coat, skirt, and slacks).
[3] The Army blue uniform is required for all officers on extended active duty for periods of 6 months or more.
[4] As required by AR 600–8–24 and chapter 17, AR 670–1.
[5] Officers will have four utility uniforms—two temperate and two hot-weather uniforms.
[6] Additional quantities are authorized as organizational issue by CTA 50–900 when required by officers for performance of official duties while assigned to units with missions that include band formations, reviews, parades, ceremonial events, and other similar events.

### C–3. Accessories
Officers also are responsible for procuring and maintaining adequate quantities of appropriate accessories, insignia, footwear, undergarments, headgear, and gloves for use with the above uniforms.

# Appendix D
# Mandatory Possession and Wear-out Dates

## D–1. Possession and wear-out dates of clothing bag items

*a.* All soldiers are required to possess all clothing bag items. The following items in table D–1 and table D–2 have either been added to the clothing bag, or were changed enough to require replacement by a new item. The item, number required, and possession dates are listed below, along with the wear-out dates for deleted or replaced items.

*b.* Initial entry enlisted soldiers will be issued these items in their clothing bag. All other soldiers must purchase them. Enlisted soldiers will be paid sufficient clothing replacement allowance (CRA) to purchase these items from the Army military clothing sales store. The CRA is paid over a period of time from the date of the introduction of the item into the system, to the mandatory possession date.

## D–2. Replacement of required items

*a.* The CRA is paid to enlisted soldiers on an annual basis to provide sufficient funds over a period of time for the replacement of required items of clothing that are prescribed for wear. The CRA is not intended to cover the cost of repair, dry cleaning, or laundering.

*b.* The initial issue represents the minimum uniform requirements. It is possible that soldiers, particularly careerists, may find it convenient or advantageous to acquire and maintain more uniforms than are provided for in the CRA. In addition, any unusual wear and tear, damage, or loss of items may result in out-of-pocket costs. Greater than average wear of one type of clothing bag item (such as the BDU) is offset by less than average wear of another (such as the Army green service uniform).

**Table D–1**
**Possession dates of clothing bag items**

| Item | Possession date |
|---|---|
| AG 415 shirt, male, poly/cotton w/pleated pockets, stand-up collar (2 SS, 1 LS) | 1 Oct 99 |
| AG 415 shirt, female, poly/cotton w/princess pleats (2 SS, 1 LS) | 1 Oct 99 |
| Army green service uniform, AG 489 Male (1 coat, 2 trousers) | 1 Oct 99 |
| Enhanced hot-weather BDU | 1 Oct 00 |
| All-weather coat, black, double-breasted, belted, 65/35 poly/cotton | 1 Oct 01 |
| Army green service uniform, AG 489 female, new style skirt and slacks (1 coat, 2 skirts, 2 slacks) | 1 Oct 03 |
| IPFU (T-shirts, 2 SS, 1 LS; 2 trunks; 1 jacket; 1 pants) | 1 Oct 03 |

**Table D–2**
**Wear-out dates of clothing bag items**

| Item | Wear-out date | Replaced by |
|---|---|---|
| AG 415 shirt, male, w/o stand-up collar SS and LS | 30 Sep 99 | AG 415, w/stand-up collar, SS and LS |
| AG 415 shirt, female, w/bust darts, w/o princess pleats, SS and LS | 30 Sep 99 | AG 415, w/princess pleats, SS and LS |
| AG 344 green service uniform, male (coat and trousers) | 30 Sep 99 | AG 489 green service uniform, male (coat and trousers) |
| Neck tab, black, female under collar hook-and-pile fastener | 30 Sep 99 | Neck tab, black, female wrap around hook-and-pile fastener |
| All-weather coat, black, unbelted | 30 Sep 01 | All-weather coat, black, 65/35 poly/cotton |
| AG 344 green service uniform, female (coat, skirt, slacks) | 30 Sep 03 | AG 489 green service uniform, female (coat, skirt, slacks) |
| PFU (SS T-shirt, shorts, sweatshirt and pants) | 30 Sep 03 | IPFU (SS and LS T-shirts, jacket and pants) |
| Hot-weather BDU | None[1] | Enhanced hot-weather BDU |
| Black oxford shoe, female, moccasin toe, leather | None[1] | Black oxford shoe, female, smooth toe, poromeric |
| Black oxford shoe, male, leather | None[1] | Black oxford shoe, male, poromeric |
| OG 408 green socks | None[1] | Black cushion-sole socks |

Notes:
[1] Item may be worn until it is unserviceable.


**Table D–3**
**Wear-out dates of optional purchase items**

| Item | Wear-out date | Replaced by |
|---|---|---|
| Female insignia | 31 Aug 00 | Large and small insignia |
| Cardigan, old style, M/F | 30 Sep 00 | Black unisex cardigan |
| Black mess and evening mess uniforms | 30 Sep 03 | Blue mess and evening mess uniforms |
| Old-style female blue jacket | None[1] | |
| Green jungle boots | None[1] | |

Notes:
[1] Item may be worn until it is unserviceable.

# Appendix E
# Clothing Bag List

## E–1. Required clothing items
Soldiers are required to possess the clothing items listed in table E–1, in the quantities shown. Soldiers may purchase and wear optional items authorized by this regulation.

## E–2. Approved optional items
Items identified by an "X" in the optional item column are authorized in lieu of the specification item. These items have been approved by the Army and contain the required certification label.

## E–3. Optional items that need not be approved
Those items identified by an "*" in the optional item column are authorized in lieu of the specification item and are not required to be certified or approved by the Army.

**Table E–1**
**Clothing bag list**

| Item | Quantity required | Specification item | Optional item |
|---|---|---|---|
| Bag, duffel | 1 | X | |
| Belt, riggers, black | 1 | X | |
| Belt, web, black, w/brass tip, male | 1 | X | |
| Belt, web, black, w/brass tip, female | 1 | X | |
| Beret, wool, black shade 1593 | 1 | X | |
| Boots, combat, Infantry | 2 | X | X |
| Buckle, belt, black | 1 | X | |
| Buckle, belt, slacks, nickel underplate | 1 | X | X |
| Cap, camo, EHWBDU | 1 | X | |
| Cap, camo, TBDU | 1 | X | |
| Cap, knit, black | 1 | X | |
| Coat, all weather, double breasted | 1 | X | X |
| Coat, camo, EHWBDU | 2 | X | |
| Coat, camo, TBDU | 2 | X | |
| Coat, camo, CW (field jacket) | 1 | X | |
| Coat, AG 489 | 1 | X | X |
| Drawers, brn, male[1] | 7 | X | X |
| Glove inserts, cold, black | 2 | X | |
| Glove, flexor, light duty | 1 | X | |
| Gloves, leather, black, unisex | 1 | X | X |
| Jacket, IPFU | 1 | X | |
| Neck tab, female | 1 | X | |
| Necktie, male | 1 | X | * |
| Pants, IPFU | 1 | X | |
| T-shirt, LS, IPFU | 1 | X | |
| T-shirt, SS, IPFU | 2 | X | |
| Shirt, AG 415, SS | 2 | X | X |
| Shirt, AG 415, LS | 1 | X | X |
| Shoes, oxford, black | 1 | X | X |
| Skirt, AG 489, female | 2 | X | X |
| Slacks, AG 489, female | 2 | X | X |
| Socks, boot, green | 7 | X | |
| Socks, black, poly/nylon | 7 | X | X |

**Table E–1**
**Clothing bag list—Continued**

| Item | Quantity required | Specification item | Optional item |
|------|------|------|------|
| Towel, bath, brn[1] | 4 | X | |
| Trousers, AG 489, male | 2 | X | X |
| Trousers, TBDU | 2 | X | |
| Trousers, EHWBDU | 2 | X | |
| Trunks, IPFU | 2 | X | |
| Undershirt, brn | 7 | X | |
| Undershirt, wht, male[1] | 2 | X | X |
| Undershirt, CW, polyester, brown 436 | 1 | X | |
| Undershirt, CW, polypro 436 | 1 | X | |
| **Cash allowances** | | | |
| Pumps, black (females) | 1 | | |
| Lingerie, nylons, underwear (females) | (As required) | | |
| Handbag (females) | 1 | | |
| Running shoes (males and females) | 1 | | |

Notes:
[1] Enlisted soldiers are not paid a CRA for this item.

# Appendix F
## Shoulder Sleeve Insignia–Former Wartime Service (SSI–FWTS)

### F–1. Applicability.
This guidance applies to soldiers of all components (Active, ARNG and USAR) that deploy during periods of service designated for wear of the SSI–FWTS, in accordance with paragraph 28–17.

### F–2. General.
*a.* There is no time-in-theater requirement to be authorized to wear the SSI–FWTS.

*b.* A deployed unit that is authorized to wear an SSI in its own right (or an organic component thereof), in accordance with para 28–16, will wear that unit's SSI as the SSI–FWTS. This is true regardless of whether the headquarters element deploys, and regardless of the number of changes to the unit's alignment or operational control (OPCON) during the period of deployment.

*c.* When a unit not entitled to its own SSI deploys, the OPCON relationship prior to deployment is terminated, and a new OPCON relationship is established. Members of these units will wear the SSI of the lowest echelon deployed unit entitled to an SSI in each of their new deployed chains of command as their SSI–FWTS.

*d.* When there is no intermediate unit that has its own SSI in the deployed chain of command, members of units not entitled to their own SSI will wear the SSI of the senior Army command in the theater as their SSI–FWTS.

*e.* Soldiers who are cross-leveled, assigned, attached, or augmenting deployed units, and soldiers who are TDY on orders through the use of DD Form 1610 (Request and Authorization for TDY Travel of DOD Personnel) will wear the same SSI–FWTS worn by members of the deployed unit(s) to which attached or OPCON. This does not apply to members of Trial Defense and CIDC, who will wear the SSI of their respective commands as their SSI–FWTS.

*f.* Soldiers authorized to wear more than one SSI–FWTS may choose which SSI–FWTS they wear. Soldiers also may elect not to wear the SSI–FWTS.

*g.* Precedence was established in Vietnam for elements organic to, or an integral part of an organization to wear the organizational SSI as their SSI–FWTS.

# Glossary

## Section I
## Abbreviations

**AAFES**
Army and Air Force Exchange Service

**AGR**
active guard reserve

**AIEP**
Army Ideas for Excellence Program

**AMC**
Army Materiel Command

**AMCSS**
Army military clothing sales store

**AMSC**
Army Medical Specialist Corps

**ANC**
Army Nurse Corps

**ARNG**
Army National Guard

**ASCC**
Army service component command

**BDU**
battle dress uniform

**CA**
civil affairs

**CMF**
career management field

**CONUS**
continental United States

**CRA**
clothing replacement allowance

**CTA**
common table of allowances

**CVC**
combat vehicle crewman

**DCS, G-4**
Deputy Chief of Staff, G-4

**DCS, G-1**
Deputy Chief of Staff, G-1

**DOD**
Department of Defense

**HQDA**
Headquarters, Department of the Army

**LI**
leaders identification

**LIN**
line item number

**MACOM**
major army command

**MOS**
military occupational specialty

**MOU**
Memorandum of Understanding

**MP**
military police

**MTOE**
modification table of organization and equipment

**NCO**
noncommissioned officer

**NFPA**
National Fire Protection Association

**NSRDEC**
U.S. Army Natick Soldier Research, Development and Engineering Center

**OCS**
Officer Candidate School

**PEO**
Program Executive Office

**PM-SPIE**
Project Manager-Soldier Protection and Individual Equipment

**PMOS**
primary military occupational specialty

**POC**
point of contact

**ROTC**
Reserve Officer Training Corps

**SDF**
State Defense Forces

**SMA**
The Sergeant Major of the Army

**SSI**
shoulder sleeve insignia

**SSI–FWTS**
shoulder sleeve insignia–former wartime service

**TDY**
temporary duty

**TOE**
table of organization and equipment

**UQCP**
Uniform Quality Control Program

**USAR**
United States Army Reserve

**USC**
United States Code

**USMA**
United States Military Academy

**WOC**
warrant officer candidate

## Section II
## Terms

**Accouterment**
Items such as medals, ribbons, insignia, badges, emblems, tabs, and tapes authorized for wear on uniforms.

**Appurtenances**
Devices such as stars, letters, numerals, or clasps worn on the suspension ribbon of the medal, or on the ribbon bar that indicate additional awards, participation in specific events, or other distinguishing characteristics of the award.

**Awards**
An all-inclusive term that consists of any decoration, medal, badge, ribbon, or appurtenance bestowed on an individual or unit.

**Badge**
An award given to an individual for identification purposes, or that is awarded for attaining a special skill or proficiency. Certain badges are available in full, miniature, and dress miniature sizes.

**Clothing bag**
Uniform items and personal clothing issued to initial entry soldiers, and which all soldiers are required to maintain throughout their military career.

**Decoration**
An award given to an individual as a distinctively designed mark of honor denoting heroism, or meritorious or outstanding service or achievement.

**Dress uniforms**
Uniforms worn as formal duty attire, or that are worn at formal or informal social functions, before or after retreat. They include the enlisted Army green dress uniform, and the Army blue and white uniforms.

**Field uniforms**
Utility and organizational uniforms, excluding the hospital duty and food service uniforms, that are worn in field, training, or combat environments.

**Gold color/gold-colored**
Includes gold plated, gold bullion, and synthetic metallic gold.

**Lapel button**
A miniature enameled replica of an award, which is worn only on civilian clothing.

**Local commander**
The commander of an installation or equivalent in CONUS, the MACOM commander overseas, and the State Adjutant General for the ARNG, as the individual who may prescribe policy on discretionary wear policies in this regulation. The local commander may delegate this authority to subordinate commanders.

**Medal**
An award issued to an individual for the performance of certain duties, acts or services, consisting of a suspension ribbon made in distinctive colors and from which hangs a medallion.

**Mess uniforms**
Uniforms worn for formal social occasions, when prescribed by the host. They include the blue and white mess and evening mess uniforms for males. For females, they include the blue and white mess and evening mess uniforms, the all-white evening mess, and the black mess and evening mess uniforms.

**Miniature medal**
A replica of a regular size medal, made to a scale ½ that of the original. The Medal of Honor is not worn in miniature.

**Optional clothing**
A uniform or clothing item which the individual is not required to own or wear, but may be worn at the individual's option, as prescribed in this regulation.

**Organizational uniforms, clothing, and equipment**
The uniforms, clothing and equipment listed in the common tables of allowances (CTA), which are issued to an individual on a loan basis and remain the property of the organization. Commanders issue organizational clothing and equipment in accordance with the allowances and directives published in the appropriate CTA. When issued, organizational clothing is worn when prescribed by the commander in accordance with Army regulations, technical manuals, and the CTA. Examples of organizational uniforms are the maternity work uniform, desert BDU, hospital duty and food service uniforms, and cold-weather clothing.

**Personal clothing**
Military-type clothing, clothing of a personal nature, and component items listed in CTA 50–900, table I, that are provided to enlisted personnel (specifically, the initial clothing bag issue).

**Ribbon or ribbon bar**
A portion of the suspension ribbon of a medal, worn in lieu of the medal and made in the form of a bar, 1 ⅜ inches long by ⅜ inch wide.

**Rosette**
A lapel device created from gathering the suspension ribbon of a medal into a circular shape. The device is worn on the lapel of civilian clothing.

**Service medal**
An award made to personnel who participated in designated wars, campaigns, or expeditions; or who have fulfilled specified service requirements in a creditable manner.

**Service uniform**
Worn in garrison environments when the wear of utility or dress uniforms is not required or appropriate. Service uniforms consist of the Army green (class A and B) uniforms.

**Silver color/colored**
Silver color includes silver-filled, silver-plated, sterling silver, silver bullion, and anodized aluminum.

**Unit award**
An award made to an operating unit, which is worn by members of that unit who participated in the cited action (permanent unit award). Other personnel serving in the cited unit, but who were not assigned to the unit during the action, may be authorized temporary wear of the award (temporary unit award).

**Utility uniforms**
Uniforms normally worn in the field, during training, or while performing duties where it is not practical or appropriate to wear a service uniform. Utility uniforms include the temperate, hot weather, enhanced hot-weather, aviation, and desert BDUs, the maternity work uniform, and the cold-weather uniform.

## Section III
## Special Abbreviations and Terms

**ABDU**
aircrew BDU

**AG**
Army green

**CW**
cold weather

**DBDU**
desert BDU

**DUI**
distinctive unit insignia

**ECWCS**
extended cold weather clothing system

**EHWBDU**
enhanced hot-weather BDU

**FCG**
foreign clearance guide (military)

**ID**
identification

**IPFU**
improved physical fitness uniform

**OD**
olive drab

**OG**
olive green

**OPCON**
operational control

**PFU**
physical fitness uniform

**RD&E**
research, development and engineering

**RDI**
regimental distinctive insignia

**RSC**
regional support command

**STARC**
State Area Command

**TASS**
Total Army School System

**TBDU**
temperate BDU

**TIOH**
The Institute of Heraldry

# Index

PIN 039557–000